THE CHASE

THE

The Chase Manhattan

CHASE

Bank, N.A., 1945–1985

JOHN DONALD WILSON

Harvard Business School Press

BOSTON, MASSACHUSETTS

HG
2613
. N54
C538
1986

Harvard Business School Press
© 1986 by the President and Fellows of Harvard College.
All rights reserved.
Printed in the United States of America.
89 88 87 86   5 4 3 2 1

Photographs Courtesy of Chase Manhattan Bank Archives

Library of Congress Cataloging-in-Publication Data

Wilson, John Donald, 1913–
  The Chase: The Chase Manhattan Bank, N.A.,
1945–1985.

  Bibliography: p.
  Includes index.
  1. Chase Manhattan Bank, N.A.—History—20th century.
I. Title.
HG2613.N54C538   1986   332.1'5'0973   86-11960
ISBN 0-87584-134-1

The paper used in this publication meets the requirements
of the American National Standard for Permanence of Paper
for Printed Library Materials Z39.48–1984.

Harvard Business School Press, Boston 02163

To Danesi

Contents

Preface

The possibility of writing a history of The Chase Manhattan Bank attracted me as I approached retirement in 1981. I had joined The Chase National Bank in 1953 and had served over the years as chief economist, director of corporate planning, and in other supervisory capacities. My work brought me in close contact with the chief executives—McCloy, Champion, Rockefeller, and Butcher—through this period. And I served as a member of the principal planning and operating committees of the bank in my later years there. These experiences provided a unique opportunity to participate in and observe at first hand the radical changes in banking as they unfolded at Chase.

My retirement in 1981 coincided with that of David Rockefeller, whose tenure had spanned the full postwar period to that time. When I suggested to both Rockefeller and Willard C. Butcher, his successor, the desirability of a history of the bank, I found them in full agreement. They requested me to undertake it, and the bank made available all records and facilities necessary for the work, while affording me free rein in the writing of it.

Other than the opening chapter concerning Chase's early years, the depression, and wartime, this history concentrates on 1945 through 1985, a truly revolutionary age in banking. Revolutions are never accomplished, however, without casualties and hardship as well as forward movement, and Chase encountered its share of all these. I have presented not only the bank's growth and progress over the years, but also have examined in some detail its setbacks. The views expressed throughout are my own and may not necessarily reflect those of the bank's past or current management.

My debts are many in the preparation of this work. At Chase, A. Wright Elliott, executive vice president for corporate communications, and Fraser Seitel, head of public affairs, provided my point of contact in the bank and offered many helpful suggestions. Elsewhere, Richard Sylla, professor of economics at North Carolina State University and former editor of the *Journal of Economic History*, was immensely helpful as editorial adviser. Within Chase, the bank's archivists, Anne H. VanCamp and Sally Ann Brazil, made available their considerable resources, as did the bank's secretary, Michael E. Carlson, with records of the board of directors. The bank's legal counsel, Milbank, Tweed, Hadley and McCloy, also opened their useful records.

In all I interviewed more than sixty Chase officers, active and retired, and used interviews with many others that are held in the Chase Archives. I am especially indebted to David Rockefeller and Willard C. Butcher for a number of interviews.

Finally, Connie F. Nieto assisted greatly in the preparation of the manuscript. And my wife, Danesi H. Wilson, with unceasing patience gave support in many ways.

New York, New York   John Donald Wilson
January 1986

THE CHASE

Introduction

This is the story of the transformation over four decades of The Chase National Bank, primarily a domestic bank, into a leading worldwide institution, The Chase Manhattan Bank. The forty years from the end of World War II to the mid-1980s witnessed a revolution in banking, in its structure, activities, and mode of operation. Chase, while unique in many respects, typified this revolution, and indeed formed a significant part of its vanguard.

Chase, up to the close of World War II, was devoted chiefly to wholesale banking, serving large business and financial institutions, including other banks. It possessed few branches abroad, operating chiefly through relationships with foreign banks. At home, its branch network was limited to Manhattan, the commercial heart of New York City, and was oriented heavily toward the needs of commerce and industry. As with other banks, its resources were generated through demand deposits, and lending continued to be influenced significantly by seasonal demands.

Over the ensuing years Chase grew greatly in size and complexity, responding to profound changes in the economic, technical, and regulatory environment. With assets exceeding $87 billion in the mid-1980s, a fourteenfold increase since the war, the bank became truly international in scope and character, operating branches, subsidiaries, and other outlets matched in number by few other banks throughout the world. Half its loans and deposits were domiciled overseas. At home too Chase spread, with branches first throughout the entire city and its suburbs, then throughout the state, and finally establishing a holding company, The Chase Manhattan Corporation, to facilitate expansion across the nation, developments duplicated by other banks.

Meanwhile the nature of Chase's activities were changing in far-reaching ways. In 1955 the bank took a decisive step into consumer banking through merger with the Bank of Manhattan, acquiring branches in New York City that dealt primarily with the needs of individuals, a market then as now regarded as a significant source of deposits as well as credit demand. To a considerable extent, banking for consumers underwent its own distinct evolution, marked by the introduction of credit cards, overdraft banking, a proliferation of savings instruments (culminating with money market accounts), and not least, radical new methods for delivering services through automation.

1

Notwithstanding this thrust into consumer banking, Chase remained principally a wholesale bank. This was the most profitable market, and successive managements maintained this orientation. Here again significant changes occurred, rendering banking both more complex and more risky. Term loans, inaugurated in the 1930s, grew in importance, and the time-honored practice of seasonal borrowing largely disappeared. Complicated cash-flow analysis became more significant than the balance sheet and collateral as the primary basis for credit judgment in an increasing proportion of loans. And credits designed for specific purposes gained in prominence—large project loans, oil production loans, ship loans, and bridging loans for construction among them. Asset-based credits still filled a special niche, especially through leasing and commercial finance for smaller businesses.

Chase initially extended credit overseas to central banks and correspondent banks for short-term trade-related purposes. Loans were not normally made to industry. By the late 1950s these practices had begun to give way, however, as prominent U.S. companies moved facilities into other countries. Foreign credit was soon being granted by a spreading network of overseas branches and affiliates, as well as by the head office. Foreign firms became valued clients. And large syndicates including many banks were organized for extending huge loans to foreign governments.

This growth in loans, both domestic and foreign, would not have been possible without the opening up of new sources of funding. Chase, even more than most other banks, emerged from World War II with large holdings of U.S. government securities. For some years the sale of these, along with growing deposits by individuals, provided funds for higher yielding loans. But by the late 1950s Chase and other banks were beginning to feel the constraint of inadequate resources. Seminal changes in money gathering rectified this problem. Domestically a long-standing policy of refusing to pay corporations for time deposits was abandoned with the introduction of negotiable certificates of deposit, supported by a secondary market for such instruments. Abroad this was complemented by the development of an overseas market for dollars—the Eurodollar market—which soon extended to other currencies. Borrowed money, rather than demand deposits, fueled the growth of the major banks. Eventually almost 85 percent of Chase's usable funds flowed from such sources.

The introduction of borrowed money on a huge scale altered the economics of banking as well as its mode of operation. And it magnified risks associated with banking. Cost of money became far and away the largest expense and required careful control. Loans of three to seven years or more, funded with short-term borrowed money, were increasingly priced with floating rather than fixed rates. As interest rates (and money costs) became more and more volatile in the 1970s, loan pricing underwent a veritable revolution. The prime rate, the key to loan pricing since the 1930s, became only one of a number of bench marks. In such circumstances careful overall management of assets and liabilities, embracing not only the head office but foreign branches as well, became imperative.

As always, Chase's activities were heavily influenced by the economic environment in which it operated. Prosperity and recession were mirrored in changing loan demand, interest rates, and asset quality. The breakdown of the international monetary system, the so-called Bretton Woods system, in the early 1970s replaced fixed relationships between currencies with shifting ones. Unforeseen shocks like the Vietnam war and the energy price explosion of the 1970s ushered in a new era of inflation, damaging both industrial and developing countries, and creating troublesome imbalances in international payments.

Banking grew increasingly risky under these developments, with the first failures of important institutions since the Great Depression of the 1930s. Chase itself did not escape unscathed, as it encountered heavy losses in the mid-1970s centered principally in credit to real estate, a rapidly expanding field in which the bank had emerged as a leader. Earnings plummeted, although never to the point of failing to cover the dividend comfortably. They recovered by the end of the decade, only to be hit again temporarily in 1982 by a large unexpected loss. The image of the bank and banking generally suffered from these and similar incidents.

Improvements in technology, bringing better and less costly ways of doing business, also left their mark on banks throughout these years. The world and the nation were growing smaller with each new development in communication and transportation. Perhaps no change exercised a greater impact than the introduction of the computer as an instrument for handling huge volumes of information. The computer revolutionized the back office operations of banks as well as the production of data for their management. And as equipment increased in efficiency and diversity, it spawned a host of new information products, many pioneered by Chase.

Hardly less important was the evolution of bank management. In 1945 Chase lacked even the semblance of a modern budget. Corporate staff was limited and forward planning nonexistent. Again necessity impelled change as activities were enlarged and became more complicated. Over the years a disciplined management process, designed to set goals, monitor performance, and exercise control over diverse activities throughout the nation and the world, was put in place. Professionals in many fields supplemented and supported staff engaged in traditional banking. But a price was paid for the increased size and efficiency, as the bank's relations with customers and staff became less personal.

Indeed the culture of Chase changed in significant ways over the years. Wholesale banking became less dominant in attracting talent and resources, as consumer banking, money management, and other functions gained in importance. The domestic and international departments, once highly autonomous, began to work closely together to serve a customer base now global in scope and character. In terms of staff management, a paternalistic approach dating from the depression years, was replaced by a more objective system of rewards for efficiency and merit. In one respect, however, Chase culture held steadfast. More than other major banks, Chase had a sense of social responsibility, and this influenced many of its actions through the years.

As Chase entered the mid-1980s, it faced a radically changed competitive environment. Banks had lost position among the host of financial institutions, as security brokers, investment companies, and foreign financial firms forged new instruments for savers and provided many borrowers with a cheaper and wider choice of funds. To a considerable degree this lagging performance by banks reflected the regulatory straitjacket in which the government had confined them after the depression trauma of the early thirties: limits on rates that could be paid and charged for money, on branching, and on permissible lines of business. Chase itself was severely hampered in its efforts to expand domestically in the 1960s and early 1970s by adverse decisions of the Federal Reserve Board. The Chase Manhattan Corporation, its holding company, was formed largely to break out of this confining web of regulation.

By the 1980s the adverse economic consequences of these regulations had become so apparent that reforms were under way. Ceilings on interest rates were lifted and lines of business broadened. The boundaries between different types of financial institutions were progressively blurred. Chase in its planning for the new environment accorded top priority to two principal markets—corporations and financial institutions (the wholesale market) and consumers (the retail market)—although it continued to court real estate, trust, and other long-standing business. Chase began to stress investment banking and developed interest rate and currency swaps, options, futures, and other complicated products for major firms. In the United States, the bank began to spread across the country, with offices to serve consumers and the middle market more directly, as well as full-service bank subsidiaries in states that permitted them. And it prepared for the day when traditional banking nationwide would be authorized. But Chase also aimed at the upper segment of its markets.

Throughout the postwar years, Chase was fortunate in its leaders: Winthrop Aldrich, an imposing figure who helped restore the image of banking in the 1930s and 1940s; John J. McCloy, an outstanding contributor to American public life, who presided over the bank's critical expansion in the 1950s; George Champion, chairman in the 1960s, a banker's banker highly respected throughout the industry; David Rockefeller, president in the 1960s and chairman in the 1970s, influential throughout the world of business and public affairs; and Willard C. Butcher, able associate of Rockefeller and chairman in the 1980s.

The contributions of these leaders and the development of the institution they have led are illustrated in the chapters that follow. This history would not be complete without an accounting of the successes and failures that marked progress, of the technological advances that altered ways of doing business, and of the external events that shaped the environment. These all form an integral part of the Chase story, one that relates how a leading U.S. bank of the 1940s grew and developed into one of the few global banking institutions of the 1980s.

PART ONE

Postwar reconstruction, expansion, and merger: 1945–1960

After a brief sketch of the early history of Chase, from 1877 to World War II, this part examines in some detail the bank as it stood in 1945 providing a backdrop for developments in following years (see Table 1). We shall see how the bank interacted with the swiftly changing economic environment, shaped by postwar reconstruction, expansion, and inflation; the Korean conflict; and alternate periods of prosperity and recession. The impact of Federal Reserve and other government policies also is surveyed.

Domestically, lending grew substantially in this period, chiefly to business, through diverse and innovative means. Loans replaced lower yielding securities as Chase's deposit base increased rather slowly, portending limits on future activity. The bank responded with a large-scale entry into retail banking through merger with the Bank of Manhattan and further expansion of its New York City branch system, thereby gaining access to increased deposits of individuals.

Internationally, Chase reconstituted its foreign activities, which had been disrupted by World War II. Foreign branches in Paris and the Far East were soon reopened and new branches established in Germany and Japan, although the international department continued to favor its prewar policy of operating chiefly through correspondent banks abroad. Few new branches were added in the 1950s, and those in Hong Kong, China, and Cuba were closed. Meanwhile trade finance, foreign exchange, and correspondent business expanded rapidly, and new financing techniques for developing countries were explored.

7

Table 1.   Statistical profile: 1877–1945.[a]

Year	Assets	Loans and Mortgages	Deposits	Capital
1877	1.0	0.6	0.6	0.3
1885	4.5	2.7	3.9	0.5
1887	9.5	5.3	8.4	1.0
1890	15	8.4	13	1.4
1895	25	15	23	1.8
1900	48	22	43	3.1
1905	67	28	60	6.0
1910	105	49	91	13
1914	150	85	135	14
1918	471	262	373	25
1920	535	321	351	40
1925	638	304	565	47
1929	1,715	885	1,248	241
1930[b]	2,697	1,536	2,074	358
1933	1,715	795	1,339	207
1935	2,351	638	2,075	222
1940	3,824	664	3,543	237
1941	3,812	802	3,535	241
1945	6,093	1,280	5,742	300

a. End of year figures expressed in millions of dollars. Exceptions to year-end date are December 7, 1887; December 13, 1895; December 13, 1900; November 9, 1905; and November 10, 1910.
b. After merger with The Equitable Trust Company of New York.
Source: Reports of The Chase National Bank of the City of New York to the Comptroller of the Currency, Chase Archives.

Significant changes in management and organization also occurred. Winthrop Aldrich retired as chairman in 1953 and was succeeded by John J. McCloy. In 1957 a new generation came to the fore, with George Champion as president (succeeding J. Stewart Baker, former head of Manhattan) and David Rockefeller as vice chairman. Modern techniques of management were introduced, and the organization was modified to accommodate the new initiatives in retail banking.

By 1960 Chase Manhattan held assets of $9.3 billion, almost double Chase's assets in 1946, making the bank the largest in the city. Loans increased fourfold, and profitability was greatly enhanced. The bank was favorably viewed by the public as it prepared to move into its new headquarters at One Chase Manhattan Plaza.

The Chase National Bank: 1877–1945

At war's end, in 1945, The Chase National Bank of the City of New York was approaching its seventieth anniversary. Founded in 1877 by John Thompson, the bank had grown with the nation through periods of prosperity and adversity. By 1945 it was the largest commercial bank in the country, and served as one of America's leading financial institutions.

Chase at this time was a product of its own unique history, as well as that of banking in general. Thompson had named the bank after his friend Salmon P. Chase, secretary of the treasury under Lincoln and father of the National Banking System.[1] Earlier Thompson had developed and sold the First National Bank of New York, and for many years he published *Thompson's Bank Note Reporter*. With experience and contacts gained from these ventures, Thompson was able to give the new Chase Bank a solid start.

It remained for Henry White Cannon, who succeeded Thompson in 1887, to set the bank on the course it would follow over the next several decades. Cannon had served as comptroller of the currency under President Chester A. Arthur and had roots in the Northwest. "He knew the Western country and he knew country bankers, and he laid the foundations for the growth of The Chase deep and wide by allying it with the undeveloped West," an associate wrote.[2] Under Cannon's leadership Chase became known as a banker's bank, serving as New York correspondent for other banks, holding their reserves, and performing a myriad of services. By 1900, in less than a quarter-century deposits had grown to $43 million, with 70 percent flowing from other banks.

A. Barton Hepburn, also a former comptroller of the currency, was appointed president in 1904 and carried forward this tradition.[3] Rapid national expansion and the favorable reputation of Chase helped swell deposits threefold to $135 million at the time the Federal Reserve System began operations in 1914, with two-thirds of that sum placed by banks. Meanwhile the bank moved aggressively in other directions, establishing relationships with commercial and industrial firms both large and small. These sources soon replaced deposits lost to the Federal Reserve, although correspondent banks continued to be a major source of funds for Chase.

Leadership in the commercial and industrial business was taken by Albert H. Wiggin, who joined the bank in 1904 as a vice president. For almost three decades Wiggin proved a dominant figure, becoming president in 1911

9

and later chairman and chairman of the governing board. He early established relationships with major corporations by adding top executives to the Chase board, while he himself served as a director of fifty companies over the years.[4] Thus by 1917, as the United States prepared to enter World War I, Chase was firmly established as a prominent wholesale bank, primarily serving large business and correspondent banks.

World War I: growth and change

World War I proved a watershed for the U.S. economy and the nation's banks. With Europe convulsed for more than four years, U.S. industry and finance were called upon for both direct assistance and to fill many gaps in the world economy. U.S. industry boomed after 1914, and inflation took hold. Internationally, the United States shifted from importing capital to exporting it. Trade with other nations flowed in increasing volume. For the time being London abdicated as the center of world finance and New York City took over.[5]

For Chase and other banks these developments created many new opportunities. After 1914 the bank's resources again grew more than threefold, to $535 million in 1920, prompted by a powerful advance in credit to commerce and industry. U.S. trade was financed on an increasing scale, shifting away from London. Banker's acceptances, issued by banks for the first time under the Federal Reserve Act of 1913, were initially reported on Chase's statement in 1916. Balances held abroad by both American and foreign firms were transferred to New York. Although the pound sterling later reasserted its primacy in international finance, New York City banks became permanently entrenched in the field.[6]

Chase also struck out in new directions in these years. National banks were not permitted to underwrite and distribute securities for corporations and governments. They could, however, perform these functions through an affiliate, owned by stockholders of the bank.[7] In 1917 Chase established The Chase Securities Corporation, one of the earliest bank security affiliates.[8] An increasing volume of corporate funds were raised through issuance of securities, and Chase, under Wiggin's direction, determined to participate in this profitable business.

The major security activity at this time, however, involved financing the U.S. war effort. As it would again a quarter-century later, the bank played a leading role in distributing U.S. war bonds, and it added substantially to its own portfolio. The sale of Liberty Bonds introduced a wide segment of the American public to the purchase of securities, paving the way for heavy sales of bonds and stocks in the 1920s.[9]

In 1919 Chase first set up its trust department, a function that had been authorized for national banks by the Federal Reserve Act. For Chase both corporate and individual trust activity flowed naturally from its regular banking business. In the early years corporate trust proved dominant, but trust investment for individuals grew steadily.[10] The bank, with aggressive leadership and a solid reputation, was thus in a good position for the advance that followed in the next decade.

The 1920s: Chase reaches out

The 1920s marked an extraordinary period in U.S. economic history. Strong growth, steady prices, and unbridled optimism finally gave way to financial excesses, culminating in the Great Depression of the 1930s. Chase was a leading player in the drama, reaching out into the city, the nation, and abroad with new facilities, by 1929 more than tripling its volume of resources.

Prior to the 1920s Chase's growth had been generated internally, but in the twenties much of it was achieved through merger and acquisition. Five banks were merged with Chase between 1921 and 1929 (see Figure 1), adding $750 million in resources.[11] The first, the Metropolitan Bank, was not large, but it brought Chase seven branches, propelling the bank on a new course.[12] National banks at this time were not permitted to establish branches, although they could maintain branches of merged state banks or trust companies where such branches were authorized. And if a state bank or trust company converted to a national charter, a national bank could merge with it.[13]

A sizable second merger with Mechanics and Metals National Bank in late 1925 increased Chase branches to eighteen in number. Wiggin observed in 1926 that the business of New York could no longer be served adequately by large banks in Wall Street and small banks uptown, that businesses of great magnitude were now located uptown and required branches to bring Chase services to them conveniently.[14] Hence, Chase branches evolved as primarily wholesale in emphasis, rather than retail.

The McFadden Act of 1927 enabled national banks to branch directly within the limits of their city, provided state law authorized state banks to do so. Chase established new branches and added others through further mergers. By the end of 1929 the bank was operating twenty-seven branches and carrying resources of $1.7 billion, making it the third largest in the city, behind National City and Guaranty Trust.[15] A culminating merger with Equitable Trust in 1930 then lifted the bank to the top position.

Meanwhile, Chase also moved abroad with facilities and credit. World War I enlarged the horizons of the bank, as trade financing expanded, and with it correspondent bank relationships. The first foreign representative

The Chase National Bank of the City of New York
1877–1955

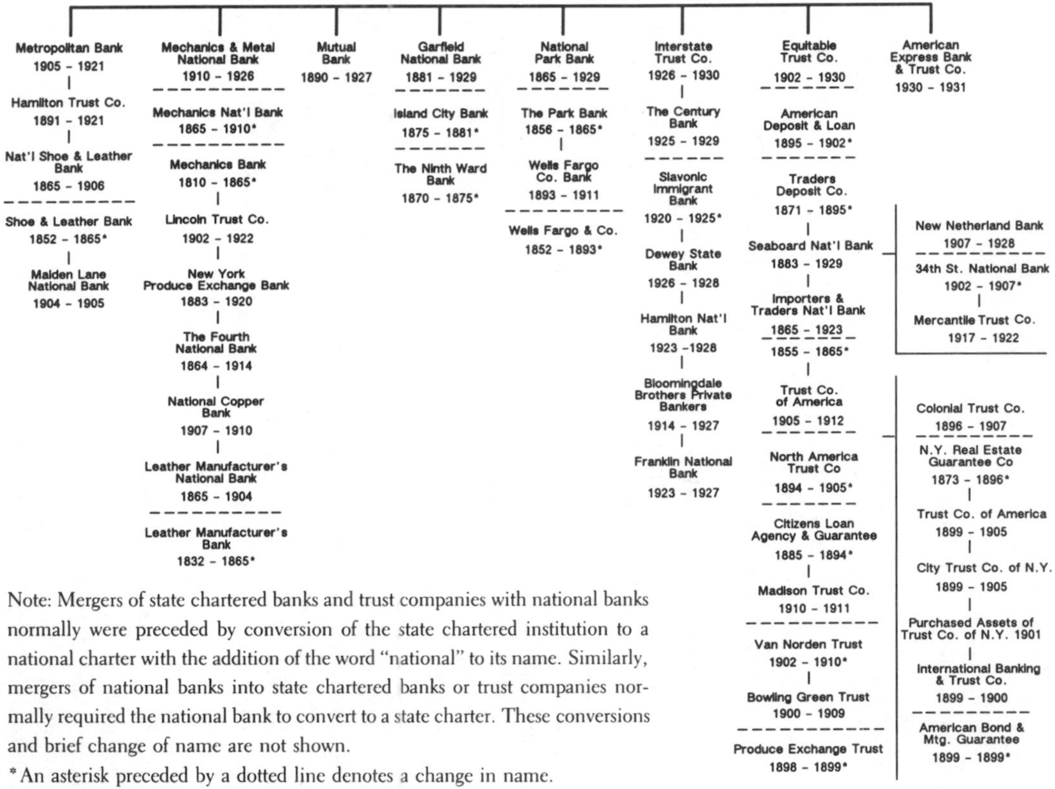

Metropolitan Bank
1905 – 1921

Hamilton Trust Co.
1891 – 1921

Nat'l Shoe & Leather Bank
1865 – 1906

Shoe & Leather Bank
1852 – 1865*

Malden Lane National Bank
1904 – 1905

Mechanics & Metal National Bank
1910 – 1926

Mechanics Nat'l Bank
1865 – 1910*

Mechanics Bank
1810 – 1865*

Lincoln Trust Co.
1902 – 1922

New York Produce Exchange Bank
1883 – 1920

The Fourth National Bank
1864 – 1914

National Copper Bank
1907 – 1910

Leather Manufacturer's National Bank
1865 – 1904

Leather Manufacturer's Bank
1832 – 1865*

Mutual Bank
1890 – 1927

Garfield National Bank
1881 – 1929

Island City Bank
1875 – 1881*

The Ninth Ward Bank
1870 – 1875*

National Park Bank
1865 – 1929

The Park Bank
1856 – 1865*

Wells Fargo Co. Bank
1893 – 1911

Wells Fargo & Co.
1852 – 1893*

Interstate Trust Co.
1928 – 1930

The Century Bank
1925 – 1929

Slavonic Immigrant Bank
1920 – 1925*

Dewey State Bank
1926 – 1928

Hamilton Nat'l Bank
1923 – 1928

Bloomingdale Brothers Private Bankers
1914 – 1927

Franklin National Bank
1923 – 1927

Equitable Trust Co.
1902 – 1930

American Deposit & Loan
1895 – 1902*

Traders Deposit Co.
1871 – 1895*

Seaboard Nat'l Bank
1883 – 1929

Importers & Traders Nat'l Bank
1865 – 1923
1855 – 1865*

Trust Co. of America
1905 – 1912

North America Trust Co
1894 – 1905*

Citizens Loan Agency & Guarantee
1885 – 1894*

Madison Trust Co.
1910 – 1911

Van Norden Trust
1902 – 1910*

Bowling Green Trust
1900 – 1909

Produce Exchange Trust
1898 – 1899*

American Express Bank & Trust Co.
1930 – 1931

New Netherland Bank
1907 – 1928

34th St. National Bank
1902 – 1907*

Mercantile Trust Co.
1917 – 1922

Colonial Trust Co.
1896 – 1907

N.Y. Real Estate Guarantee Co
1873 – 1896*

Trust Co. of America
1899 – 1905

City Trust Co. of N.Y.
1899 – 1905

Purchased Assets of Trust Co. of N.Y. 1901

International Banking & Trust Co.
1899 – 1900

American Bond & Mtg. Guarantee
1899 – 1899*

Note: Mergers of state chartered banks and trust companies with national banks normally were preceded by conversion of the state chartered institution to a national charter with the addition of the word "national" to its name. Similarly, mergers of national banks into state chartered banks or trust companies normally required the national bank to convert to a state charter. These conversions and brief change of name are not shown.

* An asterisk preceded by a dotted line denotes a change in name.

Source: *Corporate Controller, The Chase Manhattan Corporation.*

Figure 1.

office opened in London in 1923, and soon the bank began lending directly to European industries and governments, encouraged by the stability produced by the Dawes plan for German reparations.[16] In 1925 the bank purchased from the American Foreign Banking Corporation its first full-scale foreign branches—in Havana, Panama City, and Cristobal in the Canal Zone.[17] By 1929 representative offices in Paris and Berlin rounded out the bank's foreign network.

Chase Securities Corporation

The principal agent for Chase's geographical expansion in the 1920s, however, was the bank's security affiliate, The Chase Securities Corporation. A brief but severe economic depression in 1920–21 induced U.S. corporations to lessen their reliance on banks for short-term credit. Sizable profits enabled companies to finance working capital from retained earnings, and loans to commerce and industry increased relatively little over the decade. Instead, business issued securities on an increasing scale to raise necessary funds.[18] States and municipal bodies joined in seeking such finance, along with large numbers of foreign borrowers. All told, some $61 billion of securities were issued in the United States from 1922 through 1929.[19]

The flood of new issues could not be handled by the old, established investment houses. Possessing wide contacts and financial experience, banks filled the gap by creating affiliates to participate in the underwriting and distribution of securities. Some two hundred national banks were operating such affiliates in 1929.[20]

Chase Securities Corporation, as noted earlier, was one of the first bank affiliates. For ten years after its founding in 1917 it conducted a wholesale business, acting as underwriter and syndicate manager for many large issues. Capital funds grew from $2.5 million to $20.5 million in 1926, with earnings in the latter year of $3.7 million. Then in 1927 the bank announced a far-reaching change in policy.[21] Chase Securities entered the retail business, selling securities it underwrote to individuals as well as to institutions. An issue of bonds by the Argentine government was the first offering publicly advertised. Sales offices were soon organized in New York and other large cities. By 1929 Chase Securities was operating twenty-seven offices outside New York from coast to coast, as well as abroad in London, Paris, Rome, Warsaw, and Berlin. Capital escalated dramatically to $78 million.[22]

A final expansion occurred in August 1930, with the acquisition by Chase Securities of the Harris Forbes companies, headquartered in Chicago. Harris Forbes had pioneered especially in public utility and municipal issues, maintaining thirty-five sales offices in the United States and Canada, along with offices abroad. The two firms carried a peak capital of $109 million and formed one of the largest security operations in the nation.[23]

The merger proved ill-timed, however, as new security issues dropped off dramatically with the deepening of the depression. Chase Securities and Harris Forbes were consolidated into Chase Harris Forbes in 1931. Security inventory was written down, reducing capital to $55 million. Finally in the spring of 1933 Chase chose voluntarily to liquidate Chase Harris Forbes, although passage of the Glass-Steagall Act subsequently would have mandated it.[24] Capital in the end fell to $4 million, and the firm's public image was badly tarnished, along with that of other security affiliates, by revelations of management abuses, reported in public hearings before the Senate Banking and Currency Committee.[25] Thus the curtain descended on Chase's early effort to expand nationwide.

Chase acquires American Express and merges with Equitable Trust

Two further significant developments occurred on the eve of the Great Depression. The bank in 1929 acquired ownership of American Express, with its extensive travel and banking services, holding most of its stock through Chase Securities Corporation. Subsequently part of the company's banking activity was transferred to Chase, but the opposition of minority shareholders blocked transfer of the traveler's check business. In 1934, as part of the liquidation of Chase Securities, ownership of American Express, which in later years might have proved of inestimable value, was distributed to Chase shareholders.[26]

The second development was of lasting importance. In June 1930 the bank entered into its largest merger to date, with Equitable Trust Company of New York, which carried resources of approximately $900 million and ranked third among trust companies in the nation.[27] Equitable brought to Chase future leadership and strength in the international field. It operated three branches in China and Hong Kong, as well as branches in London, Paris, and Mexico City. The company's personnel and activities were to exert wide influence on the enlarged institution in the years ahead.

Somewhat older than Chase (established in 1871), Equitable had also grown by merger, the most recent in 1929, with the Seaboard National Bank. Legal counsel for Equitable in this joinder was Winthrop W. Aldrich, the son of former Senator Nelson Aldrich of Rhode Island and the brother-in-law of John D. Rockefeller, Jr., Equitable's largest stockholder. Late in 1929 the president of Equitable died suddenly, creating a void in top management at a difficult time. Rockefeller sought someone in whom he had complete confidence to head the bank, if only temporarily, and Aldrich was the logical man for the task. He agreed to undertake it, although, he hoped, not permanently.[28]

Aldrich set out immediately to strengthen the management of Equitable by merging it with Chase in June 1930, creating a bank with resources of $2.7 billion, largest at that time in the nation and indeed the world. Wiggin remained chairman of the governing board of the merged bank, with Aldrich serving as president. After two and a half troubled years, in the depth of the depression Wiggin retired. Aldrich succeeded him early in 1933 as chairman of Chase's governing board, while continuing as president. Aldrich remained at the helm for the next two decades, exercising a profound influence on both Chase and American banking generally.

Chase enters the Great Depression

The Great Depression of the thirties interrupted the growth of Chase, as it did all of banking, and it ushered in far-reaching changes in bank regulation and practice which did much to shape expansion in subsequent years. Yet Chase weathered this period well, closing the decade with substantial strength and prepared for the war that followed.

For banks the trauma reached its peak early in March 1933, when the newly elected president, Franklin D. Roosevelt, closed all banks from Monday, March 6, until Monday, March 13, in the face of a collapse in confidence. More than five thousand banks failed to reopen at the time, and from 1930 to 1933 the total in the nation fell more than one-third to 14,800.[29] Chase, with more banking relationships than any other institution, advanced funds to many of its correspondents, rescuing a number that are prominent today. It matched these actions with corporate customers as well, financing those with good management, even in the face of adversity. George Champion, chairman in the 1960s, later observed of this policy, "That's one of the reasons Chase had a long-time reputation as the number one commercial and correspondent bank in America."[30]

Bank failures led to a plethora of regulations that would affect banks in future decades. Through many postwar years Chase devoted substantial effort and resources to escape the confines then laid down. Government sought through legislation to make banks safe and stable, providing what it regarded as protection for an inherently risky business.[31] As a result of the Glass-Steagall Act of 1933, which separated investment banking from commercial banking, Chase liquidated Chase Harris Forbes and then in 1934 spun off American Express to its shareholders. Payment of interest on demand deposits was prohibited by law, and ceilings were established for time deposit rates. Federal Deposit Insurance was created to provide a safety net for depositors, and thereby to preclude any spreading panic. In addition, entry into commercial banking became highly restricted as new banking charters were subjected to a "needs test," and institutions other than banks (including thrifts) were barred from offering demand deposit and other commercial bank services.

The separation of investment banking from commercial banking was one of the most significant and controversial acts. Aldrich publicly supported this legislation, one of the earliest and certainly the most prominent of bankers to do so.[32] He was convinced that combining the two activities led to conflict of interest, and examples in major banks, including Chase itself, supported him. His stand gained national recognition, although it did not endear him to many of his peers.

At this time an incident occurred that embarrassed the bank while supporting Aldrich's view. Albert Wiggin, then retired, was called in October 1933 as a witness in hearings into Stock Exchange practices conducted by Ferdinand Pecora, counsel to the Senate Banking and Currency Committee. The hearings produced testimony concerning questionable financial relations between companies organized personally by Wiggin and by The Chase National Bank and its affiliates. Most damaging was a revelation that Wiggin's companies had realized a profit of $10 million by dealing in Chase stock between 1927 and 1932, and that a substantial part of this was gained by selling the stock short while the market was collapsing in the final months of 1929—some of these sales to a group sponsored by Chase affiliates in an effort to support the market.[33]

Chase directors had granted Wiggin a lifetime payment of $100,000 a year on his retirement. After the hearings he voluntarily gave up this payment and later made a financial settlement in a court action brought by Chase shareholders and joined by the bank.[34] Yet he was remembered by fellow officers as an outstanding banker who more than any other had been instrumental in building Chase through World War I and the twenties.

Losses and adjustments in the thirties

Chase itself did not escape the depression years unscathed. Capital funds fell from $358 million at the end of 1930 to $219 million four years later, while the capital of Chase Harris Forbes, once $109 million, was virtually wiped out. Moreover the bank's total now included $50 million in preferred stock sold to the government's Reconstruction Finance Corporation, redeemed within three years, however, by reserves accumulated from loan recoveries.

Heavy write-offs on loans were made throughout the early thirties, which contributed significantly to the reduction in capital.[35] The bank accepted equity stock in settlement of a number of debts, including securities of public utilities and a leading film corporation. Over the years most of these companies recovered, and the securities were sold at a profit.

Loans outstanding fell more than 50 percent to $638 million by the mid-thirties, then languished over the rest of the decade. It was this period, however, that gave birth to term loans, with Chase a principal innovator. These loans, which were amortized by a fixed amount each year, normally bore a maturity of eighteen months to five years, although in special circumstances they might extend as long as ten years.[36]

Deposits initially declined in step with loans but recovered sharply after 1933, fueled by large inflows of gold from abroad. Chase resources consequently approached the 1930 peak of $2.7 billion by 1936 and reached $3.8 billion in 1940. With loan demand stagnant, the bank turned to investment in government securities, and the 1940 total of $1.1 billion far surpassed loans in volume. Even so, bank reserves greatly in excess of those required continued to pile up at the Federal Reserve—for Chase, double the volume needed as early as the mid-1930s.

In these circumstances interest rates plummeted. New issue treasury bill rates averaged a minuscule fifteen basis points (less than one-sixth of one percent) from 1934 to 1940. Chase and other banks in 1933–34 adopted a base point for loan pricing, the so-called prime rate, accorded to borrowers of the highest quality. This concept of pricing was to stand unchallenged for almost four decades. Initially the prime was set at 1.5 percent, a level that endured until 1948.[37]

Chase during World War II

Aldrich, in the bank's annual report for 1942, observed, "A nation fighting for its life is not stopped by considerations of finance or credit; it is stopped only by military defeat or economic exhaustion. On that basis, the main objective of wartime finance is to provide a smoothly working mechanism for implementing the fiscal transactions involved in the all-out prosecution of the war."

Three years later, with victory achieved, he was able to report with satisfaction that "The Chase National Bank gave its full strength and energy to the prosecution of the war," providing "loyal support to the credit demands of the government while maintaining a high standard of banking service in all departments under extraordinarily difficult conditions."[38] More than one-fourth of the bank's personnel, some 1,500 in all, served in the armed forces. Forty-eight were killed; eleven had been prisoners of war; and sixteen from the Hong Kong and Chinese branches had been interned by the Japanese, eleven for the duration.[39]

Financing the war held the highest priority for Chase and other banks. From 1942 through 1945 the government raised an unprecedented $156.7 billion in eight war loans. Some $8.3 billion, or 5.3 percent of the total, was obtained through Chase, the largest of any institution.[40] The bank's own government security holdings swelled to $3.1 billion at the end of 1945, in contrast to $1.4 billion four years earlier.

Wartime financing gave a further boost to deposits, as the Federal Reserve made bank reserves readily available. Total resources grew more than 50 percent to a peak of $6.1 billion, preserving Chase's position as the largest bank in the nation. This was not a distinction it maintained for long, however, for a year later it fell to third, behind Bank of America and National City Bank.

Deposits of all banks at war's end were greatly swollen by the huge war loan account of the U.S. Treasury. At Chase alone this amounted to $1.254 billion on December 31, 1945, while a year later the account had been reduced to only $113 million. Not until the merger with the Bank of Manhattan in the mid-1950s did Chase again exceed its wartime totals in assets and deposits, although the composition of assets had changed radically by then, with a huge growth of business loans replacing investment in governments.

Chase's important role as a wholesale bank provided great breadth in sources of deposits. Excluding the war loan acccount, more than 70 percent of the bank's deposits came from businesses and individuals, with corporations responsible for the major proportion. Another 24 percent flowed from correspondent banks throughout the nation and the world. Almost all deposits were payable on demand, as Chase served as a principal clearing bank for corporations and correspondent banks. Growth in the bank's deposits and assets over the full period of the war, propelled by the needs of government, is shown in Table 2.[41]

Although loans advanced strongly, a large part of the increase represented loans against government securities. Credit to industry rose sharply in the early stages of the war, financing the expansion of capacity and adding working capital. But the government itself eventually met many of these needs directly, and corporations paid down debt as they accumulated liquidity. Yet Chase retained its position as a preeminent lender to business, with a volume and market share exceeding that of any other bank.[42]

Of the eight war loan drives carried out by the Treasury, banks were permitted to participate directly in only the first two. But many nonbank investors found it profitable to borrow against existing holdings of treasury securities in order to participate in additional new issues, a practice encouraged by the operations of the Federal Reserve in supporting the prices of government securities. This pyramiding of security purchases produced the major increase in Chase's loans, as it did with loans of all major banks.[43]

Chase's twenty-seven domestic branches contributed greatly to sales of government securities during the war years while providing an increased range of personal banking services. Special checking accounts were added for small depositors, and in 1944 the bank led in organizing a pool of credit from

Table 2.   Major assets and liabilities, The Chase National Bank, 1941 and 1945.

	Year End 1941	Year End 1945	Increase 1941–1945
	(Millions $)		(Millions $)
Total assets	3,812	6,093	2,281
Deposits	3,535	5,742	2,207
Loans	802	1,280	478
Commercial loans	618	648	30
Investments	1,685	3,382	1,697
Capital	241	300	59

Source: The Chase National Bank, *Annual Reports*, 1941 and 1945. Commercial Loans: Reports of The Chase National Bank to the Comptroller of the Currency.

New York City banks for small and medium-sized businesses.[44] For returning servicemen it established a separate unit to administer loans under the Servicemen's Readjustment Act, supplementing these with added credit facilities of its own.[45]

The bank's foreign branches in Paris and the Far East had been cut off early in the war, but its three offices in London became a welcome link with home for thousands of Americans. And its foreign department in New York, with more foreign correspondent relationships than any other bank, helped maintain the vital flow of trade throughout the Western hemisphere, aided also by its Caribbean branches.

Leadership of the bank

Through the war years and the depression preceding them, Winthrop Aldrich remained head of the Chase. He had taken over at a time when Chase's public image and that of banks generally was tarnished; but through his own personal qualities, as well as his breadth of knowledge and vision, he did much to improve the public's view of the bank. Aldrich's wartime activities on the civilian front contributed to this improvement. He served as chairman of the National War Fund, the top organization responsible for coordinating the activities of the host of civilian relief agencies then at work. And he took the lead in a number of civilian organizations concerned with wartime economic problems as well as postwar planning.[46]

Somewhat imperious in manner and austere in appearance, a man of absolute personal integrity, Aldrich inspired respect. His management style was to delegate to others the day-to-day operations of the bank, keeping informed of any significant developments. He selected top personnel, set the strategic course, and spent substantial time serving as the bank's ambassador to its many publics—business, government, and the people at large—both national and international.[47]

In such a regime Aldrich's chief lieutenants played a significant role. For eleven years prior to 1945 the president of Chase under Aldrich was H. Donald Campbell, a Seattle banker who came east as a young man in 1917 and through a series of mergers became associated with the Equitable Trust and then Chase. At the end of 1945 Campbell announced his intention to retire the following April. He was succeeded by Arthur W. McCain, who had been a vice president of Chase since 1929.[48] McCain was a man of wide experience in banking. At the time of his appointment he was in charge of the bank's commercial lending activities in the Far West, as well as in New York State and New Jersey. He had been closely identified with the financing of industrial expansion in the initial stages of the war, especially the aircraft and airline industries. Earlier he was exposed to the international side, having started with Chase in the foreign department after spending twelve years in South America with other banks. With such a background, McCain might have been expected to be a successful president. Aldrich became dissatisfied with his performance, however, and for reasons related in Chapter II, he was replaced in 1949.

Ultimate governance of the bank was in the hands of the board of directors. In 1945 the board numbered twenty-five, the maximum permitted under national banking law. It was a distinguished board, including leaders of industry and insurance, as well as representatives of John D. Rockefeller, Jr., who then owned about 4 percent of Chase's stock.[49] (A list of the directors through the years, along with their period of service, is presented in Appendix 1.) Carl J. Schmidlapp, a long-time vice president of Chase and its senior loan officer, served as an inside director, along with Aldrich and Campbell.

The board met twice a month, and its executive committee convened in alternate weeks. The directors carried major responsibilities: to ensure that the bank was effectively managed, with safety and soundness of assets, and to provide for continuity of management. In addition, the directors were required to fulfill many routine functions under the law: making appointments and promotions, recording information on bank borrowing by officers, approving loans, and the like. Much of this responsibility would be delegated over future years. All purchases and sales of investments and all loans and lines of credit where the aggregate indebtedness to the bank was $500,000 or more were reported to the board. For the most part, however, details with respect to specific transactions were reviewed by the executive committee rather than the full board.

Much of the oversight of the bank was carried out by committees, most of which met monthly and reported to the full board. In addition to the executive committee, of particular importance were the examination, trust, and salary committees. These endured over the years, while others were modified in response to changing needs.[50]

Apart from the board of directors, but appointed by it, were eight branch advisory committees, each attached to a major branch in a particular section of Manhattan. These committees, which met monthly to exchange views on the bank and pertinent issues, were designed to enlist the support and business of the prominent executives who were members.

Chase organization in 1945

In the mid-forties the organization of Chase reflected a heritage of the past modified by recent experience (see Figure 2). The principal markets served by the bank formed a cross-section of the economic life of the nation: commerce and industry, other banks and financial institutions, individuals, and governments. Moreover foreign activities, while in some ways similar to the domestic, possessed special characteristics that required separate administration.

Chase continued to emphasize three of these markets: large-scale commerce and industry (wholesale banking); relations with other banks and financial institutions; and foreign activities. The bank by no means short-changed the market for consumers and small business (retail banking), for it possessed a network of twenty-seven branches. But all except two of those branches were located in Manhattan, and much of their activity continued to be devoted to serving large business. In contrast National City Bank and Manufacturers Trust operated a much larger number of branches and placed relatively greater emphasis on the market for individuals through personal loans and savings. So too did the Bank of America in fast-growing California, where the law, less restrictive than in New York, permitted statewide branching.[51]

Much of Chase's wholesale banking business, along with its relations with domestic banks and insurance companies, was carried out through its commercial banking department. This department included seven geographic districts (one of them Canada), with an officer in charge of each. The district heads met regularly as a group to review loan applications. In this manner they maintained some continuity of treatment and equalization of rate structures throughout the United States.[52] This system of geographic districts while modified in some respects, was to persist well into the 1970s.

Yet even in the mid-1940s not all wholesale business was carried out through the districts. Certain key industries were handled in separate depart-

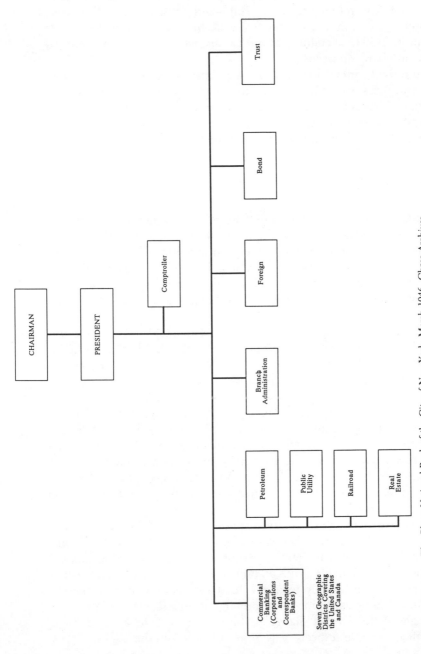

Source: Directory, The Chase National Bank of the City of New York, March 1946. Chase Archives.

Figure 2. The Chase National Bank organization, 1945.

ments, each again reporting independently to the president. Public utilities, petroleum, railroad, and real estate departments then existed also developing out of experience.

Aldrich decided in late 1931 to organize the public utilities department in order to bring together in one place the many loans Chase had outstanding to that troubled industry. Edward L. Love, an imaginative and enterprising officer with experience in investment banking, was placed in charge, and he had much to do with slowly restoring a number of utilities to financial health through the thirties and the war years.[53]

Then in 1936 Aldrich formed the petroleum department, recognizing Chase's strong position in that industry and foreseeing its critical importance to the world economy. This time he reached outside the bank and recruited Joseph E. Pogue, a distinguished petroleum engineer, geologist, and professor at Northwestern University, to head the new department. Initially Pogue knew nothing about banking, but he built an outstanding department of credit officers, petroleum engineers, geologists, and economists.[54]

In real estate too Chase held a commanding position which it was to maintain for many years. Its railroad department, however, formed in the depression years, was losing position in a declining industry and would be phased out as a separate entity early in the 1950s.

Foreign activity

Chase's foreign activities were the province of its foreign department, which shared with that of National City a position of leadership among American banks. The Equitable Trust had been especially strong in this field, with worldwide correspondent bank relationships and branches in London, Paris, Mexico, and the Far East. All this had been combined with Chase, much less active internationally but with branches in the Caribbean. Aldrich closed the Mexico City branch in 1934, much to the later regret of Chase, but retained a representative office in that city.[55] A branch in San Juan, Puerto Rico, was added in 1934.

By far the most important of the Chase branches was in London, where the bank operated three offices—the headquarters at Six Lombard Street across from the Bank of England, at Bush House in Aldwych, and at Fifty-one Berkeley Square near the American Embassy and wartime military headquarters on Grosvenor Square. The Chase branch had long been managed by a competent Scotsman, John Wallace, who was favorably known in the City and had the confidence of Aldrich.

Chase lost no time in reopening its branches in Paris, Hong Kong, Shanghai, and Tientsin once the war was over, and all were in operation by late 1945. It also moved into South Asia and the Middle East, opening representative offices in Bombay in late 1945 and in Cairo in mid-1946.[56] But the bank passed over an opportunity to establish a branch in the Philippines, again a decision regretted in later years.[57]

With the resumption of worldwide business, the foreign department soon came to be organized on both a geographical and a functional basis. The world was divided into European, Latin American, Near East, and Far East territories, with separate units also responsible for handling domestic (commodity) credits, commercial letters of credit, foreign exchange, money transfer, and other specialized activities. After the two co-directors of the department retired at the end of 1945, Charles Cain, Jr., in charge of commodity lending and originally from Equitable, was given broader administrative responsibilities. He was appointed director in 1947 and served in that capacity for sixteen years.

Trust, bond, and staff departments

One of the largest units of the bank, and one that commanded the continuing attention of the directors, was the trust department. It occupied ten floors of the bank's building at Eleven Broad Street, a block away from the head office, and employed a staff of 1,200, about one-sixth of the bank's total. The department provided a full range of trust services—personal, investment, and corporate—and carried many important accounts, including Rockefeller trusts. Chase's position in this field at the time was on a par with that of any other bank.

Still another department was concerned with investment and sale of government and general obligation municipal bonds, as well as underwriting the latter. It was run by Eugene R. Black, the son of a former governor of the Federal Reserve system, who had come to Chase from the bank's old security affiliate, Chase Harris Forbes. Aldrich also introduced Black to international activity. In February 1945 he was instrumental in organizing a $100 million credit to the Royal Government of the Netherlands, with Chase as the manager of a syndicate of fourteen New York City banks. This was the first extension of private credit to a liberated country.[58] Later Black left his mark on the international scene as president of the World Bank.

In one organizational respect, however, the bank was seriously deficient by today's standards: its staff functions were of limited scope, and it exercised few of what are now known as modern management techniques. In this it was no different from other banks, which lagged behind industry in up-to-date management practice.

Chase undertook no formal planning, although Aldrich and others were developing a strategic conception that embraced further expansion into retail banking, as well as more traditional activities. Total expenses were projected each year, but the bank lacked any real budget. A staff concerned with public relations and advertising existed, and Aldrich made good use of it. Similarly an economics staff was available, but largely for public relations and counseling to Aldrich. The important department handling personnel was adequately manned but was directed by nonprofessionals transferred from other areas of the bank.[59]

Personnel at war's end

The staff that managed and supported the bank's diverse activities by mid-1945 numbered about seven thousand. Almost half were women, compared with one-fourth in 1941. The great majority were clerical, engaged in back office support of functions at the head office and in the branches and trust department. The officer group totaled about four hundred, of whom seventy-seven were vice presidents. A large cadre of experienced personnel added strength to the staff; some 940 had been with the bank twenty-five years or more, and close to half more than ten years. The fact that two-thirds of the 1,500 personnel who had entered the armed forces returned to the bank after the war suggests that Chase maintained a satisfactory working environment.[60]

Yet Aldrich and others recognized that the bank would face a serious problem in the years ahead, since many of its officers would soon be retiring. Chase, like other banks, found itself with a surplus of personnel during the depression—the more so as a result of the merger with Equitable. Very few were added to the official staff between 1930 and 1946 other than those promoted from within. A personnel committee was formed, and on its recommendation in 1946 the bank undertook a significant forward step, establishing a management training program for which it recruited college graduates from outside the bank as well as promising clerical employees.

The first of these programs included thirty-one selected college graduates and sixteen from within the bank, most of whom had no college degree.[61] It was the second program, in 1947, however, that proved unusually valuable, producing a number of senior officers in later years, including Willard C. Butcher, eventually president and chairman. George Champion, then a vice president in the commercial banking department, provided much of the initiative for the program. Its trainees were exposed to all the major departments of the bank over a twelve-month period, and their training was supplemented by outside study and evening lectures.[62]

Recruitment and management training were matters of continuing concern to the bank in the years to come. The program was revised many times in the light of changing needs and competitive pressures. National City Bank had conducted a recruitment program as early as 1917. It and others proved to be potent competitors for able young personnel.

David Rockefeller joins the bank

The year 1946 also marked the arrival at the bank of David Rockefeller, who later as vice chairman, president, and chairman was to be influential beyond others in shaping its course. Rockefeller was thirty when he came to the bank in April 1946, after receiving his discharge from the army as a major in intelligence. He had graduated from Harvard some ten years earlier with a concentration in history and literature, and followed this with graduate study in economics at Harvard, the London School of Economics, and the University of Chicago, from which he received a Ph.D. degree. Subsequently, prior to entering the army, he served as private secretary to Mayor LaGuardia in New York City and then briefly as assistant regional director of the Office of Defense and Warfare Services. During the war he was active as an army intelligence officer in North Africa and France.[63]

Young Rockefeller, the son of John D. Rockefeller, Jr., with a record of accomplishment had many potential career paths open to him. He was influenced in his choice of banking by Joseph Rovensky, who served as co-director of Chase's foreign department, and by his uncle, Winthrop Aldrich. At the suggestion of Rovensky, Rockefeller spent the summer of 1937 with the Chase economics department, and while a student at the London School of Economics, devoted half a day each week as a trainee at the London branch of Chase. Aldrich, when traveling through Europe in 1945, met Rockefeller in Paris and again suggested that he join the bank. Rockefeller, who maintained a great interest in international affairs, chose to start his career as an assistant manager in the foreign department.[64]

Chase's special culture

Of significance to Chase or any institution of long standing is the special culture that it develops. A set of values and attitudes permeates the organization. Certain activities gain priority attention and attract the most able talent; and in the absence of change, particular ways of doing things become ingrained. The new or different is frequently resisted, even if subconsciously. This is the case especially where technological or environmental change is gradual and planning does not exist.

Chase in the early postwar years had its own special culture. The greatest value and emphasis were placed on wholesale banking—on relations with large business and domestic banks. Foreign activities were also accorded some priority, with the use of foreign correspondent banks a favored mode of operation in many areas. Major departments operated with a high degree of autonomy and independence. And in relations with personnel, a paternalistic attitude frequently prevailed. Complementing this too was a sense of social responsibility which was weighed in the balance with profits.[65]

In such an environment it was no accident that those departments that served large business—commercial banking, public utilities, petroleum, and railroad—included twenty vice presidents, whereas the foreign department had only seven and the domestic branches fourteen, all of them in branches that served major business firms. Nor did it occasion any surprise when in September 1947 four senior vice presidents were named, all engaged in wholesale banking: Carl Schmidlapp, Percy Ebbott, and Hugo Scheurmann from the commercial banking department and Edward Love from public utilities. In 1946 the new president, Arthur McCain, had also been selected from the wholesale area. Aldrich created the senior vice presidents to join him and the president in a top-level executive group dealing in matters having to do with the bank's overall management and policy.

On the foreign side the impact of the merger with Equitable Trust was still felt fifteen years later. While the Equitable had operated branches in London, Paris, and the Far East, the major thrust of its business involved relations with foreign correspondent banks. In this the Equitable had been a leader, and the concept had been carried forward into Chase. The principal activity of Chase's officers was to visit these correspondents, attract deposits, and develop reciprocal trade business with them. This contributed to the foreign department and the commercial banking department operating quite independently of each other in most respects. Indeed, relations between the two groups were marked by a certain degree of restraint and rivalry.[66]

Paternalism in employee relations was most evident in a reluctance to discharge or release employees. The bank prided itself on not releasing employees during the depression, even though it was overmanned. Officers who did not perform adequately were moved into less demanding jobs, a practice that prevailed into the postwar years.[67] Such policies and practices, while humane, were not altogether consistent with the efficiency and economy that came to be required as the protective regulations born of the depression began to erode and banking became more competitive.

Indeed many elements of the Chase culture would be tested and modified in the years ahead. The heavy concentration on wholesale banking, the emphasis on correspondent banks in foreign activities, the independence in operations of the departments, inefficiencies in manning—all these would be severely altered by the economic, political, and technological changes of the ensuing decades.

Postwar expansion and inflation: 1946–1952

As the war drew to a close, Aldrich and his lieutenants wondered what type of environment would confront the bank. Opinion at Chase and elsewhere was divided. One school, whose experience of the 1930s was still a vivid memory, felt that the huge cutback in military spending, coupled with the demobilization of 12 million in the armed forces, would cast the nation into a prolonged recession. Others saw a huge accumulated internal demand awaiting fulfillment, and a devastated world abroad requiring reconstruction. Their main concern was the possibility of inflation, once wartime controls were removed.

In any event, the transition to a peacetime economy in the United States, with the reabsorption of discharged military personnel, moved ahead with surprising ease. Unemployment never exceeded 3 million, or little more than 5 percent of the labor force, and after a brief downward turn in the first quarter of 1946, the economy began to improve. Some $146 billion of liquid savings in the hands of individuals—three times the volume six years earlier—helped power an advance of more than 11 percent in real consumer spending over a twelve-month period.

Business also stepped up its own spending greatly, drawing on a hoard of accumulated assets, larger retained earnings, and new credits as it reconverted to a postwar pattern of demand. Capital expenditures rose by more than a third in real terms, and inventories swung from liquidation to a high rate of accumulation. The long-depressed housing industry also recovered, with new starts reaching 650 thousand.

All this reflected a huge shift from government to the private sector. Government outlays on goods and services, which in the final year of the war had accounted for almost 40 percent of the gross national product, fell in 1946 by nearly two-thirds. The net result was a decline in real GNP for the year, but a rise in employment and income for the populace at large. Production and employment continued to expand through 1947 and well into 1948, with industrial output growing by 17 percent over these two years.

Meanwhile those concerned about the potential for inflation began to see their apprehension justified. The money supply had more than doubled during the war, but inflation had been suppressed through rationing of goods and a widespread system of price controls. Soon these controls began to give way. Labor became restive, and strikes interrupted a number of key industries

Table 3.   Statistical profile: 1945–1960.[a]

	Assets	Loans and Mortgages	Deposits	Capital (Millions)
1945	6.1	1.3	5.7	300
1946	4.9	1.1	4.5	314
1948	4.6	1.5	4.2	328
1950	5.3	1.9	4.9	353
1952	5.7	2.6	5.2	375
1954	5.9	2.4	5.4	397
1955[b]	7.5	3.7	6.8	526
1956	7.8	3.9	6.9	580
1958	8.3	4.1	7.4	631
1960	9.3	4.7	8.1	689

	Domestic Loans and Mortgages	Loans to Commerce and Industry	Overseas Loans	Net Operating Earnings (Millions)
1945	1.3	0.6	*	17.4
1946	1.1	0.8	*	19.1
1948	1.5	1.2	*	19.0
1950	1.9	1.3	*	18.5
1952	2.5	2.0	0.1	27.9
1954	2.3	1.8	0.1	28.3
1955[b]	3.6	2.3	0.1	42.3
1956	3.8	2.8	0.2	49.2
1958	3.9	2.7	0.2	55.6
1960	4.4	2.6	0.3	74.3

a. End-of-year figures expressed in billions of dollars.

b. After merger with The Bank of Manhattan.

* Less than $100 million.

Source: *Annual Reports* of The Chase National Bank, 1945–1954, and The Chase Manhattan Bank, 1955–1960. Loans to Commerce and Industry, Reports to the Comptroller of the Currency, 1945–1954, and to the New York State Superintendent of Banking, 1955–1960.

in 1946, resolved only by a substantial increase in wages. Price controls were loosened by midyear and abandoned altogether in the autumn. The result was a steep rise in prices, beginning in the second half of 1946 and continuing well into 1948 before leveling off. Over this period consumer prices rose an average of 34 percent, but the cost of equipment and material used by business climbed even more, with the cost of farm products outpacing all others.[1]

Chase contributes to the postwar expansion

The combination of postwar growth and inflation brought profound changes to the nation's banks, none more so than Chase (see Table 3). The bank's portfolio at war's end had been top heavy with loans against government securities; only half its loans were outstanding to business. But in 1946 the government, flush with cash and cutting back expenditures, paid off substantial debt, and many holders of securities turned to more productive investments. The result was a large reduction in security loans, replaced to a considerable degree by an increase in loans to business. By the end of 1946 loans against securities had declined to 13 percent of the total, while credit extended to business accounted for three-quarters of the portfolio.

Already in late 1945, as credit in support of war production wound down, the bank's loans for expansion of working capital and equipment for peacetime output was beginning to increase. For the next three years this wave of demand moved forward at a varying pace as business encountered large unanticipated cash needs, created more by inflation than by an advance in the real economy. Chase's loans to business rose from $648 million at the end of 1945 to $1.199 billion at the end of 1948, an extraordinary 85 percent increase.[2] Yet the bank could have done even more, if not for the fact that the new president, Arthur McCain, viewed the future with great caution and was a restraining influence on loan expansion.[3] Although Chase retained its lead in loans to business, its relative share among New York City banks fell slightly from 21.2 percent in 1945 to 20.4 percent three years later.[4] And because of the large reduction in security loans, the loan portfolio as a whole increased only 19 percent to some $1.531 billion.

Much of the credit advance took the form of term loans, not only for equipment financing but for permanent working capital as well. Many loans were revolving credits, to be drawn down when the borrower wished, frequently with the option of conversion to a term loan. Yet a return to the prewar seasonal pattern of borrowing also became evident, with industry and trade purchasing raw materials and finished goods more heavily in the autumn and winter than in the summer.

A start in installment lending

Chase at this time also moved deeper into the field of consumer banking. In May 1946 it began to provide installment credit, an activity that National City and Manufacturers Trust had carried on for some years.[5] The bank had inaugurated a program of personal loans to returning servicemen in 1945, and installment credit represented a further evolutionary step. But as Percy Ebbott later recalled, there was no one at the bank with the skill to manage an installment credit department: "Certainly an officer accustomed to lend thousands of dollars to a corporation on a balance sheet would have difficulty in lending $300 to a man and wife who had few assets, let alone a balance sheet."[6] The bank therefore hired the best number two man it could find from the installment credit departments of its competitors. So began what was to be an important new business—financing autos and home appliances, insurance premiums, property improvements, other personal needs, and even small businesses. Loans were extended at the head office and at the bank's twenty-seven branches, helping to round out Chase's retail services.

Other than special checking, the retail service stressed most frequently in advertising was the compound interest (savings) account. Thanks to the large personal liquidity built up during the war and expanding incomes, these accounts increased each year in number and size, although the aggregate constituted only a small share of Chase's total deposits. In 1947 rates on savings accounts improved slightly, with one percent paid on accounts of $5 to $2,500, and ¼ percent on accounts of $2,501 to $25,000, still far below the regulatory ceiling set by the Federal Reserve. Previously the maximum on such accounts had been $15,000, with only ⅛ percent paid on accounts of $10,001 to $15,000.[7]

Reconstruction and recovery abroad

Meanwhile an immense task of reconstruction confronted the nations of Western Europe and the Far East, the theaters of active warfare. Not only did the physical plant have to be rebuilt and adequate food have to be supplied, but trade needed to be rechanneled as well, for almost all these nations were highly dependent on imports. It quickly became apparent that the task would be doubly difficult without help from the United States in the form of supplies and financial aid.

The United States responded with a series of programs unique in history. By the end of 1946 the federal government had authorized $8.5 billion of foreign aid in grants and loans. The widely debated loan of $3.750 billion to Britain in the form of a line of credit available to December 31, 1951, was approved by midyear. Additional assistance came through a number of other channels—the United Nations Relief and Rehabilitation Agency, Lend-lease, the Export-Import Bank, and the U.S. Army in Germany and Japan. In 1946 the United States ran a surplus on its net export of goods and services of $8 billion, which in turn was covered by $3 billion of grants, $3 billion in long-term loans, and a gold inflow of $2 billion.[8]

The great bulk of long-term foreign lending in the early postwar years was carried out through the government. Private financial institutions, however, played a limited but important role. Chase in 1945 managed a loan to the

Netherlands, the first to a foreign government for rehabilitation, and in 1946 a similar although smaller loan was extended to the central bank of Norway.[9] Later, in 1947, the bank also provided a sizable credit to the Rumanian government for the import of badly needed agricultural and other food products.[10] By and large, loans to governments or central banks at this time were backed by gold.

Nonetheless, all this early assistance proved to be inadequate. By the first half of 1947 conditions in Western Europe had deteriorated seriously. Crops were poor; food shortages and political unrest were troubling Germany; strikes were occurring in France and Italy; and balance-of-payments positions were steadily deteriorating. Again the United States responded, first through aid to Greece and Turkey of $400 million. Then after midyear a plan for European recovery, the Marshall Plan, began to take shape on both sides of the Atlantic, with President Truman submitting proposals to Congress in December 1947. By April 1948 a three-year program had been launched, with approval by Congress of $5 billion in aid for the first twelve months.[11]

The European Recovery Program proved to be a turning point for Western Europe. Output in all countries increased substantially in 1948 and again in 1949, running in excess of prewar levels in most areas. This general improvement was tempered, however, by the spread of inflation. Initially prices were held in check in Europe by widespread controls. But these began to break down as early as 1947, and prices rose markedly in 1948, with the commodity inflation prevalent in the United States a contributing factor. Rising prices added to the cost of the recovery program and created balance-of-payments problems not only in Europe but in Latin America and Asia as well. By 1948 the entire free world outside the United States was complaining of a dollar shortage.[12]

Chase moves into Germany and Japan

For Chase the recovery of world trade and the expansion of economic activity abroad created new opportunities. Even in 1946 the bank was able to report that

> the volume of business handled in all divisions of the Foreign Department increased enormously. Deposits held for foreign account rose to a record total. Commercial letters of credit and other facilities for financing exports and imports were in extraordinary demand. And expansion in operations required a 70% increase in personnel and much additional working space.[13]

In London too the branches reported a doubling in commercial loans and a substantial increase in deposits. This thrust in foreign activity continued until mid-1947, when it paused until the European Recovery Program came into being.

In late 1947, at the invitation of the military authorities, the bank extended its branch network into Germany and Japan.[14] With the exception of a branch in Beirut, these were the only new countries in which Chase established branches or affiliates until the late 1950s, reflecting the foreign department's continued preference for dealing through correspondents. New facilities were located in Frankfort on the Main and Stuttgart in Germany and in Tokyo, followed soon by branches in Heidelberg and Osaka. Chase was the first bank to be invited into Germany, but was preceded by National City and Bank of America in Japan.

These branches at first largely served the needs of the U.S. military and its personnel. Then several years later, at the time of the Korean war, Chase established an additional series of special facilities in Japan, seven in all, to meet the needs of military personnel based there or visiting the country from war zones for rest and recreation. The Chase facilities exchanged yen for the scrip in which the military was paid. Some yen remained on deposit, providing useful local currency for the bank's business.[15]

Military facilities in both Germany and Japan were kept separate from the bank's main branches, which were positioned to finance growing trade with the United States. The German branches for some years did not deal directly with German firms, but worked largely through German banks. But in Japan the branches of Chase and the other U.S. banks became the depositories of the central bank reserves of that country, providing resources of high value in support of trade and other business.

Representative offices rather than branches were reopened in Rome in 1947, and in Buenos Aires for the first time in early 1948. These supplemented offices already operating in Mexico City, Bombay, and Cairo. Elsewhere activities of the branches in Shanghai and Tientsin were handicapped by stringent government regulations and by widespread economic dislocation accompanying the inflation then gripping China.

Aldrich travels to Latin America

Although the chairman of the bank had traveled to Europe frequently in the thirties and forties, he had not visited other areas of the world for the bank. But in the spring of 1947 Aldrich made a lengthy trip through Latin America, visiting Cuba, Brazil, Uruguay, Argentina, Chile, Peru, Venezuela, Panama, and the Canal Zone.[16] He wore three hats on this trip:

chairman of The Chase, president of the International Chamber of Commerce, and chairman of the President's Advisory Committee for Financing Foreign Trade, a post to which he was appointed by President Truman in 1946. Two decades later Charles Cain, Jr., who had accompanied him, recalled, "This man was superb . . . as the chairman of the bank and as president of the International Chamber . . . if I had made the trip alone I would not have seen the people I saw with Mr. Aldrich. This even included Juan and Evita Peron . . . I never knew him to be tired. This was a hard trip. . . . But when the time came to operate, he operated."[17]

The trip was a success, both for the bank and the International Chamber, and it was the beginning of far more extensive foreign travel by senior officers of the bank. Aldrich came back with a clearer understanding of the needs of Latin America and the opportunities that existed there. Shortly before the trip he had approved a $10 million line of credit for the central bank of Brazil. His biographer Arthur M. Johnson recounts a meeting of Percy Ebbott and Charles Cain, Jr., with Aldrich concerning the transaction, which illustrates the chairman's method of operation. As Ebbott remembered:

> I'll never forget one day . . . the Central Bank of Brazil needed an emergency loan. Charlie Cain came to see me about it, and I said, "Well let's go in and talk with the Chairman; it'd do him good to get in on one of these credit jobs." When [the two] went into Aldrich's office, Cain pointed out that Chase lacked a firm policy with respect to Brazil, and he recommended that the Bank extend a line of credit and stay with it. . . . Many years later Cain still remembered the dialogue with Aldrich: "I think a bank of our importance has got to be there in a big way if we're going to be an international bank. He looked at me and he said, 'What do you recommend?' I said, 'Ten million dollars.' He said, 'What do you think of the Brazilians?' I said, 'They're unpredictable. But the country is still there, and if we get frozen, some day we'll get unfrozen. But in the middle I don't want you or the directors worrying. I want it fixed.' And he said, 'All right.' And that line was never reduced or frozen.[18]

The European Cooperation Administration, 1948–1949

The foreign economic activities of the United States in 1948 and 1949 were dominated by the European Cooperation Administration (ECA). Chase supported this new agency in every way possible, circulating information to correspondents and customers on its functions and regulations and even sending officers abroad to assist major correspondents in setting up procedures. Some of these correspondent banks then designated Chase for a substantial share of the interim financing carried out under their country's allotments of aid. Chase soon became the leader in financing shipments through letters of credit made out to importers abroad. From April 1948 to August 1949 letters of credit issued by all banks under the ECA program totaled $2.2 billion, with Chase responsible for $356 million, well in advance of other banks.[19] Considerable additional documentation was required for shipments under ECA, and the business was not very profitable. Yet it served the national interest while helping cement important business relations for Chase.

By 1949 Europe was well on the road to recovery, although prices were still rising. Intra-European trade returned to prewar levels, and U.S. aid for the year amounted to $5.2 billion. The pattern of world exchange rates, however, no longer reflected underlying economic reality. In September, Great Britain initiated a necessary adjustment, devaluing the pound sterling from $4.03, a rate established in 1946, to $2.80. Other sterling area countries followed, and currencies generally were realigned.[20] Early in the year, too, President Truman announced what came to be known as the Point Four program. Designed to provide technical assistance to underdeveloped countries, it marked the start of U.S. aid to the developing world.

As a result, 1949 was the most active year Chase's foreign department had yet experienced. Currency devaluations both complicated and increased the bank's business by expanding trade financing throughout the world. And the bank continued to add to its correspondent relationships: it became the principal banking connection for the National Bank of Yugoslavia in 1948 and for the newly organized Central Bank of the Philippines in 1949.[21] In 1949 Chase also broke the financial isolation of Franco's Spain, extending its first loan to that country—a $25 million credit secured by gold.[22] Alfred W. Barth, later to head the foreign department, had carried out business for the U.S. government in Spain during World War II and was perhaps the best-known American banker in Spain and Portugal. He arranged the Spanish credit as well as the new relationship with Yugoslavia.

Closing in China and Hong Kong

In the Far East, however, trouble was brewing. The communists, coming into power in China, forced the bank's branch in Tientsin to close in August 1949, and not long afterward the Shanghai branch also ceased to do business. By April 1950 only one American staff member, Julius J. Thomson, remained, and he was told to wind up the small amount of uncompleted business.[23] As matters developed, Thomson was destined to stay in Shanghai for five years, detained as a hostage because of disagreement between Chase and the Chinese revolutionary government over the disposition of Chinese assets held by Chase, a disagreement shared by other banks and institutions that had been active in China.

A year later, with the Korean war under way, Aldrich also closed the branch in Hong Kong.[24] The status of that colony was then clouded with uncertainty. The U.S. Treasury prohibited payments and transactions in which communist China had a direct interest, and business in the Hong Kong branch had fallen off sharply. More important, Aldrich feared that a problem related to the Trading With the Enemy Act might arise similar to a disconcerting incident that occurred during World War II. The bank in 1944 (an election year) had been accused by the U.S. Treasury of conspiring to release funds illegally to several Belgian and Dutch nationals, allegedly as a result of its failure to block the account of a small company suspected of doing business with the Axis in industrial diamonds. Although the bank was acquitted in a subsequent trial, the incident received wide publicity and was highly embarrassing to the bank and to Aldrich personally, and he was determined to avoid any possible repetition.[25] Nevertheless, other banks, including National City, remained in Hong Kong, and events proved them right. Chase reopened its Hong Kong branch in 1963, when it acquired Far East offices from the Nationale Handelsbank of Amsterdam (see Chapter XI). The bank's image and position in Hong Kong had suffered, however.

Management changes in 1949

Early in 1949 a significant change occurred in top management. Percy J. Ebbott was appointed president, replacing Arthur W. McCain, who became vice chairman. Carl J. Schmidlapp, senior vice president and chief loan officer, who had been a director since the war years, was made vice chairman of the executive committee. Two new senior vice presidents were also named: George Champion, at forty-five displaying qualities of leadership in the commercial banking department, and Eugene R. Black, who would resign before the year was out to accept the presidency of the World Bank.[26]

McCain had been president for three years. Although the bank had undoubtedly moved forward in that period, there was dissatisfaction within the official staff over his leadership. Courtly in manner, a Southerner, McCain nevertheless lacked diplomacy in dealing with others, and he failed to project an image of leadership. Nor was he as capable or aggressive in his approach to banking as the competitive environment required.

Ebbott had a more outgoing personality, and he was widely respected both within the bank and without. His acquaintance nationwide with bankers and leaders of industry was unrivaled. He had been a pioneer in the development of term loans for business in the 1930s, and this was typical of his approach to

banking—to try to work out a way to help a company if it was at all creditworthy.[27] He had come to Chase by way of the Seaboard and Equitable
mergers of 1929–30, and had served as vice chairman of the commercial
banking department. Ebbott was a director of a number of companies—
Allied Stores, Nash-Kelvinator, and Moore-McCormack Lines among
them—and he encouraged other officers to accept such responsibilities,
convinced that they would benefit from the experience. He possessed a
combination of personal and professional qualifications that gained universal
approval for his appointment.

The Korean war and renewed expansion

These improvements in Chase's management had come at an opportune
time, for the bank soon entered a critical new phase of expansion. In June
1950 one of those unexpected events that overshadow all others occurred.
North Korea invaded South Korea, and the United States, as the protector of
the South, again found itself at war. Although the conflict was limited, it
soon involved forces from mainland China as well. Moreover, it sounded the
alarm in other countries, especially in Western Europe, and some contributed troops and supplies directly under the banner of the United Nations. In
consequence the war greatly influenced not only the economy of the United
States but that of the world, doing much to shape the activity of industry and
finance.

Fortunately the United States in mid-1950 was in a position to absorb the
added demands that were placed upon it. Although the upward thrust of
postwar expansion came to a halt in early 1949, and the economy experienced its first postwar recession, it turned out to be extremely mild, with
industrial production down only moderately. The recession also yielded an
unexpected dividend: prices declined for the first time since the 1930s. By
autumn economic activity had begun to recover, and in the first half of 1950
business again was headed into a normal cyclical expansion, although considerable slack persisted.

The bank mirrored this pattern in its own activity. Loans declined in 1949
for the first time since 1946, and the reduction was particularly marked in
loans to business, which fell by 19 percent. As was to be the case in subsequent periods of economic recession, many term loans on the bank's books
were prepaid, frequently by companies taking advantage of ease in the capital
markets by refinancing.[28] Because of its preeminent position in loans to large
business, the bank was prone to be more affected by this development than its
competitors, providing a source of concern to management and account
officers.

The U.S. economy in wartime: 1950–1952

Slackness in the economy and in loans to business soon disappeared under the powerful stimulus of wartime spending. In the twelve months following the onset of war defense outlays rose sharply, and the president was given wide powers over the economy, including authority to impose selective controls over consumer and real estate credit. Income tax rates were raised, and early in 1951 an excess profits tax was adopted. Wages and prices were frozen initially, and new attempts to regulate them followed.

Consumers, industry, and finance all were affected by these onrushing developments. Housing construction and the purchase of autos and household goods advanced strongly in the early stages of the conflict, then slowed under the imposition of credit controls. But output expanded rapidly in lines related to defense, and the economy exhibited surprising resiliency. Industrial production as a whole rose 40 percent in the four years following the recession of 1949. Prices also reacted less vigorously than many had anticipated. Wholesale prices rose by 16 percent, but then began to subside. The post–World War II inflation was not to be repeated, as a combination of monetary, fiscal, and credit policies helped hold the increase in the cost of living to only 12 percent over the Korean war period.

The nation's banks, Chase among them, were called upon to play a significant role in efforts toward restraint, although with mixed results. Along with other financial institutions, they administered the controls over consumer and real estate credit.[29] Such credit did grow more slowly during the war, but the relative contribution of controls, with the bureaucratic apparatus necessary to enforce them, has remained open to debate. Also playing a role was a policy of monetary restraint, pursued by the Federal Reserve, which limited the overall growth of credit, including that for consumers and real estate.

More relevant from the bank's standpoint was an effort monitored by the Federal Reserve aimed at getting banks to curb the growth of credit to business on a voluntary basis. This Voluntary Credit Restraint Program, implemented in 1951, was the first of a series that would occur in times of stress over the next several decades. The bank was asked to concentrate on loans for productive purposes and to avoid loans of a speculative character, as well as loans for such "nonproductive" purposes as acquisitions and mergers. Such a program proved difficult to administer. Some credits for working capital undoubtedly were employed in part for speculative accumulation of inventories, and not all mergers or acquisitions were "unproductive." Nevertheless, over the ensuing eighteen months Chase did turn away many loan applications.[30]

And yet the increase in Chase's loans to business in this period was among the most rapid in the bank's history. Over three years, to the end of 1952, such credit doubled to almost $2 billion, and Chase's relative share among New York City banks climbed back from 20.2 percent to 22.6 percent. Meanwhile under conditions of monetary stringency a larger portion of the nation's borrowing was directed, particularly by large business, to New York City banks, a pattern repeated on similar occasions in later years.

Initially loan demand flowed from all industries, stimulated by expanding inventories and rising prices. But as the war progressed, credits by Chase were extended in larger share to aviation and machinery industries, as well as to public utilities, in most cases for defense or defense-related purposes. The bank's loans and unused credits to aircraft manufacturers increased from $25 million to $133 million over the course of 1951 alone.[31]

At this time too a special program designed by the public utilities department to provide credit to small, independent telephone companies came to full fruition. These companies, many of them serving relatively less populated areas, lacked access to capital markets and normal commercial bank credit. The public utilities department had earlier inaugurated a program to provide term loans to assist in their expansion. By 1951 about fifty companies in twenty-three states had taken advantage of the opportunity.[32] The Rural Electrification Administration indirectly complimented the bank by complaining of unfair competition, for although the small utilities received lower interest rates from the government, they frequently were required to fulfill conditions that were unprofitable.

The bank's real estate loans also increased fairly sharply through this period, controls notwithstanding, since many involved short-term financing for large construction projects related to defense. By the end of 1952 the bank's total loan portfolio stood at $2.6 billion, compared with $1.4 billion three years earlier. Aggregate loans had doubled since the end of World War II and more than tripled since 1942, a heady rate of advance. But the growth of the bank's deposits had not kept pace. Since removal of the inflated government deposits in 1946, net deposits by 1952 had grown only $350 million, to approximately $3.7 billion. To fund its loan expansion the bank sold government securities, reducing its securities portfolio by $1 billion, but still retaining total securities of $1.5 billion.

Chase was not unique in this experience. Indeed its share of New York City deposits stood at 19 percent, some improvement since 1949 and the same as in 1945. Nevertheless the failure of deposits to grow was disturbing to Aldrich and others in the bank, who feared that banking in other areas of the country would expand while remaining relatively static in New York City. In California, for example, the Bank of America, permitted to branch statewide, had increased its gross deposits by 40 percent.[33]

The Korean war and the foreign department

The Korean war affected the economic position of the rest of the world even
more than it did that of the United States. It speeded the economic recovery
of Western Europe, unleashed a short but sharp burst of inflation in late
1950 and 1951 that disrupted trade flows and exchange markets, and led to a
shift in emphasis in U.S. aid from economic to military. Growth in Europe
was particularly rapid in late 1950 and 1951, with industrial production
rising 30 to 40 percent above prewar levels. Trade expanded greatly since
most nations needed larger imports to meet both civilian and military needs.
Chase's commercial letter of credit business rose to a new peak in 1950 and
climbed a further 40 percent in the following year. Deposit balances from
foreign banks also set a new high, strengthening the dedication of the foreign
department to the correspondent banking business.[34]

The bank in 1950 served as comanager with J. P. Morgan and Co. of two
loans to France totaling $225 million, a large transaction for that period, and
a forerunner of the balance-of-payments financing which became prevalent
in the 1970s.[35] Chase also managed a $15 million credit to the Netherlands
government in 1951, and a year later pioneered a joint credit with the World
Bank to Royal Dutch Airlines.[36] In addition the bank participated with the
Export-Import Bank in a large cotton loan to Japan, a form of joint financing
repeated frequently over the years.[37]

Limited expansion abroad

During this period Chase's foreign branch network expanded only in the
Caribbean and to a limited degree in Japan. Activities in Latin America were
now headed by David Rockefeller, promoted to vice president in 1950.
Under his direction four new branches were opened in the Caribbean in
1950 and early 1951—one in David, Panama, a rich agricultural area; two
additional branches in the Havana area; and one in San Juan, Puerto Rico.[38]

In remarks dedicating these branches, Rockefeller expressed his view concerning Chase's presence abroad, which he held throughout his career, that
branches existed not only to serve U.S. customers but to assist local business
and development of the local economy as well. For example the branch in
David extended innovative loans to help expand cattle raising in the area.

In 1950 Rockefeller traveled extensively throughout Latin America, meeting with bankers, businessmen, and government officials in seven countries.
He was impressed particularly with the potential of Brazil, and in 1952
helped establish the bank's first direct presence in that country, assisted by
Edward Love and Victor Rockhill, Chase officers experienced in investment

banking. A new venture was organized in partnership with International Basic Economy, Inc. (IBEC), to underwrite and distribute locally securities of Brazilian companies.[39] IBEC had been founded after the war by Nelson Rockefeller to promote economic growth in Latin America and other developing areas. The new company, named Interamericana de Financiamento e Investimentos, S.A., also had as minority shareholders twelve leading Brazilian banks.

Brazil lacked a capital market and was clearly in need of Interamericana's services. But the company never achieved its objectives, and in time the Brazilian partners lost enthusiasm for it. Despite this most of them later established similar institutions of their own. The company also found it difficult to acquire the special management skills required for investment banking in Latin America.[40] Confronted with these problems and lacking experience in the field, Chase finally sold out its interest in 1958 to IBEC, which converted the company into a profitable investment trust.[41] Nevertheless, after this initial effort investment banking continued to be a field of interest to Chase, and the bank returned to the activity in other ways in the late 1960s and early 1970s (see Chapter XII).

Elsewhere in 1950 Aldrich undertook the first trip by a top Chase executive to the Middle East, an area that was to grow in significance to the bank in coming years. He met the rulers, other senior government officials, and businessmen in Cairo, Jidda, Dhahran, Kuwait, Abadan, and Teheran, returning to Europe by way of Lebanon and Turkey.[42]

Later, in 1952, the bank opened its sixth representative office in Beirut, but it failed to gain a facility in what later turned out to be a highly important nation, Saudi Arabia. Oil companies were already making large investments in that country, and Chase in 1949 applied for and was granted permission by the Federal Reserve to open a branch in Jidda.[43] In the end, however, this enterprise did not come to fruition because of delays and opposition in Saudi Arabia. Chase did maintain a personal banking relationship with Ibn Saud, the ruler, and held an important depository relationship with the Saudi Arabian Monetary Agency, the country's central bank.[44] But the bank's efforts over the years to establish a direct representation in the kingdom were unsuccessful until the mid-1970s.

In London the bank moved its Berkeley Square branch into larger quarters in 1952. This made it possible to transfer accounts from Bush House, and so that branch was closed. Across the Channel in Paris the bank's branch at Forty-one rue Cambon had been operated under a subsidiary, first established by the Equitable Trust and renamed The Chase Bank. Other branches of that subsidiary in Hong Kong and China were now closed; so the bank transferred all commercial banking business in Paris from The Chase Bank to a newly organized branch of the parent, The Chase National Bank.[45] In doing so, however, it left the corpus of The Chase Bank alive, with its capital intact, available for an entirely new purpose after the middle of the decade (see Chapter VI).

The bank capitalizes on an expanding economy

Through the immediate postwar years and early 1950s Chase moved to take advantage of the new expansionary environment that followed the depression and the restraints of World War II. Loan demand once again became vigorous, and gained added impetus from the Korean conflict. Corporations borrowed on a term basis to finance working capital and equipment needs, swollen by inflation as well as expansion of output. Commercial paper, open only to a limited group of customers, was not yet a potent factor.

Relations with major business firms, along with correspondent banking, remained Chase's basic activity, providing much of its core deposits and the bulk of its loans. But the bank also increased its service to individuals, with the introduction of installment credit rounding out its retail business. But no area of the bank grew more rapidly than the international department. Chase's trade-related business increased enormously, as war-torn economies were reconstructed and trade and currency relations returned to more normal patterns. The bank continued to act abroad chiefly through correspondent banks. But with newly established branches in Germany and Japan added to those in London and Paris, cornerstones were in place for a network that would be built a decade later.

Final Aldrich years and succession by McCloy

The Korean war years brought to a close the long stewardship of Winthrop Aldrich, who would be succeeded as chairman in early 1953 by a distinguished outsider, John J. McCloy. Meanwhile, though, considerable unfinished business remained to occupy him. High on the list was Chase's New York City branch system. Few changes had been made in branches over the postwar years. Several had been closed, but new ones had opened. The bank continued to operate twenty-seven branches in 1952, all but two in Manhattan. The branches carried deposits in excess of $1.6 billion, close to a third of the bank's total.[1] Moreover, growth in deposits, slow as it was, had been centered in the branches.

Nonetheless the largest volume of branch deposits flowed from corporations, and these were not increasing. Corporations, prompted by higher interest rates and heavy needs to finance new facilities, had already begun to conserve on cash. Deposits by individuals, however, were a source of expansion, as more people began to use banks, and personal income increased. Personal checking accounts by this time accounted for a respectable share of the branch total. Compound interest accounts (savings accounts) maintained a fast rate of growth, but from a low base. Installment credit also progressed, but was relatively small in volume.

For some time Aldrich and others in senior management had been observing these trends. The bank had not lost much market share in total deposits in the postwar period, but neither had it gained. National City Bank, with sixty-seven branches scattered throughout the city, had improved its position, as had Manufacturers Trust, with seventy-nine branches.[2] Percy Ebbott expressed the view of management in a letter to a stockholder in 1951: "Naturally banks with large branch systems have benefited more from this diffusion of liquid wealth in the hands of many people than have those banks which have fewer branches and whose business in the past was predominantly of a 'big business' and 'central reserve' character."[3] Among other advantages, these growing retail deposits created surplus funds that could be used by the wholesale side of the bank in loans to business.

Chase decided to expand its branch system, especially outside Manhattan. There was an ironic aspect to this, inasmuch as in the thirties the bank had disposed of (some said given away) branches to Manufacturers Trust.[4] Money was then so plentiful and interest rates so low that Chase with its overhead could not make the branches profitable. But conditions had changed, and it soon became clear that branches could be acquired more economically through merger than by starting *de novo*. The more profitable sites in many communities already contained branches, while new branches were authorized chiefly in "underbanked" areas, frequently dependent on future growth.

Chase explored a number of possibilities. At one point Aldrich discussed with H. C. Flanigan, the head of Manufacturers Trust, the possibility of a merger between the two banks.[5] Nothing came of this, and finally in September 1950 Chase made a formal offer of merger to the Brooklyn Trust Company, a bank with $225 million deposits and twenty-three branches, only to be outbid for that bank by the institution it had courted earlier, Manufacturers Trust.[6]

First merger attempt with the Bank of Manhattan

By all odds the most attractive candidate for merger was the Bank of The Manhattan Company. That bank, with $1.2 billion deposits, was the second oldest in the city. While it possessed valued corporate customers, it also operated fifty-six branches, heavily concentrated in Queens, the borough of New York with the largest proportion of middle-class families who formed the hard core for consumer banking services. In 1951 Aldrich decided to approach J. Stewart Baker, the chairman of Manhattan, about the possibility of a merger.[7]

At the outset Baker indicated that Manhattan would not be interested in a merger, but he was willing to discuss the possibility of Chase's purchasing for cash the assets and business of the Bank of The Manhattan Company. Chase, of course, would also assume all of the deposits and other liabilities of Manhattan. Baker wanted to dispose of the bank, change the name of the surviving institution to The Manhattan Company, and continue as an investment trust with a large sum of cash to start business. This possibility had not occurred to Aldrich, but he had no objection to it. He and Baker worked out an arrangement in detail, and on August 17, 1951, signed an agreement. In addition to financial matters, the agreement provided that Chase would take over all official and clerical staff of Manhattan, except those who chose to remain with the new investment trust.[8]

Word of such a transaction could not be kept secret. Manhattan's stock started to rise, so on Monday, August 20, the two chairmen issued a joint statement confirming that discussions were under way for Chase to purchase the assets and branches of the Bank of The Manhattan Company. The story appeared on the front page of the *New York Times* the following morning. Among other details it pointed out that the transaction would make Chase the largest bank in the city, with a system of eighty-three branch offices and deposits of approximately $5.9 billion. It came as something of a shock, then, when the next day a second story appeared on page one of the *Times* with the headline, "Bank Merger Off: Talks Are Ended." The article went on to state that "J. Stewart Baker, who heads Manhattan, said that 'legal obstacles' had made it necessary to bring the talks to an end."

That was the day of Chase's regular biweekly directors' meeting. Aldrich had kept them informed of the discussions, and a special meeting of the executive committee had approved the agreement. At the board meeting Aldrich reviewed the agreement signed August 17 and then reported that on the afternoon of August 21, the day after he and Baker had made their joint announcement, the Bank of Manhattan had issued a statement that the negotiations were terminated because of legal difficulties. Baker on his own had issued the statement without consulting Aldrich.[9]

The legal obstacles to which Baker referred were related to Manhattan's charter, which had been authorized by the New York State legislature in 1799. At that time, according to Manhattan's attorneys, the common law of New York State required the unanimous consent of stockholders to the sale of all assets of a corporation. Moreover, the state constitution then in effect did not grant the legislature the right to amend a corporate charter, and the Supreme Court had ruled that in such circumstances subsequent changes in the constitution granting the right of amendment to the legislature did not apply to charters granted earlier. Hence, the reasoning went, Manhattan would need a 100 percent vote of approval from shareholders if it were to sell all its assets to Chase. The banking law of New York State, which would require only a two-thirds vote for approval, did not apply.[10]

Chase's lawyers, and Aldrich himself, with long experience in banking law, did not agree. But the damage had been done. Baker's unilateral action in issuing a public statement calling off the deal had offended Aldrich deeply, and the press made much of the matter. But Aldrich, in responding to a stockholder's question at the annual meeting the following January, commented that "the idea of uniting the two banks seemed to be a wise one last August, and as far as I am concerned, it still does seem so."[11] Four years would elapse before this effort was finally successful.

Postwar earnings trends: 1945–1952

In addition to enlarging the branch system, Aldrich was concerned with Chase's earnings performance. For him this measure was highly important, but it was not the only consideration; soundness and safety stood even higher on the scale. When in 1947 the Treasury authorized the establishment of a reserve for bad debts with an accompanying tax benefit, the bank did not hesitate to take advantage of it—more so than most other banks—even at the expense of earnings. Moreover Aldrich appreciated that banks bear a social responsibility which at times may make it desirable to undertake an activity that yields little or no profit.

And yet, even if we allow for such considerations, Chase's earnings performance in the postwar years was not distinguished, although it did improve after 1950. The final year of the war, 1945, had been unusual, in that a record $9.1 million profit on securities had swelled total net earnings and profits to $26.6 million. This figure was not approached again until 1952, Aldrich's final year as chairman. Indeed net earnings and profits initially fell off rather sharply, reaching a low point of $17.6 million in 1948, after which they recovered to $25.8 million in 1952. At this point, however, net operating earnings far offset a $2.1 million loss on securities and accounted for the full amount.

The decline in the early years reflected a steady drop in net profit on securities, with a net loss of $1.5 million in 1948 from sales of long-term bonds as interest rates started to rise, an adverse swing of $10.6 million over three years on this source of earnings. Meanwhile net earnings from operations improved very little. Operating income rose only moderately (16 percent), chiefly because of a sharp drop in income from a smaller volume of securities. And expenses continued to increase, especially salaries, which advanced 38 percent in this inflationary period (with a 15 percent increase in personnel) and accounted for 59 percent of total operating expenses.

Nineteen forty-eight marked the postwar low in total assets as well as earnings. The return on assets in the immediate 1946–1948 postwar period averaged a low forty-two basis points (forty basis points on net operating earnings alone), and the return on equity was 6.21 percent. This was somewhat less than at National City Bank, which reported greater assets and larger profits but less capital than Chase. It was not until the Korean war that Chase and other banks broke out of this flat earnings trend. At that time not only did loans and assets expand sharply, but the restraints on interest rates were loosened.

The Fed unpegs interest rates

Aldrich and other bankers had long objected to the low level of interest rates, arbitrarily suppressed through much of this time by Federal Reserve activities in support of the Treasury. The three-month bill rate, which had been pegged at 0.37 percent during the war, was permitted to rise gradually to 1 percent by 1948. By the final months of 1952 it had climbed to 2.25 percent. Long-term rates, however, had been held down to a greater degree, with long-term government bonds increasing only from an average 2.3 percent in 1946 to 2.69 percent in 1952.[12] Chase's prime rate, which had been anchored at 1½ percent throughout the war, rose first to 2 percent in 1948 and then advanced periodically to 3 percent in late 1951, with Chase initiating the industry's move to that level.[13] The rate then held at 3 percent until the spring of 1953.

The increase in interest rates in 1951 was encouraged by a far-reaching change in Federal Reserve policy. The Fed in March of that year reached an accord with the Treasury under which it was no longer obligated to support the price of government securities in the market. In effect interest rates on government securities were unpegged. The Fed still intervened in the market, but now in support of broad economic policies rather than a particular set of interest rates for the Treasury.[14]

The recovery in earnings from 1948 to 1952 was more soundly based in that it reflected gains from operations and not increased security profits. The improvement was particularly notable in 1951 and 1952, when Chase's net operating earnings rose 50 percent to a total of $27.9 million. The advance would have been even greater had not the government imposed a stiff excess profits tax to help finance the Korean war.

Chase at the time was paying not only a regular corporate income tax of 52 percent but an additional 30 percent surcharge on a considerable portion of its earnings.[15] Its tax bill almost tripled from $9.5 million in 1950 to $26.4 million in 1952, about as large a sum as its net operating earnings. Relief from the tax surcharge did not come until 1954, when it helped to support earnings at a time when the economy had weakened. Earnings that year, prior to the merger with the Bank of Manhattan, were little changed from 1952.

Return on year-end assets (as measured by net operating earnings) averaged fifty basis points in the years 1952–1954, with a return on equity of 7.5 percent. While this represented an improvement over the early postwar years, it still was not outstanding. Chase's stock, like most bank shares, sold below book value, with a modest dividend yield that was regarded as safe but was growing only slowly. Increased capital in these circumstances was generated largely from retained earnings, again a gradual process. Capital funds in 1954 reached $397 million, up from $300 million in 1945. Yet this was not greatly in excess of the $358 million in 1930, at the outset of the Great Depression. The ratio of capital to assets stood at 6.7 percent, compared with 13.3 percent prior to the depression a quarter-century earlier. Even so, this represented a distinct improvement from the ratio of 4.9 percent that prevailed at war's end in 1945.

Wide swings in profits on securities

Gains or losses from the sale of securities continued to swing widely. Thus for Chase losses on securities in 1952 and 1953 were succeeded by a gain of almost $8 million in 1954. Such abrupt shifts would become even more pronounced in some future years. They were the product of a deliberate policy adopted by the bank in the management of its security portfolio, a policy induced by cyclical fluctuations in interest rates (now accentuated by the Federal Reserve–Treasury accord), combined with the application of income tax regulations to gains and losses in a manner peculiar to banks. Capital gains were taxed at the lower capital gains rate, then 26 percent. Capital losses by banks, however, were deductible from operating income for tax purposes, which in effect reduced the loss by 52 percent.

In periods of economic weakness and easy money, such as developed in 1954, interest rates fell and prices on securities rose, encouraging the bank to realize on capital gains. Because of a need for income, reinvestment of sales proceeds tended to be in securities with a longer maturity and a higher yield. The problem developed during the next cyclical expansion, when interest rates rose and bond prices fell, creating losses in the security portfolio. But at such a time loan demand also strengthened, and the bank frequently found it necessary to sell securities to raise funds. Since the losses were tax deductible, the pain of the sale was eased. Indeed if a year was determined to be a "loss" year on security sales, portfolio managers deliberately incurred losses for tax purposes.

The bank expected that over time gains from these security activities would more than offset losses. But interest rates moved on an upward trend throughout the postwar period, and loss years were not infrequent. Moreover Chase and other banks at times came to be "locked in" with securities of long maturity and yields that eventually turned out to be lower than the cost of funds to finance them. Although the policy came under frequent review, it usually seemed appropriate for the conditions of the particular moment. Yet whether over a lengthy period the practice was indeed profitable became difficult to determine. Not until the law was changed in 1969, taxing both gains and losses at ordinary income tax rates, was it seriously modified.

The benefit program of 1952

Strong earnings in 1951–52, coupled with the high marginal tax rate, encouraged Aldrich to act on still another piece of unfinished business: improving the benefit package for employees. A new program, featuring radical changes, had been in the planning stage for some time. In 1951 a committee of senior officers headed by George Champion visited all departments and exchanged views on working conditions and personnel relations, as well as on ways to improve bank services. A new salary administration plan, based on position evaluation and providing for merit increases, was subsequently introduced, prompted in part by the need to administer salaries under the government's wartime Wage Stabilization Board. It remained to revise insurance and retirement benefits. Chase's retirement program, established in 1933, provided for payments toward an annuity, administered by Metropolitan Life and Equitable Life, to which both the bank and the employee contributed. The final retirement income was based on length of service and on the average salary received over the entire period of employment.

Victor Rockhill, then heading a small unit concerned with special projects, along with Henry MacTavish, the controller, designed the new program under the direction of George Champion.[16] It included, in addition to a more liberal pension plan, a feature new to Chase—a comprehensive profit-sharing program.[17] Other banks were to adopt a similar program that year, but few as liberal as Chase's.

The new pension plan provided that the bank pay the full cost and that the pension be based on average salary over the final five years of employment, a provision influenced by postwar inflation. The average salary was to be multiplied by 1.5 percent for each year of employment up to a maximum of forty years, or 60 percent. Penalties were assessed for retirement before age sixty-five, but these were much more modest than the discounts that had been applied under the actuarial rules of the previous system.

The new profit-sharing plan represented even more of a departure from the past. The program provided a nest egg that made a considerable difference in the eventual quality of life for many employees. It was formally named a Thrift-Incentive Plan, and included a contribution each year by the bank, as well as a mandatory contribution by the employee of 2 percent of his salary, withheld each month by the bank. Moreover, an employee could contribute as much as 6 percent of his salary, an amount eventually raised to 10 percent. The funds were held in trust and invested in various mutual funds selected by the employee and administered by the bank's trust department. Payment of taxes on the bank's contribution, as well as on earnings of the total investment, was deferred until paid out to the employee, a very considerable advantage. The bank's contribution to the Thrift-Incentive Plan was related to its net operating earnings before taxes, computed on a sliding scale, with no provision if capital funds fell greatly or dividends were reduced below the level then existing. Moreover, the maximum contribution by the bank was limited to 15 percent of salary, a level soon reached and maintained for a number of years.

The new retirement and Thrift-Incentive programs together added $5.8 million to staff expenses in 1952, or about 14 percent of the total, a sizable increment. But management was determined to get the new program under way, spurred on by an appreciation that most of the added cost that year would otherwise flow into the excess profit tax.

Management looked upon the new program as serving the dual purpose of providing more liberal and flexible arrangements for retirement while, with the new profit-sharing plan, motivating employees to work more efficiently and actively promote the interests of the bank. Over the years it appeared doubtful that the second objective had been realized. As the staff changed, employees came to accept the program as part of Chase's normal compensation package, although it did help Chase remain competitive in attracting new personnel. But additional management incentive programs, targeted to individual officers rather than the staff as a whole, eventually would prove necessary.

Organizational changes in 1952

In 1952, as Aldrich approached retirement, he initiated several changes in the organizational structure of the bank. They were not radical but were of an evolutionary character. In May, Arthur McCain resigned as vice chairman in order to accept the presidency of the Union Planters National Bank of Memphis, Tennessee, returning to the South of his early years. The vice chairmanship was allowed to lapse, leaving Percy Ebbott, president, and Carl J. Schmidlapp, vice chairman of the executive committee, as the other inside directors. Schmidlapp continued in this position until his retirement two years later.

In December, a few weeks before he was to leave the bank, Aldrich introduced a further change, one designed to define more clearly responsibilities on the domestic side as well as to improve efficiency.[18] Three new departments were established:

1. The United States department replaced the former commercial loan department. The nine geographical districts of that department were responsible for relations with commercial, financial, and many industrial corporations throughout the nation. George Champion, then senior vice president, was named head of this unit.

2. The special industries department brought together under a single executive the various specialized industry groups: public utilities, petroleum, railroad, aviation, and real estate. New to this group was aviation, which had expanded enormously during the Korean war. Edward L. Love, senior vice president, formerly in charge of the public utility department, was appointed director of this enlarged group.

3. The metropolitan department embraced all of the bank's business in New York City, including the branches, the branch administration department, the New York City district staff, the business development staff, and related activities. David Rockefeller headed this department. Earlier in September, Rockefeller had been appointed senior vice president and transferred from the international department to oversee customer relations in New York

City.[19] The new assignment introduced him to domestic affairs and provided an opportunity to broaden his administrative experience.

A New York City district had been established in 1950, with the objective of centralizing relationships with large national corporations headquartered in New York.[20] A number of these customers carried their main deposit accounts in branches, but they preferred to do business at the head office. Moreover the expertise to serve them in all respects could not be scattered throughout the branch system. The New York City district, patterned after the geographical districts in the commercial loan department, was formed as an answer. Over time accounts were transferred from the branches, although close coordination continued between the units.

The appointment of George Champion as head of the United States department held significance for the future. Then in his early fifties, Champion had developed into an outstanding banker with wide experience and strong leadership qualities. He had been born on a farm in Normal, Illinois, a heritage he did not hesitate to put to good use in speeches and other public appearances. Champion entered banking directly upon graduation from Dartmouth in 1926, where he had played on a notable football team with several All-Americans as teammates. Like so many other officers, he came to Chase through the merger with Equitable Trust in 1930. In 1931 Champion was afforded an experience that left a lasting impression and helped mold him as a banker. Along with a more senior officer, he was sent to New Orleans to help manage a troubled bank, the Canal Bank and Trust Company, a good customer indebted to Chase. He remained there for two years in the depths of the depression, contending not only with narrower management problems but also with the wider political and community relationships that arose—at times dealing with Senator Huey Long, who wielded great political power in the State.[21] Champion returned to Chase in 1933 and eventually became head of the southeastern district. In 1949 he was appointed vice chairman of the general loan committee. Within a decade he would become president and then chairman.

Retirement of Aldrich

The reorganization in December 1952 was one of Aldrich's final acts. At that time he was sixty-seven years old. The directors had asked him to remain as chairman after the customary retirement age of sixty-five, and in good health, he had found no difficulty in doing so. Yet he knew the time was approaching when he should retire. Late in the year events developed that pushed him toward a decision.

The immediate impetus came from a request by President-elect Eisenhower that Aldrich serve as ambassador to Great Britain. An invitation from the president-elect to serve in some capacity could hardly have come as a surprise. Aldrich had strongly supported Eisenhower both for the nomination and in the election. He was influential in the Republican party, especially in New York State, and his support had been of help to the general. The request came shortly after the election, which gave Aldrich time to make the necessary arrangements.[22]

His most pressing problem was to identify his successor. He and the other directors believed that the bank ought to look outside for someone with the necessary stature. Aldrich placed high priority on the ambassadorial apsect of the chairmanship—on representing the bank in high councils on any matters affecting it—more so than on skills in banking, or indeed in management. He was fortunate, then, in finding a man with the qualities he deemed most important: John J. McCloy, who recently had resigned as United States high commissioner in Germany.

McCloy was a man of unusual talent and experience. A partner in a leading law firm in the 1930s, he had gone to Washington in 1941 as a special assistant to the secretary of war, Henry L. Stimson. A year later McCloy became assistant secretary of war and served in that capacity throughout the war, participating in Roosevelt's councils along with Stimson on many matters of high policy. At war's end he retired from public life to return to the practice of law, only to return in 1947 as president of the World Bank and then to his responsibilities in Germany.

McCloy combined a keen intellect and abundant energy with much personal charm. He had been born in Philadelphia "on the wrong side of the tracks," as he put it. Yet with the help of his mother (his father had died), he graduated from the Peddie School, Amherst, and Harvard Law School, interrupting his legal studies to become a captain of artillery in World War I. McCloy's consuming interest lay in international affairs, and he was appointed to many special commissions and advisory bodies over the years by Republican and Democratic presidents alike.

Aldrich knew McCloy well and lost little time in approaching him. He invited McCloy to ride uptown from the bank's headquarters one afternoon, explained his conception of the position, and offered it to McCloy. At this time McCloy was considering several other possibilities and initially had reservations about the Chase chairmanship. But as he thought about the matter he became favorably disposed. As he later put it: "It was an institution with broad interests, wide interests, it involved of course matters of finance, trade, commerce. And in view of the work I'd been involved in as a lawyer—which in large part had been so-called financial law—together with my experience in the World Bank, it seemed to fit."[23]

McCloy accepted the position and was appointed chairman by the directors at a special meeting on December 23, 1952. The decision became effective January 19, 1953, when Aldrich retired to become ambassador. Percy J. Ebbott continued as president and Carl J. Schmidlapp as vice chairman of the executive committee.

Aldrich's contribution to Chase

Aldrich had been chairman of Chase for eighteen years and president for four years before that. His full contribution predates the period of this history. Perhaps it was greatest during the troubled period of the thirties, from which banking in general and Chase specifically emerged stronger both financially and in public recognition. A resolution of the directors, recorded in the minutes of the January 7, 1953, meeting and presented to Aldrich, states in part:

> He [Aldrich] had the statesmanship and courage to advocate the divorce of investment banking from commercial banking. He had the courage of the Chase tradition to support its banking and commercial customers who were in difficulties through the long years of their recovery. He had the imagination to set up specialized departments of great technical skill for service to particular industries. And all during this period his was a potent voice advocating policies to lead the country out of the financial wilderness. He had a conception of the Chase Bank as a great responsible financial citizen of the Republic, that should accept the risks and responsibilities of working for sound policies under which banks could best serve a free and energetic economy in the country.
>
> He leaves the Bank stronger in personnel and resources, and in better position than it has ever been to serve the country's great industries that are its customers and the great number of banks for which it acts as correspondent.

The bank certainly was a stronger, better organized institution in 1952 than in 1945. Its staff had expanded to more than ten thousand from seven thousand. Its cadre of senior management had been strengthened and enlarged, with provision made for the future through new recruitment. Loans to business had more than tripled to $2 billion, and foreign activity had grown tremendously. Services to individuals, too, had been broadened, with the start of consumer lending. And in such other activities as trust and bond distribution and investment, Chase stood among the leaders.

Chase was perceived by the public as a premier bank—perhaps *the* premier bank—in part because of the recognition of Aldrich as a leader in both banking and civic affairs. And yet there were challenges. Bank of America and National City Bank were growing more rapidly and were better positioned for the future in some markets. Chase had not yet enlarged its domestic branch system. And abroad, while it had established branches in Germany and Japan, the bank continued to rely chiefly on relations with correspondents. No less significant, the earnings performance of the bank had not been outstanding. The basic culture of the bank, molded under Aldrich, remained intact but would require modification under new management in the years ahead.

The recession of 1953–54

Before Aldrich departed, McCloy asked him if any major problems confronted Chase. Aldrich responded that the bank was in good shape, but that two shortcomings required action: it needed a citywide branch system in order to compete effectively with other banks possessing such a system, and it required a new building to bring together and manage effectively the nine thousand employees now scattered in nine buildings in the downtown area.[24]

Over the next few years McCloy spent considerable time on both of these problems. In 1953, however, he found that all would not be positive for banking in the period immediately ahead. President Eisenhower, acting early to redeem his campaign pledge, brought the war with Korea to a close in July. There followed a period of economic adjustment which left its imprint on Chase and other banks. Fortunately the letdown in economic activity proved to be relatively mild, as real gross national product fell only 1.4 percent in 1954.

Contra-cyclical action by the Federal Reserve helped in this regard, and in implementing it the monetary authorities influenced the position of the banks. From a monetary policy of active restraint in 1952 and early 1953, the Federal Reserve moved first to neutrality and then, by late 1953, to active ease. Reserves Chase was required to hold against demand deposits were reduced from 24 percent to 22 percent in July 1953 and then to 20 percent in August 1954, while reserves against time deposits were cut from 6 to 5 percent. Supplementing this were declines in the Fed's rediscount rate from 2 to 1¾ percent in February 1954, and again to 1½ percent in April. But perhaps of greatest import was an aggressive open market policy which pumped reserves into banks so that total bank credit in 1954 rose by $11 billion, more than in any year since World War II, chiefly through purchase by banks of government securities.[25]

Impact of the recession on Chase

The changed economic environment again affected activity at Chase and other New York City banks. Loans at Chase fell about 8½ percent over the two-year period, turning again to expansion in the final months of 1954 as economic growth resumed. Along with other banks Chase raised its prime rate from 3 to 3¼ percent in April 1953, only to return to 3 percent in March 1954.[26] But money market rates, especially those on commercial paper, fell to a greater degree, and more customers were encouraged to turn to that market, starting a trend that became of increasing concern to the bank over future years. Easier conditions in the capital market also encouraged corporations to lengthen debt structures and pay off or reduce bank loans.

There were exceptions to this loan weakness, including credit to petroleum companies and commodity dealers. Consumer credit also continued to advance, and the bank actively sought to expand its lending to small business through correspondents around the country.[27] But with three-fourths of Chase's portfolio representing loans to business—chiefly large business—it felt the recession more keenly than other banks.

Yet in terms of total assets the bank managed to more than offset the decline in loans by a huge increase in holdings of government securities, made possible by the expansionary policy of the Federal Reserve. As a result assets at the end of 1954, prior to the merger with Manhattan, approached $6 billion for the first time since 1945.

Foreign developments, 1953–1955

In 1949 recession in the United States had caused widespread difficulties abroad. It was feared that history would repeat itself in 1953 and 1954, that "if the U.S. economy sneezes, the rest of the world will catch pneumonia." Fortunately this did not happen. The economies of Western Europe took the end of the Korean war in stride. While industrial production declined in the United States, it rose by 9 percent in Western Europe. World commodity prices remained relatively firm, and exports to areas other than the United States continued to expand. Restrictions on the flow of trade and payments between nations were gradually relaxed, and dependence on dollar aid was greatly reduced.[28]

Chase's foreign department continued to prosper in the favorable international environment, with strength in Western Europe helping to sustain U.S. exports. Commercial letters of credit, collections payable in other countries, remittances to and from the United States, and foreign exchange transactions all expanded, especially in 1954.[29] In this year too the bank entered into a path-blazing credit transaction, joining the U.S. Treasury and the International Monetary Fund in providing $30 million to the government of Peru, enabling that country to establish a fund to stabilize the Peruvian sol in foreign exchange markets. Chase's share amounted to $5 million. The credit was not supported by collateral, but the Peruvian government agreed to adopt a program of fiscal reform laid out by the IMF. The agreement with Chase represented the first instance in which a private bank had participated with the IMF in such an arrangement, later to become commonplace.[30]

Large dollar balances held from foreign banks at the head office proved most profitable for the foreign department. The total was a jealously guarded secret, but Chase was known to be the largest correspondent for both foreign and domestic banks. Balances from the two sources amounted to $1.311 billion on September 30, 1954, almost one-fourth of all deposits.[31] Well over half was from foreign institutions. How profitable these balances really were no one knew, for they were employed to process transactions, and there was no reliable data on costs. Nevertheless, with interest rates still relatively low, many banks maintained surplus funds on deposit with Chase.

Deposits at foreign branches were less than those of correspondent banks, amounting to $445 million. Still this was a respectable total and far in excess of loans of $120 million.[32] Few changes occurred in the foreign branch network over the two years. A fourth office was added in Cuba, bringing total branches to seventeen in eight countries, supplemented by additional military banking facilities in Japan and Germany and representatve offices in five countries.

Chase on the eve of merger

Thus, on the eve of its merger with the Bank of Manhattan, Chase remained in a strong position. Third in assets among banks in the nation, Chase continued to be predominantly wholesale in character, still leading all others in loans to business and correspondent banking. Similarly its international department, universally recognized for expertise and worldwide relationships, complemented the domestic. The bank's officer cadre had been tested by long experience, and a new chairman, outstanding in public life, was at the helm. But deposits, the fuel for growth, were lagging. The bank hoped to rectify this problem by diversifying further into retail banking. Although its first attempt in 1951 had floundered, the bank would soon try again.

The merger with Manhattan

McCloy was not idle on the urgent matter of establishing a citywide branch system. It soon became clear that this could be accomplished only through merger, yet the possibilities for doing so were increasingly limited. Between 1949 and 1952 nine banks in New York City were absorbed by larger ones, and a proposed merger between Manufacturers Trust and New York Trust fell through.[1] Then in 1954 the Chemical Bank, with deposits of almost $1.8 billion, added a further $776 million through merger with Corn Exchange Bank Trust, lifting Chemical from tenth to sixth place among the nation's banks.[2] Chemical also acquired seventy-nine additional offices throughout the city, increasing its total to ninety-eight. Many of these branches were small and not of high quality, but they gave Chemical a wide base to build upon.

The obvious choice for Chase continued to be the Bank of The Manhattan Company; but the failure of the proposed merger in 1951 had left such a legacy of bad feeling that McCloy initially believed it futile to pursue this possibility. He considered other banks and rather surprisingly decided to approach J. P. Morgan and Company. While a merger with Morgan would not solve the branch problem, McCloy believed that sooner or later Morgan would need to merge, and that its prestige, management, and customer base would benefit Chase. He found George Whitney, the chairman, willing to discuss the matter. McCloy later recalled that Whitney inquired about management and where it would rest. "I said we would sit down and try to figure out what the best management of this bank would be, taking account of all the personnel. I said that means I am quite prepared to step aside if, as a result of that analysis, it would seem that others should conduct the affairs of this bank."[3]

As matters developed, it was not necessary for McCloy and Chase to face this issue. Other senior officers at Morgan, especially Thomas Lamont and Harry Davison, learned of the conversations and strongly objected, claiming that they would never merge with anyone, and least of all with Chase. It was not until six years later, in 1959, that Morgan finally merged with Guaranty Trust Company, a bank three-and-one-half times Morgan's size, but an institution which Morgan nonetheless dominated.

The Bank of The Manhattan Company

After failing to make headway with Morgan, McCloy finally determined to try once again with the Bank of The Manhattan Company.[4] More than any other prospect, Manhattan fitted Chase's needs for a bank of high quality, with personnel of similar caliber, and with a branch system and business that complemented Chase's.

Manhattan looked back on a considerably longer banking history and tradition than did Chase, founded in 1877. The charter of Manhattan dated from 1799, making it the second oldest banking institution in the state of New York, after the Bank of New York. Originally the charter was granted for the operation of a company to supply water to the city of New York. But the charter also contained a clause, inserted without the knowledge of supporters of The Bank of New York, including Alexander Hamilton, that permitted the company to use any of its capital not required in the water business "in the purchase of public or other stocks, or in any money transactions or operations not inconsistent with the laws and constitution of the State of New York."

It was this clause that provided for the genesis of the Bank of The Manhattan Company. While construction of the water system moved forward, the company also quickly organized an "office of discount and deposit," which opened for business on September 1, 1799. Aaron Burr was among the leaders who obtained the charter, and the new office became the object of some controversy because of the manner by which it had been authorized. Burr was quietly dropped as a director in 1802, and had no connection with the company at the time of his duel with Alexander Hamilton in 1804.

Over the years the company's water business did not fare well, and by 1840 the city-owned Croton water system had completely superseded it. In contrast, the banking operation became an immediate success, expanding its business in the city and opening branches in Poughkeepsie and Utica in upstate New York. These branch offices were maintained from 1809 to 1819, but distance from the head office made control by management difficult and they were finally closed.

The bank successfully weathered the economic vicissitudes of the nineteenth century. During the panic of 1873 and the depression that followed, Manhattan continued to pay its normal dividend of 5 percent. It also maintained close relations with state and city governments, still in effect at the time of the merger. At the outbreak of World War I in 1914, Manhattan carried deposits of $94 million. These doubled by 1920, and again in the ensuing decade, rising to $404 million in 1930.[5]

Development of Manhattan's branch system

By 1900 the bank had become a national institution and was engaged in international business. But it also gave consideration as early as 1911 to establishing branch offices throughout the city in order to serve individuals and small business while gathering deposits that could be used for loans to commerce and industry.

The first step in this direction was taken through merger in 1918 with the Bank of the Metropolis, which was converted into a branch at 31 Union Square (see Figure 3).[6] Meanwhile Manhattan also acquired stock (permitted by its unusual charter) in the Bank of Long Island, which operated branches especially in the expanding borough of Queens. It assumed complete ownership of this bank in 1920 and began concentrating on Queens. The borough grew rapidly and Manhattan grew with it, both through merger with small banks and branching *de novo*. By 1930 Manhattan possessed seventy-eight branches, with representation not only in Queens and the central city but in the other three boroughs as well. It paid no interest on small deposits during this period, but the convenience of its location resulted in surplus funds for use in loans and investments by the head office.

The thirties, with low rates of return on loans and investments, proved to be a difficult period, forcing Manhattan, like other banks, to close a number of branches. But adversity also instigated innovation and change. Manhattan turned more to the provision of services for its local customers—special checking accounts, consumer and personal loans, home mortgages—a truly retail business. At the start of World War II the bank continued to operate fifty-six branches, a number little altered (fifty-seven in 1954) at the time of merger.

Manhattan's branches enabled it to grow more rapidly than Chase in the postwar years. The number of families using banks continued to increase, and personal savings and incomes were expanding. Manhattan's deposits rose more than 20 percent from 1945 to 1954, whereas Chase had not yet regained its earlier total. But the distribution of assets differed. Manhattan's loans increased by only two-thirds, while those of Chase climbed by more than 80 percent, with the major advance representing loans to business. Each bank showed a loan-deposit ratio of about 45 percent. And yet, as Champion later observed: "It [Manhattan] was a gem for Chase to get hold of to take care of commercial customers, which the Bank of Manhattan didn't have in great numbers. At that time the Guaranty Trust Co., which had only one branch uptown, was having a very difficult time getting money to take care of their customers. But we had it. That gave us a combination that was wonderful."[7]

Champion went on, however, to praise Manhattan for its handling of

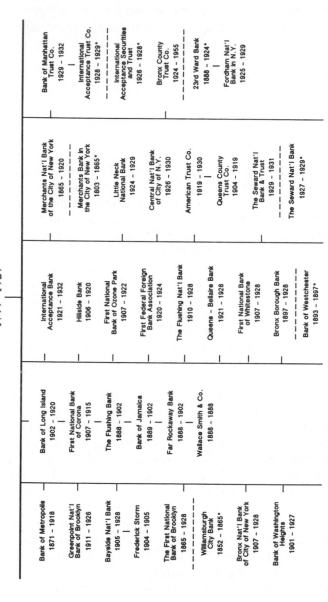

BANK OF THE MANHATTAN COMPANY
1932–1955

PRESIDENT AND DIRECTORS OF THE MANHATTAN CO.
1929–1932*

BANK OF THE MANHATTAN CO.*
1799–1929

Bank of Metropolis 1871 – 1918	Bank of Long Island 1902 – 1920	International Acceptance Bank 1921 – 1932	Merchants Nat'l Bank of the City of New York 1865 – 1920	Bank of Manhattan Trust Co. 1929 – 1932
Greenpoint Nat'l Bank of Brooklyn 1911 – 1926	First National Bank of Corona 1907 – 1915	Hillside Bank 1906 – 1920	Merchants Bank in the City of New York 1803 – 1865*	International Acceptance Trust Co. 1928 – 1929*
Bayside Nat'l Bank 1905 – 1928	The Flushing Bank 1888 – 1902	First National Bank of Ozone Park 1907 – 1922	Little Neck National Bank 1924 – 1929	International Acceptance Securities and Trust 1926 – 1928*
Frederick Storm 1904 – 1905	Bank of Jamaica 1889 – 1902	First Federal Foreign Bank Association 1920 – 1924	Central Nat'l Bank of City of N.Y. 1926 – 1930	Bronx County Trust Co. 1924 – 1955
The First National Bank of Brooklyn 1865 – 1928	Far Rockaway Bank 1888 – 1902	The Flushing Nat'l Bank 1910 – 1928	American Trust Co. 1919 – 1930	23rd Ward Bank 1888 – 1924*
Williamsburgh City Bank 1852 – 1865*	Wallace Smith & Co. 1888 – 1888	Queens – Bellaire Bank 1921 – 1928	Queens County Trust Co. 1904 – 1919	Fordham Nat'l Bank in N.Y. 1925 – 1929
Bronx Nat'l Bank of City of New York 1907 – 1928		First National Bank of Whitestone 1907 – 1928	The Seward Nat'l Bank & Trust 1929 – 1931	
Bank of Washington Heights 1901 – 1927		Bronx Borough Bank 1897 – 1928	The Seward Nat'l Bank 1927 – 1929*	
		Bank of Westchester 1893 – 1897*		

Note: Mergers shown with national banks normally were preceded by conversion of the national bank to a New York State charter with elimination of the word "national" from its name. These conversions and brief changes in name are not shown.

* An asterisk preceded by a dotted line denotes a change in name.

Source: *Corporate Controller, The Chase Manhattan Corporation.*

Figure 3.

those large companies that were its customers. He mentioned the courage and forebearance of a management that supported good customers in trouble during the thirties. And he pointed to Manhattan's acumen in early assisting such successful companies as States Marine Corporation, with its Far Eastern shipping, and the tanker operations of D. K. Ludwig. These and others continued as valued customers of the enlarged bank.[8]

Negotiation of a merger

McCloy did not know J. Stewart Baker well, and he thought long and hard about the best approach for reopening discussion of a possible merger between Chase and Manhattan. At Manhattan's annual meeting in December 1953 Baker again was asked about the possibility of a merger and again denied that any was contemplated. McCloy reviewed the 1951 attempt and as a lawyer was not impressed with the legal opinion that under Manhattan's charter a 100 percent concurrence by stockholders would be required for Manhattan to sell its assets or merge into another bank. He thought that the opinion might have been prepared at the last moment as a means of getting out of the merger. Although there were ways to handle the charter issue, the matter had received wide publicity, and litigation might well develop. So, as he later related, "I made up my mind that if the merger was worth doing, it was worth putting it around the other way. Instead of having the Bank of Manhattan merge into Chase, have Chase merge into the smaller Manhattan."[9]

McCloy admitted that leaving the national banking system and giving up the sole name of Chase, which was known favorably worldwide, would be painful. But he was impressed by the Manhattan charter, for most of the major New York banks operated under the state system. "So," he recalled, "I put on my hat and went to see Stewart Baker. I remember those early meetings in his apartment uptown. I broached to him the idea of merging under the Manhattan charter. A good bit of his reticence, if not his opposition, was, I think, broken down by that first approach with the idea that we were ready to move that way."[10]

In spite of his repeated denials that Manhattan was open to a merger, Baker realized that the bank could not stay as it was—primarily a retail bank in a world where the trend was toward more balanced institutions, frequently referred to as "department stores of finance." And he recognized that Chase and Manhattan complemented each other to an exceptional degree. Chase's major strength was in its wholesale business, national and international, but with an understanding of the retail, while Manhattan operated forty-eight of its fifty-seven branches in areas of the city not covered by Chase, especially in fast-growing Queens. This complementarity would ease the pain of the merger. Chase was the most logical partner for Manhattan, as Manhattan was for Chase, and Baker knew it.

It was decided early that the name of the merged institution would be The Chase Manhattan Bank, and that the head office would be located at Eighteen Pine Street, Chase's head office. There remained the hard bargaining on financial arrangements and agreement on the placing of key personnel.

Both McCloy and Baker had at their sides tough-minded controllers: for Chase, Henry J. MacTavish, a somewhat irascible and unyielding Scotsman who was nearing retirement; and for Manhattan, Charles A. Agemian, an astute financial man of Armenian heritage who would play a significant role with the bank during the sixties. As a result of their interplay, under guidance from the chairmen, an acceptable formula emerged: each share of Chase stock was to be exchanged for 1¼ shares of Manhattan.[11] Some 12 million shares were thereby created for the merged bank, with a capital account of $150 million. The addition of large surplus and undivided profits, swollen by upward adjustments in a number of Chase assets, brought total capital funds to $515 million.[12] The new bank also began with a strengthened position in reserves, including a reserve for bad debts of $70 million, more than 2 percent of loans outstanding.

Shareholders were rewarded with a sizable increase in the dividend. Dealers in bank securities, reviewing the merger terms, were unanimous in their approval. They pointed out other longer-term advantages to shareholders, especially creation of a more rounded bank with a potential for greater growth and increased efficiency.

Management of the merged institution

Baker was concerned about the placement of key personnel, and McCloy was also sensitive to this issue. Baker himself, as head of the smaller parent institution, felt that he should possess some form of coordinate authority with McCloy. He was a handsome, proud man with complete integrity, sixty-one years of age, whose family had been associated with Manhattan since its founding in 1799. His great-grandfather was one of the original shareholders, and he had succeeded his father, Stephen Baker, as chairman in 1932. He sought and gained assurance from McCloy that Chase's adoption of the Manhattan charter was not just a gimmick, soon to be negated with Chase dropping the Manhattan name and reverting to a national charter.[13]

The problem of coordinate authority was resolved by Baker's becoming chairman of the executive committee of the board as well as president. McCloy continued as chairman of the merged institution, and the by-laws named both as chief executive officers. Baker remained with the merged institution only until the end of 1957, when he retired. He was an able banker but somewhat more cautious than a number of his new Chase associates. McCloy later was to say, "The arrangement went along all right. There was no fundamental difference in policy. Mr. Baker was quick to take up matters with me, and I with him, and he taught me a lot about banking. I benefited from the association."[14]

Percy Ebbott, Chase's president, agreed to stay with the merged institution as vice chairman of the board, although he had already passed the age of retirement. Graham B. Blaine, vice chairman of Manhattan, was also expected to continue in a similar position. Illness forced Blaine to become inactive, however, and he did not long remain on the board. Four executive vice presidents were named: George Champion, Edward L. Love, and David Rockefeller from Chase and Lawrence C. Marshall from Manhattan. Marshall, who had served as president of Manhattan, assumed direction of the metropolitan department, which included the enlarged domestic branch system. David Rockefeller, in turn, was placed in charge of all staff activities, a function that he quickly moved to revitalize. Meanwhile Champion and Love continued to direct the bank's wholesale activities.

Other functions that remained under direction of Chase officers included the international, trust, bond, and real estate departments. Shortly after the merger was proposed, and two and one-half months before it was consummated, joint committees were set up by the two banks to plan its implementation. All personnel were retained, and the actual joining went smoothly, a process helped by David Rockefeller and Lawrence Marshall, who were designated to work on the human aspects of the merger.[15]

The board of the merged bank was to include ten directors from Manhattan and fifteen from Chase, which required each bank to retire nine members from its existing board. McCloy recalled that this posed one of the most disagreeable tasks of his tenure at Chase.[16] The resulting board, however, was one of exceptional quality (members are listed in Appendix I). Moreover, some former directors not included in the new board continued to be associated with the merged bank as members of a newly constituted trust advisory board, which met monthly and provided counsel to the trust department on investment policy.

Board approval and public announcement

Agreements on financial and management aspects of the merger were completed before any public announcement. Meanwhile conjecture had been aroused by a statement by Baker at Manhattan's annual meeting on December 7, 1954, that the possibility of a merger of other banks into the Bank of The Manhattan Company was under consideration.[17] The price of both Chase and Manhattan stock began to react, and by the new year the press was reporting that merger talks were under way, although neither Chase nor Manhattan provided official confirmation.

Not until its regular meeting on January 5, 1955, did the Chase board take any action on the merger, although McCloy had kept the directors informed of the negotiations. At this meeting he reported in detail on the agreements reached, and stated that a definitive document would be drawn up and submitted shortly to the boards of both banks for ratification. The directors at that meeting then approved in principle the program of merger, subject to later approval of the formal merger agreement.

With many both inside and outside the two banks now informed of details, news of the merger could not be kept confidential. Consequently, directors of each bank met separately a week later and approved an announcement to the press. Prior to this announcement the full staffs of the two banks were informed by internal memoranda. On Friday, January 14, the New York press carried the story of the proposed merger as a major feature. A two-column heading on the front page of the *New York Times* read: "2d Biggest Bank Planned by Chase and Manhattan," with subheads declaring the merger to be a record, and that it reversed a formula which had failed in 1951. An inside page gave not only details of the merger but lengthy histories of the two banks and biographical sketches of the principal officers. The following day a *Times* editorial concluded:

> The Chase-Manhattan merger may be said to be a logical reflection of the present trend in metropolitan banking which emphasizes consumer financing, saving accounts and small checking accounts. In a sprawling city such as New York this puts a handsome premium on branch affiliates. And in addition to its rich historic background the Manhattan Company brings to this merger no fewer than fifty-seven of these valuable properties, or more than twice Chase's present total.

Joinder of two banks

The announcement to the staff and the press emphasized that the Chase Manhattan merger was not a takeover of one bank by another but a true joinder of two complementary institutions. Total resources of the merged bank (see Table 4) were about $7.6 billion, with deposits of $6.86 billion, second in size only to the California-based Bank of America ($8.3 billion). Among New York City banks Chase Manhattan would now vault ahead of its major competitor, National City Bank.

But Chase's margin was not as great as had initially been anticipated. In October 1954 National City brought to market the largest single offering of new bank shares ever made to that point, raising $131,250,000 of new

Table 4.   The Chase Manhattan Bank: combined assets and liabilities as of December 31, 1954.[a]

	The Chase National Bank	Bank of The Manhattan Company	The Chase Manhattan Bank
Assets			
Cash and due from banks	$1,446	$442	$1,887
Total investments	2,015	494	2,509
less: reserves	6	6	12
U.S. government securities	1,435	473	1,908
State, municipal, other securities	574	15	589
Loans, discounts, and mortgages	2,379	668	3,047
less: reserves	49	13	62
Banking houses	32	10	42
Accrued interest receivable	15	—	15
Customers' acceptance liability	66	38	104
Other assets	10	36	46
	$5,908	$1,668	$7,576
Liabilities			
Deposits	$5,379	$1,480	$6,858
Foreign funds borrowed	3	0	3
Acceptances outstanding	102	39	142
less: in portfolio	31	—	31
Other liabilities	58	52	110
Capital	111	27	150
Surplus	239	50	300
Undivided profits	47	20	44
Total capital funds	397	97	494
	$5,908	$1,668	$7,576

a. Figures in millions of dollars. Adjusted to reflect pro forma capital stock and surplus accounts.

Source: The Chase National Bank-Bank of The Manhattan Company. Analysis of the Proposed Plan of Merger. M. A. Schapiro & Co., Inc., February 23, 1955, p. 2.

capital.[18] Shortly thereafter, in March 1955, National City announced that it would obtain the First National Bank of New York, with deposits of $556 million, through acquisition of the latter's outstanding stock. The combination produced a bank with $6.3 billion total deposits, closing about half the gap with the newly merged Chase Manhattan, and it made the renamed First National City Bank an even more potent competitor.[19]

Chase Manhattan's capital funds of $515 million after the merger provided it with a lending limit to a single customer slightly in excess of $50 million, ahead of First National City by a small amount. And in terms of loans and mortgages outstanding, the new bank emerged by far the largest in New York City, with a total exceeding $3 billion. Manhattan, with its extensive branch system, increased the proportion of consumer and small business loans in Chase Manhattan's portfolio, but the merged bank remained the leading lender to business by a substantial margin.

In earnings too Chase Manhattan stood premier among New York City banks. At the end of 1954 the combined net operating earnings amounted to $39.1 million, with Chase providing about four-fifths of the total and Manhattan one-fifth. The new bank at this point also surpassed others in the rate of return on average book value: 8.03 percent, compared with 7.24 percent for National City Bank, with net operating earnings of $33.8 million.[20]

Combining the branch systems

Manhattan's citywide branch systems made it a prime attraction for Chase. The complementarity of the two networks eased the task of gaining approval from the regulatory authorities. Moreover the banks could well argue (and did) that the combination introduced greater competition into the New York banking scene, where twelve banks operated branches, but only six (see Table 5) maintained networks outside Manhattan.[21]

In many respects Queens, with rapid growth and high levels of income, constituted the most desirable area for branching outside of Manhattan. Here Chase Manhattan was exceptionally well situated. The network in the borough of Manhattan was also strengthened with no duplication. Only in Brooklyn was Chase's single branch near one of Manhattan's, and the two were combined.

In the Bronx the network was further enlarged by a transaction Manhattan had under way at the time of the merger—the acquisition of Bronx County Trust Company. This small bank carried deposits of about $71 million and operated nine offices throughout the borough. The transaction, which gained little public attention in the light of the much larger mergers and consolidations, was accomplished ten days prior to the merger of Chase and

Table 5.   Distribution of banking offices by boroughs, December 31, 1954.

	Manhattan	Bronx	Brooklyn	Queens	Richmond	Total
Chase National Bank	27	1	1	0	0	29
Bank of Manhattan-	10	5	8	35	0	58
The Chase Manhattan Bank	37	6	9	35	0	87
Manufacturers Trust	37	18	41	16	0	112
Chemical Corn Exchange Bank	65	12	9	10	2	98
National City Bank	41	5	17	8	1	72
Bankers Trust[a]	17	10	8	7	0	42

a. Figures for Bankers Trust include seventeen branches of that bank at the end of 1954 and twenty-five branches of the Public National Bank, whose proposed merger into Bankers Trust was carried out on April 8, 1955.
Source: The Chase National Bank-Bank of The Manhattan Company. Analysis of the Proposed Plan of Merger. M. A. Schapiro & Co., New York, N.Y., 1955.

Manhattan, and it raised the total offices of the combined bank to ninety-six, with fifteen in the Bronx.[22]

Approving a merger

Approval of the merger required orchestration on many fronts—directors, stockholders, and regulatory authorities. Among regulatory agencies, approval of the New York State superintendent of banks was most important, covering all aspects of the merger. But the Federal Reserve Board, New York's attorney general, the commissioner of Internal Revenue, and authorities in certain states and twelve foreign countries where Chase operated branches or representative offices were also involved. Beyond this at least tacit concurrence was required from the attorney general of the United States.

Even in the rumor stage the proposed merger was denounced in Congress as a violation of the antitrust laws. Representative Emmanuel Celler of Brooklyn, chairman of the House Judiciary Committee, issued a statement on January 3, saying, "This is too big a merger . . . it would give an all powerful oligarchy a stranglehold on New York banking."[23] Celler wrote to Stanley Barnes, assistant attorney general for antitrust, requesting that he warn the banks that their merger might violate the antimerger provisions of the Clayton Act. Barnes requested information from the two banks, which their attorneys sent him.

Meanwhile McCloy, in his opening statement at Chase's annual meeting on January 25, attacked the anticompetition allegation head-on. He pointed out that fourteen thousand commercial banks were at work in the nation, engaged in competition at all levels, not only among themselves but with alternative sources of finance as well. Moreover, he said, "it is part of the competitive system that alert institutions must keep pace with the larger needs for credit in our national economy."[24] These needs were changing and growing as a result of shifts in population and income. People were moving from the inner city to outer areas, and from old industrial centers to the West and South, carrying income with them. If Chase was to grow and adequately serve the needs of its customers, it must move with them.

The banks buttressed McCloy's contentions with a lengthy analysis and statement of the economic benefits of the merger, prepared by their economists and controllers.[25] They demonstrated how the two banks complemented rather than duplicated each other: they shared very few borrowers, their deposits flowed largely from different sources, and their foreign and trust businesses differed. This information, along with that on the complementarity of branches, was perhaps most persuasive to the regulatory authorities. The statement, which was submitted to the Department of Justice, the attorney general of New York, the superintendent of banks, and the Federal Reserve, undoubtedly did much in the end to help resolve the allegations.

State action

The key role in the approval process was played by the New York State superintendent of banking. A law passed in 1950 provided a two-way street for mergers between national banks and state banks: if the surviving bank operated under a state charter, the state regulatory authorities had full jurisdiction; if the survivor was a national bank, the comptroller of the currency handled the matter.

The superintendent in New York at this time was George A. Mooney, a former reporter on banking for the *New York Times*. Mooney proceeded carefully in the approval process, guided by a statement of policy set forth in the banking law:

> Banking organizations shall be supervised and regulated . . . in such a manner as to insure the safe and sound conduct of such business, to conserve their assets, to prevent hoarding of money, to eliminate unsound and destructive competition among such banking organizations and thus to maintain public confidence in such business and protect the public interest and the interest of depositors, creditors, shareholders and stockholders.[26]

The statement of policy said nothing about maintaining competition. Indeed it set criteria that seemed to take precedence over competition. In this, however, the statement was at variance with sections of the New York business law that required the state's attorney general to prevent the establishment of monopoly.[27]

Jacob K. Javits, the state attorney general, recognized his authority in this regard and quickly sought and obtained information concerning the merger. On February 8, less than a month after the announcement, he phoned attorneys for the banks and informed them that he was not contemplating any action. But he left the door open for action in the future if the public interest required it. Not until the last moment, March 28, did he put his conclusion in writing and send it to the superintendent. Nevertheless the superintendent had apparently already been in touch with the attorney general, for on February 3 he called Henry MacTavish, the Chase controller, and told him that he knew of no reason why the banks should not go ahead and call their stockholder meetings.[28]

Yet the superintendent continued to evidence concern. He retained outside legal counsel, Rosenman Goldmark Colin and Kaye, to advise him on the legality of the merger. And on February 25 he wrote the banks asking them to obtain a letter of clearance for the merger from the Department of Justice. He then followed this with a request on March 7 for economic data showing whether competition would be increased, decreased, or unaffected, not only in total but for various products, functions, and facilities. Moreover he asked that benefits from the merger for customers, stockholders, and employees be spelled out in detail. The banks responded only in part by forwarding their statement of the economic benefits of the merger.[29]

Position of the Department of Justice

The superintendent's request for a letter of clearance from the Department of Justice placed the banks under some pressure. Their attorneys now found it desirable to meet with Assistant Attorney General Barnes to convey the superintendent's request. Barnes responded that he would take the matter under consideration, but he then offered a rather revealing comment. He remarked that he was disturbed by the fact that there seemed to be no statutory mandate for federal supervisory authority over the competitive aspects of bank mergers.

In this he was only partially correct. Certainly the Sherman Antitrust Act applied to bank mergers as to mergers in industry. Later in July, months after Chase and Manhattan had merged, Barnes informed a congressional committee that the Justice Department was investigating the merger to determine whether an antitrust suit should be filed under the Sherman Act.[30] The likelihood that any such suit could be successful appeared remote enough as to suggest that the statement and the investigation were rooted more in politics than in law.

Much more restrictive as an antitrust measure was the Clayton Act, which since 1950 had been extended to mergers as well as to the acquisition of stock or assets. This act was designed to prevent mergers that might substantially lessen competition or tend to create a monopoly in any section of the country. But in passing the act, Congress had specifically exempted banks, at least in part on the grounds that they were adequately regulated by banking authorities. It occasioned no surprise, then, when on March 23, eight days before the merger, Barnes wrote to Bennett of Milbank, Tweed, Hope and Hadley outside counsel for Chase, stating that the Justice Department concluded that it did not have jurisdiction to proceed under section 7 of the Clayton Act and did not "presently plan to take any action on this matter."[31] This was at best a backhanded letter of clearance, but it was conveyed immediately to the superintendent.

The County Trust (White Plains) affair

Even as the letter from Barnes was en route, the superintendent raised another question related to antitrust matters. On the same day he wrote to Baker calling attention to a minority stock interest that Manhattan held in the County Trust Company (White Plains), the largest bank in Westchester County. This investment aroused concern in the Superintendent. He raised a question as to the propriety of the merged bank's continuing to retain such stock in the light of "Rockefeller interests" holding a substantial investment in a competing bank, the National Bank of Westchester, as well as in The Chase National Bank.[32]

Baker and McCloy, in a carefully worded but somewhat icy response, denied that Manhattan controlled County Trust (it owned 6.6 percent of the outstanding stock), and they emphatically denied that the Rockefeller brothers or any interests connected with the Rockefeller family controlled The Chase National Bank. They indicated that the bank would be pleased to continue to hold the County Trust stock as an investment (which was possible under Manhattan's charter). But they added that the orderly and prompt consummation of the Chase Manhattan merger was of such importance that if possession of the stock constituted an impediment, they would pledge not to vote the stock without the superintendent's consent.

This clearly put their concerns in perspective. In acknowledging the reply the superintendent stated, "I have noted the commitment you have made— and deem it a satisfactory disposition of the matter."[33]

Final act of the merger

While the jockeying on antitrust was under way, the more important clearance from other agencies moved ahead. Favorable tax rulings on the exchange of stock were obtained. And the Federal Reserve indicated that it would approve the merged bank's continued operation of existing domestic and foreign branches, as well as holdings of certain Chase investments, although some values were adjusted upward. But not until March 30 did the Federal Reserve officially convey its approval of the merger.

More difficult to obtain was permission from banking authorities in other countries to transfer Chase's foreign branches to Manhattan. The problem was new to these authorities, and they were inclined to treat the branch of the merged bank as being established anew. This could have required additional capital in some instances and would have entailed a time-consuming procedure of revising existing contracts.[34] Only through a maximum effort by Roy C. Haberkern, Jr., of Chase's legal counsel, Milbank, Tweed, Hope and Hadley, working through local counsel in the various countries, were the transfers accomplished.

The stage was now set for the concluding act of a process that had been initiated almost three months earlier: approval by the stockholders and final approval by the superintendent. Stockholder meetings held by both Chase and Manhattan on March 28 resulted in an overwhelming vote in support of the merger.

Finally the superintendent received from outside counsel the written opinion for which he had been waiting. The opinion reviewed all the federal and state laws bearing on the merger and concluded that the superintendent did indeed have authority to approve the merger; that the Clayton Antitrust Act did not apply; that the Sherman Antitrust Act was not violated; and that the section of the New York business law that prohibits establishment of a monopoly was not violated since the attorney general had declined to bring action on the matter.[35]

Thus armed and protected, on March 31 the superintendent approved the merger. Officers of the two banks worked into the night putting their accounts together, although the task was eased by earlier preparation of *pro forma* statements. On April 1, 1955, newly named, The Chase Manhattan Bank opened for business.

Significance of the merger

The merger with Manhattan provided the single most important event in Chase's postwar history. It committtted the bank solidly to retail business within the city and gave it the impetus to expand into the suburbs and upstate. The merger constituted the first significant modification in Chase's early postwar character, which had concentrated heavily on wholesale banking. But the merger represented only a modification, for many in senior management still regarded the principal value of the new branches to be as a source of surplus funds for use in lending to business, rather than the retail business itself.

Overnight the merger elevated Chase to the top position among New York City banks, and second in size in the nation only to the Bank of America. Within a few days end-of-quarter statements were published, showing Chase Manhattan with almost $6.9 billion deposits, compared with $6.3 billion for First National City and $5.4 billion for Chase alone three months earlier. But this emphasis on size was to prove a mixed blessing. It fueled a contest between the banks in which size became an end in itself. Eventually this contributed to actions by Chase that produced heavy losses, especially in the mid-seventies, before size as an objective came to be placed in more reasonable perspective. Meanwhile the addition of Manhattan's branches enabled the bank to achieve a more rapid rate of growth over the next few years than would otherwise have been possible.

Prior to the merger considerable conjecture had arisen in the press and among bank analysts concerning possible advantages to the enlarged institution of Manhattan's special charter, and particularly its ability in the past to make investments in other banks. The investment in stock of County Trust Company (White Plains) constituted one example. But the merged bank found it difficult to make effective use of any unique provisions in the Manhattan charter, and indeed the charter finally proved a handicap to expansion and was abandoned in 1965 (see Chapter IX).

Impact of the merger on legislation

The Chase Manhattan merger focused the attention of regulatory authorities on control over bank mergers and acquisitions, and it aroused public interest and the concern of both Congress and the Department of Justice over the issue of bigness in banking and its impact on competition. Representative Celler's effort to apply the Clayton Antitrust Act to banks was a direct outgrowth of the merger. [36]

McCloy, who had been asked to testify on this proposed legislation, submitted a statement in July to the antitrust subcommittee of the House Judiciary Committee, although he did not appear personally. He pointed to the limited number of bank mergers in the total banking system, and he denied that competition had been diminished. He cautioned against making competition the overriding criterion for judging a merger, and objected to placing in the hands of the Justice Department the enforcement of prohibitions against bank mergers. Many in Congress agreed with McCloy's point of view. The issue was hotly debated, and not until 1960 was the landmark Bank Merger Act finally adopted. This required all mergers of federally insured banks to be approved by federal regulatory agencies, and then with competition only one of the criteria.

Meanwhile the Chase Manhattan merger eased the way for a companion piece of legislation: the Bank Holding Company Act of 1956. This act brought bank holding companies, except those controlling only a single bank, under effective federal control for the first time, with the Federal Reserve the regulating agency. Affiliation of banks with a holding company (with the exception of a few "grandfathered" existing companies) was restricted to banks located in the same state as the holding company's head office. The criteria governing acquisitions included "whether the effect of the acquisition . . . would be to expand the size or extent of the bank holding company system involved beyond limits consistent with adequate and sound banking, the public interest, and the preservation of competition in the field of banking."[37] Congress determined that concentration in banking called for preventive action, and students of the legislation concluded that fear of size was a dominating consideration.

These two legislative acts for many years denied Chase any opportunity to acquire sizable New York institutions or banks in other states. This proved later to be a severe handicap to the bank's strategy for expansion.

More immediately, however, the movement toward consolidation of banking in New York City was not ended. If anything, the success of Chase and Manhattan in combining helped encourage it, for bank mergers at this time proved advantageous. They opened up new sources of deposits for growth, increased capital and the maximum loan limit to large corporations, and could yield large economies in overhead and duplicating operations. Within the next six years Chemical Bank acquired New York Trust Company, J. P. Morgan joined with Guaranty Trust, and Manufacturers Trust merged with Hanover Bank. The Department of Justice, its patience exhausted, sought first to enjoin and then to break up the Manufacturers-Hanover merger. It failed, but that merger proved to be the final one among major New York City banks.

The postmerger bank: 1955–1960

The half-decade following the merger was among the most fruitful periods Chase Manhattan experienced. The newly enlarged bank was reorganized and modern management techniques introduced. New businesses were launched—not all successful, but innovative in varying degrees. Construction began on the landmark building that became the headquarters at One Chase Manhattan Plaza. Important additions were made to the domestic branch system, and the issue of branching into the suburbs was finally resolved. On the international side, a modest start was launched on broadening the overseas network. Meanwhile the basic business of the bank—loans, deposits, and a host of other financial services—continued to expand, propelled by economic growth in the United States and abroad. Earnings too increased in an almost unbroken progression. The bank's deposit base grew more slowly than loans, however, and the funding of future expansion came to be recognized as a major problem.

The Bower report

In order for the bank to prepare adequately for the changes that lay ahead, a more effective organizational structure was necessary. Shortly after the bank announced its plans for the Manhattan merger, David Rockefeller had suggested to McCloy that the organizational structure should be reexamined and that outside assistance would be desirable. McCloy agreed, and a management consultant, Gerald A. Bower, was retained.[1]

Bower was a rather unusual consultant. He had spent thirty years with General Electric, finally serving as staff assistant to the president on matters related to management organization. Bower brought along no assistants. Rather he asked that a group of officers who knew the bank be assigned to work with him. The recommendations of this group would then be presented to a committee of senior officers, which in turn would transmit final recommendations to McCloy and Baker.

Bower began work on May 1, 1955, a month after the merger. McCloy and Baker appointed Hamilton T. Slaight to serve as chairman of the working group. A vice president from the public utility division with long and varied experience in the bank, Slaight carried out this difficult assignment with tact and energy. The group fashioned for the first time a statement of objectives for the bank, couched in very general and broad terms—too broad in the light of later experience. An introductory section set forth the goals:

> Chase Manhattan Bank has as its primary objective the maintenance and enhancement of its position, nationally and internationally, as the leading commercial banking institution in the world . . . The Bank will conduct a commercial banking business and provide trust facilities recognized as second to none in scope, quality and value—all in a manner consistent with the best interests of the public, the Bank's customers, its employees and its owners.[2]

Subsequent sections elaborated on these objectives, still in general terms:

- The bank would carry out all activities involving funds entrusted to it in accordance with sound banking and investment principles designed to ensure overall safety of funds.
- It would provide a full range of commercial banking and trust facilities for anyone with a sound and proper need for them, seeking to expand its activities aggressively.
- The bank aimed to provide employment at attractive pay, opportunity for individual development and advancement, means of acquiring personal security, and motivation to contribute constructively to the bank's objectives.
- For shareholders it sought to produce maximum revenues while conducting its business efficiently so as to "realize a satisfactory return on equity . . . and maintain a desire . . . to retain present holdings," as well as to encourage increasing ownership.

The explicit assumption in the introduction that Chase Manhattan led in national banking could certainly be defended; the bank carried more business loans and possessed more correspondent bank relationships than any other bank. But the assertion of world leadership in international banking could be strongly disputed, especially by First National City. Even so, the bank aimed to be an all-purpose institution within limits set by law and regulatory authorities, and to excel in all respects. This posed a huge challenge, and one that eventually proved impossible to fulfill completely.

Revised organizational structure

The organizational structure that was finally adopted adhered closely to the recommendations of Bower and his working group. The bank's activities were brought together under seven components, each differing from the other but each in itself comprising related activities: United States, metropolitan, international departments, investments and financial planning, bank development (renamed planning and development), trust department, and operations department (see Figure 4).[3] Only two of these were new management units: investments and financial planning, and bank development. The former included the bond and the real estate and mortgage loan functions, with the executive head also serving as the bank's chief financial officer, responsible for capital planning, among other matters. John B. Bridgewood, who had served as head of the trust department since 1953, assumed this new assignment.

The establishment of the bank development department constituted one of the major changes introduced by the Bower study. For the first time the bank recognized the need for a number of specialized staff functions as an aid to effective management. Rockefeller, who had long been aware of this need, assumed direction of this function. Initially it embraced all existing corporate staff—advertising and public relations, economic research, employee relations, and operations—and added several new specialties, including marketing, management development, and organizational planning, the latter soon filled by an outside expert, States M. Mead, formerly of Cresap, McCormack and Pagett. Still another activity, special investments, was carried out by the unit devoted to special projects, under Victor E. Rockhill.

Operations and employee relations soon formed a separate department. Under the direction of Harold F. Moeller, an officer with experience in all phases of branch administration, computers were first introduced into operations in 1959, inaugurating one of the most significant developments of the postwar period (see Chapter XX).[4]

The Bower report suggested that the staff units should share a common responsibility for planning. Under Rockefeller's direction the first formal efforts at long-range planning were begun. Staff heads reporting to him met each month outside the bank for a half-day to exchange views and review plans. Hamilton Slaight, chairman of the Bower committee working group, became the first officer charged with long-range planning, a function at this stage in its infancy within banks and corporations. In 1957 the central focus of bank development was formally acknowledged by a change in name to planning and development.

Improving the line departments

No less important than the two new departments were improvements in existing line departments. At George Champion's instigation, the introduction to the Bower report stated, "We want to emphasize the importance of

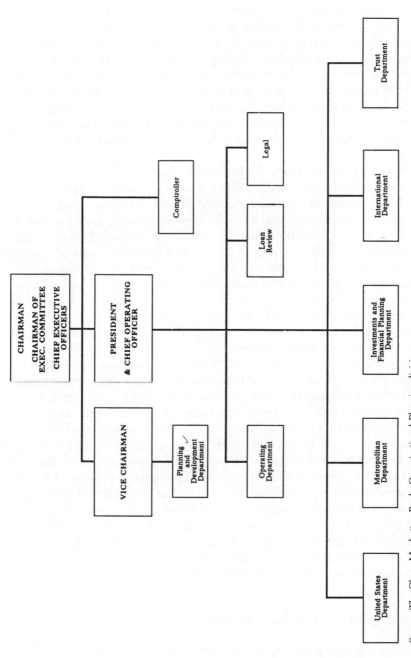

Source: The Chase Manhattan Bank, Organizational Planning division.

Figure 4. The Chase Manhattan Bank organization, 1957.

the continuing need for men with the right qualifications to fill the positions for developing and maintaining profitable business and good customer relations. This has been aptly referred to as 'our need for bankers.' "

Three changes were common to all these departments: delegation of greater responsibility (including lending authority) to officers down the line; introduction of a new cadre of middle management to reduce the span of control of executives to effective proportions; and the insertion of staff units to improve coordination, planning, and administration. By and large these departmental staff positions were concerned with marketing, operations, and personnel, which had been carried out in part previously in a less formal manner.

Prior to the reorganization, the business of the United States department had been handled by nine separate districts, all responsible to George Champion. The reorganization added the public utilities, petroleum, and aviation divisions from the former special industries department, now disbanded. Apart from these special industries, the country was divided into ten geographical districts instead of nine, but separated into three regional groups, with a vice president in charge of each group reporting to Champion.

Lending limits were assigned down the line, including to junior officers. Responsibility was fixed on the individual, rendering unnecessary a number of committees that had previously approved loans. Altogether seven loan committees were disbanded, with only the general loan, international, and commodity loan committees continuing.

The metropolitan, international, and trust departments underwent changes in varying degrees similar to those in the United States department. But the Bower committee made one observation concerning the international department that highlighted a problem cited earlier. After concluding that the department should continue to operate as an autonomous unit, the committee stated, "It is our opinion that there could be better liaison between the International Department and other Departments of the Bank."[5] The committee recommended that the executive of the international department move his office to the same floor as the other departmental executives, and that a staff marketing position be established with specific responsibility for building up liaison with the rest of the bank. The marketing effort was soon under way, but it was not until six years later, when the bank moved into its new headquarters, that the head of the international department joined his fellow executives in an adjoining office.

The comptroller and loan review

The Bower committee introduced still another organizational change which grew in significance over the years: the establishment of a central point of surveillance in the bank over the quality of credit. The officer in charge of this function also acted as the principal liaison with examining authorities, and was placed in charge of "loan workouts"—difficult or bad loans that required considerable renegotiation, participation in creditor reorganization committees, and other time-consuming tasks. The committee pointed out that recent examinations had placed $79 million of loans in a "classified" status, and an additional $242 million as "specially mentioned"—this out of a total portfolio of $3.047 billion.

These activities had been conducted in several different areas of the bank, although a substantial part had been performed by the comptroller's department through a credit review division. The Bower committee concluded that such work was not normally a part of the comptroller's function. McCloy and Baker agreed, and established a new position, loan review officer. Henry MacTavish, the Chase comptroller, was named to this post, opening the way for the appointment of Charles Agemian, formerly comptroller at Manhattan, to that position in the merged bank.

Reflecting in later years on the report of the Bower committee, Rockefeller commented that "it was something of a turning point in the bank's history."[6] It marked the introduction into the bank of modern management techniques, still at times in rudimentary form. And it placed the bank in a position to handle the explosive growth that lay ahead. Not until the end of the 1960s was a similar comprehensive examination of the bank's organizational structure again undertaken.

Growing diversity in credit

The merger had enlarged the bank's customer base and increased the loan portfolio to $3.1 billion, higher by almost 30 percent than that of Chase alone. But even as the two banks came together, the merged institution entered another period of unusual credit expansion. The economy recovered strongly from the post–Korean war recession of 1954, powered first by a revival in consumer spending and then by a boom in capital investment. In three years loans grew by almost $1 billion to more than $3.9 billion, the bulk of it to commerce and industry. Then after a pause during the brief recession of 1958, the advance resumed. By 1960 credit had climbed to $4.7 billion, a rise of 50 percent since the 1955 merger and a volume that began to strain the bank's resources.

A trend that had emerged since the end of the war was becoming more evident: a growing demand on the part of business for term credit. To some degree this was fostered by the bank itself, as officers trained in the technical aspects of such credit emphasized its usefulness as a flexible instrument tailored to meet the needs of specific customers. Many medium-sized firms without access to security markets made use of it. In 1960 some 56 percent of all loans to commerce and industry carried an original maturity of more than one year.[7] Maximum maturities normally ran from five to seven years, with term loans frequently combined with revolving credits. Companies often borrowed to finance new equipment, amortizing their loans through increased production or savings in costs. Credit demand consequently was linked closely to fluctuations in capital spending.

Public utilities remained an area of strength for the bank. Stand-by term loans employed for bridge financing—covering the period of construction of a new plant until long-term financing was arranged—became more widely utilized. Commitments were made prior to construction and funds drawn down only as needed. In the petroleum industry, oil production loans constituted a growing instrument; these were loans secured by oil in the ground and amortized from the sale of yearly output from wells already producing. Smaller independent firms raised money in this manner for further drilling. Chase's expertise in these transactions, with its combination of geologists, economists, and credit officers, was matched by few peers.

The domestic branches more than held their own in lending, as their assets grew almost 50 percent in these years. Many major corporate accounts continued to be handled through the branches, and they financed local business, both large and small, frequently lending against inventory. Certain branches specialized in credits to industries centered in their area. Ship loans, for example, were the province of the branch at Twenty-five Broadway. Fleets, both cargo and tanker, were expanding, and Chase was a leading lender. Credit was extended against the value of the vessel as well as assignment of a charter, with term loans of five to six years financing 70 percent of cost.[8] Longer-term financing arranged through an insurance company might supplement this. Normally a tanker or a vessel carrying bulk cargo would be under charter to a particular corporation, arranged prior to the loan and providing assurance through the loan agreement of repayment on a regular basis.

Although Chase continued to maintain its share of business loans among New York City banks, institutions in other areas were expanding credits somewhat more rapidly. Regional banks in particular were becoming more effective competitors, frequently invited into such a position by national corporations operating throughout the country. Treasurers of such corporations normally took the initiative in planning a sizable borrowing, naming the banks to be included in a syndication. Chase often acted as the agent in such a transaction, disbursing funds to the borrower, distributing interest payments to the lender, and gaining a certain prestige in the process.

Demand deposits fail to keep pace

Demand deposits continued to grow only slowly in the second half of the fifties, with average net balances advancing at a rate of 2.3 percent annually.

In consequence loan-deposit ratios rose substantially. From a mere 22 percent in 1945, when government securities dominated bank assets, the ratio more than doubled to 55 percent in 1955 and rose to 61 percent in 1959. Management observed in the annual report for that year that "loan/deposit ratios have reached a point where banks must be increasingly selective in their lending."

Chase was not unique in this respect. Other New York City banks faced the same problem, and the city's share of national deposits continued to erode, to 16.6 percent in 1959 from 18 percent five years earlier and 23.2 percent at the end of the war.[9] The New York City Bank Clearing House appointed a special committee in 1959 to study the matter, with Marus Conrad, a Chase vice president concerned with correspondent bank relations, as a member. The committee identified a number of troublesome trends. Other regions were growing more rapidly than New York, and within the metropolitan area the suburbs were siphoning off population, particularly the more affluent. (New York City banks could not yet branch into the suburbs.) Even more serious was the tendency of corporations and individuals to conserve on deposits in response to higher interest rates. Similarly, correspondent banks increasingly channeled funds into the Federal Funds Market, to the detriment of New York City balances.

By and large these trends would persist into the future, stimulating a reexamination of policies forbidding the payment of interest on certain types of time deposits, especially those from corporations (see Chapter VIII). Meanwhile Chase Manhattan, maintaining a greater volume of business with corporations and correspondent banks than its competitors, felt the trends keenly.

Upsurge in savings

The shortfall in demand deposits was alleviated to some degree by a dramatic advance in savings accounts. Higher rates paid on these accounts induced individuals across the country to shift funds into them. Chase had not been strong in this field, but the merger with Manhattan provided a wider base to build upon. Nonetheless, savings at the end of 1955 amounted to only $174 million, putting Chase considerably below First National City and Manufacturers Hanover.

An unexpected opportunity soon developed for Chase to improve its position. Interest rates rose in 1955 and 1956, propelled by a strong economic recovery. Partly in response, the Federal Reserve in December 1956 increased the ceiling rate banks could pay on passbook savings from 2½ to 3 percent.[10] Almost immediately Chase lifted its rate to the new ceiling on deposits of $5 to $10,000, and it advertised the fact widely. Rather surprisingly, none of its major competitors followed suit. Indeed not until July 1 of the following year did other major banks match Chase's move, setting a rate of 3 percent on savings up to $25,000.[11] The bank promptly increased its maximum to the same level.

The response for Chase was electrifying. Its savings more than doubled through 1957, and by the end of 1958 rose to $500 million. Over two years the number of accounts increased from 235,000 to 350,000, many of them new to the bank, with depositors adding other services as well. By this time the bank had become a leader in retail savings along with First National City. It acted to sustain this position in 1959 by becoming the first to pay interest from day of deposit to day of withdrawal on accounts that maintained a minimum balance until the end of the quarter.[12] Savings jumped again to $633 million in 1960. The lesson was not lost on the bank, which has maintained an aggressive posture on personal savings ever since.

Chase was less fortunate, however, with other time accounts. For the first time the bank felt the restraining effect of Regulation Q (under which the Federal Reserve set maximum rates) on international time deposits.[13] The Federal Reserve had established ceiling rates of 3 percent on time deposits of six months or more, with lower rates for shorter maturities. By 1959 these rates were no longer competitive with those in foreign money markets, and the international department lost deposits. The bank formally petitioned the Federal Reserve for an increase in ceiling rates only to have its request denied. An issue was thus posed that would arise more than once in the years ahead.

In the international field too loans moved ahead more rapidly than deposits, intensifying the squeeze on loanable resources. Continued prosperity and expanding trade lifted the need for foreign financing. By the end of the fifties international loans and customer acceptances at both the head office and overseas branches exceeded $900 million and accounted for about one-fifth of the bank's outstandings.[14] Many governments were extended term credit by the bank for balance-of-payments, trade, and development purposes, while Chase branches abroad found new customers in the growing number of U.S. firms moving overseas. The bank now extended credit to these subsidiaries, at times on a term basis, a significant advance from the early 1950s. Establishment of the European Common Market in 1958 and the European Free Trade Area in 1960 accelerated this trend, and in the latter year the bank placed a consultant in the Paris office to advise U.S. firms on opportunities for trade and investment.

Managing the security portfolio

In an environment of rising loan demand, slow deposit growth, and fluctuating interest rates, managing the security portfolio became increasingly important. John B. Bridgewood, executive in charge of investments and financial planning, supervised this responsibility, with the day-to-day activities carried out by the bond department. As president, Baker and subsequently Champion took a keen interest in this aspect of banking. At weekly meetings they met with heads of major departments to review changes in the bank's security position and consider strategies for the future.

Priority in managing the portfolio was given to providing adequate liquidity—funds necessary to finance daily or seasonal shortfalls in deposits—as well as growth in loans. Chase Manhattan, as the largest clearing bank for other banks in the nation, was subject to wide deposit swings, which the "money desk" sought to anticipate. If the bank needed funds, it sold securities with short maturities either directly or through repurchase agreements, or it bought federal funds, the surplus reserves of other banks. Chase was already buying and selling such funds on a growing scale as a service to its correspondents.[15] The bank also provided overnight loans to security brokers and dealers, and the volume could be adjusted from day to day. Still another source of funds, borrowing from the Federal Reserve Bank of New York, was seldom utilized. Chase sought to stay out of the Fed whenever possible.

Aside from providing liquidity, the security portfolio constituted an important source of income, second only to loans, both through interest earned and in favorable circumstances through capital gains. Here the results were heavily influenced by monetary policies of the Federal Reserve. In periods of monetary restraint (as in 1956–57 and again in 1959) the volume of securities declined and interest rates rose, while in periods of ease (1958 and 1960) securities expanded and interest rates fell. By and large the expansionary influence proved the more powerful, and income from securities increased over the period. The overall trend of interest rates, however, was upward (with government security prices moving lower), so capital gains were difficult to achieve. In only one year, 1958, were they realized. Unlike a number of other major banks at this time, Chase did not act as a dealer in securities of the U.S. government. Not until 1969 did the bank undertake this activity. Meanwhile, it bought and sold exclusively from its own portfolio, serving customers in this manner or through dealers. The bank did, however, act as an underwriter and dealer in the general obligations of states and municipalities. In this field it held a paramount position, and John Linen, who headed the activity until 1958, was a recognized authority on New York City finances. Underwritings expanded greatly to finance schools, roads, and other public works around the country. The peak for the period was achieved in 1958, encouraged by a decline in interest rates, when the bank either managed or participated in syndicates that bid successfully for new issues with a value of $2.4 billion.[16]

Improvement in earnings and capital

In one other acid test, the bottom line, the bank showed marked improvement. Net operating earnings rose from $42.3 million in 1955 to $74.3 million in 1960, an advance of 75 percent. Although resources increased, more important, the bank was able to channel a larger proportion of assets into higher-yielding loans during intervals of strong economic expansion. And it did so in a climate of rising interest rates. As the prime rate moved up, the average rate earned on loans and securities climbed from 2.96 to 4.5 percent over the five-year period.

On two key measures—the return on assets (ROA) and the return on equity (ROE)—the improvement was impressive. As we have seen, return on assets was extremely low in early postwar years, little better than forty basis points. The measure rose with the increase in interest rates during and after the Korean war and in 1955 stood at fifty-six basis points (based on year-end assets). By 1960 ROA had climbed to eighty basis points, the highest in the years covered by this history, although a peak not long retained. Moreover this performance lifted the return on equity from 8 percent in the mid-fifties to almost 11 percent in 1960, double the level ten years earlier. The price of the bank's shares on the security market advanced in response to these gains and in the second half of the fifties exceeded book value.

This higher share price enabled the bank to raise capital for the first time since the 1920s through sale of stock on the market. In 1956 shareholders were given the right to subscribe to 1 million shares at a price about 6 percent above book value. The offering proved a complete success and provided $46.4 million for the capital account.[17] With help also from increased retained earinings, capital funds grew to $689 million by the end of 1960, larger by a third from the total of the merged bank in 1955. Supplementing this was a reserve for loan loss of $113 million. The two amounted to 8.7 percent of assets, a comfortable margin but one that would erode with the rapid expansion of assets in the years ahead.

The public view of the bank

The bank not only projected a strong financial image in the late fifties; it also remained favorably regarded by the general public. A survey by *Business Week* magazine in the mid-fifties reported that the bank led all others in general reputation in the business community, as well as in interpreting to the general public the free enterprise system and the part played by banks in that system.[18] McCloy contributed to this positive image, speaking out on public issues, taking the lead in the struggle for change in banking laws, and participating in a wide range of outside activities. Over the years he appeared

Illustrations

Salmon P. Chase, Secretary of the Treasury, 1861–1864, for whom the bank was named.

104 Broadway, first home of The Chase National Bank, 1877–1887.

John Thompson, founder and Director
of The Chase National Bank, 1877–
1891; President, 1884–1886.

40 Wall Street, first
home of the Bank of
the Manhattan
Company, 1799–1839.

The Fourth National Bank, 1864–1914, included through subsequent mergers in The Chase National Bank and located at the site of the bank's head office, 1928–1955.

Henry White Cannon, President, The Chase National Bank, 1886–1904; first Chairman, 1904–1911.

15 Nassau Street, home of The Chase National Bank, 1887–1896.

A. Barton Hepburn, President, The Chase National Bank, 1904–1911, and Chairman, 1911–1917.

77–83 Cedar Street, home of The Chase National Bank, 1896–1914. New York Clearing House above.

Albert H. Wiggin, President, The
Chase National Bank, 1911–1917;
Chairman, 1918–1930, and Chairman
of the Governing Board, 1930–1933.

57 Broadway, Chase National Bank head office, 1914–1928.

18 Pine Street (behind Federal Hall, first capitol of the United States), head office of The Chase National Bank, 1928–1955, The Chase Manhattan Bank, 1955–1961.

Winthrop W. Aldrich, President, The Chase National Bank, 1930–1933, Chairman of the Governing Board, 1933, and Chairman, 1934–1953.

John J. McCloy, Chairman, The Chase National Bank, 1953–1955, and Chairman, The Chase Manhattan Bank, 1955–1960.

J. Stewart Baker, Chairman, Bank of The Manhattan Company, 1932–1955, and President, The Chase Manhattan Bank, 1955–1956.

One Chase Manhattan Plaza, head office, 1961—.

"Group of Four Trees," Jean Dubuffet, Chase Manhattan Plaza, 1974.

George Champion, President, 1957–1961, and Chairman, 1961–1969.

David Rockefeller, President, 1961–1969, and Chairman, 1969–1981.

Willard C. Butcher, President, 1972–1981, and Chairman, 1981—.

frequently before committees of the House and the Senate. In 1958 he was elected chairman of the Ford Foundation, the largest in the world, and he also served as chairman of the Council on Foreign Relations. Champion and Rockefeller too were active on the outside, speaking on issues and participating in many organizations.

Publications issued by the bank dealing with the domestic economy, foreign economies, and trends in energy added further to its reputation. So too did a permanent exhibit, Moneys of the World, in effect a small museum, unique of its kind, including more than 75,000 pieces of money, with coins ranging from the ancient Greek to the modern. The collection contained many odd species of money, not the least a large stone weighing 175 pounds once exchangeable for ten thousand coconuts or a wife on the island of Yap in the western Pacific. In 1956 this exhibit moved to a ground-floor space fronting on Sixth Avenue in the RCA building, where it was visited by many thousands each year.[19] It remained there until 1978, when the bank lent the collection to the Smithsonian Institution with the intention of later donating it.

The bank's contribution program

The bank's image was also enhanced by its contribution program, which it regarded as an important aspect of its responsibility to the communities it served. Chase for many years under Aldrich contributed to a few leading charitable organizations. In 1945 the selection, heavily influenced by war needs, included the Red Cross, the National War Fund, and the Greater New York Fund, for a total of $365,000, or a bit less than 1 percent of earnings before taxes.[20] The number of recipients increased over the immediate postwar years, although the dollar amount declined somewhat as earnings fell. By the time of the merger, the recipients had swelled to twenty-eight in number. Hospitals, health agencies, civic organizations, and a few educational institutions became beneficiaries, while disbursements rose to $404,000. With the subsequent reorganization of the bank, a contributions committee was formed, chaired by David Rockefeller. This committee now submitted to the directors for approval an annual budget setting forth the organizations to receive donations and the amounts, as well as a contingency fund. For some years after 1958 the committee channeled many grants through a foundation established to facilitate giving.

A major program developed at this time involved aid to education.[21] Grants were extended to a limited number of private universities, selected both on the basis of excellence and as a source of present and potential management personnel. Similarly, grants were awarded to three state and regional associations representing fifty-six smaller colleges and universities in

New Jersey, New York, and New England. Supplementing these was a matching gift program whereby the bank matched gifts up to a total of $1,000 by members of the staff (soon extended to directors and retirees) to colleges, universities, and private secondary schools. Some $175,000 was set aside for this educational program in 1958, its initial year.

By 1960 the contributions budget was raised to $950,000—not quite 0.7 percent of earnings before taxes—with a wide range of social welfare, educational, cultural, health, and other public service organizations of significance to the bank as beneficiaries. The program continued to expand through coming years in line with increased earnings, adding many new recipients as it adjusted to changing social needs (see Chapter XXI).

Evolution in senior management

Through this period of growth McCloy continued as chairman, although changes in senior management were soon undertaken to ensure a proper succession. Stewart Baker first opened the way in 1956 by suggesting to McCloy and the board that he retire as president while remaining as chairman of the executive committee. In doing so he would continue for the time being to share responsibility with McCloy as chief executive officer, but would relinquish what were in effect the tasks of a chief administrative officer. At the same time Percy Ebbott agreed to leave the board in order, as he put it, "to make room for younger management." The directors noted in a resolution at the time of Ebbott's retirement that throughout his long and eventful career he "labored with profit to his masters and distinction to himself."[22] He was designated chairman of the trust advisory board and invited to continue to attend meetings of the directors, although not as a voting member.

The actions of Baker and Ebbott made it possible to introduce the next generation of top management. Accordingly on December 12, 1956, the directors elected George Champion president and David Rockefeller vice chairman of the board, effective January 1.[23] The by-laws were altered so as to designate the president as chief administrative officer, with general supervision over the operations of the bank, subject to direction of the board, the chairman, and the chairman of the executive committee (see Figure 4). The vice chairman, in turn, was to assist the chairman and the chairman of the executive committee in carrying out their duties as chief executive officers. In this capacity Rockefeller continued to devote attention to planning and development, and major corporate staff functions related to this activity reported directly to him. He also retained primary responsibility for overseeing the bank's new building, on which construction was just beginning.

The appointment of Champion and Rockefeller to these posts represented a natural evolution. As noted earlier, Champion had spent his entire business life in banking, and was widely and favorably known among his peers. In 1958 he was elected president of the Association of Reserve City Bankers, a mark of distinction within the profession. The directors knew him as an officer experienced in all phases of banking, although concentrated chiefly on the domestic wholesale side. He had served as chairman of the general loan committee after the retirement of Carl Schmidlapp, and was recognized as a sound but not overly cautious judge of credits.

Rockefeller was eleven years younger than Champion, with ten and one-half years' experience in the bank. Hard working and involved in many outside interests and commitments, he had served in both domestic and international fields. Rockefeller was interested in the professional aspects of management and recognized the need to introduce modern techniques on a wider scale. He was highly qualified to be responsible for planning and development.

The designation of Champion as president left open the top position in the United States department, to which the directors named Walter E. Dennis, an able banker and manager with long experience at Chase.[24] Earlier Frank G. Ross had succeeded John Bridgewood as executive of the trust department when the latter took over new responsibilities in investments and financial planning. With the appointment later of Harold Moeller as executive for operations and employee relations, the departmental organization was complete for the remainder of the decade. Lawrence Marshall remained in charge at the metropolitan department and Charles Cain, Jr., at the international department. All departmental heads now carried the title of executive vice president.

Baker did not remain long as chairman of the executive committee and co-chief executive officer. He chose to retire altogether from active participation in management at the end of 1957 but continued as director. The position of chairman of the executive committee was abolished for the time being. The directors, in paying tribute to Baker, pointed out that he had served with the bank for thirty-nine years, during most of which he was an executive officer, including successively president and chairman of the board of the Bank of The Manhattan Company, and president and chairman of the executive committee of The Chase Manhattan Bank. The directors went on to say, "By his character and integrity he has greatly enhanced the reputation and position of the Bank in the community and the nation; in this respect worthily following the tradition of effective leadership which his father established before him."[25] The Bakers, descendants of one of the founders of the Bank of Manhattan in 1799 and its chief managers for more than a half-century, were now retired as a family from its executive leadership.

Growth in basic business and earnings

With a new organization and revamped management in place, Chase strengthened its operations and increased its capacity to move into new fields. The bank's basic business—the extension of credit—had grown markedly in the five years following the merger. But the squeeze on deposits continued, and loan-deposit ratios rose to a point that concerned management. A lag in deposit growth in New York City was particularly unsettling, for it accorded an advantage to regional banks in other areas.

For Chase the problem was somewhat alleviated by an unusual expansion in savings accounts, encouraged by a rise in the ceiling rate set by the Federal Reserve. The bank benefited from an aggressive posture in this business and would pursue a similar policy in the future. Still, more extreme action would be necessary, especially enlarging the area for branching (see Chapter VI) and opening up the market for time deposits.

On one other count Chase and other banks reported marked progress: bank earnings rose to a new peak, benefiting from increased loans and wider margins. Bank stock prices advanced strongly, and for the first time since the 1920s Chase was encouraged to raise equity capital in the market.

Exploring new fields

The Bower report in 1955 declared that Chase Manhattan should aim to be the premier bank in the world, excelling in all fields. This posed a large challenge, and it impelled the bank to search for ways to continue to advance. Change was in the air, and competitors were also seeking new avenues for expansion. In 1957 First National City announced plans to form a holding company, and through this to acquire County Trust Company in White Plains, the largest bank in Westchester County. As matters turned out, the combination failed to gain necessary approval from the Federal Reserve, but it signaled First National's aggressive posture. Later Chemical acquired New York Trust, and Morgan merged with Guaranty. On the international side First National City widened its thrust overseas, while Bank of America accelerated its movement abroad. All this occurred against an economic backdrop that encouraged growth in bank facilities and resources, both at home and in other nations.

Expanding the domestic branch system

For the newly merged Chase Manhattan an immediate challenge lay in further expanding its domestic branch system, rounding out representation in the city and pressing for the legislative approval to move into the suburbs. This would help in gaining badly needed deposits to finance loans and widen the market for other retail services. By 1960 the bank was operating 105 branches, up from ninety-six at the time of merger in 1955. But its competitors were busy too. Manufacturers Trust operated 119 branches, an increase of seven, and First National City grew to eighty-eight from seventy-three.

Chase's expansion at this time was accomplished largely through merger. In July 1957 the bank acquired the Staten Island National Bank and Trust Company, with five offices and assets of $35.6 million.[1] This was followed in early 1959 by merger with the Clinton Trust Company, which operated four offices on the West Side of Manhattan and held assets of $42.6 million.[2] Chase had not been represented in either area, which was a major consideration. Nevertheless the stockholders did not all agree on the importance of Staten Island. One stockholder asked what the bank could expect to gain from the merger, describing the borough as "a desolated bit of real estate and

89

an industrial desert." Baker, who was serving as chairman at the meeting in the absence of McCloy, responded that the bank was obtaining five sites, five franchises, five opportunities to do business, and that it would be difficult and costly to accomplish this in any other manner. He added that surveys showed the population of Staten Island doubling by 1975.[3] On this count he proved to be somewhat optimistic, for the population grew only about 50 percent, but this was in the face of a decline for the city as a whole.

Breaking into the suburbs

New York City itself, however, was not the main target. Chase aimed to break into the immediate suburbs. This was the area of rapid growth, now drawing many of the middle-income families out of the city. But the banking law divided the state into nine banking districts and confined branching to the district in which a bank had its head office. The suburbs fell into different banking districts from the city.

First National City's attempt to circumvent this rule in 1956 by acquiring County Trust in adjoining Westchester raised an immediate outcry from suburban banks. The state legislature quickly responded by establishing a joint committee to revise the banking law. It adopted legislation in early 1957 that temporarily barred holding companies from acquiring additional banks lying outside the banking district of their head office.[4] The problem was further complicated by competing interests of the thrift institutions, savings banks and savings and loans. The legislature found itself caught in a political crossfire and was unable to reach agreement. Hearings were held in 1957 and again in 1958 and in 1959, but not until 1960 was an acceptable compromise fashioned.

McCloy had early stated Chase Manhattan's position: New York City banks should be able to move into the suburbs, and to do so through branching rather than holding companies. But if the bank was left with no other choice, it would seriously consider following the latter route. The argument put forth by the bank was simple but compelling:

> The entire Metropolitan area now constitutes one integrated social, economic and trade center. Population boundaries have disappeared; stores at the center have established branches in the outer regions; and there is a ceaseless flow of workers, commerce and communications between all parts of the area.[5]

No institution could long remain vital and dynamic, the bank asserted, if it was artificially shut off from a primary area of natural growth.

This argument was buttressed by a promise of positive benefits for the suburbs, a range of services that New York City banks could bring to the outer areas that would not otherwise be easily accessible: larger loans, specialized trust services, foreign services, nationwide credit information, and the backing of $3 billion in capital funds. Little was said about reduced rates for installment loans, but rates were lower in the city than in the suburbs, and this proved to be one of the tangible benefits.

McCloy testified before the joint legislative committee in March 1957, and in his absence from the country a year later, David Rockefeller journeyed to Albany to testify. Then in September 1959 and finally in February 1960 McCloy again appeared before the committee, which by this time was headed by a new chairman and included new members.

The governor and the vice chairman

Meanwhile another element was introduced into the debate: the relationship of David Rockefeller to the new governor of the state, Nelson A. Rockefeller, his brother. At hearings of the joint committee for bankers on Long Island in early September 1959, Arthur T. Roth, president of the Franklin National Bank, claimed that David Rockefeller was the chief proponent of change in the banking law and, as the *New York Times* reported, "charged that the State Banking Department and the legislative leaders were following the dictates of the state's largest bank, Chase Manhattan."[6]

Two days later, when the joint committee met in New York City, McCloy entered a sharp rejoinder. He asserted that the name of David Rockefeller had been introduced into the hearings deliberately. "We all know that another man named Rockefeller holds a position of high honor in this state . . . the imputation was quite clear, that some undue influence was used, that some connivance occurred. This is a very tawdry suggestion."[7]

McCloy employed the term *tawdry* advisedly, for it was a matter of public record that the Rockefeller brothers owned about 19 percent of the stock of the National Bank of Westchester, the second largest bank in that county. Chase Manhattan itself still possessed a 6.6 percent stock interest in County Trust, White Plains, which had been a subject of contention with the state superintendent at the time of the Manhattan merger. And the governor was reputed to own stock in Chase Manhattan. In actual fact Nelson Rockefeller had long been a shareholder in the Chase National Bank and at this time held about eighteen thousand shares of Chase Manhattan stock.[8]

To avoid any appearance of conflict of interest, the governor quietly disposed of this holding in January 1960, several months before action was taken on the bill. Then in May, after branching legislation had been adopted, the Rockefeller brothers took similar action with stock of the National Bank of Westchester. They offered their 19 percent interest in the bank to other shareholders, specifically stating that this was done to avoid any misunderstanding or constraints on the bank.[9]

The Omnibus Banking Act of 1960

The logjam on banking legislation was finally broken at 1:07 A.M. on March 22, 1960. The legislature at that late hour adopted what had become known as the Omnibus Banking Bill, "Omnibus" because it included provisions also contained in a number of separate bills. Governor Rockefeller signed it into law a few hours later.[10] The act sanctioned statewide bank holding companies, but it required any acquisition across banking district lines to be approved by a three-fifths vote of the State Banking Board. Previously the state had exercised no control over bank holding companies, although approval for acquisitions had been required from the Federal Reserve since 1956. Chase Manhattan had opposed statewide holding companies, while First National City supported them.

Meanwhile the apprehension of upstate bankers over this holding company provision was relieved to some degree by a preamble to the act which declared it to be the policy of the state "to prevent statewide control of banking by a few giant institutions." Although apparently harmless and irrelevant at the moment, this policy statement would later become a club held over the head of New York City banks.

Of more immediate concern to Chase was the enlargement of the New York City district for branching. Here the bank gained the immediate objective it had been fighting for. New York City banks were permitted to branch into Nassau and Westchester Counties (although not yet into nearby Suffolk and Rockland), and Nassau and Westchester banks could branch into New York City. Savings banks and savings and loans also gained more liberal branching privileges, not only in New York City but upstate as well.

Nevertheless this branching privilege was circumscribed by a provision buried in small print. Section 105 of the law, previously in effect, barred banks from branching into any community with a population of 1 million or less that already contained the head office of another bank. This would forestall Chase from moving into many of the most desirable locations. Moreover the act established criteria for approval of mergers of state commercial banks. Again these criteria would become relevant for Chase and other New York City banks in the not too distant future, especially a requirement that competitive as well as banking factors be applied in approving bank mergers.

Aftermath of the Omnibus Bank Act

In the immediate aftermath of the Omnibus Bank Act, officers responsible for branch expansion scoured the suburban countryside for new locations. But so did other New York City banks. The superintendent of banks, G.

Russell Clark, made it clear that he had no intention of relaxing standards for new branches, and he announced as basic policy that he would not permit large New York City banks to merge with any major banks in the suburbs.[11]

Applications under the law for new branches could be submitted as of July 1, 1960. Chase requested three locations in Nassau and added a fourth at Hartsdale in Westchester. Eight New York City banks applied to open twenty-two new branches, an impossible situation for the state superintendent and the comptroller of the currency, who acted upon national bank requests. In early August the bank's first suburban branch, at Great Neck Plaza in Nassau, was approved. Later the branch in Hartsdale also gained acceptance, but the other two branches in Nassau were denied.[12]

The Chase Manhattan Charge Plan

The bank in late 1958 also buttressed its retail business by introducing a significant new service: The Chase Manhattan Charge Plan (CMCP). In effect this represented a forerunner of the bank credit card, which would become commonplace by the end of the following decade, and it constituted a pioneering venture in the New York market. On the West Coast, Bank of America began a similar service, and the two banks shared experience and operating information.

The plan operated in a simple manner but involved much paperwork.[13] Cardholders made purchases on credit from participating merchants, who in turn deposited the sales slips with the bank. The bank then sent the cardholder a single bill once a month for all purchases. Cardholders who settled their accounts within ten days incurred no additional charge; otherwise they paid an interest charge of 1 percent a month on the unpaid balance. Credit was extended for a maximum of five months.

Merchants gained from the plan by receiving immediate credit to their accounts when they deposited sales slips with the bank. They incurred no credit risk and were able to provide a modern charge account service at low cost. Sales volume was expected to benefit. In turn merchants compensated the bank for its credit and bookkeeping work with a service charge, which the bank deducted when sales slips were deposited. The basic charge was 6 percent, but with refunds graduated according to volume it averaged about 2 percent.

Chase advertised the new service heavily and solicited cardholders by mail. After a year of operation the bank announced that 350,000 consumers and 5,300 retail merchants were participating in the plan, although the estimated number of consumers included several for each card. Sales volume charged against the card increased, but the average volume per cardholder remained moderate. By 1960, the second year of operation, volume had risen to about $25 million.[14]

Yet the plan was losing money, and projections undertaken in 1961 did not see it turning profitable in the period ahead. The number of cards outstanding leveled off at about 160,000, and credit losses were relatively high. Larger stores did not join the plan, choosing instead to protect their own credit operations. Only Korvettes among large retailers was finally induced to become a member, but solely by providing it with a very low discount on sales. Most merchant members were relatively small retailers, largely sellers of apparel and household goods.

Chase's experience appeared to run counter to that of other banks that had started similar services, including Bank of America, whose card operation was turning profitable. George Roeder, who had succeeded Marshall as head of the metropolitan department, and Charles Agemian, the comptroller, traveled to the West Coast to look into reasons for the difference.[15]

One obvious factor was the size of the market. Bank of America operated with branches statewide and with a higher average income potential. In addition there appeared to be a difference in principle and even in business philosophy. In its accounting Chase Manhattan charged to CMCP all direct costs associated with the operation, but Bank of America did not do the same. Advertising and promotion were heavy costs, but Bank of America absorbed these in a general advertising budget for retail services. Similarly, funds used by CMCP to pay merchants and to finance outstanding credit were charged the central pool rate, the transfer rate for funds between departments. At Bank of America the credit card incurred no charge for such funds, utilizing cost free part of the surplus funds generated by the retail side of the bank.

No doubt Bank of America sharpened its cost accounting as time passed. But its card survived and went on to become the basis for the nationwide VISA system, a highly profitable venture. It was aided too by the bank's ability over the next few years to computerize many operations, thereby reducing large clerical costs.

Chase stayed with its accounting principles, which had the virtue of more accurately measuring the cost of remaining in the business. Early in 1962, slightly more than three years after the plan's inception, the decision was taken to sell the business. George Champion delivered the initial announcement at the annual meeting of stockholders on January 30.[16] The buyer was Uni-Serve, a new corporation formed for the purpose by Joseph P. Williams, who had gained experience in the credit card field on the West Coast. In effect, Uni-Serve purchased the receivables for $9 million and took over 160,000 cardholders and 5,300 participating merchants operating some 6,700 retail outlets. Uni-Serve moved the operation to Queens, which offered the benefit of lower employee costs. Over the next few years the company expanded into other areas and added travel and entertainment outlets.

In late 1965 the operation was sold to American Express, which looked upon the card as a complement to its own travel and entertainment card.

Meanwhile, Chase remained interested in credit cards, although initially on a nationwide basis. Finally, with the passage of time and much study, the bank repurchased Uni-Serve, by then a much larger multipurpose company, paying American Express $25 million for the business (Chapter X).[17]

In the end the decision to close out the Chase Manhattan charge plan was Champion's. He was supported by Roeder and Agemian, but Marshall, then vice chairman, preferred to continue. Rockefeller, more concerned at the time with international expansion, did not hold strong views on the matter. Certainly the projections and the arithmetic supported the decision. But it also reflected in some immeasurable degree the continuing culture of Chase, reflecting the preeminence of wholesale banking and the reluctance to make a large and risky investment in an innovative instrument on the retail side.

American Overseas Finance Corporation

Other fields for exploration were open on the international side. In the mid-1950s U.S. economic relations with other countries reached a turning point. The industrial nations, especially Germany and Japan, had recovered from World War II. Economic aid to the industrial world ceased, but was replaced to a limited degree by aid to less developed countries. U.S. exports encountered stiffening competition in world markets, and save for a boom year in 1957 did not increase greatly. Meanwhile imports continued to expand, and the nation's trade surplus dwindled.

In surveying trade finance, Chase recognized a need by U.S. exporters of machinery and equipment for medium-term credit (one to five years). Although Chase and other commercial banks did not yet readily make term loans for foreign business, other industrial nations had established official institutions for this purpose which frequently accorded their exporters a competitive advantage. The Export-Import Bank fulfilled this role in the United States, but considerable time and trouble were involved in obtaining such credit. Moreover the Ex-Im Bank charter dictated that it also assist private sources of finance.

The planning and early organization of the new venture were in the hands of Victor Rockhill, who was then heading the small special projects unit. Rockhill in early 1955 enlisted the help of Norbert A. Bogdan, a man with considerable experience in international finance, who was subsequently appointed president of the new American Overseas Finance Corporation (AOFC), organized under the Edge Act of 1919 to provide greater flexibility to institutions financing international business. Four other major banks joined Chase in ownership.[18] McCloy served initially as chairman, and Rockefeller, who had taken a special interest in the project, was a director. The five banks fully subscribed to an original $10 million of common stock.

The importer, the exporter, AOFC, and the Export-Import Bank all contributed to arrangements for financing by AOFC—the importer with a down payment, AOFC and the exporter with the remaining credit, and the Export-Import Bank through a partial guarantee. The new corporation started in a promising manner. A number of trade deals were financed, and Bogdan sought to establish export lines of credit for manufacturers. Moreover, some months after the founding of AOFC, the Federal Reserve made even more flexible the powers of Edge Act corporations, permitting them to take various forms of equity as a supplementary payment to interest. By the end of 1956 AOFC held total assets of about $11 million, nearly all arising from export transactions, as well as commitments to buy paper amounting to $22,255,000.[19]

Quite early, however, the corporation found that on certain transactions the Export-Import Bank was emerging as an active competitor. This directly violated a written agreement Rockhill and Bogdan had negotiated with the Ex-Im Bank as one of the considerations for establishing AOFC. The problem finally came to a head in early 1957. AOFC had nearly completed negotiations with Thyssen of Germany, involving export of U.S. equipment to that company when Bogdan, to his surprise, discovered that financing had already been arranged on more favorable terms with the Export-Import Bank.[20]

McCloy and Bogdan flew to Washington to review the matter, meeting first with Samuel Waugh, president of the Ex-Im Bank. They failed to obtain his assurances that the bank would not seek to finance transactions AOFC was willing to handle. They next visited George M. Humphrey, secretary of the treasury, who was known as a staunch proponent of free enterprise. To their consternation Humphrey in effect told them that if private enterprise was unable to compete with the government in this type of financing, then there would be no room for private enterprise. McCloy, deeply disturbed by his attitude, walked out.[21]

The other partners also became concerned about the competition between AOFC and the Export-Import Bank. They saw companies with the highest credit rating turning to the Export-Import Bank because of lower rates. The partner banks decided to sell AOFC, although it continued to be a profitable business. A buyer was found in Nelson Rockefeller and the International Basic Economy Corporation, to whom the ability of AOFC to hold equity as well as to extend credit was a distinct advantage. Rockefeller enlisted other partners to form a new corporation, American Overseas Investing Company. In June 1957 it acquired AOFC by issuing to the owner banks $10 million in five-year serial notes, the amount the banks had initially invested.[22]

Chase International Investment Corporation

Although AOFC required considerable time and effort, the bank's principal international activity outside normal banking was a fully-owned subsidiary called the Chase Bank, soon to be renamed The Chase International Investment Corporation (CIIC). The Chase Bank, which operated under an Edge Act charter, originally served as the company through which the Chase branches in Paris and the Far East were held. It carried a capital of $6 million, to which an additional $10 million was eventually added.

Aldrich originally conceived the idea of using the Chase Bank as a vehicle for what he called productive financing abroad, an activity different from such normal types of business as making guaranteed loans to foreign governments and banks or short-term financing of foreign trade.[23] It was through the Chase Bank that the investment in Interamericana in Brazil was undertaken (see Chapter II). Responsibility for the Chase Bank was lodged with Edward Love and Victor Rockhill in special projects rather than in the international department. McCloy, as much an internationalist as Aldrich, embraced the concept and encouraged Love and Rockhill to move ahead with it. Rockefeller also took an active interest and later became chairman of CIIC.

As an Edge Act corporation the Chase Bank could engage in equity financing outside the United States, as well as provide loans, both long and short term, and other types of finance. This degree of flexibility was denied to commercial banks for operations within the United States. Aldrich and Rockhill held the conviction that if the Chase Bank were to take advantage of its special powers, it should do so in a manner that would contribute positively to the process of economic development, a view shared by both McCloy and Rockefeller. This led the Chase Bank, and finally its successor CIIC, to concentrate on financing enterprises in less developed countries, a worthy but somewhat risky process. As Rockhill later put it, "*Pro bono publico* was an element. It wasn't on top of the arch, but it certainly was trying to help other economies stabilize themselves. . . . We wanted to make money in the process, but it wasn't just to make money."[24]

Activities of the new Chase Bank were simplified in the spring of 1956, when the Federal Reserve changed certain regulations governing Edge Act corporations. The revisions separated nonbanking from banking corporations, the latter being permitted to accept deposits but not make equity investments. Chase Manhattan chose to qualify the Chase Bank as a nonbanking corporation, and in August 1957 the name was changed to the Chase International Investment Corporation.[25] Meanwhile an experienced investment banker, Robert H. Craft, was retained to head the new company.

CIIC's method of operation

CIIC early developed a technique of operation. Its investments for the most part involved new projects, preferably in an underdeveloped country. These usually were made with a know-how partner, normally a U.S. corporation possessing skills and experience in the business. High priority was accorded to projects that employed local materials and labor and saved or earned foreign exchange for the host country. The Edge Act did not sanction any project that operated in the United States, although a project could export to this country. CIIC also utilized a lengthy checklist of requirements, including adequate power, labor supply, transportation, water, and the like. Not infrequently, however, new or unforeseen problems developed.[26]

Craft began operations in 1956 with a small staff, and he succeeded over the next several years in carrying out some significant transactions. One, in partnership with Lazard Frères, involved establishing the Industrial and Mining Development Bank of Iran (IMDBI), which later fell victim to revolution. IMDBI was the first development bank to be organized by private interests, and it became a prototype for development banks in other countries, with CIIC a founding participant in a number of them.[27]

Craft departed to some extent from the philosophy conceived for the institution. As an investment banker, he sought projects that would earn a profit regardless of their contribution to economic development. One investment in particular, involving the purchase of equity in a reorganized refinery in Puerto Rico, turned out to be highly profitable, yielding several million dollars in a year or two. But it tied up the scarce resources of CIIC. Craft also found it difficult to coordinate and even accommodate his activities to those of the larger parent. CIIC was a relatively small operation and was destined to remain so; its assets never exceeded $35 million. It could not ignore the much larger interests of the international department. The fit between Craft and the bank was not good, and he was succeeded as president in 1959 by Victor Rockhill.[28]

A further change of some significance occurred in 1959, when CIIC formed a Canadian subsidiary, named Arcturus, through which many of its transactions were channeled for tax purposes. The bank was fortunate in enlisting an outstanding Canadian, Graham Towers, former governor of the Bank of Canada, to be chairman of Arcturus. Towers proved to be helpful not only to CIIC but to the parent bank as well.[29]

One project carried out through Arcturus in 1960 illustrates both the accomplishments and the problems of CIIC. With know-how partners from both Switzerland and Italy, CIIC took the lead in organizing Nigerian Textile Mills in Lagos, the first major private industrial project with an American interest in Nigeria. CIIC supplied about one-fourth of the initial capital of $4.25 million for a complete spinning and weaving plant. Housing and training programs were provided for African workers. But the project depended on public power, which proved to be uncertain, causing shut-downs. Only after some years did the government permit the company to establish its own power supply. Moreover two of the Nigerians selected as local directors were jailed for revolutionary activity. They refused to resign, and a special stockholders' meeting was called to discharge them.[30]

And yet, unlike certain other projects, the Nigerian mill in the early years was quite profitable and paid an attractive dividend. In the 1960s, when the government ordered the sale of stock to Nigerians, a possible opportunity was provided to divest a considerable proportion of the investment at a substantial profit; but only a small proportion was sold. By the early 1980s the partners continued to own about 60 percent and did not find it propitious to sell.[31]

These problems, however, lay in the future. In the early 1960s Rockhill and his associates, never a large staff, explored and undertook projects in many areas, always attempting to hold to CIIC's basic philosophy of assisting in the process of economic development.

Expanding the foreign branch system

In the late 1950s Chase began gradually to break away from its mode of delivering traditional banking services overseas. In only one country, Lebanon, had a branch been opened since 1947. Charles Cain Jr., head of the international department, and his deputy, Alfred Schumacher, remained wedded to correspondent banking, convinced that the bank would lose sizable deposits if it moved aggressively abroad to establish branches. McCloy doubted their conclusion and Rockefeller frankly disagreed with it. Baker and Champion were undecided. A task force formed to examine the problem delivered its recommendation in mid-1957: Chase should establish a wider network of foreign branches.[32] Not until the early sixties, however, was the policy pursued with vigor, as related later.

Nevertheless a start was made in South Africa, a country that impressed Victor Rockhill and John Watts, in charge of Africa, as possessing great economic potential. South Africa did not permit foreign banks to open branches, so it was necessary to organize a subsidiary, The Chase Manhattan Bank (South Africa). This in turn required the approval of the Federal Reserve, and a new Edge Act subsidiary for banking, the Chase Manhattan Banking Corporation (later the Chase Manhattan Overseas Banking Corporation), was formed as the parent. Over the years CMOBC became the holding company for Chase Manhattan's interests in many foreign banks and other financial institutions. The first, however, was the South African bank, operating from headquarters in Johannesburg. The new bank was formally opened in February 1959,[33] with a second branch added in Cape Town the same year and a third in Durban in 1962. The opening, attended by David Rockefeller, occasioned no public comment. But only a few years were to pass before operations in South Africa became a contentious issue.

While action on South Africa was under way, the bank tried seriously to break into the Far East. James A. Jacobson, in charge of that area, had long considered acquiring the Mercantile Bank, a British overseas bank with a large number of branches in former British territories in the Far East. Mercantile needed an infusion of capital and better management. Not everyone was enthusiastic about the venture. Cain and Schumacher, however, finally were persuaded to recommend it to McCloy, who then began negotiations to acquire the bank.

It appeared that the negotiations might be successful when Chase made what was later regarded as a tactical error. Senior officers felt it advisable to inform Lord Cromer, head of the Bank of England, of the bank's intentions. Rather than welcoming Chase's intervention, Cromer responded with a letter suggesting an unacceptable alternative—that the bank acquire several branches from the Chartered Bank. Meanwhile he encouraged the Hong Kong and Shanghai Bank in a successful attempt to take over Mercantile. This caused disappointment and some ill-feeling within Chase. Later McCloy was to say, "I had the feeling that perhaps if I had been a little more aggressive and acted a little more promptly, I could have accomplished it. But there was a good deal of dragging of feet and objections here that took up some time in the early stages of negotiations."[34]

Expansion and retrogression in the Caribbean

The Caribbean continued to be a major area of operations for Chase Manhattan. A third branch was opened in Puerto Rico in 1956, followed by a fourth two years later. Thirteen of the bank's twenty foreign branches were now located in the Caribbean. These branches conducted retail operations to a much greater degree than other areas, in effect making them an extension of activities in the United States.

In 1959 an opportunity arose to move into a new area, the Virgin Islands. The West Indies Bank and Trust Company, operating four offices in the territory, became available, and Chase Manhattan was the successful bidder. The bank was purchased with Chase shares bought on the open market, an unusual transaction arranged by Charles Agemian.[35] This added branches in St. Thomas, St. John, and two in St. Croix. Although not large, the acquisition proved to be a useful and profitable addition to the bank's network over the years.

Unfortunately this acquisition was soon offset by a setback in Cuba. Fidel Castro came to power in 1959. The U.S. government was quickly at odds with Cuba and took measures against it. On the night of September 16, 1960, militiamen who were bank employees moved into the branches of Chase Manhattan and the other two U.S. banks "to protect our places of employment." Within twelve hours Castro signed a decree nationalizing the branches of all three banks.[36]

The Havana branch had been acquired by Chase National Bank in 1925, one of that bank's first foreign ventures, and four offices were now in operation. Capital was raised to $4 million in 1957, and the branch was moderately profitable. But the bank also did business with Cuba from the head office. Two years before nationalization, in August 1958, Chase had extended a $30 million loan to two institutions of the Cuban government. The loan was fully covered by collateral in the form of U.S. government securities held in New York. At the time of nationalization $10 million of this loan remained outstanding, but the Cuban authorities, perhaps inadvertently, had left collateral in excess of $17 million with the bank. In addition the Cuban National Bank had placed time deposits of $2.5 million with the bank. Chase immediately took over the collateral and time deposits and applied these not only to payment of the loan but also to offset its loss of capital and unremitted earnings, as well as in compensation "for goodwill and going concern value of the Cuban branches confiscated."[37]Cuba lost little time in suing Chase Manhattan (and First National City, which had a similar although smaller loan), for the return of what it called excess capital. This suit dragged on for many years, and the bank established a reserve to cover the principal. A decision was finally handed down in early 1980, almost twenty years later, with Chase awarded $6.9 million, or most of what it had been seeking. Meanwhile, it had earned interest on the extra funds, which it was not required to relinquish.[38]

The loss of the Cuban branches was a blow, but it did not halt expansion in the Caribbean. Indeed even while the Cuban revolution unfolded, the bank established both a branch and a trust affiliate in Nassau, Bahamas. At the end of 1960 Chase continued to operate twenty-five overseas branches, fifteen in the Caribbean.

The bank reaches out in the 1950s

Expansion of Chase's foreign branch system, although not as yet pursued aggressively, marked a further effort to respond to changes in the external environment. With a clearer vision as to where it was heading, the bank moved solidly into retail business on the domestic side, first through the Manhattan merger, then through additions to its metropolitan network, culminating with its entry into the suburbs.

Innovative enterprises were started, albeit without much success. The first bank credit card in New York City, the Chase Manhattan Charge Plan, was established, only to be abandoned as unprofitable in the early 1960s, a somewhat cautious approach to innovation that typified Chase. Internationally the bank began a new source of medium-term credit for trade purposes, but ran afoul of unexpected competition from the Export-Import Bank. Soon Chase was providing such credit directly through its international department. And the bank successfully launched a new subsidiary designed to cooperate with others in furnishing equity and other capital for projects in developing countries. Modest in scope and never really profitable, Chase International Investment Corporation nevertheless planted the seed from which some worthwhile ventures eventually grew.

The creation of One Chase Manhattan Plaza

A major accomplishment of the McCloy years was the construction of the bank's new head office at what is known as One Chase Manhattan Plaza. This addressed the second problem that Aldrich had identified for McCloy: to bring together in one location personnel scattered in nine different buildings. Such dispersion produced inefficiency in back office operations and made more difficult normal working relations between departments. No less important, it complicated the task of management oversight.

McCloy lost little time in beginning to consider alternatives. Early in 1953 the head of Chase's real estate division, John J. Scully, was authorized to discuss plans for a new building with architects. The firm he initially engaged envisaged a rather conventional skyscraper and in the end was not retained.[1]

Meanwhile the bank faced a basic question critical not only for it but for the future configuration of the city: whether to move uptown or remain downtown. Already many firms, including good customers, were deserting Wall Street for Park Avenue. The bank retained Ebasco Services to make a study of the matter, and McCloy conducted his own survey, speaking with bankers and businessmen, even seeking counsel from the City in London.

The heads of other banks, all then located downtown, felt in general that it was better to stay there, maintaining the cohesion of the financial community. Most positive in expressing this view was Howard Shepherd, chairman of First National City Bank. "Oh, of course we are going to stay downtown," he told McCloy. No commitments were made. But four years later, when First National City announced plans to move uptown, McCloy was informed by Shepherd, whose view had not prevailed.[2]

Ebasco, weighing the pros and cons, recommended that the bank remain downtown. The operating advantages were there. The New York Clearing House for banks was downtown, as were the Federal Reserve Bank and the Stock Exchange. If Chase Manhattan were to move, the financial core of the city might well become fragmented. The value of the bank's investment in existing buildings would then depreciate.[3]

The directors were divided on the matter, so McCloy made the final recommendation: stay downtown. "It was not an easy decision," he later recalled, and he advanced with a sense of history a further consideration. "Downtown was the hearthstone of the city. It was here where the Old

Federal Building was first set up, where Washington took his oath of office, in which the Bill of Rights was adopted, which was just across Pine Street from our Eighteen Pine Street building. The tip of Manhattan had a great tradition and it had real beauty, at the confluence of two rivers. It seemed to me that it had some significance not only to the city but to the nation to keep in existence this area, where, in and out of those narrow streets for a period of a century, the progress of the country had been financed."[4] At that time and ever since it has generally been acknowledged that Chase Manhattan's new building revitalized and anchored the financial district.

What kind of building?

The next step was to determine the most suitable site and type of building. The problem of the site called for decisive action. At the rear of the bank's head office, across Cedar Street, stood an almost empty block containing the abandoned headquarters of the Mutual Life Insurance Company of New York, one of the firms that had moved uptown. The block had subsequently been acquired by the Guaranty Trust Company.

One morning in February 1955 David Rockefeller was called at home by William Zeckendorf of Webb and Knapp, a leading real estate broker and builder in New York City, who informed him that Guaranty Trust was on the point of selling the Mutual Life building and land. Rockefeller and Zeckendorf conveyed this information to McCloy, and it was confirmed by William L. Kleitz, president of Guaranty. Kleitz gave the bank twenty-four hours to make a counteroffer. The following day the bank agreed to purchase the property, formally closing the contract on February 23 for payment of $4,425,000.[5]

Chase now owned the Mutual Life block, its Eighteen Pine Street headquarters, and most of the other buildings in the same block. It also owned and occupied other properties, especially Fifteen Broad Street, the former head office of Equitable Trust, which along with an adjacent building served as the headquarters for the trust department.

The board quickly authorized demolition of the Mutual Life building, and architects and engineers were engaged to draw up plans for a new building on that block. The choice of architects was of critical importance. The board sought out Skidmore, Owings and Merrill, the firm that had recently completed for Manufacturers Trust a branch on Fifth Avenue of modern design which was attracting favorable attention. More than many other architects, they were regarded as having a concept of what the future architecture of the city should be.

Rockefeller met with Nathaniel Owings, and asked that the firm draw up several preliminary sketches, one showing the remainder of the Pine Street block utilized for a separate building, along with a building on the Mutual Life block, and a second showing a single building on the Mutual Life block with the space on Pine Street remaining open as a plaza. This latter would require the city to close and deed to Chase the block on Cedar Street separating the two properties.

The architects submitted sketches, and a debate followed within the bank and on the board as to the most desirable type of building. A number favored a conventional skyscraper, while some preferred the plan for two buildings. Others, led by Rockefeller, argued for the more modern and dramatic approach. The Ebasco report, he recalled, had recommended that the bank stay downtown, but that "we should do so in a sufficiently definitive and dramatic way that people would recognize as a decisive move on our part, which would change the climate and preserve Lower Manhattan."[6] A large modern building with an open plaza in crowded Wall Street might accomplish this.

Rockefeller gained support from both Owings and Zeckendorf. McCloy also came to favor the modern plan, and in the end this was selected. But first, agreement was needed from the city to close Cedar Street and to grant variances from the setbacks normally required for the upper floors of high buildings. Many city authorities were involved, but the key official to persuade was Robert Moses, commissioner of parks and member of the planning commission. Moses, an imaginative builder himself, favored the plan, and the city finally gave its approval.[7] The way was now open for the architects and engineers to work on detailed plans and cost estimates. A contract was signed for razing the old buildings on the Mutual Life block, a task that began in mid-1955 and was completed in the spring of the following year.

Selling off existing properties

The bank meanwhile set about disposing of many of the real estate parcels it then owned. The very fact that it intended to remain downtown and construct a large new headquarters strengthened property values and improved its own negotiating position. The first sale involved the old head office at Eighteen Pine Street, an excellent structure built in the mid-twenties. The bank had simply outgrown it. Chemical Corn Exchange, seeking a better head office, purchased the property for $15 million and the transfer of two small parcels of real estate. Chemical thus became the neighbor of Chase Manhattan on the plaza and through renovation and tasteful decoration of the Pine Street structure contributed to the plaza's attractiveness.[8]

A second major sale concerned the headquarters of the trust department at Fifteen Broad Street, a thirty-eight-story building erected in 1928 by Equitable Trust, connected to a smaller structure fronting on Wall Street. The two surrounded the landmark building at Broad and Wall which housed the Morgan Bank. Morgan was the natural buyer in the circumstances but drove a hard bargain. The price of $21,250,000 was secured by a purchase money mortgage with a final maturity in 1995 and an interest rate of 3½ percent.[9] The rate bothered Champion and others at the bank, and some years later Chase bought out the mortgage.

Other properties were disposed of, including an interest in the land under Forty Wall Street, the former headquarters of the Bank of Manhattan. Many of these transactions were carried out by Zeckendorf, who frequently arranged trades of other properties in order to consummate a final sale. Altogether a total of $63 million was realized from property sales. This along with a subsequent mortgage went a long way toward financing the new structure.

Planning the new building

More than a year was devoted to planning the new building, and actual work on the foundation was not started until early 1957. Meanwhile the public needed to be informed. The story first broke in the *New York Times* on November 8, 1955, with a front-page headline, "Chase Manhattan Planning a Downtown 'Rockefeller Center.'" The article described the concept of a plaza and building, but because the necessary approval had not yet come from the city, the bank was not in a position to supply detailed information. Not until the following March was the bank able to give details.[10] It then unveiled an architect's model and revealed certain of the main features:

- The plaza would cover about 70 percent of the 2½ acre site. Beneath it, but at street level on the William Street side, would be the public banking floor of Chase Manhattan's head office.
- Customers would look out from this floor to a sunken pool in the center of the plaza.
- Floors below the main banking floor would house a cafeteria and recreational facility for employees, as well as large operating departments. An auditorium would be located on the plaza floor.
- The head office would rise sixty stories, 810 feet above the level of the plaza, a simple rectangular shaft 281 by 107 feet.
- Each floor would have a uniform open area of more than thirty thousand square feet. Four floors would be devoted to mechanical equipment. The total usable floor area of the project, including space under the plaza, would be more than 1.7 million square feet.
- About fifteen thousand people would work in the building. To move them and an estimated ten thousand visitors per day, twelve escalators and forty-two elevators would be installed.

• Visually and structurally the most striking feature of the proposed building would be the rows of external metal-sheathed columns rising unbroken from the plaza to the top of the building.

Stewart Baker in releasing the details commented, "Although the plan is
unconventional in its use of open space, it represents a highly advantageous
use of the bank's property from an economic viewpoint. The conventional
approach of a set-back building on one of the blocks in the site would result
. . . in less efficient space, a more costly type of construction, and little or no
room for expansion. In short, the loss of economic space involved in the
Plaza is compensated for by the space gained in the design of the building
made possible by the Plaza."[11]

The tall external columns, made of steel and sheathed in anodized aluminum, were indeed striking and unusual—so much so that McCloy and the
architects asked the board to review the design at an early stage. The board
did so and gave its approval.

A cost problem

After the bank initially reviewed the project with the architects, an estimated
cost of $55 million was presented to the directors. But costs rose as plans
developed, and a revised estimate of $75 million emerged. The directors took
a deep breath and approved the revision. Accordingly McCloy was greatly
disturbed when in the early summer of 1956, before any work had actually
begun, he was informed that the cost of the project would considerably
exceed that figure. He called for a halt on all work so that the board might be
given realistic estimates and a choice of alternatives.

The architects and engineers wrestled with the problem for three months
and finally came to the board with four choices, only two of which were
given serious consideration: the original design of a sixty-story building with
plaza, and the same plaza and building but fifty stories tall rather than sixty.
The directors took an even deeper breath and approved the sixty-story building, now estimated to cost $91,317,000. With land, furnishings, and special
facilities, the total capital investment was placed at $121,800,000.[12]

This estimate was more realistic, although in the end it proved again to be
too low. There were unexpected cost overruns, especially, as we shall see, for
the foundation. And outlays for furnishings and special facilities ran higher
than budgeted. The final cost after completion of the plaza was nearly $145
million.[13] Twenty-five years later the building was conservatively valued at
more than three times its original cost, and represented a sizable undervalued
asset on the bank's books.

With such huge sums involved, the problem of financing was addressed
early. The sale of existing properties yielded about half the initial estimated

need for funds, and another $60 million was raised through a mortgage, an exceptional deal, with a thirty-year basic repayment period at 4 percent interest.[14]

The bank was reluctant at this time to show on its statement of condition a large increase in investment in banking houses. To avoid this, as well as for management purposes, in 1957 it created a subsidiary, The Chase Manhattan Realty Corporation, which owned the building and served as the mortgagee. Prior to the new building project, the value of banking houses was reported at $59 million, but by 1962 banking houses, including branch premises, were carried at $92 million, somewhat more than initially estimated. Changes in New York City tax laws subsequently made it desirable to dissolve the real estate subsidiary and hold title to the property directly. The bank chose to pay off the mortgage in these circumstances, and investment in banking houses rose to $149 million at the end of 1963. Meanwhile total assets had increased by $4.6 billion, or 60 percent and capital funds by almost 50 percent, and the enlarged total occasioned no comment.

Construction begins: excavating the foundation

The most troublesome phase of the project proved to be the foundation. Turner Construction Company was selected as the general contractor for the building itself, but Moran, Proctor, Muser and Rutledge engineered the foundation, with the Foundation Company undertaking the work. David Rockefeller was placed in charge of the project for the bank, assisted by John Scully, who, although not in the best of health, worked tirelessly. From the outset Walter Severinghaus ably served as project architect for Skidmore, Owings and Merrill, while Gordon Bunshaft was responsible for design.

Some 225,000 cubic yards of earth were removed in the course of excavating the foundation, the largest in downtown New York up to that time. The major problem, however, turned out to be water—not surprisingly, since it was known that an underground stream flowed through the area. Bedrock was some ninety feet down, and wet sand had been encountered little more than halfway at the east end of the site. Normal practice in the past had been to utilize laborers, called sandhogs, working under pressure in caissons, a process similar to digging tunnels underwater. But the sandhogs, tightly unionized, were on strike for higher wages and refused even to quote a figure for their labor. It was then that the engineers resorted to an innovation previously tried in Europe. Chemicals were pumped into the ground around the wet area, turning the sand into a low-grade cement sufficient to hold back the water.[15]

By the end of 1957 a perimeter wall of concrete seven feet thick and in some places nearly eighty feet deep had been constructed around the entire

Mutual Life block. The foundation work was now about 75 percent complete. The schedule called for construction work on the basement floors to begin in the spring of 1958 and above-ground steelwork in the fall. But this was not to be. Citywide strikes interfered, and the foundation was not completed until the autumn of 1958. Costs, constantly revised upward, amounted to approximately $16 million, close to one-third more than initially estimated.

Erecting the superstructure

Building the foundation and basement required almost two years. Above-ground work on the building would need another two. By the start of 1959 the steel framework of the sixty-story tower began to climb skyward. The construction schedule called for the erection of steel at the rate of three floors every two weeks, a rate that surprised sidewalk superintendents. For once plans were fulfilled. By the spring of 1959 the rising structure had become a familiar landmark, visible from the harbor, the city's immediate environs, and points as distant as Newark across the New Jersey meadows. The swift ascent finally reached its climax with the topping out of the steel on September 9, an event witnessed by the bank's senior officers at a reception for two hundred guests.[16] Convening in a temporary lounge on the sixth floor, they watched on closed-circuit television as Stewart Phillips, a Mohawk Indian wearing a feathered headdress, swung the final steel column into place. Then, following steelworkers' tradition, an American flag was run up on a pole 826 feet above ground.

The pouring of concrete floors, the installation of the aluminum skin, and the insertion of storm-proof windows quickly followed the steelwork, so that by the end of 1959 the facade of the tower was assuming its planned dimensions. Meanwhile a problem that had troubled the bank in the course of construction—the selection of suppliers from competing companies which were good customers of the bank—had come to a head. An acute situation in this respect arose in connection with the elevators.[17] The bank early established a policy of competitive bidding with awards to the lowest bidder. Two companies were in active contention for the elevators: Westinghouse and Otis. Westinghouse had long maintained a major relationship with Chase and was a highly valued client. Andrew W. Robertson, chairman of the finance committee of Westinghouse, served as a director of the bank, and McCloy sat on the Westinghouse board. Westinghouse was certainly the preferred bidder under the circumstances.

McCloy sensed early that Westinghouse might not take the competition seriously. He urged them to sharpen their pencils on their estimates, but they came in with a bid substantially higher than Otis's. McCloy discussed the matter with the directors, who unanimously agreed that the contract should be awarded to Otis. Westinghouse was surprised and chagrined. Robertson resigned from the board, and the company distributed its banking relationship among a number of institutions, including Chase. McCloy was tempted to resign from the Westinghouse board but was persuaded by its officers to remain. Later, after he retired from the bank, he proved of immense value to the company in helping to settle a critical lawsuit brought against it by the government.

Other problems were not so acute. Suppliers by and large understood the low-bid policy, but much explanation and attention to relationships was nonetheless necessary. One significant decision concerned the choice of the metal skin: anodized aluminum or stainless steel. Both had staunch advocates. Aluminum was finally selected as being more economical, easier to maintain, and more likely to retain its shiny appearance.

As the building rose, certain aspects attracted more than normal attention. A major one was the vault, more than three-quarters of an acre in size and weighing almost a thousand tons. It was anchored to bedrock ninety feet below ground by scores of heavy steel bars, to keep it, the explanation went, from being swept away in the event of a tidal wave such as had occurred in lower Manhattan a century and a half earlier.[18]

Moving in

Although the bank expected to move into its new headquarters early in the autumn of 1960, it was not until late January 1961 that the move began. Completion of the building had again been delayed by four citywide strikes of construction unions, one of which lasted eighteen weeks.

Careful planning went into preparation of the interior and the move. Even before the steel framework rose, a full-scale mock-up of a portion of the building was constructed in Garden City on Long Island.[19] Two stories high, it provided a means for testing materials and furnishings, as well as partitioning and internal arrangements. The comparative effect of stainless steel and aluminum as a skin material was first tried there. Later various lighting units and types of furniture were examined. The architects played a role in all this. The interior motif was modern, in keeping with the exterior style.

The bank planned to occupy all underground floors, the first thirty-five floors, and the sixtieth floor, where official dining rooms were located. The remaining floors were to be leased to outside tenants. An average rental of approximately $8.50 per square foot was established, which at the time was high for the area. McCloy and others were concerned that the bank might price itself out of the market, but Scully reassured them and he proved correct. By May 1961, when the big move was completed, all space had been leased to some fifty-three leading financial, business, legal, and other professional firms. [20]

The opening of the building received worldwide publicity, which continued throughout the year. *Architectural Forum* carried a thirty-page cover story stating, "The building is already proving to be one of the boldest, and quite possibly one of the soundest, investments to be made on Wall Street in many years." *Forbes* magazine, in a cover story on the bank, called the building "a superbly efficient working tool, quite apart from the fresh and hopeful cast it has given to the old financial district." And *Time* magazine carried a special four-page color portfolio featuring the art and other decoration of the new building. [21]

For McCloy, who retired as the bank entered the new structure, completion of the building marked the fulfillment of a major objective, but it was not accomplished without a degree of tribulation. Looking back on the period he later remembered: "There was a time when the building was the first thing on your desk every day and you could hardly look at anything else, because there always seemed to be a new problem and a new headache. But now as I see the beauty of the building, and the concept of the building, and the development of the plaza, it really is occupying the position we hoped it would." [22]

The art program

The art and interior decoration in the new headquarters drew attention from all sectors of the media, from other business firms, and especially from artists themselves. The program developed out of a need to provide decoration in a building that lacked moldings, friezes, and other detail to furnish warmth and life to the interior. Large expanses of blank wall required some type of relief. The architects felt strongly that in a modern building with modern furniture, works of art would enliven the surroundings in the most suitable manner. [23]

A laboratory for experiment was at hand in a new branch at 410 Park Avenue, then under construction. It too was of modern design and would serve as an uptown headquarters. A Sam Francis mural was commissioned for an informal board room on the fourth floor, and other contemporary art was added. The results bore out the promise, and the program was adopted for the new building.

A committee to make selections was established, with Rockefeller serving as chairman and McCloy as a member. The architects were represented by Gordon Bunshaft, design partner for the building. But a majority of the members were outstanding authorities from the art world: Alfred H. Barr, a founder of the Museum of Modern Art, and Mrs. Dorothy Miller, also of that institution; Robert B. Hale of the Metropolitan Museum; James Johnson Sweeney, former director of the Guggenheim Museum; and Perry Rathbone of the Museum of Fine Arts in Boston. All were strong personalities, frequently holding different views.

McCloy, when first approached by Rockefeller about the use of modern art, admitted that there was much about it he did not understand. Later he said that he had enjoyed the committee and had gained confidence in his own judgment as he listened to the differences of opinion among the experts.

Many of the early selections were abstract art, attractive compositions of color and form in space. These were reasonably priced within the limits of the budget set by the bank (an initial outlay of $500,000 was authorized for the program). Artists who even then had established reputations were represented: Pierre Soulages, Adolph Gottlieb, Josef Albers, Jack Youngerman, Milton Avery, Larry Rivers, and Alfred Jensen among them. Many others were less well known. To be included in the Chase Manhattan collection became a mark of distinction, adding both to the artist's reputation and the commercial value of his or her work.[24]

From the outset plans called for renewing and strengthening the collection through a system of donations and acquisitions. Works were donated to museums and other institutions, with the savings realized on taxes devoted to acquiring new works. Turnover occurred in this manner over future years, although not as extensive as anticipated.

Not only contemporary art was acquired. Folk art, simple and primitive in form, also complemented a modern building. Although American art was featured, the bank as an international institution sought works from other countries as well. Eventually sixty or more countries came to be represented. It was not unusual for Rockefeller on his many trips abroad to spend an hour or two in a gallery or shop, frequently sending back a tapestry, painting, or sculpture for consideration by the committee. Normally he was accompanied by other officers, many of whom acquired an interest in and taste for art in the process.

As the program gained recognition at the head office, the branches, both domestic and foreign, sought to share in it. This increased the demand for art and kept the committee active over the years. The bank became known as one of the leading corporate supporters of art, and Rockefeller served as a founder of the Business Committee on the Arts, a nonprofit organization devoted to stimulating business support.

Occasionally a stockholder questioned the cost of the program. Initial outlays were kept well within the $500,000 limit and were regarded as modest for the purpose. Twenty-five years later a total of about $10 million had been spent,[25] but the actual value was conservatively estimated to be substantially greater.

As it moved into its new modern building the bank also adopted a new symbol. The old symbol of a map of the United States with an inset globe, used since the merger with Manhattan, failed to project an appropriate image. A number of firms were invited to submit designs, and that of Chermayeff and Geismar Associates was accepted—an abstract octagonal form highly modern in appearance and effect.[26] The symbol, displayed widely in advertising and as a decoration on the bank's buildings and offices, came to signify Chase Manhattan around the world.

Construction of the plaza

The move across the street into the new headquarters was completed by the spring of 1961. The second phase, construction of the plaza, could now begin. All the buildings in the Pine Street block except the former headquarters were to be demolished. The task, which required almost a year, proceeded without incident. The plaza and the three floors beneath it were then finished on schedule in spring 1964. No unusual problems were encountered here either. Dedication ceremonies on May 6, with Mayor Wagner in attendance, took an unusual form. A country-fair party, replete with popcorn, balloons, flower-filled carts, a hurdy-gurdy, circus acts, and a twenty-five piece band, attracted thousands of the bank's friends to spend a most unbanklike lunch hour.[27]

The plaza remains today an extraordinary feature of downtown New York—a large, open area in the midst of tall buildings, graced by a monumental sculpture. A large sunken garden on one side provides daylight to the main banking floor below and includes a decorative pool with water playing over huge sculptural stones brought from Japan. In the summer the plaza is the scene of lunches, concerts, and other entertainment, and at Christmas the trees it holds are decorated with many lights.

The large sculpture provides a crowning touch to the plaza. Installed in 1972, it was made available permanently to the bank through a gift from David Rockefeller. Like the building it too is modern. Called *Group of Four Trees*, the work of the French artist Jean Dubuffet, it consists of four stark trunks with huge, curving black and white leaves.[28]

The plaza was the forerunner of other open space created in the area over the following years. Structures erected in the past two decades now dot the financial district. Entire sections have been revitalized, the World Trade Center, Battery Park, and parts of lower Broadway among them. A large new plot of land has been reclaimed from the Hudson with tall buildings rising on it. The process of regeneration is never ending. But for Lower Manhattan it was set in motion by the Chase Manhattan Bank and its imaginative new headquarters and plaza. Without this and the bank's forceful leadership, the future of the downtown financial district almost certainly would have taken a different turn.

PART TWO

The 1960s: radical change at Chase and in banking

T he 1960s witnessed the most far-reaching changes in banking since the 1920s (see Table 6). The form of organization, the source of funds, and even the bank's functions were heavily influenced by economic, regulatory, and technological developments.

Chase was led at this time by George Champion as chairman and David Rockefeller as president, succeeding John J. McCloy. The bank early adopted new sources of funding as a basis for expansion, utilizing negotiable certificates of deposit (CDs) and the Eurodollar market for the purpose. Borrowed money soon came to dominate the cost structure, enhancing the need for careful liability management. The new funding supported a further huge advance in loans, encouraged by extraordinary growth in the world economy and trade between nations. Even so, the bank incurred its first severe credit crunches in 1966 and 1969, as the Federal Reserve arbitrarily slowed credit expansion in an effort to control inflation aggravated by the war in Vietnam.

Chase lending abroad increased even more rapidly than domestic lending. Controls over the U.S. balance of payments were progressively tightened, diverting international credit demand to foreign sources. The bank prepared itself well to meet these needs, building a unique network of foreign facilities by 1970. Affiliates or branches now served much of the developing world as well as most industrial countries.

At home the bank spread its branches into New York City's adjacent suburbs, but was blocked by regulatory agencies from moving upstate. In the process Chase Manhattan converted to a national charter to improve its flexibility for expansion. It aggressively pursued consumer banking by introducing personal overdraft accounts and acquiring Uni-Card, the largest credit card in New York City. Late in the decade the bank weighed the advantages of forming a holding company (see Part Three).

Table 6.   Statistical Profile, 1960–1970.[a]

	Assets	Loans and Mortgages	Deposits	Equity Capital
1960	9.3	4.7	8.1	.689
1961	10.1	5.1	8.9	.718
1962	10.9	5.4	9.6	.749
1963	12.1	6.5	10.7	.772
1964	13.0	7.2	11.4	.811
1965	15.3	9.4	12.9	.828
1966	16.0	10.0	13.8	.860
1967	18.0	10.4	15.8	.900
1968	19.4	11.0	16.7	.953
1969	22.2	13.0	19.0	.997
1970	24.5	13.9	21.2	1.105

	Domestic Loans and Mortgages	Loans to Commerce and Industry[b]	Overseas Loans	Net Operating Earnings
				(Millions)
1960	4.4	2.6	.262	74.3
1961	4.8	2.7	.332	70.5
1962	5.0	2.8	.358	72.1
1963	6.0	3.2	.501	77.5
1964	6.6	3.3	.604	84.7
1965	8.5	4.6	.918	92.2
1966	9.1	5.3	.941	98.6
1967	9.3	5.7	1.1	105.5
1968	9.7	6.0	1.3	119.5
1969	11.4	6.8	1.6	114.6[c]
1970	11.2	6.6	2.7	133.0

a. Year-end figures, expressed in billions of dollars.

b. Excludes short-term money market instruments in the form of bankers acceptances.

c. The reduction in net operating earnings shown for 1969 reflected a change in bank accounting. Henceforth the provision for loan losses was included as an operating expense. Previously banks were permitted to add to the reserve for loan losses by a transfer from net operating earnings, with an accompanying tax benefit up to a maximum amount established by the Internal Revenue Service. Under this accounting arrangement Chase's net operating earnings for 1969 would have been $122.5 million, representing an increase of 2.5 percent over 1968, rather than the decline of 4.1 percent reported. A new all-inclusive earnings measure also was introduced at this time, designated as net income, and representing net income after taxes and after security gains and losses. In place of net operating earnings, banks now reported income before security gains and losses. This was regarded by bankers and security analysts as the preferred measure of operating performance.

Source: The Chase Manhattan Bank, *Annual Reports*, 1960–1968; The Chase Manhattan Corporation, *Annual Reports*, 1969–1970. Loans to Commerce and Industry, Reports to the New York State Superintendent of Banking, 1960–1964, and to the Comptroller of the Currency, 1966–1970.

Growth powered by a revolution in funding

The sixties proved to be a period of far-reaching change for Chase and other banks. The world economy expanded through most of this period, encouraging substantial growth in credit demand that strained the bank's resources. The early years turned out to be unusually benign, with the U.S. economy advancing by almost a third from 1960 to 1966 while prices remained remarkably stable, an interval viewed later with nostalgia. Investment flourished, and loan demand increased steadily.

Abroad too economies advanced vigorously. The European Common Market and the Free Trade Association, both in their early stages, provided impetus to foreign trade and investment. Around the globe Japan accelerated its remarkable climb to prosperity. And in the developing world many countries embarked on the process of industrialization, Brazil, Taiwan, and Korea among them.

Two developments, however, emerged to mar the economic scene. Escalation of the Vietnam war after middecade pushed the U.S. economy to its limits and ushered in a new era of inflation. Interest rates rose to record heights, and banks were forced to ration credit, in spite of new sources of funding. Restraints were particularly severe internationally as the United States encountered a growing deficit in its balance of payments with a loss of gold and build-up of foreign dollar holdings. New government controls on capital movements profoundly influenced the course of events at Chase and other leading banks.

New management

Chase in this critical decade was guided by George Champion as chairman of the board and David Rockefeller as president and chairman of the executive committee, succeeding John J. McCloy, who retired at the end of 1960. They were backed by Lawrence C. Marshall, vice chairman of the board.

McCloy had prepared for this transition with care. Almost a year before his anticipated retirement date of March 1960, the directors appointed a special committee to consider the matter.[1] The problem was not easy. Two men were obvious candidates for the position of chief executive: Champion, then president, and Rockefeller, vice chairman. Both were able and favor-

117

ably known, and both aspired to the position. Moreover they complemented each other. Champion was the more experienced banker, and was widely known throughout the profession. Rockefeller, younger and with great responsibilities and diverse interests outside the bank, was better known to the general public. In the end the special committee and the board postponed a final decision and asked McCloy to remain as chief executive through 1960. McCloy agreed, and subsequently continued to serve as a consultant to the bank after his retirement.[2]

The matter was finally resolved by a decision to designate both Champion and Rockefeller chief executive officers, dividing between them major areas to which each would give special oversight. To have done otherwise would undoubtedly have led to a resignation, and each had much to contribute.

The new management was formally announced October 21, 1960, to be effective at the start of the new year. The announcement, after naming Champion and Rockefeller to their respective positions, went on to state:

> Each will be concerned with and responsible for all aspects of the Bank but each will supply special leadership in certain areas of his total responsibility. Mr. Champion will give particular attention to the operational and lending policies of the Bank, to the investment of funds in its portfolio and to its fiduciary responsibilities. Mr. Rockefeller will give particular attention to forward planning with emphasis on manpower, facilities and markets, to activities abroad and to domestic expansion.[3]

This division of responsibility was the result of discussions between Champion and Rockefeller. Rockefeller finally put it into writing and Champion agreed to it.[4] Both men were able and strong willed. The division in actual practice was not as clear-cut as it appeared. Particularly on vital matters concerning expansion, both would need to be involved. It remained to be seen how the system of dual chief executive officers would develop.

McCloy's accomplishments

As he retired McCloy could look back on significant accomplishments during his tenure. He had realized the two major objectives laid down by Aldrich eight years earlier. The bank now operated an extensive branch system in New York City and had begun to move into the suburbs. And the head office staff would soon come together in a single building. Moreover these accomplishments were achieved in a manner that helped propel the bank into a more visible position of leadership. In the relatively short space of eight years its loans had grown by four-fifths and total assets by three-fifths. Capital funds increased 85 percent and net operating earnings rose more than 150 percent. All this progress was helped greatly by the merger with Manhattan. Chase Manhattan was now the largest bank in New York and second to Bank of America in the nation. Its prestige had, if anything, been enhanced over the decade.

The culture of the bank had undergone change, nurtured not only by McCloy but by Champion and Rockefeller as well. But the change was less than appeared on the surface. Domestic wholesale banking remained the most important and favored business and continued to attract a high proportion of the most able talent. Retail banking had been brought to the fore by the Manhattan merger and played an accepted but subordinate role. It was, on the international side that the bank continued to lag.

Internally McCloy was leaving the bank much better organized. Responsibility was delegated down the line, and younger men were coming to the fore. A better rapport developed between the domestic and international sides of the bank, in part because officers in each department needed help from the other as American business began to invest heavily in other countries. The corporate staff was broadened and operated more effectively, although planning remained in its infancy, and the centralized personnel function, while competent, lacked a certain degree of professionalism.

McCloy continued as a director and a member of the executive and international committees. He served on the board until 1966, when he automatically retired because of the age limitation, but his ties to the bank remained close, in part because he returned to the firm that served as legal counsel to the bank, soon renamed Milbank, Tweed, Hadley and McCloy. And his talents were again put to use in the public sphere by Presidents Kennedy and Johnson.[5] It was this fusion of the public and the private that the directors noted when in a moving tribute to him they stated:

> Mr. McCloy's wise counsel and warm humanity have left indelible marks on this Bank. Indeed, its very name spells a tribute to his far-seeing leadership under which two renowned institutions were merged to form The Chase Manhattan Bank.
>
> The optimism and determination that marked his tenure at the Bank have been equally evident in the broader field of world affairs, and his notable accomplishments in this field have been a source of pride to all of us.[6]

A funding problem

As Champion and Rockefeller came into command, they were confronted with a major decision concerning funding. Mention was made earlier (see Chapter V) of the slow growth in demand deposits at major New York City banks and their failure to keep pace with the increase in loans. In 1960, with credit demands slowed by a minor recession, the loan-deposit ratio at Chase stood near 60 percent. The ability to sell off large amounts of government securities to raise loanable funds no longer existed. Nor was the outlook for demand deposits at all promising. While Chase and other banks could now move into the more rapidly expanding suburbs, the process would be gradual. And with interest rates continuing at a high level, corporate treasurers and other customers intensified their efforts to cut back on excess balances.

The stage was thus set for change. It was introduced in February 1961 by First National City Bank with an announcement that henceforth it would issue time certificates of deposit in a negotiable form to corporations, public bodies, and other organizations, and that these could be traded in a secondary market.[7] Such certificates of deposit were not new, having existed for many years as a companion to time deposits on open account.[8] The new element involved their negotiability and the creation of a secondary market in which investors could redeem certificates for cash. An illiquid investment thus became liquid, making the negotiable CD an alternative to commercial paper or Treasury bills as an investment.

A few regional banks had already begun to offer CDs to corporations, but money market banks with a large corporate clientele resisted the practice. Chase Manhattan, along with others, feared that providing such an instrument would result chiefly in shifting balances from non–interest demand accounts to interest-bearing time accounts, and that the policy in the end would not be profitable. Projections made as part of the planning process tended to bear out this conclusion.

Even so, to remain competitive Chase shortly made available its own negotiable CD to select customers, as did other major banks. Yet Champion and other members of senior management continued to view the new instrument with caution. For the first year Chase lagged behind other banks in issuing negotiable CDs, but as loan demand picked up, the bank began to utilize the instrument more actively. Over the next few years it became a major source of deposit growth, and by late 1965 negotiable CDs amounted to $1.5 billion.[9]

Indeed, although its future importance was only dimly perceived at the moment, the adoption of the negotiable CD had a far-reaching impact on the way Chase and other major banks did business. A huge new pool of funds was opened to the bank, providing added impetus to lending. Moreover, liquidity needs could now be met by bidding for funds in the market rather than holding a large volume of low-yielding government securities. But these advantages were realized at a cost not only of added expense but also of increased risk. Efficient management of funding became highly important. And the bank was given further incentive to determine the true cost of services that in effect had been subsidized for years by low-cost demand deposits.

One element of risk, already evident with other time deposits, soon became apparent: the restraining influence of Regulation Q, under which the Federal Reserve set the maximum rates that could be paid on CDs. Toward the end of 1961 market rates on short-term instruments rose above the ceilings on all time deposits save those of six months and longer.[10] This limited the ability of banks to compete for funds, although the restraint at this stage was not severe. Over the next few years the Federal Reserve revised upward its ceiling rates, but the threat remained that the monetary authority might employ Regulation Q as a means for credit restraint. Later in the decade the threat became reality.

Birth of the Eurodollar market

Even before the negotiable CD came into existence, another source of funds, the Eurodollar market, developed abroad. This vied with CDs at home in importance and heavily influenced future operations of the bank. Something of a mystique surrounded this market from the outset, and it is helpful to provide a brief background concerning its nature and the circumstances that propelled its growth throughout the sixties.[11]

Eurodollars were (and are) nothing more than deposits denominated in dollars and placed in banks outside the United States. They are not demand deposits, but rather negotiable or nonnegotiable time deposits whose maturity may vary from overnight to more than a year. Since the ultimate means of dollar payment must be a demand deposit, and these are lodged in banks within the United States, Eurodollars are linked to demand deposit accounts at banks in the United States in somewhat the same manner as domestic time or savings accounts. Hence, they do not constitute "money" in a narrowly defined sense, but they can be readily liquidated and are a close substitute.

The Cold War had provided the market with its initial impetus in the midfifties. The Soviet Union and other Eastern bloc countries, requiring dollars for trade but concerned that balances could be blocked within the United States, lodged them in offshore accounts with the London affiliates of East European banks and in British merchant banks. The practice was not prohibited by British exchange and banking controls; rather, the Bank of England found reason to encourage its use more widely. Because of the pound's chronic weakness, controls had been placed on sterling financing of world trade, and the dollar became the favored currency for settling trade and other international transactions. The new market was helpful to British banks as well as to others, and the Bank of England left it free of restrictions. London quickly became the market center.

A number of circumstances combined to expand the market throughout the 1960s. Higher rates could be paid on Eurodollars (as is the case today) because they required no mandatory reserves or Federal Deposit Insurance premiums. Nor were Eurodollars subject to interest ceilings under Regulation Q. Continued U.S. balance-of-payments deficits encouraged foreign governments to relax restrictions on foreign transactions. Concurrently, regulatory action by the U.S. government to halt the payments drain drove U.S. corporations and banks to use Eurodollars to finance credit needs abroad.

The market operated efficiently and grew rapidly as corporations, banks, and central banks, both U.S. and foreign, channeled dollars into it. By 1965 Eurodollars totaled more than $14 billion on a gross basis. Over the next five years the market increased more than fourfold and escalated through the 1970s.[12]

Chase Manhattan, as a leading dollar-based bank with a well-established branch in London, was exceptionally well placed to take advantage of this new facility, yet once again it was somewhat slow to act. There were conceivable risks involved in a build-up of Eurodollar deposits in London; for example, regulations or controls could be imposed by either British or U.S. authorities, making it impossible to obtain the dollars necessary to repay obligations as they came due. No lender of last resort existed for the market, as did the Federal Reserve for bank activities in the United States. Charles Cain, Jr., head of Chase's international department, was reluctant to engage the bank actively in the market, but Alfred W. Barth, soon to succeed Cain on the latter's retirement, was more favorably disposed. He obtained Champion's permission in 1961 to take on initial deposits of no more than $100 million, a limit that was soon increased.[13]

Offshore markets developed in other currencies over the next few years, but the Eurodollar remained paramount. Chase became a leading participant, employing the market for all aspects of international banking—for placement of surplus funds, as a source of funds for loans or for bank liquidity, and as a means of currency trading and hedging foreign exchange risks. Chase held an advantage in intermediating Eurodollars—acquiring funds at a particularly favorable rate and relending them at a higher rate to banks less favorably situated or at longer maturities, transactions known as "placings."

Eurodollars also served as an alternate source of funds for domestic purposes, a function that later became critically important. In the absence of exchange controls or other special regulations, rates between the domestic and Eurodollar markets were linked, with freedom from reserves and FDIC insurance accounting for a normal upward margin in Eurodollar rates. But unusual circumstances frequently intervened, providing opportunities for arbitrage. Liability management at Chase assumed added dimensions, directed from New York to take advantage of these opportunities and to coordinate money-gathering on a worldwide basis.

Loan expansion in the early sixties

The development of new sources of funding enabled the bank to market vigorously its principal products, loans and mortgages. Not until 1966 were serious constraints placed on extension of credit, and the volume outstanding increased each year. By the end of 1966 total loans and mortgages exceeded $10 billion, more than double the outstanding volume at the start of the decade.

Increased capital outlays by business again created a need particularly for term credits. Such loans now rose to almost 60 percent of the loan portfolio to commerce and industry, still the most important market for the bank and one that was geographically widespread.[14] A survey of corporate customers in 1961 revealed that about half the loans outstanding were extended to firms located in almost every state outside New York, another third to firms with head offices in New York City, and about 15 percent to subsidiaries and other companies in foreign countries, including loans by foreign branches.[15]

The bank meanwhile adopted a more aggressive approach to marketing. Eugene B. Mapel, a well-known specialist in marketing techniques, joined the corporate staff in 1959 as marketing officer. Mapel lost little time in organizing a series of courses designed to improve the sales efficiency and abilities of contact officers. All officers with account relationships were exposed to these courses over several years. The emphasis was on active selling rather than the more passive approach of earlier years.

The bank in these years reached beyond its nucleus of existing customers and extended loans to many new companies. A number of these credits did not represent full relationships requiring normal deposit balances, but were referred to as "income" loans.[16] Projections of cash flow, along with the balance sheet, were highly important in making credit judgments. Prudence and safety were never ignored, but the interest rate on such loans was considerably higher than the average, with a fee for financing frequently adding to income.

Yet the bank's traditional markets continued to dominate. Loans to petroleum companies and public utilities remained the largest in volume, accounting in 1963 for one-third of credit extended to business.[17] And lending to machinery, chemical, aerospace, and a wide range of other industries also expanded. The bank at this time strengthened its organization for lending to many of these complex industries by adding a corps of technical experts. Included were specialists in mining, electronics, metals, chemicals, textiles, transportation, and agriculture, with others added later.[18] These technical directors were available to all departments and traveled widely with loan officers, identifying loan opportunities and helping assess risks.

In one form of corporate finance—leasing—Chase was handicapped in comparison with its principal competitor, First National City. Banks chartered in New York were not authorized to hold title to equipment, as were national banks, and therefore could not engage directly in this activity. The business was growing rapidly, and Chase in 1963 sought to alleviate the problem by organizing an independent company, Lease Capital, to own equipment and market leasing services in cooperation with the bank.[19] Chase provided money to the new firm to acquire equipment leased to customers. But since the bank was barred from ownership, it failed to share in any residual values at the termination of the lease, one of the more profitable aspects of the business. The bank continued to lend to other lessors as well as to Lease Capital. Later, after conversion to a national charter, it entered leasing directly.

Balance-of-payments controls and international lending

Credit assistance to American business for overseas activity entered a period of great growth at this time. The late fifties and sixties were years of rapid movement abroad by U.S. industry. While tariff walls were slowly crumbling between countries of the Common Market and within the European Free Trade Area, they remained restrictive to outsiders. American corporations responded by establishing facilities within the confines of these trade groups. By 1964 direct investments abroad by U.S. firms had risen to $44 billion, and were increasing at a rate of almost $4 billion annually.[20]

Chase played an important role in financing this expansion, at both the head office and its foreign branches. The former reluctance of the international department to lend to companies overseas virtually disappeared as good domestic customers requested such accommodation. International credit offered by the department at the head office doubled over the first half of the decade to $1.4 billion, while loans at foreign branches more than tripled to $900 million.[21] Growth in the London branch was especially rapid, supported by the burgeoning Eurodollar market.

Balance-of-payment controls by the government gave added impetus to international lending. In July 1963 President Kennedy proposed the so-called interest equalization tax on purchases by Americans of foreign securities with a maturity in excess of three years, increasing the cost of such financing by approximately 1 percent.[22] The immediate effect was to shift credit demands from the security markets to commercial banks, and foreign loans by Chase increased substantially over the following eighteen months.

Partly because of the bank loophole, the balance of payments failed to improve, leading President Johnson in February 1965 to adopt even more restrictive measures.[23] This time they fell on banks as well as other financing institutions and corporations. The interest equalization tax was extended to foreign loans with maturities of one year or more at head offices of U.S. banks. More severe, a maximum limit was imposed on all foreign loans at the head office, whatever the maturity. Initially the limit was set at 105 percent of the dollar volume of foreign loans outstanding at the end of 1964. The 1964 base was retained over the life of the program, with the maximum limit raised to 109 percent in 1966–67, after which it was lowered.

This program, labeled somewhat euphemistically the Voluntary Foreign Credit Restraint Program, was administered by the Federal Reserve. Chase reported quarterly on foreign credit outstanding and lived within the guidelines, sometimes scrambling toward the end of a quarter to get down to the maximum. But unlike most other banks, Chase possessed one great advantage: it could lay off foreign credits to its branch in London or to a branch established in Nassau, which possessed a tax advantage. The supply of Eurodollars was sufficient to finance them at both locations.

Real estate and assistance to small business

Corporate lending was not the only area of strength in the first half of the 1960s. Credit in support of real estate also flourished, growing fivefold to more than $1 billion in 1966, the largest increase of any commercial bank in the city. Stable mortgage rates and a growing population encouraged widespread construction of new housing and commercial facilities. Chase had long been a leader in construction loans and other funds for commercial properties. It now became more active in providing mortgages for homeowners, impelled by expansion of its domestic branch system into outlying areas. Branch customers were given priority in such lending, and by 1966 the total had swelled to $300 million, more than a fourth of all real estate and mortgage credit. Losses on these home mortgages in the future proved to be minor in good times and bad.

Home mortgages were now increasing more rapidly than installment lending in the field of consumer finance. Even so, Chase gained position in installment loans, although it lagged considerably behind First National City. Outstandings approximated $250 million by the end of 1965, surpassing Manufacturers Hanover and accounting for 19 percent of the market.[24] The bank placed relatively more emphasis on this type of credit for small business than its competitors, and it introduced installment financing for personal and corporate aircraft.

Chase applied more stringent credit standards to automobile and personal loans than First National City, which had standardized its approach to such credit, applying a point system to various factors for approval. This enabled it to delegate lending authority more widely through its branch system. Chase moved in this direction but retained a higher degree of centralized control, resulting in fewer losses but a smaller portfolio.

Chase did take the lead, however, in one other form of finance for small business. In 1962 it became the first New York City bank to establish a small business investment company, The Chase Manhattan Capital Corporation.[25] Organized with an initial capital of $3 million, the company expanded its capital base to $17 million in 1970. Credit was extended to companies starting in business, some with an initial capital as small as $5,000. Borrowers represented a wide range of service and manufacturing lines. Risks were high and administrative costs large per transaction, but the corporation served a useful purpose, especially in the troubled environment of the later years of the decade. It proved difficult to support, however, on the basis of profitability.

Beginning of credit restraint

By 1965 the U.S. economy had shifted into high gear. The tax cuts of 1964 set off a surge in both consumer and business spending. Capital outlays continued to rise, and inventories were expanding. Military outlays too began to increase as a result of the hostilities in Vietnam. Prices started to advance after four years of remarkable stability, and the Federal Reserve moved from mild ease to mild restraint in monetary policy.

For banks the result was a skyrocketing demand for credit, supplemented by heavy lending abroad to overseas subsidiaries of U.S. corporations. Loans at Chase rose by 31 percent in 1965. Credit increased in all markets—business, consumers, real estate, and overseas—and as the bank entered 1966, the demand appeared unabated. Champion and Rockefeller were concerned about this pace of expansion. Lines of credit and commitments outstanding, large in volume, were now being drawn upon. For the first time serious questions arose about the ability of the bank to fund loan demands.

A review of deposit growth over the previous five years was not entirely encouraging. The increase had occurred almost entirely in savings and time deposits; net demand deposits continued to display no growth. Savings had maintained their strong advance, more than doubling over the period. These received further stimulus in early 1965, when Chase became the first bank to introduce savings certificates of six- and twelve-month maturity, permitting payment of a higher rate of interest.[26] But the major increase in time accounts occurred in certificates of deposit, both negotiable CDs and non-negotiable certificates to individuals, smaller business, and other institutions. Negotiable CDs by the end of 1965 had risen to $1.5 billion, and other time deposits to $1.8 billion.[27] These could be vulnerable if market interest rates rose above the ceiling rates for time deposits established by the Federal Reserve.

Meanwhile, interest rates were beginning to stir. By and large, rates had remained unusually stable for five years. Short-term money market rates advanced from around 3 percent to 4 percent between late 1960 and 1965, but long-term rates increased very little.[28] And the bank's prime rate had not moved from the 4½ percent level to which it had descended in August 1960, the longest period of stability in the postwar years. Although margins had narrowed, banks were under public pressure not to change the rate. But in the autumn of 1965 the cost of CDs began to increase, and in early December, Chase finally raised its prime to 5 percent.

Surveying these trends in deposits and rates, and confronted with a continuing strong loan demand, Chase decided to embark on its own program of credit restraint. It no longer aggressively sought new customers, and it attempted to discourage loans not thought to contribute to increased productivity. High on the list of the latter (as had been the case during the Korean war) were loans to finance acquisitions, as well as loans of a speculative nature. The bank was reluctant also to extend credit for refinancing of debt held by other institutions, or to make loans that depended on the future sale of securities for repayment. A list was drawn up of eighteen types of loans that were to be discouraged. Emphasis was on the word *discouraged*, not *prohibited*, for good customers. And no restraints were placed on installment credit or loans to small business.[29]

The credit crunch of 1966

Loan restraint slowed down the credit advance in the first half of 1966 but did not halt it. Throughout the year the bank turned down loan requests totaling $2 billion, but loans still increased another $700 million and for the first time reached $10 billion, with most of the larger volume extended to business. Yet the bank was apparently exercising more restraint than its competitors, for its market share declined a bit.

Meanwhile, the Federal Reserve in December 1965 provided at least temporary relief for time deposits by raising the maximum rate for various maturities, although the top rate for savings remained unchanged. But continuing strong credit demands soon induced the Fed to turn to more active restraint, and costs for negotiable CDs moved higher. Chase increased its prime rate in March and again in June. By July money market rates exceeded the ceiling rate on time deposits.

Chase now faced the prospect it had feared: a run-off in negotiable CDs and other time deposits. The Federal Reserve held firm and indeed signaled its intention by increasing reserve requirements on time deposits in excess of $5 million. Events reached a climax in August 1966, when interest rates climbed to their highest level since the 1920s, and conditions in the money market threatened to become disorderly. Chase for the fourth time in twelve months raised its prime rate, this time to a record 6 percent.[30]

Champion and others at the bank were deeply disturbed by this turn of events. It fulfilled their apprehension over the growing dependence on time deposits under maximum rates set by the Federal Reserve. After reviewing the bank's position at a weekly meeting—its restraint on loans to customers and now the restraint on funding—one top officer observed, "Banking isn't fun anymore." Indeed banking had changed radically from the forties and fifties.

Unlike other banks Chase had an outlet for relieving the pressure: it could turn to the Eurodollar market, acquiring deposits in London and transferring them to New York. The Federal Reserve placed no restrictions on this escape hatch. From a peak of $1.6 billion in the spring of 1966 negotiable CDs fell to $1 billion by year's end, while takings of Eurodollars for use in New York rose by an almost equivalent amount.[31]

Savings deposits, restricted to a 4 percent ceiling, fell off by $200 million, attracted away at one point by a U.S. Treasury offering at 5 percent, a rate dealers labeled "the magic fives." Chase countered by cultivating the market for smaller-denomination nonnegotiable CDs, as well as by stressing consumer time deposits. A new "Nest Egg" deposit account, started in January, permitted a customer to deposit $1,000 or more on ninety-day notice, earning a premium rate of 5 percent. By scrambling for funds in these markets, the bank was able to sustain its volume of savings and small time deposits.

In September the Federal Reserve issued a special letter that only added to the unease.[32] It requested that banks slow their loans to business, and coupled this with what many interpreted as a veiled threat to restrict access to the discount window for those who failed to comply. President Johnson soon followed with proposals for fiscal restraint by the government, including suspension of the investment tax credit.

At this point signs began to appear that the peak pressures has passed. Growth of credit slowed and money market rates eased after September. In December the Federal Reserve withdrew its special letter issued only three months earlier. The credit crunch of 1966 had ended.

A brief respite

The respite that followed was destined not to be long lasting. The unpopular Vietnam war escalated in 1967 and 1968, pushing the economy upward after a brief pause in early 1967. Inflation gathered strength and would remain troublesome.

Late in January 1967, during the low point in activity, Chase took the lead in reducing its prime rate, a development featured in the press. This proved to be one of the few reductions in a five-year period, for the cut was restored late in the year.[33] Rates then moved steadily upward to record peaks through 1969 and into 1970.

Domestic loans grew only a moderate 7 percent in 1967–68, the smallest advance in the sixties, as both corporations and banks sought to restore badly needed liquidity. This lull was not experienced by the international side of the bank, however, as new problems erupted abroad. The Arab-Israeli conflict of June 1967 sent shock waves through world financial markets. The British pound, which had survived several previous crises, finally was devalued from $2.80 to $2.40. The bank, caught by surprise, suffered a loss, although not a serious one.

Meanwhile the U.S. balance of payments, which had recorded a small improvement in 1966, deteriorated anew in 1967. Expenditures abroad for Vietnam rose, and the capital outflow increased with heavier borrowing by Canada and Japan, accorded favorable treatment under existing regulations.

The president reacted with the announcement of even more stringent balance-of-payments controls. Banks were asked to reduce their foreign credits at the head office to 103 percent of the volume in 1964 (the base year) from the previous ceiling of 109 percent, and to concentrate these reductions particularly on credits to Western Europe. The program remained voluntary, but the Federal Reserve was given standby authority to invoke mandatory controls if necessary. [34]

For Chase's international department this in effect imposed a decline in credits to foreigners, met again by selling certain foreign credits to its overseas branches, especially in London and Nassau. But the new program also increased the demand for credit at branches and newly acquired affiliates abroad. Mandatory limitations were now placed on the outflow of corporate funds for direct investment, forcing greater borrowing overseas. Chase loans in foreign branches rose 17 percent in 1967 and advanced a further 50 percent in 1968 and 1969 to a total in excess of $1.5 billion, six times the aggregate at the start of the decade.

The credit crunch of 1969

This expansion overseas was soon matched at home, creating a credit crunch that exceeded even that of 1966. By the start of 1969 credit demands had begun to escalate, propelled by rising inflation and wartime government spending. Interest rates also climbed to new peaks. By midyear Chase had raised its prime rate three times, the last in June by a full percentage point to an unprecedented 8½ percent. [35] Yet rates in the commercial paper market rose even higher. The flow of credit into that market began to shift into banks, already beset with heavy demands from business.

The problems of money center banks were compounded by policies pursued by the Federal Reserve as it moved toward ever-increasing tightness. Reserve requirements were raised and the discount rate increased. But most important, the monetary authorities decided not to change Regulation Q ceilings on large CDs and other time deposits. A set of graduated ceilings had been put in place in April 1968, ranging from 5½ to 6¼ percent for different maturities on time deposits of $100,000 and more. These ceilings again fell far below market rates. As in 1966 Chase and other banks began to lose deposits, and Chase again turned to the Eurodollar market, expanding its takings from London, Paris, Frankfort, and Nassau.

The deposit drain proved even more severe than in 1966 and continued well into the fourth quarter of 1969. Savings and other time deposits at the head office declined by $1.2 billion, but deposits in foreign branches rose by an unprecedented $2 billion, an increase of two-thirds in a single year. Part of this advance was used to finance loan expansion abroad, but the great bulk was transferred to the head office. After rates on Eurodollars rose to 10 or 11 percent during the final six months, the bank was paying more for these funds than it was receiving in interest on many loans. The Federal Reserve added to the expense by placing a 10 percent reserve requirement on all net borrowings from foreign branches above the amount in a base period.[36]

A program of loan restraint

Chase was squeezed for funds during the 1969 credit crunch, not only because of the drain in domestic time deposits but also because loan demand remained exceptionally strong. The bank again installed a loan restraint program, the third in the postwar period. Some $2.5 billion of creditworthy loans was turned away during the year.[37] But in spite of this, loans increased by almost $2 billion to a total of $13 billion. Again a great proportion of these credits went to business. The bank found, as it had earlier, that restraint on business loans was hard to impose when a large volume of commitments and lines of credit was already outstanding.

Moreover restraint was made doubly difficult by the Federal Reserve's working at cross purposes. The board's chairman was charged as part of an anti-inflation program to avoid increased costs to business by holding down bank interest rates. Concurrently he pursued a tight monetary policy. The result was a distortion in the structure of rates, with the bank prime rate far below money market and bond rates. Credit demands that should have been met in other markets were diverted to banks.

The erroneous belief persisted among politicians that the bank prime rate stood apart and could be isolated from other rates. The House Banking Committee initiated an inquiry into the increase in the prime rate after Chase's move to 8½ percent on June 9, 1969. The committee chairman, Congressman Wright Patman of Texas, implied that the rate had been increased solely to enhance the bank's profits. David Rockefeller, testifying for Chase, vigorously denied this, stating, "We raised our prime rate on June 9 because of the necessity of preventing a flood of loans into the bank. . . . Neither costs nor earnings played a part in the decision." Rockefeller went on to say that he found "profoundly disturbing the accusations that the banking industry has failed to cooperate with the national objective of combatting inflation," and he named a number of steps Chase had taken to retard the increase in loans. [38]

Only in 1970 was this second credit crunch brought to an end with the first real recession in more than a decade. The 1969 experience was discouraging, coming so soon after a similar episode in 1966. The new funding sources that had appeared so promising could be severely limited in their application under existing policies of the Federal Reserve. Not until those policies were changed and Regulation Q dropped as an instrument of monetary restraint would the expectation of stable funding sources be fulfilled.

A slowdown in earnings growth

With a tripling of loan volume throughout the sixties, a substantial increase in earnings was to be expected. Earnings did grow, but at a slower pace than in the latter half of the fifties. Net operating earnings in 1969 were reported at $115 million, but the accounting basis on which this was figured changed for banks that year. Applying the previous accounting procedures (which excluded provision for loan losses as an expense) resulted in earnings of $123 million—double those of ten years earlier. Gains were achieved each year, although that was small in 1969. On this count the bank fared somewhat less well than its principal competitors, First National City and Bank of America, which exhibited stronger earnings trends. [39]

Champion's early concern about the profitability of negotiable CDs and other borrowed money was in one sense borne out. Although total earnings increased, profit margins were reduced. Return on assets fell from a peak of eighty basis points in 1960 to an average of fifty-eight basis points in the late years of the decade, while return on equity, on the other hand, rose slightly to about 12 percent.

The cause of this changed financial performance was not difficult to ascertain. It lay in the escalating expense of the new funding sources, which revolutionized the cost structure of the bank. Within a few years borrowed money had become the dominant element among costs, and by 1969 amounted to double the aggregate of salary expense. The cost of borrowed money could be controlled only within narrow limits, since it was subject principally to market forces, some unpredictable. Personnel expense, by contrast, constituted a budget item subject to management determination, and it was monitored closely.

On one other count the rapid growth of borrowed money altered Chase's financial structure. Capital funds did not keep pace with assets, even though the aggregate doubled during the sixties to $1.4 billion. In consequence the ratio of capital funds to assets declined to 6.1 percent from 7.4 percent in 1960. Moreover capital funds now included long-term notes as well as equity. Equity alone stood at 4.5 percent of year-end assets, a relatively low percentage. Nevertheless, under guidance from Champion, a conservative banker who remembered well the troubled thirties, the bank also built up its loan loss reserve substantially, adding a further margin of safety.

The introduction of debt obligations into Chase's capital structure first occurred in June 1965. The provision of longer-term debt was not new; the comptroller of the currency, James J. Saxon, had first authorized it for national banks in late 1962. But no major New York City bank had offered such an issue. Champion, after reviewing the bank's capital position and earnings trend, recommended in May 1965 that the bank raise $250 million additional capital, and that it do so by issuing long-term capital notes, subordinated to deposits and most other debt. The issue, with a twenty-five-year maturity and 4.6 percent interest rate, came to the market on June 9 and soon sold out without loss.[40] Three years later this was followed by an offering of $150 million in long-term convertible capital notes at a rate of 4⅞ percent.

Although the new capital notes were listed on the New York Stock Exchange, they were preceded by a listing several months earlier of Chase Manhattan's common shares, the first bank stock to be added to that leading exchange in a number of years. Actually stock of The Chase National Bank had been traded on the exchange for a half century prior to 1928, when, with a number of other banks, management chose to delist it, hoping to avoid speculation and achieve greater price stability.[41]

The occasion for reexamining this policy arose when legislation extended to securities traded over the counter the same registration, disclosure, and other regulations that applied to securities listed on the stock exchanges. A major advantage of not listing on the exchange was thus removed. Chase shares were widely held, and the bank concluded that trading on the exchange would broaden the market.

The market first opened on Chase Manhattan stock on March 16, 1965. The initial trade to appear on the tape was a purchase of one hundred shares by George Champion at a price of $69.63 per share (substantially above book value) to add to his personal holdings.[42] The stock fared relatively well over the next few years as earnings moved upward. Nonetheless, growing reliance on borrowed money altered the profit profile of the bank, introducing new elements of risk and volatility. These would become more evident in the difficult decade that followed.

Impact of funding sources

The new funding sources introduced in the 1960s exercised a pervasive impact on banking—on loan expansion, on costs and liability management, and on earnings and capital structure. Chase's loans at home and abroad grew at an even more rapid rate than in the 1950s. Yet the attempt of the Federal Reserve to control loan growth through interest rate ceilings on time deposits caused major banks to adopt a cautious approach on expansion. The credit crunches of 1966 and 1969 remained a vivid memory.

Use of interest rate ceilings as an instrument for credit control proved faulty in significant respects. Distortions developed in the pattern of credit demand and interest rates, and the burden of restraint fell unevenly on different banks. Chase with access to uncontrolled Eurodollars and foreign branches, was able to circumvent restrictions in a way not available to many. These and other shortcomings became apparent to the Federal Reserve, which began in 1970 to free large time deposits from maximum ceilings on interest rates (see Chapter XIV). The credit crunch of 1969 thus proved to be the last of its kind.

Development of the Eurodollar market also set international banking on a new course, encouraged perhaps inadvertently by U.S. balance-of-payments controls of the 1960s. The dollar became the paramount international currency, with Eurodollars directly beholden to no regulatory authority. As dollar-based institutions, Chase and other U.S. banks held an advantage in utilizing this new resource. Henceforth the bank possessed a flexibility in funding credit demand in many countries where it operated branches or affiliates.

The profit picture of banks was also altered by the new sources of funding. Profit margins were narrowed, and banks were impelled to increase earnings through a larger volume of assets. In doing so they leveraged off capital, and Chase was no exception. Moreover, long-term borrowing, with interest costs tax deductible, became an attractive source of capital, marking a significant change in the bank's capital structure.

Expansion into the suburbs:
early attempt upstate

C hase and other New York City banks entered the sixties expecting a fairly rapid expansion into the suburbs, now authorized by passage of the Omnibus Banking Act. Events showed them to be overly optimistic. Two problems immediately arose, and for Chase a third. First, Nassau and Westchester, the counties adjacent to New York City, were well served by banks, and new locations acceptable to the regulatory authorities were difficult to discover. Of the four branch applications initially submitted by Chase, only two gained approval.

No less serious was the second problem, the section in the New York banking law that barred banks from branching into any community with a population of 1 million or less that contained the head office of another bank. This forestalled New York City banks from moving into twenty-one of the most desirable locations, including Hempstead, Garden City, and Glen Cove in Nassau, and White Plains, Mount Vernon, Yonkers, and New Rochelle in Westchester.[1] New York City banks sought throughout the decade to have this provision modified, but not until the next broad overhaul of branching regulations in 1971 did they succeed.

Third, Chase shared an additional handicap with other state-chartered banks. The comptroller of the currency, who regulated national banks, demonstrated greater liberality in approving branch applications than the state superintendent. Over the first two years of the new act, First National City gained approval to open eleven branches in Nassau and Westchester out of fifteen applications. Chase made twelve applications but received only five approvals. Chemical Bank, also state chartered, was even less successful.[2]

James J. Saxon, the comptroller, held liberal views regarding branching and bank regulation generally. Little coordination existed between his office and that of the state superintendent. He acted expeditiously, but the state acted slowly. These differences were among the factors that later persuaded Chase to convert to a national charter.

Plan for merger with Hempstead National Bank

Chase sought a way out of this impasse through a merger. Lawrence Marshall, as vice chairman, and George Roeder, as head of the metropolitan department, guided the effort, and went about addressing the problem carefully. Approval was required not only from the state superintendent but also from the Federal Reserve Board. The legislative effort to involve federal authorities in all bank mergers, first set off by the merger of Chase with Manhattan, finally culminated in the Bank Merger Act of 1960. This empowered the Federal Reserve Board to pass on mergers of all state-chartered banks that were members of the Federal Reserve System. (The comptroller continued to approve mergers of national banks.) The act set forth specific criteria to be applied; prominent among them was the effect on competition.

Marshall was convinced that no merger could gain approval unless the target bank was relatively small. He finally approached the Hempstead National Bank, with its head office in Hempstead in Nassau County, carrying deposits of $72 million (4 percent of the county total). More important, Hempstead possessed fifteen offices strategically located in central and southern Nassau County. Nassau was dominated by two large banks: Franklin National Bank and Meadowbrook National Bank, operating eighty-one branches (half the total) and holding two-thirds of all deposits in the county. A case could be made that the injection of Chase on a larger scale would increase competition rather than reduce it.

Hempstead National Bank had grown more slowly than many others in Nassau, and its chairman, Bruce Wood Hall, was open to an approach from Chase. Agreement was reached on an exchange of Chase shares for those of Hempstead, providing shareholders of the small bank with a sizable premium. Hall was to become a director of Chase and serve as chairman of the bank's Nassau advisory committee. The agreement was publicly announced on June 28, 1961.[3]

Chase prepared the application for merger with great care. In many respects the transaction represented a test case with respect to both the ability to expand expeditiously into surrounding areas and the attitude of state and federal authorities toward any merger of more than marginal significance by New York City banks. Unfortunately Chase was not alone in testing the waters at this point. About one month before the announcement, although not before the negotiations, Chemical Bank New York Trust Company had announced plans to merge with Long Island Trust Company of Garden City, also in Nassau. Long Island Trust, with $140 million deposits (6.5 percent of the county total), had fourteen offices and ranked third among banks in Nassau, while Hempstead ranked fourth.[4]

Both mergers would be in the hands of the banking authorities at the same time. Moreover, further complicating matters, First National City had earlier filed an application with the comptroller of the currency to merge with the National Bank of Westchester, second largest in that county, with $216 million in deposits and twenty-two offices.[5] Somewhat ironically, this was the institution from which only a year earlier the Rockefeller brothers had withdrawn a substantial investment in order to avoid any implication of impropriety on the part of the governor. These three mergers, planned simultaneously, might suggest to the authorities a pattern for the future.

Approval was obtained from Chase and Hempstead shareholders in late August, and the applications were submitted to the authorities. On October 4, 1961, the state superintendent approved both the Chase-Hempstead and Chemical-Long Island Trust mergers. In the case of Chase and Hempstead, the superintendent found that no significant competition would be eliminated, nor were smaller banks likely to be seriously affected, but rather benefits would accrue to the public, among them lower charges on loans and other services, and more convenient availability of Chase's broad range of services.[6]

There remained a decision from the Federal Reserve Board. Several months passed with no word. Finally, late in December 1961, some four months after submitting the application, the bank was notified that the board would order a public proceeding on January 19, 1962, at which proponents and opponents of both mergers could be heard.

The hearing before the Federal Reserve Board

Again long hours were spent in preparing the bank's case. David Rockefeller would appear as Chase's principal representative, but Marshall believed that it would be helpful to have several qualified witnesses voicing an independent opinion. As a result, Francis A. Florin, a retired deputy superintendent of New York State banking, testified that it would not be possible to build a branch system *de novo* to compete effectively with Franklin National or Meadowbrook. Ernest Hackwitz, president of First National Bank of Farmingdale, a small Long Island bank with a single office, then presented his judgment that the Chase-Hempstead merger would not alter the ability of small banks in the area to survive and prosper. And Roger F. Murray, a highly respected professor of banking from Columbia University, analyzed the competitive aspects, concluding that both the Chase and Chemical mergers would help restore competitive balance without creating additional institutions of overriding influence.[7]

These independent judgments were supported by Rockefeller, who presented an array of statistics and charts on existing relationships between Chase and Hempstead.[8] The evidence showed minimal competition between the two banks. Indeed competition within Nassau County would be enhanced by the proposed merger, for Chase would be a more potent competitor to the two dominant banks in a number of locations where Hempstead offered the closest alternative facility.

Yet even with increased competition, Rockefeller contended, no valid reason existed to assume that any of the smaller Nassau banks would be driven out, or that their ability to compete be seriously affected. Their favorable growth trend in recent years gave evidence of their health and viability. Rockefeller concluded that the Chase-Hempstead merger would indeed be in the public interest, that it would stimulate competition and provide badly needed economical banking services in an area of dynamic industrial growth.

But witnesses also appeared in opposition. Two of them—Arthur Roth, chairman of Franklin National Bank, and Sidney Friedman, executive committee chairman of Meadowbrook—had long fought the expansion of New York City banks into the suburbs. Perhaps more significant were negative opinions lodged by the comptroller of the currency and the Department of Justice. Under the Bank Merger Act of 1960 the Federal Reserve was required to seek opinions from the two agencies as well as the Federal Deposit Insurance Corporation concerning competitive aspects of merger proposals that came before it.

In December 1961 the comptroller had rejected the application of First National City to merge with the National Bank of Westchester, a much larger joinder involving more questionable competitive aspects. Now he opposed both the Chase and the Chemical mergers.[9] As for the Justice Department, it had consistently sought jurisdiction to approve or deny bank mergers on the basis of competitive factors alone. It occasioned little surprise when the department concluded that the proposed merger would eliminate substantial existing and potential competition between Chase and Hempstead, a judgment opposite to that returned to the board by the Federal Deposit Insurance Corporation.[10]

The Federal Reserve denies the merger

On April 30, 1962, some eight months after the application was submitted, the Federal Reserve finally handed down its decision. It was negative, not only for Chase and Hempstead but also for Chemical and Long Island Trust.[11] The board recognized that Nassau was growing rapidly and required increasing banking service, especially in the wholesale field. But it reasoned that these needs could be filled effectively by Franklin and Meadowbrook. Moreover Chase and other New York City banks served major business concerns out of their New York offices, where experts in a range of industries and banking techniques were concentrated. As for the retail field, the board remained unconvinced that Hempstead's services were inadequate.

But it was in weighing the competitive factor that the majority of the board came down strongly negative, and the governors appeared to strain to do so. They acknowledged that the merger would mean greater competition for

Franklin and Meadowbrook. And they said that greater competition was desirable. But increased competition in this respect, they claimed, would be outweighed by other effects, notably the probable impact on smaller banks (which was unproven) and the elimination of Hempstead as a competitor.

On balance, then, the majority of the governors concluded that "the opening of de novo branches, although a slower route than merger, would reduce a risk to the Nassau banking structure which provides local workers, commuters, businesses, and large-scale commercial and industrial enterprise with a variety of banks of different sizes and types."[12] They had come down on the side of the comptroller and disagreed with the superintendent of banks of New York State.

Expansion of the branch system

The mood at Chase was one of great disappointment but not shock, for the length of time that passed before a decision was announced suggested that the governors entertained doubts. Chase had no choice now but to set about establishing new branches from the ground up, a process in which they were handicapped by the home office protection provisions of the law and the relatively rigid standards of the state superintendent. Even while waiting for the decision on Hempstead, the bank moved ahead in Westchester, opening its first three branches. After the decision on Hempstead, Chase opened four new branches in Nassau, bringing the total to six. Meanwhile the bank also found opportunities for new offices within the city, especially in Manhattan and Brooklyn.

By the end of 1964 the branch system had swelled to 130 offices, compared with 105 four years earlier. But First National City had been even more active, adding almost twice as many branches as Chase. It now matched Chase's total, overcoming the lead created by the Manhattan merger. Moreover First National City had been especially busy in the suburbs, opening thirty-seven offices, in contrast to eleven for Chase.[13]

It became apparent that First National City was pursuing a different, more aggressive policy, geared to longer-term development and with less immediate concern for profit. Branches were established in locations that Chase had projected could not earn their way in more than a decade, and in some instances offices appeared to be opened solely for reasons of prestige. Chase's planning guidelines normally called for a new branch to become profitable within five years, although this period might be extended to seven or eight years in the suburbs, especially in developing areas where the population had to grow to create profitability.

Profitability was also influenced by elements of cost as well as by internal pricing arrangements. For example, Chase charged new branches for overhead—the costs of management, central staff, accounting, and other units, whose services were shared by all revenue-earning departments. Not all banks allocated such costs to a new branch, judging that it would earn its own way initially if it covered only those costs that it incurred directly.

Internal pricing was significant, since many branches (and the branch system as a whole) generated more funds through deposits than they employed in loans. These excess deposits were in effect "loaned" to a central pool, from which they were "reloaned" to operating units that utilized more deposits than they generated. The price paid to the supplying area for such funds, along with the cost charged to the borrowing area, was a subject of much discussion among different departments, since it strongly affected their relative profitability. Chase's domestic branch system was particularly valuable, since it produced a large net surplus of funds for use in other areas of the bank for loans and investments. In the mid-sixties this surplus amounted to more than $1.5 billion and accounted for a substantial portion of branch income.

There thus was room for considerable difference between banks in judging a branch's profit potential. Chase was conservative in its approach. First National City was not, choosing to establish itself strongly in the marketplace even at the expense of near-term profit. This difference in policy prevailed throughout the decade. By 1968 Chase was operating 143 branches, but First National City had 168, more than double the number at the start of the sixties. And in the suburbs Chase with fourteen offices lagged considerably behind First National City with a network of thirty-seven. Chemical Bank too had been aggressive and nearly matched Chase in total branches, with a larger number in the suburbs.[14]

The disparity in numbers was viewed with unease in some quarters of the bank, but senior management supported existing branching policy. And there was reason to believe that First National City had become concerned about the profitability of its new branches. Meanwhile Chase Manhattan managed to retain its share of the market in most retail services and even to gain in some. In early 1968 it held 30 percent of the savings account balances of New York City banks, a larger share than in the first years of the decade and slightly exceeding that of First National City. And its share of installment loans had risen substantially. Only in the number of retail accounts, both savings and checking, and not in dollar volume had First National City improved its position relative to Chase.[15]

Chase moves to form an upstate holding company

Even as the bank expanded into the suburbs, it sought also to move upstate. McCloy in testimony on the Omnibus Banking bill in early 1960 indicated that the bank had no interest in such a move. But in the autumn of 1963 E. Perry Spink, president of the Liberty National Bank and Trust, third largest in Buffalo and a long-time correspondent, asked Chase if it might be interested in forming an upstate holding company. The bank studied the matter and gave some encouragement to Spink. He persuaded two other banks, Central Trust Company in Rochester and Lincoln National Bank and Trust in Syracuse, also Chase correspondents, to join in the venture, and in the spring of 1964 they formally approached Chase. The banks were of modest size, and they believed that forming a holding company would enable them to bring to their customers the many specialized services of Chase.

Upstate banking at the time was dominated by one institution: the Marine Midland Corporation, with prominent affiliates in all banking districts outside metropolitan New York as well as an anchor bank in the city itself. Throughout the 1930s and 1940s Marine Midland's affiliates expanded through merger and internal growth, establishing branches widely in their respective districts. Marine Trust of Western New York, its affiliate in Buffalo, carried deposits of almost $1 billion, the largest in the area and 50 percent of the city total, and the affiliates in Rochester and Syracuse ranked second in size. Marine Midland, as the sole bank holding company, was the only institution with facilities that covered much of the state. In 1961 Morgan Guaranty had attempted to form a rival with six leading banks upstate, only to be turned down by the Federal Reserve.[16] Nevertheless, banking observers generally felt that the regulatory authorities would welcome a competitor.

Chase in its studies saw benefits in an upstate holding company and was prepared to act affirmatively. Upstate New York was growing more rapidly than the city, in both population and banking deposits. Moreover an advantage would be gained in relations with customers who operated facilities in various areas of the state, a marketing asset which Marine Midland put to good use. And sooner or later statewide branching was likely to be adopted. A holding company with branches in place would put Chase in a highly favorable position.[17]

The three banks that had approached Chase occupied a moderate position in their markets. Liberty, with $272 million in deposits, held 14 percent of the Buffalo total. Central Trust, the smallest of four banks in Rochester, carried deposits of $128 million, some 11.5 percent of the city total. And Lincoln National in Syracuse ranked third, with deposits of $150 million, or 23 percent of the total. Together the three banks operated fifty-six branches in the state's most populous areas outside New York City.[18]

The aggregate of $550 million in deposits was dwarfed by Chase's $10.7 billion. But the addition of Chase would make the new holding company the largest in the nation. This in itself was certain to draw fire from such members of Congress as Wright Patman, chairman of the House Committee on Banking and Currency, and Emmanuel Celler, chairman of the House

Judiciary Committee. But the bank was convinced that it could put a strong case for approval to the regulatory authorities. After preliminary discussions with both state and federal agencies it felt encouraged to move ahead. The board had been informed of the approach, and on July 15, 1964, it authorized the bank to enter into negotiations.

Problems in organizing the holding company

There then ensued a lengthy period of frustration for Chase and its potential partners. Problems immediately arose concerning the precise method of structuring the holding company. The directors had authorized the bank to proceed with the conventional form, under which Chase and the three upstate banks would become separate affiliates under a "top" holding company. But for Chase, operating under the Manhattan charter granted in 1799, this posed legal difficulties. A dissenting stockholder might possibly enjoin a transaction whereby Chase would give up its charter, the same uncertainty that had blocked Chase's initial effort to merge with Manhattan.

In the face of this problem the bank decided to explore an alternative suggested to Rockefeller by the comptroller of the currency, who had regulatory authority over two of the upstate banks.[19] Chase would not be required to give up its charter or its individual identity. (This aspect of the plan appealed greatly to Champion and Rockefeller, who had been hesitant about placing the bank itself under a holding company.) Rather an upstate holding company would be created to which only the three upstate banks would be affiliated. All of the stock in the holding company as well as the stock of the three banks would then be held in trust by three trustees for the beneficial ownership of all Chase Manhattan stockholders. Chase would provide the trustees with an initial capital of $3 million, as well as Chase Manhattan stock to be exchanged with the shareholders of the three banks for their existing stock. Directors of the holding company would be selected by Chase stockholders. Chase would distribute all dividends paid by the holding company to stockholders of Chase. Stockholders of all four banks would be required to approve the plan. Since Chase would be regarded as a holding company affiliate under both state and federal laws, it would be necessary to obtain approval for the transaction from the Federal Reserve Board, as well as the state superintendent and the state banking board.

The reason for creating the trust and these rather elaborate arrangements was to by-pass provision in the National Bank and Federal Reserve Acts prohibiting purchase by any member bank of the Federal Reserve System "for its own account of any shares of stock of any corporation." Legal counsel was not certain how the arrangement would be viewed by the Federal Reserve Board. So in December a lengthy memorandum was presented to the board outlining the plan and seeking their views as to its acceptance.[20]

Although the memorandum appeared persuasive, it failed to convince the board. In late February, after a lengthy delay, they responded in the negative. One reason had to do with certain conditions attached to the trust agreement between Chase and the trustees of the upstate holding company, conditions dictated by the Internal Revenue Code. If the exchange of Chase stock for the three banks was to be tax free, the trust agreement had to stipulate that Chase itself would be entitled to all dividends of the trust and upon its termination would be entitled to its assets. This, according to the Federal Reserve, made Chase, and not Chase stockholders, the beneficial owner of the trust. Thus the plan would result in purchase by The Chase Manhattan Bank of corporate stock for its own account in violation of the prohibition contained in the law. The letter from the Federal Reserve concluded, "If this plan to establish a bank holding company system were submitted to the Board . . . the Board would be compelled . . . to deny the application."[21]

Postponing formation of the holding company

The response from the Federal Reserve was a bitter disappointment. The bank immediately reviewed the alternatives open to it. If it were to persist in the effort to affiliate with upstate banks, a top holding company would be necessary. But the old Manhattan charter remained a stumbling block. This could be resolved by converting to a national charter, a step that had been under consideration for other reasons as well. The lawyers believed that such a conversion could be undertaken without encountering the same legal problems that had plagued the bank in the past. Under a national charter, conversion to a holding company affiliate could be accomplished by approval of two-thirds of the stockholders. The decision was taken to pursue this course.

Unfortunately this would involve a further delay. A year had passed since the upstate banks first came to Chase, and eight months since the initial announcement of plans for the holding company. The upstate banks were becoming restless. The managements of the four banks decided to shelve the plan for a holding company for the time being, and they made a public announcement to that effect in March 1965.[22]

The debate on reconversion to a national charter

The holding company problem was merely the immediate impetus for converting to a national charter. The matter had been under consideration for some time. As early as 1963, Dewey, Ballantine, Bushby, Palmer and

Wood, legal counsel on questions related to the charter, submitted a memorandum on the advantages and disadvantages of changing to a national charter. Subsequent staff studies were undertaken. Champion and Rockefeller were prepared to act quickly.

The directors had discussed the matter on several occasions and then went into it more deeply at their meeting on March 24, 1965. Champion, in a letter to the directors, had set forth reasons why conversion was desirable whether or not the bank formed a holding company.[23] He pointed out that the state charter was restricting Chase in a number of ways. The bank could not enter the leasing business directly. Recently it had explored the possibility of issuing traveler's checks and discovered that as a state bank, it could not market its checks satisfactorily in a number of other states. Indeed, because national banks were not generally subject to state "doing business" laws, they were able to engage in a wide variety of transactions extending across state lines without the prohibitions or complications faced by state banks. Moreover federal law gave national banks substantial protection against multistate taxation, whereas no such protection was available to state banks. All these advantages were available to First National City and Bank of America but not to Chase.

Then again, state banks were placed in double jeopardy on many regulatory matters. They were required to obtain approval not only from state authorities but also from the Federal Reserve Board on new branches and mergers, whereas in most cases national banks need look only to the comptroller of the currency. Moreover the comptroller in recent years (and especially the current comptroller, Saxon) had adopted more liberal standards on many matters than either the state or the Federal Reserve Board.

There were a few disadvantages. Chase Manhattan served as fiscal agent for the state, a function long performed by the Bank of Manhattan, and this appointment most likely would be sacrificed, although the loss would not be serious. Also troublesome in some respects was the necessity of reverting to cumulative voting for directors, as required by the National Banking Act. But The Chase National Bank had lived with cumulative voting for many decades, and a return to it would remove a source of contention among some stockholders.

Finally the problem of the holding company was at issue. After reviewing again the background of the holding company, Champion set forth various methods by which it might be established. All posed some risks and difficulties, in part because of the special nature of the Manhattan charter. But the method that entailed the least risk, that could be accomplished by only a two-thirds affirmative vote of stockholders at all stages, first involved converting to a national charter.

Events intervened to postpone any final decision. Most serious, a respected director and former president, J. Stewart Baker, who had opposed establishing a holding company under any conditions, took even stronger exception to vacating the old Manhattan charter. He put his objections in writing for distribution to the other directors. Baker reviewed the long history of the charter and the many legal opinions that any effort to give it up could be successfully enjoined by a dissenting stockholder. He recalled that McCloy's first promise in initiating discussions of a possible merger between Chase and Manhattan was that the merged bank would operate under Manhattan's charter. "This was never questioned in preliminary conversations, in formal negotiations, or in the operations of the merged bank, as far as I know, until it was suddenly and without warning placed before the directors. . . . This is such a drastic move that it would seem that the reasons for it must far outweigh the disadvantages."[24]

Baker rejected the arguments put forth to support conversion, pointing to other large New York banks that were conducting business successfully throughout the country. And he set forth a list of disadvantages to a federal charter several of which Champion had not named, among them a smaller limit on loans to a single borrower, for national banks could not include undivided profits as part of capital in determining the limit. Nor could they apply the limit separately to a company and certain subsidiaries, such as General Motors and General Motors Acceptance Corporation.

Chase decides to reconvert

The other directors did not take Baker's views lightly. They remained concerned that conversion might be challenged in the courts. Champion and Rockefeller sought a new opinion from Dewey, Ballantine, which had originally advised Baker against the Chase-Manhattan merger in 1951. This time the opinion was conveyed by the senior partner himself, former New York Governor Thomas E. Dewey: namely, that Chase Manhattan could convert to a national bank by an affirmative vote of two-thirds of the stockholders. The relevant federal law stated: "Any bank incorporated by special law of any state . . . or organized under the general law of any state . . . may by the vote of shareholders owning not less than 51% of such bank . . . be converted into a national banking association. . . . Provided, however, that such conversion shall not be in contravention of the state law."[25]

The Bank of The Manhattan Company had been incorporated by special law. Under common law, with a charter such as Manhattan's, a profitable corporation could not sell its assets or go out of business if any stockholder objected. But no case existed applying this rule to a conversion of a state bank into a national bank. No sale or disposition of assets was proposed, and no transfer or termination of the business was involved. Conversion would merely result in the continuation of the same institution as a national bank. Moreover this view was supported by past court decisions.

The matter was brought to the directors for final resolution on July 14. The wider public interest was involved, for since Chase was the nation's largest state bank, conversion to a national charter inevitably would be viewed in some quarters as a blow to the dual banking system.

Again Champion dispatched a lengthy letter to the directors repeating the advantages and disadvantages of conversion and referring to Stewart Baker's objections. He concluded that

> the basic advantage of a national charter is that it will permit the Bank greater flexibility in its operations, including the establishment of new services which cannot be carried out effectively under a state charter. Our two largest competitors, First National City and Bank of America, hold such an advantage today, and we have become increasingly aware of its significance.[26]

The directors had been exposed to the problem for some months. After further discussion they approved the conversion, with Stewart Baker asking to be recorded in the negative. A press release announcing the decision was issued immediately, and the story was carried on the front page of a number of newspapers.[27] The comptroller was reported to be overjoyed. "It's an old friend coming home," he said. But the state superintendent, who would be required to approve any holding company application, issued a statement regretting the action.[28] He would sorely miss Chase's $13 billion of assets.

At a special meeting on September 22, 1965, the stockholders gave their overwhelming assent: 16,890,000 for the change and some 55,000 against. No dissenting stockholder petitioned the court to block the conversion. On the following day Champion went to Washington to receive the new national charter from the comptroller. It bore the same number as that of the former Chase National Bank. The new bank would be officially named The Chase Manhattan Bank, National Association, or N.A. for short. The old Manhattan charter was a thing of the past.

Proposed affiliation with Liberty National

With conversion to a national charter, the way was now open to form a top holding company with Chase and the three upstate banks as affiliates. But almost eighteen months had passed since the original agreement, and competitors had not been idle. The previous spring three other holding company proposals had been announced, one an upstate regional organization anchored by Security Trust of Rochester, and two others by Bankers Trust and Irving Trust in New York. The latter included the Merchant's National Bank and Trust in Syracuse. Chase's upstate bank proposal no longer stood as the sole potential competitor to Marine Midland.

In the face of these changes Perry Spink, head of Liberty National Bank and initially the prime mover in organizing the upstate group, decided to withdraw. Since Liberty was the most important upstate bank in the plan, and Buffalo the major upstate economic and banking center, the proposal was no longer attractive to the other participants. Top officials of the four banks decided to abandon the proposal. A public statement was issued to that effect on October 6, 1965.[29]

Meanwhile Spink had informed Chase that Liberty alone would be willing to enter into a holding company with Chase under an organizational arrangement that would in effect make Liberty an affiliate of Chase. The arrangement called for Chase to make a voluntary exchange offer for Liberty stock, conditioned on the receipt of at least 80 percent of the Liberty shares. While this might result in a small minority ownership, the problem was not expected to be serious. Liberty would then continue to operate as an autonomous bank with its own board of directors. Chase expected to own the Liberty stock directly, but if the regulatory authorities desired, an intermediary corporation would be interposed.

The arrangement was similar in certain respects to the previous one to which the Federal Reserve had objected. But there now was one significant difference: the comptroller, and not the Federal Reserve, would be required to approve formation of the holding company, since only a single affiliate was involved. And the comptroller had informed Chase that he would rule that the bank could acquire the Liberty stock, either directly or indirectly "for purposes properly incidental to the business of banking." Approval also would be required from the New York State superintendent and the banking board. Nevertheless the bank was not completely free of the Federal Reserve, for it would need to obtain from the board of governors a permit to vote the Liberty shares at meetings of shareholders. Normally this was issued rather routinely.

On October 20, 1965, the directors of Chase approved the acquisition of Liberty as an affiliate, with an exchange of shares again providing a highly favorable margin for Liberty shareholders.[30] The public announcement, following only two weeks after announcement of the abandonment of the holding company, stressed that Liberty would be an affiliate of Chase and would retain a high degree of autonomy. And it stated that the association with Chase Manhattan would put Liberty in a much stronger position to assist in the economic growth of the Buffalo area.

Again the Federal Reserve objects

Once again the bank sought clarification from the Federal Reserve Board, asking it to declare either that Chase would not be considered a holding company affiliate (in which event a permit to vote Liberty stock would not be necessary) or to issue a voting permit. This time the answer came back fairly promptly, but again it was disappointing. According to the board the transaction would cause Chase "as a business" to hold the stock of and control a bank within the meaning of the Banking Act of 1933. The holding of such stock would itself be a violation of the law. Beyond this, the transaction appeared to be inconsistent with the policy of Congress as reflected in federal laws limiting the geographical expansion of national banks. It would enable Chase to conduct a banking business in places where branches were not permitted (even in another state), and this without the express approval of the comptroller. Thus the public interest would not be served by granting the permit.[31]

The Federal Reserve was not alone in raising questions about the Chase-Liberty affiliation. The superintendent of banks in California filed a brief with the New York banking board opposing the Chase plan as illegal. So too did the Independent Bankers Association, a view seconded by Representative Patman. One of the most thorough analyses of the proposed transaction appeared in *Bank Stock Quarterly*, a respected publication of M. A. Schapiro and Co., a leading underwriter and dealer in bank securities. If the affiliation were approved, the article reasoned, it "could render obsolete the traditional merger and holding company methods."[32] Of particular concern was the fact that neither the Federal Reserve, the comptroller, nor any other federal agency would be called upon to pass judgment on competitive and other aspects of the affiliation.

The fact that the affiliation would not be judged on its merits by his office also came to be of concern to the comptroller. He therefore advised Chase in mid-December that the proposal would fall within the scope of the 1960 Bank Merger Act—that it represented an "acquisition of assets" under that act and was not to be consummated until Chase had obtained the approval of his office.

This opened the way for other federal regulatory agencies to file their views with respect to the competitive aspects of the transaction. Both the Justice Department and the Federal Reserve informed the comptroller that the effect on competition would be adverse, the Federal Reserve stating that "the proposed acquisition would eliminate whatever competition now exists between the two banks, as well as a sizable independent bank in upper New York State, which has indicated an ability to provide effective competition on its own."[33]

New York State has the final word

Meanwhle the state superintendent of banking continued to process the Chase-Liberty application. He asked for additional information on the need for various types of services Chase would render upstate, as well as other alternatives open to Chase and Liberty. Chase quickly returned an answer to all these queries.

Nothing more was heard from the superintendent. Then on February 16, 1966, he exploded an unexpected bombshell. He denied the application solely on the grounds that it would be illegal—that it would be in violation of federal laws barring banks from acquiring the stock of another. "As a factual matter," the superintendent added, "the business of banking in New York State doesn't permit a bank to own stock in any other bank as envisaged by Chase." The superintendent in effect agreed with the Federal Reserve Board and his fellow superintendent in California and disagreed with the comptroller.[34]

The reaction at Chase was one of surprise and distress. The bank immediately stated publicly that it was "still convinced that its proposal was very much in the public interest" and that it would "continue to study the situation in order to determine how this public interest might best be served."[35]

Chase abandons plans for a holding company

The superintendent left the door open for a resubmission of the application in a different form, placing Chase under a top holding company. Champion and Rockefeller informed Spink that they would be willing to proceed in this manner. The Directors had originally approved such an arrangement almost two years earlier and agreed to it once again. This would require Federal Reserve Board approval inasmuch as two banks would be under the holding company.

Doubts soon arose about gaining such approval on the basis of the Federal Reserve's narrow interpretation of anticompetitive factors. The governors had already informed the comptroller that they regarded an affiliation between Chase and Liberty as having an adverse impact on competition. Then in early April the Federal Reserve approved the applications for holding companies with Irving Trust and Bankers Trust as anchors.[36] In doing so they expressed reservations about the competitive impact of the arrangements, which involved banks much smaller than Chase and Liberty. Spink was especially reluctant to undergo another lengthy process that might end in failure. So in early May 1966 Chase and Liberty announced that they were terminating their attempt to establish a joint relationship.[37]

Frustration by regulation

So ended a half-decade of efforts by Chase Manhattan to expand its domestic facilities through merger, an endeavor frustrated at every turn by the regulatory authorities. Chase's very size was a handicap. It conjured up images, mistaken to be sure, of excessive power and even monopoly. At both the federal and state levels regulatory authorities were groping toward a determination of what the structure of banking in New York State should be. Gradually it became clear that they would seek to prevent the major New York City banks from achieving a significant position elsewhere in the state through merger or acquisition. The policy set forth in the Omnibus Banking Act "that appropriate restrictions be imposed to prevent statewide control of banking by a few giant institutions" was being pursued with a vengeance. Later, in the 1980s, circumstances would change, persuading the regulatory authorities to relax their grip and permit Chase to accomplish what it had tried unsuccessfully to do two decades earlier (see Chapter XXII).[38]

Traveler's checks, credit cards, and consumer banking

C hase complemented its drive for geographical expansion in the 1960s with a persistent effort to develop new services, especially in the consumer field. The bank wanted to be innovative, but in this respect it was not outstanding. The name Chase Manhattan symbolized solid quality and public responsibility rather than innovation. Still, the bank sought to strike out in new directions, exploring new products and markets. Two of the more important of these in the 1960s were traveler's checks and credit cards, which became interrelated over time.

Traveler's checks

Chase Manhattan provided traveler's checks to customers as a service. Although one of the largest purveyors of this instrument in the country, the bank did not issue its own checks but sold those of American Express. Only three major U.S. banks issued such checks—First National City, Bank of America, and First National Bank of Chicago, with the latter commanding only a small share of the market.

Chase had explored issuing traveler's checks in the past but had consistently backed away from it. For a period in the late 1920s and early 1930s The Chase National Bank owned the American Express Company and operated it as a subsidiary (see Chapter I), but the Banking Act of 1933 forced its divestiture. Late in the forties Aldrich became interested in reacquiring parts of the company related to banking but found this to be impractical. Then in 1956 and again in 1959 committees within the bank examined the advisability of Chase's issuing its own check.[1] Both times they concluded that the business would not be profitable.

Yet First National City and Bank of America seemed to find it advantageous. Moreover Chase could perceive that the business was expanding. More people were traveling for longer periods, both within the United States and abroad. Champion and Rockefeller decided in 1963 to take a fresh look at the market and its potential. The bank mounted a market research study in depth, interviewing correspondents, thrift institutions, and other sellers of checks, as well as individuals, corporations, and other buyers of checks. The research was conducted both within the United States and in other countries.

The survey was nearly complete when one of those accidents that change the course of events intervened. The American Express Company fell victim to a gigantic fraud.[2] The future of American Express was thought to be in jeopardy. Chase not only sold American Express checks; it was the company's major banker, clearing its checks and providing it credit. Champion and Rockefeller did not want to add to the problems of its long-time customer, so the bank set aside for the time being any formal consideration of entering the traveler's check business.

Chase's charter poses obstacles

Still, work continued at the staff level on a Chase traveler's check. But again, as in the case of the proposed upstate holding company, Chase's state charter posed problems. It was no accident that the only banks issuing such checks operated under a federal charter. Legal counsel reported that Chase would encounter great difficulties in a number of states under "doing business" laws if it were to attempt to sell checks directly, and in two important states, Illinois and Pennsylvania, it would be barred altogether. National banks were not subject to these restrictions.

The bank could avoid some of these problems if it could conduct the traveler's check business through a separate subsidiary. A domestic subsidiary was not permitted under the banking law, but an Edge Act subsidiary might be formed if it could be shown that the traveler's check business was primarily international in character. The bank explored this alternative, even visiting the Federal Reserve in Washington to discuss it. In the end, however, no formal application was made. The problems of American Express were still, at the end of 1964, an inhibiting factor. Moreover the bank at this point was seeking to resolve its differences with the Federal Reserve over formation of the upstate holding company.

A positive recommendation

Not until the summer of 1965, two years after the first studies, was a decision to enter the traveler's check business formally considered by Champion and Rockefeller with their senior staff. By then the bank was planning to convert to a national charter, and the ability to issue traveler's checks was one of the considerations. The director of corporate planning submitted a memorandum summarizing the studies and recommending entry into the business.[3]

The studies showed that Chase was well positioned to carry out the business. Not only could it market a large volume through its own domestic offices and foreign branches and affiliates, but it possessed an unparalleled network of correspondent banks that might be enlisted as sales agents. These correspondents largely carried American Express checks, but surveys indicated that a considerable number would be willing to carry and even to "push" a Chase check. Moreover the Chase name was favorably known, and surveys of users and establishments suggested that there would be no problem with acceptance of a Chase check.

Any reservations about entering the business stemmed from its uncertain prospects for profit. Income arose from two sources: fees charged for the sale and "float," or checks paid for and outstanding but not cashed. This float represented deposits that could be used for loans or investments. Since demand deposits were growing only slowly, First National City and Bank of America were perceived as possessing an advantage with this source of funds.

But the studies also recognized that the growth of traveler's checks, and hence of income, was being challenged by a rapidly expanding new instrument, the general purpose credit card. Indeed discussions over previous months had turned increasingly toward the credit card as a favored instrument. Even as the question of traveler's checks moved toward a decision, exploration of a possible credit card began.

In view of this uncertainty a very conservative estimate of the growth in traveler's checks was adopted—little more than half the rate subsequently achieved by major issuers over the next few years.[4] This estimate, along with the income foregone from the American Express account, suggested that the business would be only marginally profitable. But there also were intangibles. A major element of cost was advertising and promotion. The bank's image worldwide could be enhanced by the issuance of its own check. And some felt that if the bank was to be a leading all-purpose institution, it could not afford to stay out of the business.

After considerable deliberation a tentative decision was reached in August 1965 to issue a Chase traveler's check. The decision was not, however, an enthusiastic one. The metropolitan department, which regarded American Express as one of its major accounts, was strongly opposed. Moreover, major attention had now shifted to the possibility of a Chase credit card. The two products were interrelated, and the organization for one might influence the organization for the other. So once again implementation of the traveler's check was set aside for the time being.

A decision reversed

For the next two years Chase devoted considerable attention to the credit card field. Champion and Rockefeller did not push development of a Chase traveler's check, in part because of potential interconnections with the credit card. Rather they agreed to delay while an alternative course was explored—namely, the possibility of entering into a special relationship with American Express that would meet some of the bank's objectives.

The idea was put forth in September 1965 by Charles Agemian, who now served as head of the bank's operations department as well as controller. He felt that a special relationship might be established "through which each would benefit from the best of the other's special capacity to handle certain aspects of the travelers check, money order and credit card business."[5]

Agemian contended that Chase held a particular advantage in handling the back office activities—the clearing and reconciling of checks, the computation of float and outstandings, the billing for credit card users, and the like—especially through use of electronic data processing. American Express, by contrast, possessed special know-how in sales and service, business promotion for new accounts, collection, and protection against fraud. And most important, it possessed the outlets for traveler's check sales, although Chase might be of help through its worldwide correspondent relationships.

Chase could be compensated for its activities by receiving a share of the sales proceeds, the proportion to be negotiated. But beyond this the bank wanted its name in some form on the American Express check—perhaps "payable through the Chase Manhattan Bank," or some similar manner. In this way the bank would gain recognition for being associated with the business.

Agemian was commissioned to explore this proposal with American Express. That company had recovered remarkably well from the salad oil fraud and was no longer negotiating from a position of weakness. Its officers expressed interest in having Chase handle their back office activity. Months passed in mutual study of the matter. The company, however, remained adamantly opposed to changing the design of its check so as to accord Chase public recognition of a relationship. Negotiations were finally broken off with many at Chase convinced that American Express had merely played for time, hoping to forestall Chase from becoming a competitor.

Almost three years passed since the first survey of the business. A new study in 1967 revealed that the market had grown far in excess of earlier expectations.[6] Correspondent banks were now less willing to sell or "push" a new Chase check. The business still would be only marginally profitable after accounting for loss of income from the sale of American Express checks.

A final meeting was held in early 1968. The indifferent earnings prospects were weighed against such potential intangible benefits as enhancing the bank's image, providing another tool to promote correspondent and corporate relationships, and yielding another source of deposits through float. The metropolitan department remained adamantly opposed to forfeiting its profitable relationship with American Express. Credit cards, not traveler's checks, represented the wave of the future. The earlier decision was reversed, and the bank dropped consideration of the business. More than a decade would pass before Chase finally issued its own traveler's check, and then only in a cooperative program with other members of the Visa credit card group.

Agreement with Diners Club

The credit card soon came to be viewed by some in senior management as possessing greater potential than traveler's checks—not the retail card, which Chase had launched unsuccessfully early in the decade, but the general purpose card, used for travel and entertainment on a national and international scale. Billings on general purpose cards were growing more rapidly than sales of traveler's checks.

Three major companies were in the business in 1965: American Express, Diners Club, and Hilton Credit Corporation, which issued the Carte Blanche card. With conversion to a national charter, the bank would be able to explore acquiring one of these cards. The comptroller indicated that he would approve such an acquisition as a proper incident to the business of banking, and that it could be operated as a separate subsidiary.

The initial choice was Carte Blanche, the card with the smallest number of cardholders and establishments. (The Hiltons and Hilton Hotels were customers of the bank.) An inquiry was launched, and somewhat to the bank's surprise it was learned that Hilton Credit was already far advanced in discussions with First National City of a plan whereby the latter would acquire 50 percent interest and working control of Carte Blanche, a disappointment to Chase. A formal announcement of this acquisition came in early September 1965.[7]

The bank then turned toward exploring in depth the possible acquisition of Diners Club, the company that had first launched a general purpose card in 1950 and ranked with American Express as a leader in the field. Diners was also a customer of Chase, and Alfred Bloomingdale, its head, had recently approached the bank about the possibility of cooperating in issuing a traveler's check as a supplement to its card, a major reason for Chase's postponing issuance of its own check.

Diners had 860,000 cardholders, with billings of almost $200 million (30 percent of the market).[8] Moreover it operated twenty offices in the United States and franchised its card to companies in a number of foreign countries. The cardholders, the offices, and the foreign franchises would all be useful for traveler's checks as well as credit cards, and many costs could be shared. In addition credit cards were still in their infancy. They would undoubtedly serve as the basis for new forms of credit arrangements in the future, and it was important that Chase play a role in this development.

There were problems with Diners, to be sure.[9] Its management was not strong, and neither were its administrative controls. It operated several custom credit cards for retail establishments whose receivables required examination. And its clerical employees, unlike the bank's, were unionized. This would require that it operate as a separate subsidiary, with employee relations clearly distinct from Chase's. Nevertheless the positive aspects outweighed the negative, and the bank decided to acquire Diners.

Bloomingdale proved willing to consider a proposal. He felt that the company would be unable to finance the growth that loomed ahead, and he was concerned about competitive advantages possessed by American Express and First National City. Subsequent negotiations led to an agreement for Chase to purchase Diners Club shares for $56.5 million, or some 18 times Diners' estimated earnings for the year.[10] The announcement on November 17, 1965, occasioned no surprise, for the bank had indicated earlier that it was discussing with Diners some form of relationship. At the time only a "memorandum of intent," approved by both boards, was signed, for one hurdle remained to be surmounted.

Justice looks at the Diners Club acquisition

The hurdle was the Department of Justice. The First National City-Carte Blanche transaction was known to be under scrutiny by the antitrust division. Several days prior to the Chase-Diners announcement, John J. McCloy, former chairman and now a partner in Milbank, Tweed, Hadley and McCloy, called the attorney general and informed him of the pending transaction. He indicated that the bank intended to submit an economic memorandum to the department concerning the proposal, and he assured the attorney general that substantial time would elapse before any closing.

The memorandum went out on December 29, 1965.[11] Much of it was devoted to competitive aspects of the transaction. Chase was not engaged in the credit card business, so little or no direct competition existed between it and Diners. Moreover *de novo* entry into the field was not practical because of anticipated heavy losses, an expectation supported by Chase's previous experience with a retail card. As for Diners, it required strengthening in finance and management if it were to remain a viable competitor in the period ahead.

The letter could hardly have been delivered before the Department of Justice went to court to stop the joinder of First National City with Carte Blanche, a much smaller transaction. The department claimed that the transaction would violate the Clayton Antitrust Act by eliminating potential competition between First National City and Hilton Credit Corporation and hence "would tend to substantially lessen competition in the credit card field." Moreover it would serve to lessen competition in retail banking in the

New York City area. First National City was said to be "especially qualified" to enter the general purpose credit card business on a national and international scale on its own, and "such entry is likely if the proposed merger is enjoined."[12]

The Department of Justice filed its suit on December 30, only a day before First National City was scheduled to acquire a controlling interest in Carte Blanche. A court-approved agreement on the following day permitted the transaction to be effected, but only on condition that Carte Blanche be operated as an independent entity, apart from the bank, so that it could be divested if Justice were to win its suit.[13]

All this could hardly be called promising for the Chase-Diners Club proposal. Nevertheless the bank persisted. A profusion of files and documents relating to Chase's early credit card experience was dispatched to Justice, and at its request a memorandum was submitted detailing the estimated costs of entering the business *de novo*. The break-even point was projected to be in the sixth year, but only after start-up costs and accumulated losses of $33 million, including a charge for interest. Even then the billings on a Chase card would be little more than half those currently estimated for Diners. The bank reiterated that it had no intention of entering the business *de novo*.

Chase was anxious to get the matter settled, so early in April 1966 McCloy called Turner, the assistant attorney general for antitrust, and asked if Justice had reached any decision. Turner responded that he had recommended to the attorney general that the department institute a proceeding against the transaction, that he could not find that the Chase-Diners proposal differed sufficiently from that of First National City and Carte Blanche. The department would not seek a temporary injunction, but would discuss procedures that would enable it to effect a divestiture in the event of a court decision in favor of the department. A few days later Turner called again to say that the attorney general had accepted his recommendation.[14]

Chase and Diners Club immediately decided to terminate the proposed acquisition, announcing on April 12 that the Department of Justice had advised that it would institute antitrust proceedings to block the transaction. While they both felt that the proposed affiliation would be in the best interests of each, as well as in the public interest, "the prospects of extended litigation has convinced us that it would not be desirable to pursue the project any further at this time."[15]

Thus Chase incurred its third regulatory setback in two years in its effort to expand domestically. The press was not reluctant to point this out, and the image of the bank suffered. Yet the decision to terminate the Diners acquisition proved to be correct. First National City's litigation with the Department of Justice dragged on for several years, with the bank finally agreeing to divest Carte Blanche. Meanwhile the uncertainty and restrictions on relations between the bank and the subsidiary prevented effective development of the Carte Blanche card.

The check guarantee card and overdraft banking

A new task force was soon formed to recommend what further action should be taken on a credit card now that a major acquisition was ruled out. In addition to the general purpose card, attention was to focus on two other instruments: a check guarantee card and a local retail card, somewhat similar to the one Chase had abandoned earlier in the decade. A number of banks issuing local cards managed to turn a profit, with BankAmericard in the lead. A wave of enthusiasm for this new service swept over the banking community, and Chase decided to consider it among other alternatives in spite of its earlier disappointment.

New surveys of the market again revealed formidable problems in undertaking *de novo* a general purpose card, and so the bank decided to drop any further consideration of that possibility.[16] Bank customers in the metropolitan area, however, did appear interested in a check guarantee card.[17] There was already available a retail charge card from Uni-Serve, the successor to the Chase Manhattan charge plan. The check guarantee card, pioneered by Security First National of Los Angeles as an alternative to the Bank-Americard, guaranteed that any checks written up to a certain amount by a Chase depositor would be honored by the bank. Such a card was not available in the New York market, and the cost of providing it was relatively small. In May 1967 Chase became the first New York bank to furnish this personal banking service. Cardholders were also automatically enrolled in another recent service, an automatic overdraft on a checking account, named Cash Reserve.

Cash Reserve stood by itself as a service but was judged to be a highly desirable adjunct to any form of credit card. The bank had planned to make such a service available to selected holders of Diners Club cards if it had acquired that company.[18] The service provided an individual line of credit ranging from $500 to $5,000 to creditworthy depositors. The report on borrowing was combined with the deposit account in a single statement to the depositor each month. Cash Reserve also had the advantage over installment credit of reducing the number of small loans under installment credit, which were unprofitable because of administrative costs.

Although a check guarantee card represented a step toward returning to a local charge card, the task force, with considerable uncertainty and disagreement, recommended against providing a charge card at the time.[19] Even with Cash Reserve and other added features, the profit potential was not persuasive. Such a decision incurred the risk that another bank, most likely

First National City, would be the first to offer a local card, but such a development would not necessarily deter Chase from future action. The metropolitan department, responsible for consumer services, was assigned the task of continuing to observe and study the possibility of offering a retail credit card at a later date.

Explosive growth in credit cards

Chase's check guarantee card proved a considerable success from the outset. Cash Reserve was a promising new product. But the metropolitan department, as it monitored developments, became increasingly impressed with the explosive growth in retail credit cards unfolding throughout 1967 and the first half of 1968. At this point Bank of America had franchised its retail card into thirty-three states and claimed 8 million cardholders, thereby building a nationwide network by which local retail cards could be honored through interchange. Other networks sprang up linking cards in various regions—the Midwest Bankcard Group and the Western States Bankcard Association among them. Of the one hundred largest banks, three-fourths were issuing retail cards or had the possibility under study.[20]

Among New York banks First National City led the way, inaugurating its Everything Card in August 1967. Then in 1968 Manufacturers Hanover, Chemical Bank, and Marine Midland, with its subsidiaries throughout the state, announced plans to issue cards as part of a new regional association, the Eastern States Bankcard Association, which would link up with other regional groups to form a nationwide network called Master Charge, competitive with BankAmericard. But the major retail card in the city, now well established, was Uni-Card, sold by Chase more than six years earlier and resold to American Express in late 1965.[21]

The bank formally reviewed its position in late summer 1968. It recognized that the check guarantee card contributed a valuable component to its checking account service, especially when tied to overdraft banking. But check guarantee was no substitute for a retail card, which provided quite a different service to both merchants and individuals. Indeed some banks now offered both.

Four alternatives appeared open to Chase. It could join the newly formed Eastern Bankcard Association (with its Master Charge card) as a founding member, along with Manufacturers Hanover and Chemical Bank New York Trust. It could proceed with a completely new card, benefiting from the experience of others and improved techniques. Or better yet, the bank might attempt to reacquire Uni-Card from American Express. The fourth alternative, to do nothing, was quickly ruled out. Not only did competitive developments now mandate a retail card, but the bank sensed that the technology relating cards to different phases of consumer banking was rapidly changing. Preauthorized payments, automated bill paying, and electronic deposits and cash dispensing were waiting in the wings. Chase needed to be on the cutting edge of these developments.[22]

The Eastern Bankcard Association urged Chase to become a member. The bank appreciated that it would undoubtedly occupy a paramount position in guiding the future development of the association. The interchange among merchant establishments, the sharing of some costs, and the joint research efforts made this course more appealing than starting *de novo*. Another possibility, joining BankAmericard, was not even considered. Aside from the fact that Chase was reluctant to identify itself so publicly with a leading competitor, Bankers Trust had agreed to be the New York anchor for that card.

Chase purchases Uni-Card

The more the Bank looked at Uni-Card, the more appealing it seemed.[23] Uni-Serve Corporation had remained a customer of Chase, and the bank was well acquainted with its progress. It had grown well over much of the period and now possessed more than 750,000 billing units (in excess of 1 million cards) and close to eighteen thousand retail outlets. Cardholder volume for the year was estimated to be $113 million. And the operation was profitable, earning almost $2 million before taxes. Most of Uni-Serve's activity was located in the New York City area, but it also had cardholders and merchants in states throughout the Northeast, principally in Massachusetts, New Jersey, and Pennsylvania. In that sense it carried the potential for becoming a regional card.

American Express also hinted that it was willing to consider a sale, since it foresaw weakness in its competitive position in the future. It lacked the ability to provide loans to cardholders and to engage in nationwide interchange relationships. Better to concentrate on its highly successful travel and entertainment card along with traveler's checks.

Discussions were initiated, and in December agreement was reached on a sales price of $25 million plus the cost of receivables, which at the closing stood at a post-Christmas high of $77 million. American Express carried its investment in Uni-Serve at almost $24 million, and the bank's projections showed an after-tax return of 10 percent on the price. James H. Harris, senior vice president in the metropolitan department, who carried out the negotiations, was prepared to bid higher if necessary. The bank was well satisfied with the outcome.

The transaction was announced publicly on December 18, 1968. The bank did not play down the fact that it was repurchasing a property it had sold early in the decade, but the purchase price was not revealed. Thomas W. McMahon, Jr., executive vice president in the metropolitan department, issued the announcement, rather than Champion or Rockefeller.[24]

Chase thus emerged as the leading provider of bank credit cards in the New York area, with its own card operated under competent management. Questions naturally arose within the bank concerning the possible attitude of the Department of Justice. Since Chase was buying back an operation it had initiated, and integrating it into the bank's ongoing activities, legal counsel doubted that the department would seek divestment.[25] In these circumstances it was decided not to inform the Department of Justice other than through public announcement. A new president was moving into the White House, and leadership in the department was in transition. This might have been one reason why Justice never sought additional information concerning the transaction. For once the regulatory authorities failed to react.

Uni-Card converts to Chase BankAmericard

Over the next two years Chase experienced somewhat less success than had been projected for Uni-Card. Its cardholders continued to account for more than 25 percent of the total in the New York metropolitan area. But the sizable profits anticipated failed to materialize. The cost of money to finance receivables rose under the credit crunch of 1969 and continued to be higher than anticipated. Moreover, New York State placed an upper limit on interest rates. Although the profit margin remained positive, greater volume would be needed.

It soon became apparent that the bank was operating at a disadvantage which would increase in the years ahead. Uni-Card basically served local needs. It did not provide outlets on the national and even international scale offered by two emerging competitive systems, Master Charge and Bank-Americard. Chase attempted to franchise Uni-Card to other banks, but with little success. By 1971 projections suggested that future growth of Uni-Card in its existing form would be inadequate.[26]

Five major banks in the city offered Master Charge. Only one, Bankers Trust, had franchised BankAmericard. Market surveys revealed that growth prospects would be considerably improved by converting Uni-Card to Bank-Americard. By now BankAmericard had become widely franchised and was managed by National BankAmericard, a company separate from Bank of America, although the latter continued to play a major role in its management. This separation encouraged Chase to drop its earlier reluctance to team up with a major competitor.

In July 1971 a team of four from Chase met with senior officials of National BankAmericard and Bank of America to discuss a possible conversion. Not unexpectedly, they found that BankAmericard would welcome Chase and was willing to make concessions in its normal franchising costs and procedures. Chase would be second in size only to Bank of America in the group and could join the directorate of National BankAmericard.

Early in 1972 Chase announced that Uni-Card would join the National BankAmericard system: "Our cardholders will have immediate national and international coverage and our merchants will be able to accept credit card purchases from persons in all 50 states and a large part of the world." The announcement added, "This is a good move for all parties concerned."[27]

It did prove to be a good move. The number of merchant outlets available to the bank's cardholders swelled from forty thousand in the northeastern United States to more than 1 million throughout the nation and in seventy foreign areas. Cardholder receivables more than doubled to $350 million by late 1975, and the bank retained its premier position in the New York market.

The credit card had traveled far and fast since Chase first explored the business in the early sixties, and in many respects it possessed unique attributes. For banks and consumers it combined a means of payment with a medium for extending credit. Consumers could better manage their business, and banks could extend credit more economically. For sellers it transferred credit risk to an institution specializing in that business. And it freed Chase and other banks from the limited confines of branching, enabling them to spread nationwide and even internationally to serve consumers.

Two significant products

BankAmericard eventually outgrew its name, and in 1977 became Chase Visa. Thus the credit card and overdraft facilities developed into two of the most important consumer products introduced by Chase in the years of this history. A third, automated teller machines, would follow in the mid-1970s.

In all of these developments Chase was an early participant, although not a front runner. Its cautious approach was epitomized by the decision to issue a check guarantee card while awaiting further evidence of the profit outlook for credit cards. Yet once that outlook became clear, Champion did not hesitate to approve the reacquisition of the card he had sold almost a decade earlier.

The bank early concluded that the credit card held more potential than traveler's checks, and in this it was perceptive. Nevertheless Chase's failure to establish its own traveler's check in the mid-1960s, while not serious from a profit point of view, concerned those who had favored it. Neither Champion nor Rockefeller pushed vigorously for a decision, and the opportune moment passed. Both men at the time were more involved with geographical expansion, especially the successful building of Chase's network abroad.

The internationalization of Chase Manhattan:
the developing world

Chase's major and most successful expansion in the 1960s was in its overseas network. At the start of the decade the bank was operating twenty-four branches in eleven countries or foreign areas, supplemented by representative offices (not permitted to take deposits or make loans) in seven others. By 1970 it was operating directly in seventy-three areas, with branches in twenty-five, affiliated institutions in forty-four, and representation in four. In the short span of a decade, the number of areas in which Chase maintained facilities had more than quadrupled.[1]

Chase was well aware of the dramatic trend toward internationalization in American business. Increasingly its leading customers sought credit for expansion overseas. Surveys revealed foreign business to be of major interest to domestic customers. A 1957 study by the bank had urged that the network of foreign branches be expanded, and this had been adopted as policy. But the international department, wedded to correspondent banking, had not pursued the matter vigorously.

The succession of Champion and Rockefeller ushered in a change, bringing much greater emphasis on overseas expansion. The division of responsibility between the two accorded Rockefeller special concern with this activity, and he was keenly interested in it. Yet Champion had to be heavily involved, too, since the development of the bank's international posture was central to its entire business. Champion returned from a lengthy trip through the Far East in 1959 with a better appreciation of the ramifications of Chase's international position.[2] He supported international expansion, but there remained a fundamental difference between his views and Rockefeller's.[3]

Champion saw foreign branches as being of value chiefly to service U.S. customers as an extension of its domestic business. Rockefeller, in contrast, was a true internationalist. He viewed the bank's offices worldwide as serving customers from all nations, not only the United States but also the countries in which the offices were located, and throughout the world. As the bank moved to internationalize during the sixties, this difference in concept and objectives would cause disagreement between the two executives and slow the process.

A strategic decision

The bank's strategy as it unfolded laid initial emphasis on developing countries, especially in South America and Asia. Those areas, while politically unstable and prone to inflation, had strong trade ties with the United States and were growing fast. First National City and British overseas banks maintained branches in most large nations, but Chase had only representative offices in Argentina, Brazil, Mexico, Venezuela, and India.

At the outset the bank faced a major policy decision: should it establish branches or should it attempt to acquire local banks? From a management point of view, branches were preferable. They could be controlled more easily, and their resources could be more readily directed toward specific objectives. Moreover their full earnings and balance sheet were reported as part of the bank's assets, whereas those of an affiliated institution were not necessarily consolidated.

A number of factors, however, weighed against creating a branch system *de novo*.[4] For one thing, starting a branch in every country would require a large number of specially trained personnel, and these were in short supply. For another, no new branch would have a meaningful deposit base for some time, and in the inflationary environment of many countries, especially in South America, U.S. subsidiaries urgently needed to finance in local currencies. Finally, and most important, many South American governments were extremely cool toward the establishment of new facilities by foreign banks.

For these reasons, in South America, Chase planners decided to seek an interest in local banks rather than build a branch system. They judged—though this proved erroneous—that joining with local citizens in ownership would afford a measure of protection against government encroachment. In Asia, where local banks were less well established, Chase continued to eye the possible acquisition of networks from British overseas banks.

Spreading across South America

To implement its strategy in South America, Chase acquired an interest in banks in five countries (Brazil, Venezuela, Peru, Colombia, and Argentina), and another in Honduras in Central America (see Table 7). Of these the most successful through the years was Banco Lar in Brazil, which initially developed and financed real estate, and had added a small commercial banking department shortly before Chase acquired its interest. Banco Lar carried assets of only $28 million and capital funds of $1.7 million, but it operated thirty-one offices in fourteen cities and enjoyed a solid reputation.[5]

As the first such acquisition, Banco Lar was something of a guinea pig. In

Table 7.   Chase acquisitions in Latin America, 1962–1968.

Country	Bank	% Initial Participation	Year Acquired
Brazil	Banco Hipotecario Lar Brasileiro (Banco Lar)	51	1962
Venezuela	Banco Mercantile y Agricola	51	1962
Peru	Banco Continental	51	1965
Colombia	Banco del Comercio	43	1967
Argentina	Banco Argentino de Comercio	47	1968
Honduras	Banco Atlantida	51	1966

Source: Chase Manhattan Bank Archives and *Annual Reports*.

this role it almost failed to clear its first test: approval by Chase's directors. A preacquisition audit turned up accounting practices that, while legal in Brazil, were questionable by American standards.[6] Some directors were disturbed, and the board was divided on the acquisition. Rockefeller, however, strongly supported the purchase, backed by Alfred Barth of the international department and Charles Agemian, the controller, who had visited and examined the bank. In the end the directors approved the affiliation, which took effect in April 1962.[7]

The immediate task called for the conversion of Banco Lar into a full-fledged commercial bank. Paul Lakers, Chase's representative in Brazil, guided the process and eventually headed the management. The story of this transformation and the subsequent flourishing of Banco Lar could form a history in itself. By 1965 assets had expanded by 75 percent. A large portion of the loan portfolio was commercial in character. Real estate was being profitably sold. By the end of the decade the transformation was nearly complete; active management was in Chase's hands. After a period of small losses, earnings grew. Gradually over the years Chase increased its share of ownership to 99 percent.[8]

Initially Chase arranged for a subsidiary of Dresdner Bank, Deutsch Sudamerikanische Bank, to acquire a 10 percent interest in Banco Lar, but with no part in management. This partner, it reasoned, could produce business with German firms active in trade with Brazil. Similar small participations were acquired by Deutsch Sudamerikanische in other South American affiliates, only to be eventually bought out by Chase.

In the 1970s Banco Lar blossomed, making Chase a leading foreign bank serving Brazilians, Americans, and customers from all nations. By 1983 assets totaled $1.1 billion, a far cry from the $28 million twenty-one years earlier.[9] A long-anticipated change in name to Banco Chase Manhattan was planned for 1986.

Banco Lar Brasileiro, Rio de Janeiro.

Buenos Aires.

Tokyo, 1974–1986.

Hong Kong, 1930s.

First suburban branch, Great Neck, Long Island, 1961.

Treasury Department, One Chase Manhattan Plaza, 1976.

Executive's office at 1 Chase Manhattan Plaza. Painting is by Josef Albers.

Meeting room at 410 Park Avenue. Sam Francis mural is in background.

Frankfort, 1947–1972.

Frankfort, 1972—.

*Lombard Street, London,
1937–1969.*

Woolgate House, London, 1969—.

Paris, 41 rue Cambon, 1973.

Geneva

Milan

Problems with nationalism

Affiliations in other South American countries came to be influenced in varying degree by nationalistic acts that limited ownership. One of the most successful financially was Banco Mercantile y Agricola in Venezuela. In June 1962, when Chase acquired its 51 percent interest, Banco Mercantile held assets of $71 million, and with fifteen offices was one of five institutions dominating the financial scene.[10] It proved to be a profitable venture from the outset, and soon became a valuable link in Chase's international network.

Political developments in the late sixties, however, disrupted this beneficial arrangement. Venezuela joined other neighboring countries in an Andean Pact concerning political and economic relationships. Among other things, the pact called for foreign ownership of banks to be limited. Over subsequent years Chase was required to reduce its interest in Banco Mercantile to 19.74 percent. Banco Mercantile continued to expand rapidly and proved highly profitable, but with Chase's interest reduced to less than 20 percent, its influence on management waned. In 1980 Chase sold its share in Banco Mercantile at a substantial capital gain.[11]

Chase's affiliation with Banco Continental in Peru was even more brief. That bank stood as the fourth largest in the country when Chase acquired its interest in 1965.[12] Under Chase leadership, Banco Continental performed well over the next few years and grew to be the nation's second largest. Unfortunately its very prominence made it a political target. Peru's democratic government, unable to cope with economic ills, was ousted by the military, and in August 1970 Peruvian officials informed Chase that, in the national interest, the government would acquire control of Banco Continental.

A delegation headed by a Peruvian general came to New York to negotiate the purchase. If Chase refused to sell, the bank would be taken over forcibly by the government.[13] The matter was placed in the hands of William S. Ogden, then in charge of Chase's activities in Latin America, assisted by Gardner Patrick, Chase's chairman of Banco Continental. Tough negotiations followed. In the end Chase's interest was sold for more than double its investment, but Chase was left without any representation in Peru.[14] A decade elapsed before the bank returned with a representative office, followed by a branch in 1984.

In Colombia, Chase fared better, although not without adjustments. Banco del Comercio, affiliated in October 1967, represented the country's fourth largest bank, with assets of $79 million and 121 offices. A well-run institution, it also participated in warehousing operations in Colombia, Peru, and Panama. Chase contemplated a majority ownership of 51 percent, but in view of nationalistic sentiment reduced this to 43 percent.[15] But

Colombia too was a member of the Andean Pact, and through the seventies, as Comercio's capital expanded, Chase was gradually forced to reduce its share to about 35 percent.

Banco del Comercio developed into one of Chase's more successful affiliates through the 1970s. The top management remained unchanged, with an able president, Camilo Herrera Prado, staying in that position. The bank sustained its strong growth through the seventies, but Chase's limited participation raised continuing questions concerning its value. These were reinforced in the 1980s when the Colombian economy encountered problems and Banco del Comercio fared less well.

Argentina proved more difficult. Chase tried for some years to arrange an affiliation in that country, but prospective partners either demanded unreasonable premiums or proved unappealing because of weakness in management and loan portfolios. As early as 1961 the bank discussed a possible joinder with the founder of Banco Argentino de Comercio, but had failed to complete the deal before he died. Then in 1968 his widow reached an agreement with Chase.[16]

Banco Argentino ranked eleventh in Argentina, carrying deposits of $30 million, and operating fifteen branches in Buenos Aires and thirteen outside the capital. Since banks under foreign control operated under legal constraints, Chase, through a more complicated agreement than usual, initially took a minority position but in effect held de facto control. Within a few years, however, changes in the law encouraged the bank to increase its ownership to almost 70 percent.

The new affiliate remained Argentinian in character, although Chase soon provided a new general manager, José Leon. The return of the Peronists to power in 1973 brought a new wave of nationalism to Argentina. Legislation was passed under which Banco Argentino was to be nationalized, although U.S. banks with branch systems were permitted to remain. In 1974 Banco Argentino was placed under the control of Banco de la Nacion. Over the next three years negotiations with the central bank concerning compensation and other matters related to Chase's ownership dragged on. Meanwhile, the bank's performance deteriorated under Argentine management.[17]

Finally, in August 1977, Chase resumed control of Banco Argentino, and ownership was subsequently restored under a new law. Through recapitalization and purchase of foreign-held shares Chase achieved almost complete ownership. The name was changed in 1979 to Chase Bank S.A., and by 1980, with quality restored and assets exceeding $300 million, The Chase Bank occupied a respectable place in Argentinian banking.[18] The offices of the subsidiary were converted to branches of The Chase Manhattan Bank in 1982.

Affiliation in South America

Thus in South America affiliation proved only partially successful. In Brazil, the most important nation economically, Banco Lar provided a charter and base on which Chase was able to build a highly useful facility. In Argentina, after considerable travail, The Chase Bank S.A. emerged as a helpful adjunct to the network. The ability to acquire almost complete ownership, with freedom to manage and receipt of the full reward, was of critical importance. Chase's limited ownership in Colombia's Banco del Comercio reduced the bank's interest in that institution, and the same problem in Venezuela led to divestment. Affiliation in Peru foundered on nationalism, although not without eventual profit for Chase.

In Central America too nationalism and local politics proved an inhibiting factor. The area was much less important economically, but in the mid-1960s the major countries banded together in a fledgling Central American Common Market. Chase decided to participate, and chose as its instrument Banco Atlantida in Honduras, the largest and best capitalized bank in Central America, with assets of $42 million.[19] Chase saw Atlantida as the centerpiece for representation not only in Honduras but also in other members of the common market.

As events unfolded, Banco Atlantida was never able to carry out the plans envisaged for it. Competing interests in other countries blocked all efforts to branch or even affiliate across international borders. While Banco Atlantida was profitable, its limited scope kept it from contributing greatly to Chase's world network. Subsequently it became part of a holding company, Inversiones Atlantida, also engaged in other financial businesses, and in 1974 Chase reduced its interest in Inversiones Atlantida to 25 percent. [20]

Spreading out in the Caribbean

Meanwhile Chase also continued to give attention to the Caribbean, the area that for years formed a major segment of its foreign branch network. Chase held a leading position in the Caribbean at the start of the 1960s, but it was confined largely to areas closely associated with the United States. The bank operated fourteen branches in Puerto Rico, the Virgin Islands, and Panama, and added a fifteenth in Nassau, the Bahamas. Over the next decade Chase built on its strength in these areas, but also spread out to nearby Trinidad, the Dominican Republic, British Guiana, and Tortola in the British Virgin Islands.[21]

The greatest expansion in terms of assets, however, occurred in Puerto Rico, where Chase stood among the premier financial institutions. It operated five branches in that country and opened a sixth in a new fourteen-story headquarters in the Hato Rey section of San Juan in 1969. This new headquarters became a regional center, housing computers to handle many of the accounting functions for branches throughout the eastern Caribbean.

Meanwhile Mexico, the most populous country south of the U.S. border, continued to prohibit foreign banks from either branching or affiliating. Chase was forced to rely on a busy representative office, regretting its decision in 1934 to close the bank's branch then operating (see Chapter I).

Entering the developing countries of Asia

In the Far East a primary strategic objective lay in Southeast Asia, an area rich in rubber, tin, lumber, coconut products, and spices, and blessed with the energetic commercial centers of Singapore and Hong Kong. The effort in the late 1950s to enter the area through acquisition of the Mercantile Bank, however, had ended in failure. It began to appear that direct branching would be necessary, and this posed a problem of manpower.

In 1962 chance intervened. Chase was presented with an opportunity to purchase the Far Eastern branches of the Nationale Handelsbank, a subsidiary of Rotterdamsche Bank in the Netherlands, a close correspondent of Chase. Nationale Handelsbank had operated an extensive network of overseas branches, but the major portion, in Indonesia, had been nationalized, and only offices in Bangkok, Singapore, Hong Kong, and Japan remained.[22] Chase did not want the Japanese branches, for it was already well represented there. They would need to be closed or sold. C. F. Karsten, senior managing director of Rotterdamsche, indicated that he would cooperate in any attempt to dispose of them.

Although Nationale's branches were small (combined assets totaled $31 million), the undeniable advantage of this purchase was in acquiring a business in operation with management personnel on the job. These personnel, trained in language and banking skills in the Netherlands for overseas service, were highly competent and distinguished themselves in other locations in years to come.

The disposition of the Japanese branches held up negotiations until Karsten suggested that Continental Bank in Chicago might be interested.[23] That proved to be true. Chase and Continental soon reached an agreement—implemented, however, only after the Bank of Tokyo was accorded the reciprocal privilege of operating a banking facility in Chicago. Late in 1963, more than a year after talks began, Chase took over branches in Bangkok, Singapore, and Hong Kong. The bank paid Rotterdamsche a premium of $1.5 million, but in turn it sold the Japanese branches to Continental for $1 million.[24] The whole transaction proved to be a consummate bargain.

Shortly thereafter the bank established a new branch in Kuala Lumpur, the capital of Malaysia, linked by trade and historical ties to Singapore. In 1967 it added Korea to the network and in 1968 Indonesia, a country that offered favorable opportunity for modern banking. Less fortunate was the bank's branch in Saigon, established in 1966, the first full-service branch of an American bank in Vietnam. A victim of the war, it was evacuated in 1975 under crisis conditions.[25]

Thus by the end of the 1960s Chase had established a network of nine branches in seven developing areas of Asia, complementing its long-standing branches in Japan.

Branch	Year Acquired or Established
Hong Kong	1963
Bangkok	1963
Singapore	1963
Kuala Lumpur	1964
Saigon	1966
Seoul	1967
Djakarta	1968

Chase facilities in the Philippines and Taiwan would follow in the early 1970s.

Change of strategy in Africa

In Africa at the start of the decade the bank operated branches in Johannesburg and Capetown in South Africa. Others were organized in Lagos, Nigeria, and Monrovia, Liberia, in 1961. South of the Sahara Africa was vast, with only small pockets of industry. Institutions organized by the former colonial powers dominated the banking scene. In the British areas these included the Standard Bank, the Bank of West Africa, Barclay's Overseas Bank, and Grindley's.

Heading the Standard Bank in the early sixties was Sir Cyril Hawker, a former official of the Bank of England. In 1965 he arranged to merge the Bank of West Africa with Standard, creating a combined institution of almost 1,100 branches in seventeen countries with deposits of more than $1.5 billion. In doing so Standard acquired as stockholders three of the London clearing banks that formerly held stock in the Bank of West Africa—the Midland, Westminster, and National Provincial banks. Combined they now held 10 percent of the Standard Bank.[26]

Sir Cyril sought to broaden this tie with the industrial world by enlisting the participation of an American bank, and he approached Chase with this in mind. The proposal attracted both Champion and Rockefeller. Though it required that Chase give up its branches and lose its public identity in South Africa and Nigeria, it opened up substantial local resources that could be utilized through joint marketing arrangements.

Chase wanted a 25 percent participation, but Sir Cyril believed that Chase's share should never exceed the combined holdings of the British clearing banks. After lengthy discussion it was agreed that Chase and the clearing banks could purchase stock on the open market, raising the ownership of each to about 15 percent.[27] Chase's initial investment came to almost $21 million, but this was offset in part by Standard's payment for Chase's branches in South Africa and Lagos. Chase retained its branch in Monrovia, since Standard expressed no interest in Liberia.

By the autumn of 1965 the Chase branches were converted to Standard, but with a plaque that identified each as formerly a branch of The Chase Manhattan Bank. Officers employed by Chase were assigned to work with Standard in South and West Africa, marketing and handling business with U.S. customers. In London, Champion and Victor Rockhill were appointed directors of the parent bank, with a Chase vice president, Charles E. Fiero, designated as principal liaison and adviser to the chairman. Fiero's role was of critical importance, and he discharged it with distinction.

Standard merges with Chartered Bank

Hawker meanwhile sought a wider geographical role for Standard. With this in mind in 1969 he engineered a merger between Standard and the Chartered Bank, another leading British overseas bank which operated branches chiefly in Asia.[28] Chartered maintained facilities in all the Asian countries in which Chase was located, which reduced its value to the bank. Moreover the merger diluted Chase's stock interest in the top holding company, renamed the Standard and Chartered Banking Group, leaving Chase in the end with only 12 percent.

Potentially more troublesome, Chartered also owned a small bank in California, the Chartered Bank of London in San Francisco. Under law Chase could not own stock in another U.S. bank, either directly or indirectly. Chase had voted to approve the merger of Standard and Chartered and at the time had received agreement in writing that the merged bank would adjust its U.S. operations if necessary so that Chase could remain a shareholder.[29]

Although Chase sought from the Federal Reserve an exception that would permit Standard and Chartered to retain its California bank, protracted negotiations proved futile. Chase was given until 1975 to dispose of its interest in Standard and Chartered if it continued to be in violation of the law. Notwithstanding its written agreement with Chase, Standard and Chartered was reluctant to give up the California bank, located in a prime market. Chase finally was forced in May 1975 to sell its interest and break the tie with Standard and Chartered, which by this time had become a bank with assets well in excess of $8 billion. Midland Bank, one of the three London clearing bank shareholders, was the buyer at a price of $78.7 million, yielding Chase a profit of $43.6 million. [30]

Chase was not entirely reluctant to abandon the arrangement. Relations between managements of the banks had deteriorated to some degree. [31] And by the mid-1970s Chase was becoming restless with its lack of identity and freedom of initiative in Africa. Over the rest of the decade it would rebuild its own network in countries of promise south of the Sahara.

Changing policy on South Africa

In South Africa, Chase did not again establish a banking affiliate but carried on with a representative office, a decision initially motivated in part by political considerations. From 1965 through the early 1980s the bank was a prime target for demonstrations, threatened boycotts, and other protests by groups opposed to the apartheid policies of the South African government, who demanded that the bank withdraw completely from relations with customers in South Africa. [32]

Chase responded to these protests in various ways over the years. In the late 1970s the bank issued a comprehensive statement of its position at that time, which it reiterated in the early 1980s. Chase would not extend credit to the government of South Africa or to government-related organizations or to projects that supported the policy of apartheid. But it would also not withdraw completely from economic relations with South Africa. To do so, Chase contended, would be incompatible with the welfare of the blacks. Their most promising road to a better life was through growth and prosperity of the South African economy, which was increasingly dependent on black labor for its well being. American corporations could lead the way in improving working conditions and interracial relations. [33]

Finally, in 1985, as racial unrest escalated, Chase modified its policy and reduced lending to private business in South Africa. The bank did not announce the change publicly, although the fact became known through the marketplace. The decision was taken for reasons of country risk rather than political ones. Credit would continue to be granted to subsidiaries of American corporations that adhered to antiapartheid principles in employment, but then only with guarantees of the parent company.

The internationalization of Chase Manhattan: *the industrial world*

W hile Chase moved ahead with its network in the developing world, it remained relatively passive in the most important markets of all—the heavily industrialized nations—where no new branches or affiliates had been established since the late 1940s. Other American banks were embarking on energetic programs of expansion in Europe, but Chase with branches only in London, Paris, and West Germany, was unable to take advantage of the growing interconnections between economies in the European Common Market and the Free Trade Area.

Cognizant of the problem, Champion and Rockefeller designated Charles E. Fiero, head of the credit department and later liaison officer with Standard, to lay out a plan of action. Fiero was joined by a new recruit, Tilghman B. Koons, and in 1963 the two produced a report that greatly influenced Chase's global expansion for the rest of the decade.[1]

Fiero and Koons rejected the alternative of standing still; Chase was already losing position. Branches in the three main trade centers of Europe supplemented only by correspondent banks did not meet the needs of U.S. customers on the Continent. Fiero and Koons favored the strategy of acquiring affiliates rather than branches, and for many of the same reasons that prevailed in South America. They noted again that management personnel were scarce and that branches could not immediately command the sizable resource base vital to lending. Through affiliates the bank could serve both U.S. subsidiaries and local national businesses. Indeed, they recommended that Chase seek to affiliate with large banks even in countries where it already operated branches.

Champion and Rockefeller were willing to explore affiliating with German and French banks. But after lengthy and frustrating talks with Crédit Commercial de France, the largest private bank in France, and several banks in Germany, including Berliner Handelsgesellschaft, the bank dropped its attempt to move en masse into those large countries and turned to the smaller ones. In the meantime, it also weighed possible action in Canada.

Canada and the Toronto Dominion Bank

As an extension of the U.S. market and the nation's most intimate ally, Canada seemed to be a natural field for expansion. But since the government forbade foreign banks from setting up branches in Canada, the strategic problem was finding a suitable affiliate already chartered.

Rockefeller, who strongly favored a relationship with an existing bank, visited Canada in the spring of 1963 prepared to bring up the matter with Allen Lambert, chairman of Toronto Dominion, the smallest of the major banks but with assets of $2.2 billion and six hundred branches throughout the country. Somewhat to his surprise, Lambert himself raised the possibility of Chase's acquiring a 25 percent interest in the bank. Chase's international exposure and technical competence, Lambert said, would fortify Toronto Dominion.[2]

As the two banks conducted exploratory talks, however, the philosophical differences between Champion and Rockefeller surfaced. Champion doubted that Chase would gain increased relationships with leading businesses by joining forces with a Canadian bank. After all, he contended, many of Canada's largest firms were subsidiaries of U.S. corporations and were already being financed in the United States. Champion commissioned John Hooper, a respected credit officer, to conduct a survey, and after thorough research Hooper came back with the negative answer Champion had expected. Rockefeller, on the other hand, saw the Toronto Dominion partnership not only adding to the effectiveness of the worldwide network but also enabling Chase to share in the future development of the Canadian economy. The required investment was sizable, and the difference in view not quickly resolved.

Meanwhile a new, strongly nationalistic Canadian finance minister took office. First National City's entry into the country through the Mercantile Bank had fanned opposition to any foreign participation in Canadian banking, and by the time Champion agreed to the investment, it was too late. Lambert informed Chase that a partnership was no longer feasible.[3] The opportunity evaporated, and Chase did not penetrate Canada until the 1970s, and then only on a limited basis.

Expanding in Europe

In Europe's smaller nations Chase made up for lost time over the second half of the 1960s. Seven countries received new Chase facilities, affiliations with other banks in Belgium, the Netherlands, Austria, and Ireland, a wholly owned subsidiary in Switzerland, and full-service branches in Greece and Italy (see Table 8).

Table 8.   Chase expansion in Europe, 1966–1969.

Country	Bank	% Initial Participation	Year Acquired or Established
Belgium	Banque de Commerce	49	1966
Austria	Osterreichische Privat-und Kommerzbank, A.G.	75	1966
Netherlands	Nederlandse Credietbank	17½	1967
Ireland	The Chase and Bank of Ireland (International)	50	1968
Switzerland	The Chase Manhattan Bank (Switzerland)	100	1969
Greece	Chase Manhattan branch, Athens	100	1968
Italy	Chase Manhattan branch, Milan	100	1969

Source: Chase Manhattan Bank Archives and *Annual Reports*.

In Belgium the Bank found a cooperative partner in Banque de Bruxelles, the second largest in the country, then headed by Louis Camu, a sophisticated banker well known to Rockefeller. Banque de Bruxelles owned close to 100 percent of the stock of a subsidiary, Banque de Commerce S.A., with offices and branches in Antwerp, Brussels, and Ostend. The bank carried assets of $79 million and did a limited international business. Camu proposed that Chase become an equal partner in this institution.[4] An agreement in principle drawn up for cooperation between Banque de Bruxelles and Chase stated that Banque de Commerce would focus on the business of foreign subsidiaries operating in Belgium and would deal with the international business of Belgian firms that might be handled through Chase's network. Each bank would have an equal stock interest in the affiliate, with Banque de Bruxelles providing the chairman and Chase the managing director.[5]

Once joint ownership was consummated in March 1966, Banque de Commerce fared well under Francis L. Mason, a seasoned officer from the international department, as managing director. But the division of activities with Banque de Bruxelles set forth in the initial agreement failed to materialize. Its Antwerp branches operated with considerable freedom from the head office, and they did not relinquish any international business. Banque de Commerce continued as a relatively small Belgian bank, serving the middle market and smaller business. Over time it also developed relationships with subsidiaries of leading U.S. corporations and came to be identified as Chase's bank, active in its international network.[6]

Within three years deposits of Banque de Commerce increased by more than one-third and loans by two-fifths. The bank expanded during the seventies, with assets exceeding $700 million in 1983. In 1975 Chase sought to acquire Banque de Bruxelles's interest of nearly 50 percent. After an initial rejection by the Federal Reserve, approval finally was gained in May 1978, and Chase assumed almost full ownership. With later changes in name, the bank was known in the mid-1980s as Chase Banque de Commerce in French areas and Chase Handelsbank N.V. in Flemish areas.

Having entered Belgium, Chase turned next to the Netherlands, a country with a long history of trade, stability, and industriousness, and strong ties to American business. Here, as in Belgium, Chase received assistance in its search from a friendly institution, Pierson, Heldring and Pierson (PHP), a leading investment bank.

Engaged with Chase on another venture, PHP acted as a middleman, and for a time as a partner, in bringing Chase together with a medium-sized bank, the Nederlandse Credietbank N.V., with headquarters in Amsterdam.[7] Credietbank operated more than sixty branches and agencies throughout the Netherlands and carried deposits of $120 million. Because it was expanding strongly, needed additional capital, and wanted to develop an international capability, it was willing to permit Chase to acquire a substantial minority interest. Chase wanted at least 35 percent, but opposition from the central bank limited the initial investment to 17½ percent, raised to 30 percent within a few years.[8]

Chase began its association with Nederlandse Credietbank in January 1967, and over the years the two banks developed a highly satisfactory relationship. The chief general manager, Jacques Delsing, a talented executive, cooperated well with Chase, and the bank went out of its way to meet the needs of Chase customers. Credietbank moved ahead expeditiously, and during the 1970s and early 1980s grew to be the fourth largest in the Netherlands, with assets of more than $4.5 billion and one hundred branches blanketing the country. Some 30 percent of its commercial and industrial loans represented credits extended to customers of Chase.[9]

By the early eighties Chase owned 31.5 percent of Nederlandse Credietbank. Then in late 1983 Chase agreed to acquire a 100 percent interest at an attractive price (see Chapter XXII). The Netherlands banking authorities, who two decades earlier had limited Chase to 17½ percent, now posed no objection to full ownership.[10]

A difficult affiliation in Austria

In 1966, some months before joining Nederlandse Credietbank, Chase acquired a controlling interest in a small Austrian bank, Osterreichische

Privat-und Kommerzbank, A.G., a bank founded by the Austrian Christian Labor Union and directed by ranking members of the conservative Austrian Peoples party. Austria was a low priority area for Chase, but the bank had been approached by a third party inquiring whether it might have an interest in purchasing Privat-und Kommerzbank.[11]

Largely because no other opportunity might arise, Chase pursued the offer. The Christian Labor Union wanted to retain a 25 percent interest, and this was thought to be politically advantageous. Chase's 75 percent interest was purchased in May 1966 for $1.154 million with payment of a further $120,000 for an option to purchase the remaining 25 percent if Chase desired. Assets at the time amounted to only $7.8 million.[12]

Chase had hardly installed its own representative when a financial scandal revealed that large bad credits had been extended by Privat-und Kommerzbank to companies headed by a man with strong political ties. To cover them and also to establish a new head office in Vienna's financial center, Chase provided a further $1.475 million to Privat-und Kommerz-bank in late 1967, booked as a "dedicated deposit." In effect the "dedicated deposit" transaction permitted the bank to remain solvent, but at the expense of Chase's total contribution of $2.75 million. That the bad credits were not uncovered prior to the initial investment disturbed Champion and other Chase executives, who believed that the bank had failed to act with its usual diligence.

In 1969 Chase took up its option for the additional 25 percent, renamed the bank Osterreichische Kommerzialbank (the "O.K." bank), and then sold 25.5 percent interest to Girozentrale und Bank der Osterreichischen Sparkas-sen of Vienna, an institution owned by some five hundred Austrian savings banks. For some years this partner provided substantial funding support to the Chase Bank.[13] Later this became unnecessary, and in 1984 Chase took over complete ownership.

Today the bank is known as The Chase Manhattan Bank (Austria). In the early seventies it eliminated accounts of individuals and most small and middle-sized businesses in order to concentrate on multinational firms. The bank became a useful member of the Chase network, serving foreign affiliates and generating income from foreign exchange and classical busi-ness. But in one respect the location proved disappointing: Vienna failed to develop into the busy entrepôt for trade and economic relations with the communist nations that Chase had initially anticipated.

Still another small country of some interest to Chase was Ireland. Although Chase projections suggested that a branch would be unprofitable for a number of years, an attractive alternative became available. The Bank of Ireland, once the bank of issue and the nation's largest, expressed interest in a joint venture. Its able new management, headed by Governor Donal S. A. Carroll, believed that an association with Chase would help counteract any threatened inroads by a First National City branch, recently established, and would enable them to gain knowledge of modern techniques and management from a leading American bank.[14] An agreement was then reached in 1968 to establish The Chase and Bank of Ireland (International), with each partner holding 50 percent.

To form the basis for the venture, the Bank of Ireland separated from its group a wholly owned one-unit bank, rather inappropriately named the National City Bank, with offices in Dublin and assets of $17 million. The bank had originally been established by the Irish Republican Army but had long since become part of the Bank of Ireland family. New branches now were to be opened in the Shannon Industrial Park area and in Belfast in order to be close to U.S. and other foreign industrial investments. The Bank of Ireland would encourage the transfer to the joint venture of the accounts of U.S. and other foreign corporations, as well as much of the overseas business of its Irish customers. Chase would contribute new capital and provide the chief executive, while the Bank of Ireland would hold a majority on the board and nominate the chairman.[15]

The new bank opened for business in August 1968, and for a few years made solid progress. Over time, however, Chase's partner, the Bank of Ireland, acquired skills of its own in multinational banking and was not content with its subordinate role in the joint venture. With superior resources and a dominant position in the banking market, it attracted an increasing number of direct multinational relationships. In 1979 it proved best for both partners that Chase purchase the Bank of Ireland's 50 percent interest. The bank was renamed The Chase Bank (Ireland), and fully integrated into Chase's international network. By 1983 its assets approached $250 million.

A new bank in a leading center

Considerably more important to Chase than Ireland or Austria was Switzerland, long one of the world's great financial centers. Chase maintained especially close correspondent relations with the major Swiss banks, and in 1964 it opened a representative office in Geneva. Largely because of these connections the bank had not established a banking facility. But as other American banks strengthened their presence in Switzerland, Chase recognized that it would need direct representation as an integral part of its worldwide network.

Acquisition of an existing bank was considered, but no suitable institution was available. So Chase set about forming a new bank, designed to carry out wholesale operations and engage in other functions normally associated with Swiss banks—trust activities for individuals and such investment banking functions as private placements, loan syndications, and sale of securities. The new bank, named The Chase Manhattan Bank (Switzerland), opened in March 1969 with capital of $5.8 million, under Karl R. Lasseter, Jr., as general manager.[16]

Even before the new bank opened, a problem concerning Switzerland's bank secrecy laws arose. In granting Chase permission to invest in the Swiss subsidiary, the Federal Reserve Board stipulated that the bank make available adequate information for the Fed's examiners, to be maintained at the head office. But to comply fully would have placed the Swiss subsidiary in violation of Swiss law. This impasse was not resolved until 1973, when the bank agreed to seek signed waivers to the secrecy laws from enough customers to furnish the Federal Reserve a basis for examination. Such information would be maintained in Geneva rather than at the head office. Getting these waivers proved to be a handicap, although not a critical one.[17]

The new bank performed profitably, and after nine months assets reached $47 million, with loans of $16 million, chiefly to U.S. and other foreign subsidiaries. Since the volume of loans was limited by law to ten times capital, the bank placed heavy emphasis on its fee-based services—trust business, sale of Eurobonds, and stock brokerage—in order to remain profitable.[18]

By 1983 the bank's assets were almost $500 million with a net worth of $47 million. Foreign exchange in this money center became especially profitable, and the bank developed into an essential link in the Chase network. Correspondent bank relations were not noticeably damaged by the operation of this direct facility.

Branching in Italy and Greece

Establishment of the Swiss affiliate left only Italy among major European countries uncovered with a facility. The bank maintained a representative office in Rome, but again sought a suitable partner with an existing deposit base. It approached Banca Nazionale dell' Agricoltura, the only privately owned bank with a national branch system. Talks occurred intermittently over several years before Chase terminated them.

Finally in 1969, after loss of valuable time, the bank established a branch in Milan. Soon branches were started also in Rome and Bari. Headed by Frank E. Salerno from the head office, the Italian branches developed adequate sources of funding through the purchase of excess funds from small banks and from the money markets. The branches fared well and were regarded as superior in meeting the needs of Chase to a minority participation in an affiliate.[19]

Branches were also organized in Greece in Athens and Piraeus in 1968 and 1969. In Spain, where branching by foreign banks was not permitted, the bank continued to operate only a representative office. Thus by 1970, with the exception of Scandinavia and the Iberian peninsula, Chase had facilities in place all across Western Europe. As in Switzerland, the establishment of the bank's own facilities did not seriously disrupt correspondent relations elsewhere in the region. In the Soviet Union and Eastern Europe too relations with correspondents expanded, and in 1969 Chase participated in forming a Yugoslav joint development bank.[20]

Across the world in Australia

Another industrial nation, Australia, remained relatively neglected by Chase for a number of years following World War II, although some of its leading banks were good correspondents. Chase International Investment Corporation nudged the bank toward a more active role with an investment in 1961 in a large agricultural project in Western Australia.[21] Then as mineral and other resources began attracting U.S. corporate customers, Chase officers gained more direct acquaintance with the area.

The bank established a representative office in Melbourne in 1965, and in the spring of that year the bank's head office sponsored a day-long seminar on investment opportunities in Australia. Some two hundred senior executives from major corporations gained first hand information from an Australian delegation headed by Harold E. Holt, treasurer of the commonwealth and later prime minister.[22] Spurred on by the seminar's success, the bank sought a more active role in Australian financial affairs.

This proved difficult, for the Australian government did not permit foreign banks to branch or to acquire a meaningful share of an Australian commercial bank. It was possible, however, to invest in "near-bank" financial institutions that provided a wide range of credit and other services. In 1969 Chase finally took this route, joining two leading Australian financial institutions— the National Bank of Australasia, the country's third largest trading bank, and A. C. Goode and Co., a major brokerage firm—to provide the services of a merchant bank. Two separate companies were organized. One, Chase N.B.A., was newly formed to provide medium-term loans, leasing, and investment banking services. For the other the partners acquired an existing company owned by A. C. Goode, All States Commercial Bills, which engaged in short-term money market activities and in discounting commercial bills.[23]

The two companies began business in December 1969, with Chase providing one-third of the capital for the Chase-N.B.A. group and 45 percent of All States's capital. Both companies earned a profit in the first year, and within five years the Chase-N.B.A. group carried assets of almost $200 million, with All States Commercial Bills adding a further $67 million.[24] The companies continued to prosper over the years, but Chase preferred to operate a full-service commercial bank. This finally became possible in 1985, when Australia opened its doors to a limited number of foreign banks. Chase then joined the Australian Mutual Provident Society, the nation's largest insurance company, to form Chase-AMP Bank. To avoid conflicts of interest, participations in Chase-N.B.A. and All States were sold.

Merchant banking: an early attempt

The Australian venture was not Chase's first attempt at merchant banking. The bank had long been interested in the business. Rather paradoxically U.S. commercial banks were barred from major merchant banking activities within their own country, but they could engage in such activities abroad. Chase's unsuccessful partnership with a Brazilian investment firm in the 1950s had ended with the bank selling its interest (see Chapter II). Chase International Investment Corporation performed merchant banking on a modest scale, but Rockefeller in particular believed that Chase should engage more actively in the business, and he took steps in the mid-sixties to organize a new international investment bank with Chase as principal partner.

The time was favorable because growing balance-of-payments constraints were forcing U.S. subsidiaries and other multinationals to rely on European sources of capital. Once allied with leading European banks and investment houses, Chase would be in a position to finance customer needs through the international bond market. To meet this objective Chase lined up five prestigious partners: N. M. Rothschild in London; Banque de Bruxelles and Banque Lambert in Brussels; Pierson, Heldring and Pierson in Amsterdam; and Skandinaviska Enskildabanken in Stockholm. Lengthy discussions were held with members of the group, and agreement was seemingly reached.

A final organizational meeting in the autumn of 1966, however, turned out to be a disappointment. Even as an announcement for the press was prepared, the representative from Stockholm Enskilda Bank asked to see Rockefeller privately and informed him that his bank wished to withdraw.[25] It had been close to Morgan Guaranty over the years and feared that cooperating with Chase in the new venture might jeopardize that relationship. The deal collapsed, but in the light of subsequent developments the failure was probably fortunate.

The formation of Orion

Chase's first successful move into international merchant banking occurred in 1970, the culmination of several years' discussion with two potential partners, the Royal Bank of Canada and National Westminster Bank of Great Britain. The move was labeled internally "the Grand Alliance." The three banks had foreseen the need for large agglomerations of capital to meet the expanding requirements of business and government, but felt that such needs would overtax the resources of any single bank, whereas a working arrangement among the three would strengthen the capacity of each.[26]

Various relationships were considered, but in the end two forms of organization were determined to offer the most promising start: a medium-term lending bank to provide Eurocurrency loans of five- to ten-years' range to multinational corporations and governments, and a merchant bank to advise multinational companies, engage in underwriting and placement of bond issues and consortium loans, and provide other services traditionally offered by merchant banks.

In late October 1970 the banks (by then joined by Westdeutsche Landesbank) formally announced their plan of organization.[27] Three separate units were created, all under the name The Orion Group:

- Orion Bank, Ltd. (OBL), the newly formed merchant bank, capitalized at £10 million
- Orion Term Bank, Ltd. (OTB), for the provision of medium-term Eurodollar financing, also capitalized at £10 million
- Orion Multinational Services, Ltd. (OMSL), a marketing service, liaison, and new projects staff

The addition of Credito Italiano (1971) and Mitsubishi Bank (1972) fortified the consortium but reduced Chase's share in the merchant bank from 32 to 20 percent and in the term bank from 25 to 20 percent.

John C. Haley, head of Chase's activities in Central and Eastern Europe, took charge of Multinational Services and became chief executive officer of the group. Multinational Services performed a coordinating role between the merchant bank and the term bank, as well as between the parent banks and the consortium.

Within three years the term bank had become one of the world's largest consortium banks and a major participant in the Eurodollar market for syndicated medium-term credits.[28] The merchant bank, which developed more slowly, provided an advisory service on corporate finance (but was less active with mergers and acquisitions), took small equity positions in connection with underwriting and loans, and entered the secondary trading market for Eurobonds.

By 1974, with the growth of the petrodollar market, Chase itself was becoming more directly involved in many of Orion's activities. The record of this development and of the competition between Chase and the consortium bank it fostered is related in Chapter XV.

The major branches: mainstay of the network

Notwithstanding the great effort put into expansion through affiliates and branches in many new countries, the bank's major overseas branches in London, Paris, Frankfort, and Tokyo continued to dominate the system. Of the $5 billion in foreign branch deposits in 1969, these four branches accounted for more than two-thirds.[29]

The leader was the London branch, with deposits of $2 billion, swollen because it had become a center through which Eurodollar funds were raised for use at the head office. This activity had become one of the most important functions of the London branch. Each morning Barry Sullivan, then the branch manager, or his money market deputy, spoke with the New York executives to determine amounts to be raised and rates to be offered.[30] London then passed along instructions to Paris and Frankfort. The London office also acquired dollars and sterling for its own use and helped fund credits for other branches and affiliates.

The volume of foreign exchange transactions surged, and the branches adopted a more aggressive lending policy. New managers and young credit officers, trained in the United States, replaced their more cautious predecessors. Chase's German branches led other American banks in extending credit in that country.[31] The Paris branch stood second only to Morgan Guaranty, and the London branch was gaining rapidly on First National City.

Some credits were extended in dollars, obtained through the Eurodollar market, but for the most part loans were funded in local currency raised in the money market or through special lending arrangements with other banks or the central bank. Stringent balance-of-payments controls in the United States resulted in the transfer of foreign loans from the head office to the branches, especially London, but with volume restricted later in the decade.

On the other side of the globe, in Japan, the branch also made good progress, carrying on the largest and most profitable activity of the three American banks located there.[32] The three banks continued to be depositories for a large portion of Japan's central bank reserves. Although in dollars, the deposit at Chase of more than $100 million was carried on the books of the Tokyo branch.

Much of the activity of the Japanese branches was directed toward financing trade with the United States. The large central bank balance initially served as collateral for opening letters of credit for Japanese banks to finance U.S. imports. And a sizable volume of financing was carried out through bankers acceptances. During the sixties the branch began to provide dollar term loans to Japanese companies, funded out of New York and guaranteed by Japanese banks. These loans provided compensating balances in yen, available for local credit. Other yen deposits were generated through military banking facilities and limited swap arrangements with the central bank. But a shortage of yen placed a major constraint on the branch.[33]

The international advisory committee

In 1965, with its worldwide network growing, Chase formed an international advisory committee to provide further counsel on its foreign activities. The group included eleven chief executives from foreign nonfinancial firms and ten from the United States, with Champion, Rockefeller, and the head of the international department as ex-officio members.[34] Meetings were held twice a year, with discussions covering economic, business, and political trends, as well as matters of special concern to the bank, such as corporate planning, personnel policies, options for expansion abroad, and the like. The exchange of views proved open and candid.

As the committee's first chairman, the bank selected John H. Loudon, recently retired as chief executive of Royal Dutch Shell. Loudon had unquestionable prestige and a wide knowledge of international business and was acquainted with corporate leaders. Other original members were also prominent in their countries and their fields, among them Lord Cole of Unilever, Giovanni Agnelli of Fiat, Wilfrid Baumgartner of Rhône-Poulenc, and Taizo Ishizaka, head of Keidanren in Japan. From the United States came William Blackie of Caterpillar Tractor, Carl Gerstacker of Dow Chemical, William Hewitt of Deere, and David Packard of Hewlett-Packard. Successors through the years were no less distinguished. Normally the committee traveled abroad for every third meeting. These sessions provided an opportunity to meet with political leaders as well as senior business executives, most of whose companies were customers of the bank.

The international advisory committee more than fulfilled the objectives set for it. And it provided ancillary benefits. Its well-publicized meetings in foreign countries brought the bank the favorable attention of government and public alike. Moreover, foreign members on occasion rendered valuable assistance in their own countries. Although the committee required an outlay of money and time, Champion, Rockefeller, and their successors concluded that it constituted a highly useful addition to a truly international institution and was worth the effort.[35]

Progress with the network

The formation of the international advisory committee symbolized Chase's progress in building its overseas network, covering seventy-three areas by 1970. The bank had gone far toward meeting its objective of fulfilling the needs of customers worldwide. Subsidiaries of U.S. corporations were major customers, complementing relationships at the head office. But the network also attracted local companies. It held an advantage especially for firms concerned with transferring credit and funds between operations in different nations, a process made increasingly feasible by the convertibility of major currencies and growing freedom from exchange controls.

Benefits from this worldwide network as a whole were greater than the sum of its parts. Chase, for example, was able to strengthen a relationship with Renault in Paris because it could extend credit in Venezuela while taking compensation in Paris.[36] More than one new account was gained at the head office because of the ability to accommodate customers through affiliates in the Netherlands, Belgium, or Brazil. The rewards for such relationships were not always fully revealed in the accounts of the affiliates or branches that contributed to them, but to the overall corporation they were tangible.

All told the bank had expended almost $72 million to acquire a share in affiliates and other associated financial institutions in developed and developing countries. These institutions possessed combined assets of nearly $5 billion and deposits of over $4 billion by the end of the 1960s.[37] They formed an integral part of the Chase network which could not have been constructed so swiftly or comprehensively in their absence.

Still there were disadvantages to the affiliate system. The direct financial return on investment was relatively low, in part because at that time only remitted dividends were included as income. In 1969 the return averaged 4.3 percent, far below the bank's 11 percent return on its total capital.[38] Moreover, the lack of full ownership limited the bank's ability to integrate affiliates fully into its network. Partnership with Belgium's Banque de Bruxelles and the Bank of Ireland had not worked out as planned. Through the years therefore the bank sought to expand its ownership to 100 percent. Nevertheless, where feasible, branches came to be the preferred instrument.

The progress of the branch system had in itself been extraordinary. From 1960 to the end of 1970 deposits in foreign branches grew tenfold to almost $7 billion, accounting at the latter date for almost a third of the bank's aggregate. Loans advanced at a similar pace to $2.7 billion, representing a somewhat smaller proportion of the bank's total.[39] A considerable volume of overseas deposits, acquired in the Eurodollar market, was transferred to the head office, avoiding serious problems for the bank during the credit crunch of 1969.

On the earnings side the contribution was more modest, amounting in 1970 to $21 million after taxes (including earnings of affiliates), or 16 percent of all earnings reported.[40] Over the next few years, as we shall see in Part Three, the bank would move to diversify its facilities and activities in many countries. Deposits, loans, and earnings overseas would all increase greatly and finally come to surpass the domestic.

Adjusting to a world of heightened risk: 1970–1976

World banking grew increasingly risky over the first half of the seventies. Inflation and recession, breakdown of the international monetary system, the OPEC energy crisis, disruption of payments between nations all left their mark on Chase. Interest rates and exchange rates became highly volatile. Assets moved sharply upward, more so abroad than in the United States. Earnings also advanced, but so too did loan losses. The bank in 1975–76 experienced its most difficult times.

Notwithstanding this troubled environment, Chase continued to expand its activities and facilities. Establishment of its holding company in mid-1969 provided added flexibility. Offices for loan production, real estate credit, and international services were located in selected cities, and the bank's branches spread out over New York State. But its major effort to expand nationwide, through merger with Dial Financing Corporation, was denied by regulatory authorities.

International expansion outdid domestic as the bank rounded out and diversified its network of branches, affiliates, and subsidiaries. Few major countries remained uncovered, and those chiefly because of legal restrictions. Through Rockefeller's initiative Chase opened up relationships with the Soviet Union and the People's Republic of China. And the bank greatly expanded its role in merchant banking through fully owned subsidiaries headquartered in London and Hong Kong.

Troubles in 1975 and 1976 affected all banks, but more so Chase because of its paramount position in real estate, a field especially hard hit.

185

Table 9.   Statistical profile, 1970–1976.[a]

	Assets	Loans and Mortgages	Deposits	Equity Capital
1970	24.5	13.9	21.2	1.105
1971	24.5	14.3	20.4	1.176
1972	30.7	17.0	25.0	1.262
1973	36.8	22.1	29.9	1.348
1974	42.5	27.8	34.7	1.446
1975	41.4	28.6	33.9	1.621
1976	45.6	30.7	37.6	1.667

	Domestic Loans and Mortgages	Domestic Commercial and Industrial Loans[b]	Overseas Loans	Income Before Security Gains (Losses) (Millions)
1970	11.2	6.6	2.7	133.0
1971	11.0	6.4	3.3	147.7
1972	12.9	6.2	4.4	148.3
1973	13.9	6.9	8.2	164.7
1974	17.3	9.2	10.5	182.0
1975	16.6	7.6	12.1	156.6
1976	17.2	6.6	13.5	105.1

[a]Year-end figures, expressed in billions of dollars.
[b]Excludes short-term money market instruments in the form of bankers acceptances.
Source: Annual Reports of The Chase Manhattan Corporation. Domestic Commercial and Industrial Loans, Reports to the Comptroller of the Currency.

Net loan charge-offs and nonperforming loans rose to extraordinary levels, with real estate accounting for the major share. The Chase Manhattan Real Estate Trust moved toward bankruptcy. And in New York City a crisis in finances, which Chase and other major banks helped greatly to resolve, added to the problems. Earnings fell off substantially, although never to a point of threatening the dividend. While the bank's image suffered, policies were put in place to engineer the subsequent recovery and renewed expansion of the late 1970s. (See Table 9 for a statistical profile covering the years 1970–1976.)

Changes in top management also occurred in this period. Rockefeller took over as sole chief executive in early 1969 with the retirement of Champion. Herbert P. Patterson was then appointed president, but was succeeded in October 1972 by Willard C. Butcher.

Reorganizing under a holding company

Chase in the late 1960s undertook a major change in organization, unrelated to its foreign expansion. A top holding company, The Chase Manhattan Corporation, was established, with The Chase Manhattan Bank as its dominant affiliate. Soon the first nonbanking affiliates, closely related to the bank itself, were put in place. Meanwhile other significant organizational changes occurred. Champion retired in early 1969 after reaching the mandatory age, leaving Rockefeller as sole chief executive. Herbert P. Patterson was appointed president, with John B. M. Place and George A. Roeder, Jr., vice chairmen. The bank then reviewed and revamped its organizational structure, positioning itself more effectively for the future.

Initially The Chase Manhattan Corporation was created as a one-bank holding company. Such an organization was not a new idea; a number of industrial and retail companies owned single banks. For banks, however, one-bank holding companies possessed a singular advantage: they fell outside the scope of Federal Reserve regulation, which applied only to holding companies owning at least 25 percent of two or more banks.[1] Commercial banks sought to exploit this advantage, seeking to escape from the bonds of federal regulation.

Union Bank of Los Angeles led off this organizational change among larger banks, becoming the first to form a one-bank holding company. Major banks in North Carolina soon indicated their intention of taking similar action. Then in July 1968 First National City surprised the banking world with an announcement that it too would establish such a company in order to broaden its range of services.[2] A veritable stampede toward this type of organization quickly developed. In less than a year seventy banks had either formed one-bank holding companies or announced their intention of doing so, including all major banks in New York City not already under holding companies—except Chase.

Unlike the others, Chase was in no hurry to make this change. The unsuccessful experience with a holding company in the mid-1960s had made Champion and Rockefeller cautious, and Champion especially had always been reluctant to see the bank diminish its identity within such an organization. Nevertheless, the bank undertook a new study to determine what might be accomplished by converting to a one-bank holding company.

187

Advantage of a one-bank holding company

The one great advantage, it soon became apparent, was added flexibility: in the types of service that could be offered, in management, and possibly in financing.[3] The holding company could escape some of the restrictions and regulations that increasingly affected banks in competition. Such services as factoring, leasing, and credit cards could be operated out of offices located in various parts of the country, unhampered by geographical restrictions on banks as deposit institutions. Moreover, a range of entirely new services might become open to a holding company, not all necessarily closely related to banking.

This last possibility conjured up in the eyes of the general public (and some in Congress) an image of major banks taking over large industrial corporations, railroads, or other businesses. No bank had such a plan in mind. But the thought that it could legally be possible spurred Congress to start work immediately on legislation to control one-bank holding companies, adding a large measure of uncertainty to the future. For a national bank like Chase, affiliation with any other company required approval of the comptroller, who generally had been sympathetic to broadening the range of activities for banks.

Such new services as insurance, mortgage banking, broadly based computer services, management consulting, and even savings and loan institutions might be open to bank holding companies. First National City Corporation announced plans to acquire the Chubb Corporation, a major insurer engaged in property, casualty, and life underwriting, only to drop the venture after the Department of Justice threatened suit.[4] Chase, with the heads of three major insurance companies as directors, seemed unlikely to engage in that industry.

The bank did, however, want to broaden its activities in factoring, leasing, real estate, and computer-based services. It was especially interested in real estate, for forecasts by its economists suggested that a huge expansion lay ahead in demand for mortgage and other real estate financing. The real estate department saw advantages in entering the mortgage banking business as well as sponsoring a real estate investment trust, a relatively new organization for raising and investing funds.

Nor was the bank unmindful of the possible future use of a holding company to expand upstate, following the path it had attempted a few years earlier, only to be frustrated by regulatory authorities. The corporation would no longer be a one-bank holding company, but the distinction sooner or later would probably disappear. Antitrust considerations, however, limited the potential for acquisitions, and expansion upstate no longer constituted a reason in itself for forming a holding company.

Meanwhile the study suggested other advantages in flexibility, although none was compelling. If a new business was to be organized in a separate affiliate, it might attract and compensate management in a manner that would be difficult to carry out under the salary and benefit structure of the bank. On the financing side, the holding company might issue commercial paper unhampered by statutory borrowing restrictions on the bank. And it could possibly carry a higher ratio of debt to equity, depending on the nature of its nonbanking affiliates. Internationally too the holding company might be helpful, although the wide powers accorded to Edge Act corporations reduced its usefulness in this respect.

Establishment of The Chase Manhattan Corporation

None of these advantages in flexibility would have impelled Chase to initiate the trend toward one-bank holding companies. Nevertheless, Rockefeller and new, younger management about to take over saw the potential benefits of greater flexibility and were concerned that other banks might gain competitively. Champion and a majority of the directors were reluctant to move into this new organization, but recognized that the bank needed to keep open its competitive options. So after thorough discussion the directors on January 8, 1969, approved the establishment of The Chase Manhattan Corporation, with The Chase Manhattan Bank its sole bank affiliate.[5] On June 4 the new holding company came into being.

First moves toward diversification

Rockefeller at the annual meeting in March 1969 assured stockholders that the holding company would restrict its investments to fields closely related to banking and finance. There was no intention to become a conglomerate. He mentioned specifically that the bank hoped to broaden its activities in factoring, credit cards, and real estate financing, and would investigate computer services related to financing.[6]

Chase had already entered the factoring business in December 1968, with the acquisition of Shapiro Brothers, a leading privately owned firm engaged in factoring and general commercial finance, areas of more rapid growth at that time than conventional bank loans to business. Shapiro, which dated back to the late nineteenth century, was active especially in textile financing. It maintained a subsidiary, Berkeley Finance Corporation, based in Boston and operating in New England. Shapiro realized an annual volume in factoring and commercial finance of $435 million.[7] It was set up as the Shapiro Factors Division of the bank under the metropolitan department, and Berkeley Finance in effect became a loan production office, generating credits that were made at the head office.

Shapiro Factors was retained within the bank rather than transferred to the holding company. Its activities were further expanded later in 1969 by the acquisition of Interstate Factors Corporation, a subsidiary of Reeves Brothers of New York City, which contributed an additional volume of $230 million.[8] In the course of a year, Chase had become a substantial participant in the factoring business.

Although Shapiro Factors remained in the bank, Chase lost little time in making use of the new holding company. In September 1969 it reached agreement to acquire Dovenmuehle, a moderate-sized mortgage banking concern based in Chicago.[9] And in October the corporation announced that it would acquire United States Leasing International, with headquarters in San Francisco.[10] Both operated in fields of priority for the bank.

Rockefeller and the executive office were conscious of limits placed on acquisitions by antitrust considerations. Dovenmuehle appealed to the bank in this regard as being of acceptable size and quality. It specialized in originating loans and mortgages on homes, apartments, and office buildings, with a volume in the current year of around $60 million. Moreover it serviced for customers a mortgage portfolio of some $355 million. The acquisition was completed in December 1969, and the company continued to operate as an autonomous, wholly owned subsidiary of the corporation.

United States Leasing was substantially larger, with a net worth of $23.5 million. It aimed primarily to assist medium-sized and small business in acquiring equipment, with leases outstanding to 47,000 firms. In this respect it complemented Chase's own leasing, which dealt largely with big ticket items such as aircraft, locomotives, and computers. The firm maintained forty offices throughout the United States and Canada, and also owned interests in leasing companies in the United Kingdom, West Germany, Sweden, and Japan. The company had expanded rapidly, with yearly earnings increasing an average of 20 percent over the previous five years. Chase agreed to pay a substantial premium through an exchange of shares that involved a small dilution in Chase earnings.

Problems with holding company legislation

The acquisition of United States Leasing, approved by both parties and announced to the public, was held in abeyance while Congress debated the regulation of one-bank holding companies. Here a marked difference arose between the House and the Senate. Firms threatened with competition from bank holding companies lobbied intensively, and insurance agents, travel agents, and other small businessmen descended in droves on the Capitol. They found a sympathetic ear in Congressman Wright Patman, chairman of the House Banking Committee.

George Roeder, Jr., now vice chairman of Chase, testified before the House committee in May 1969, urging that any definition of the scope of permissible activities for a holding company be as flexible as possible in order to accommodate the changing needs of the economy.[11] He suggested a number of permissible fields, all related to finance. And he pointed out that it made little sense to impose a geographic limitation on holding company subsidiaries that were not deposit-gathering institutions, for to do so would place them in an impossible competitive position against firms operating free of such restrictions.

The House, spurred on by Patman, took little heed of the testimony of Roeder and others. It passed what in effect was punitive legislation.[12] Although geographic restrictions were not imposed, one-bank holding companies would be specifically prohibited, with minor exceptions, from engaging in such activities as insurance, equipment leasing, accounting, data processing, and travel agencies. Moreover, companies that had acquired subsidiaries in these fields since May 9, 1956 (the date of the previous Holding Company Act), would be required to divest them or get out of the banking business. The bill came as a surprise, for the full Banking Committee had overridden its chairman and recommended much more liberal legislation. But Patman, aided by the lobbyists, had rewritten the legislation from the floor.

Passage by the House came only a week after Chase and United States Leasing announced plans for their affiliation. A large element of uncertainty had suddenly been introduced into the transaction. The Senate was still to be heard from, and there were signs that it would be more lenient. But neither Chase nor United States Leasing could be sure, and it was not clear when the Senate would act. United States Leasing in particular would be inconvenienced by delay. Therefore, toward the end of January 1970, three months after announcing the proposed joinder, the two parties decided to terminate the arrangement.[13]

Chase Manhattan Mortgage and Realty Trust

Action by most banks on holding company affiliates remained frozen while Congress continued to debate legislation. Chase, however, was confident enough about the position of real estate to announce in April 1970 that it would organize and sponsor a closed-end real estate investment trust.[14] The trust had been strongly recommended by Raymond T. O'Keefe, executive vice president in charge of the real estate department, who agreed with the bank's economists that the demand for real estate financing would grow greatly in the 1970s. Many creditworthy opportunities would be available that the bank itself could not meet, the more so since it had to rely increasingly on short-term borrowed money. Establishing the trust would open up another large source of funds, and the bank, as adviser, would provide the bulk of the investments, earning a sizable fee in the process. Other Chase subsidiaries could also cooperate, especially Dovenmuehle and Housing Investment Corporation, a mortgage banking subsidiary active in Puerto Rico, acquired by the bank in 1969.

The trust went to the market for its initial capital in June 1970, offering a package that raised $100 million—$60 million by an issue of shares of beneficial interest and $40 million through convertible debentures.[15] The bulk of the trust's financing, however, was to be short-term, primarily bank loans and commercial paper. The shares (similar in many respects to equity) were listed on the New York Stock Exchange, appearing in the stock tables just under The Chase Manhattan Corporation, and the debentures were carried in the tables on bonds.

Although Chase had no ownership of the trust, the two were clearly identified in the eyes of the public. The directors agreed that the name Chase Manhattan could be used so long as the trust operated under an investment advisory agreement with the bank or one of its subsidiaries. And they approved of Chase officers becoming directors or officers of the trust, provided that a majority of the directors were not associated with Chase. The initial trustees included a number of men prominent in real estate. O'Keefe served as chairman, and Adam C. Heck, a vice president with long experience in the accounting and operations side of the bank, retired to take on the presidency. Heck immediately set up a small headquarters in Boston, since the trust was organized under the laws of Massachusetts.

At the outset the bank, as adviser, provided the trust with a sizable group of real estate investments from its own portfolio.[16] The trust's investments in the early stages were primarily relatively short-term construction loans, but it intended to reach out into intermediate and longer-term financing of office buildings, apartments, and shopping centers. It would also extend loans against land and provide funds for real estate development, financing the various steps necessary to convert unimproved land into finished sites for residential or commercial buildings. Over the next few years the trust entered into all these forms of investment, most of which were obtained by the real estate department of the bank, acting as adviser, with help from Dovenmuehle and the Housing Investment Corporation.

The trust came on the scene at a propitious moment. Real estate had suffered under rising interest rates over the previous several years, but now it was entering a boom period. Moreover, the trust possessed a major advantage for investors, inasmuch as most of the income it distributed to holders of certificates was exempt from federal income tax. Its assets grew to $750 million within three years, and its share price more than doubled. But it also contained the seeds of trouble that would emerge later under difficult and unforeseen conditions.

The Bank Holding Company Act of 1970

Congress did not resolve the one-bank holding company problem until December 1970, more than a year after the House adopted its punitive legislation. Meanwhile, attention had concentrated on the Senate, with favorable results. In the spring Rockefeller appeared before the Senate Banking Committee as a member of an unusual panel that also included the heads of First National City, Bank of America, and Wells Fargo.[17] The panel urged the Senate not to place banks in a legislative strait jacket, as had the House, but to provide flexibility to meet the needs of a growing and complex economy. They assured the senators that their banks had no desire to spread into fields unrelated to finance.

The senators took these suggestions to heart. The final legislation contained no list of prohibited activities, although it did place one-bank holding companies, along with multibank companies, under regulation of the Federal Reserve Board, which was to determine the activities permissible for bank holding companies. These were required to be bank related, and in this respect the new law employed language similar to that of the 1956 act: "so closely related to banking or managing or controlling banks as to be a proper incident thereto."[18]

The board was also required to find that an affiliation would result in public benefits, such as greater convenience, increased competition, or gains in efficiency, that would outweigh such possible adverse effects as undue concentration, decreased competition, conflict of interest, or unsound banking practices. And the act provided a more liberal framework for "grandfathering" nonapproved activities, with those started before June 30, 1968, not requiring early divestment.

In general the new act resembled that of 1956 in many respects. The distinction between one-bank and multibank holding companies had been removed. But it remained for the Federal Reserve to determine the activities permissible for bank holding companies. The suspense did not last long, but the resolution was disappointing. Within three months the Federal Reserve published its list.[19] Traditional activities in which Chase was most interested were included, mortgage banking, factoring, leasing, and consumer financing among them. So too was advising a real estate investment trust. But such pathbreaking fields as insurance (other than credit insurance), management consulting, and savings and loan institutions were missing. Approval of any acquisition of meaningful size would be difficult under the criteria set forth in the law. Moreover the bank was restricted by law in its lending to other affiliates in the corporation, although it could provide funds directly to its own subsidiaries. All this limited the usefulness of the holding company, especially in the early years.

An exception arose in the field of financing. Federal Reserve ceiling rates did not apply to commercial paper issued by a bank holding company. The credit squeeze of late 1969 and early 1970 was relieved to some degree through the sale of loans by the bank to the holding company, which the latter financed with commercial paper. Initially the directors placed a limit on the volume of such paper, but this soon was removed, leaving management to exercise prudent judgment.

Retirement of Champion

Shortly after the decision to form the holding company, George Champion retired as chairman. Both he and Lawrence Marshall, vice chairman, reached the mandatory age in early 1969. David Rockefeller became chairman and sole chief executive officer.[20]

Champion had left his mark on the bank for more than a generation. He had come up through the ranks in the old commercial loan department to become president and then chairman, and was widely and favorably known in financial and business circles. Champion was conservative, both in banking and in his political views. In many respects he was a banker's banker, with a nose for bad credits that kept the staff on the alert. To the wider public he was a staunch advocate of free enterprise and minimal government intervention, speaking out often on these themes. But he also possessed a human touch—a good golfer, bridge player, and companion. And he never lost interest in the staff down the line. It was Champion who in the early postwar years started the management training program and headed the committee that introduced innovative personnel policies.

The bank had grown considerably under the joint stewardship of Champion and Rockefeller. Assets had more than doubled in the eight years, 1961 to 1969, from $9.3 billion to $19.4 billion, with deposits increasing from $8.1 billion to $16.7 billion. First National City had grown a bit more rapidly and now exceeded Chase slightly in published figures; but Chase remained the larger domestic bank, while First National City gained its margin through foreign branches. Many of Chase's foreign affiliates, however, were excluded in such accounting.

Comparative size was given close scrutiny by Chase. Little concern was felt about Bank of America (the nation's largest), for it was regarded as a different type of institution, a huge savings bank, among other things, with its statewide system of branches in California. But First National City remained a prime competitor. Chase could not ignore size as one objective in planning, and concern was expressed that First National City seemed to be growing more rapidly. Nevertheless, quality and leadership in markets of its choosing held priority among Chase's objectives with both Champion and Rockefeller.

Champion never lost his preference for the wholesale side of banking, and it continued to form the backbone of Chase's business. He had favored the merger with Manhattan and expansion in retail branches, but had not pushed retail business with the same aggressiveness as First National City. The latter had moved ahead of Chase in number of domestic branches, and Chase continued to lag in consumer loans, although its relative position had improved.

In one highly important respect, however, the Chase culture changed dramatically during the joint tenure of Champion and Rockefeller. The bank departed from its propensity toward foreign correspondent banking and engaged vigorously in building a worldwide network of branches and affiliates. Here Rockefeller had been the principal architect, at times with only reluctant agreement from Champion, whose approach had been highly conservative. But in one respect Champion's conservatism played a healthy role: he insisted on quality in management for foreign branches and affiliates, and he made extensive changes among personnel to provide it.

Champion remained a director after retirement, serving on the examination and compensation committees, but he left the board in late 1971 under changed rules governing the retirement of directors. The board adopted a resolution expressing its gratitude for Champion's long and valuable service.[21] The bank also honored him by establishing an annual award of $50,000 over a five-year period, The George Champion Award for Community Service, to be given to a nonprofit institution in the New York area in recognition of Champion's efforts over the years on behalf of numerous community organizations.[22] Champion began a new career devoted to public service as chairman and chief executive of the Economic Development Council of New York City. Under his leadership the council assumed a larger role in city affairs and pointed the way to many improvements in the city's government and economy, benefiting business generally.

The new management

The new team—David Rockefeller, Herbert Patterson, John Place, and George Roeder—formed an executive office with overall responsibility for management of the bank.[23] The group was young, with an average age of forty-seven. The three who now joined Rockefeller at the top had benefited from varied experience. Roeder and Place had spent their early years in the United States department, the breeding ground for past leadership, but Patterson had risen through the ranks in the international department, although dealing largely with its U.S. and Canadian business. In the 1960s all three were prepared for larger responsibility by heading departments new to each.

Rockefeller, ever oriented toward techniques of modern management, sought through the executive office a means of better delegating authority while ensuring coordination. Although as chief executive he held responsibility for the entire bank, he intended to concentrate on the development of long-range strategy and plans as well as on the bank's external relationships. This left for Patterson the huge task of overseeing the bank's operations and dealing with internal problems. Patterson would be aided in this by the two vice chairmen, Place supervising the three major banking departments and Roeder the other line departments. The four members of the executive office met regularly each week with a planned agenda and gathered together on call to settle ad hoc problems.

The management changes in 1969 were a landmark. The prewar generation of bankers passed from the scene, and the postwar generation took over leadership. Other positions that opened up in the senior executive ranks were filled with relatively young men. Two were of notable importance: Leonor F. Loree II was appointed head of corporate staff and a key aide to the president, and Willard C. Butcher took charge of the international department, gaining further experience that later would serve him well as president.

Internal reorganization of the bank

With new management and senior officers at the helm, Rockefeller determined to undertake a thorough examination of the internal organization of the bank. No comprehensive study had been made since the work of the Bower committee following the merger of Chase and Manhattan in 1955 (see Chapter V). A number of important ad hoc changes had been introduced over the years. The vital back office operations of the bank (discussed in Chapter XX) were brought together in a central unit in 1963 to take maximum advantage of the revolutionary new computer equipment then being introduced. In 1964 a new department, fiduciary investment, was separated from trust in order to handle more effectively the burgeoning pension trust business. And in 1965 a department of credit and loan standards was established to serve as the focal point within the bank on lending policies and practices, as well as a center for preparing Chase for new types of financing opportunities. Lending had become so extensive and varied, with authority delegated down the line, that written policies had to be laid out carefully in a manual for loan officers.

The bank also brought together in a single investment banking department its portfolio investment, money gathering, Wall Street relations, and government and municipal bond operations. The latter activity was augmented in 1969 when Chase became a dealer in U.S. government securities, in addition to its long-standing dealing in general obligations of states and municipalities.[24] Despite these changes, the structure of the lending departments, the basic business of the bank, remained unchanged.

McKinsey and Company were retained as consultants to help review the internal organization. A number of problems were apparent. Wholesale banking relationships were carried out by the United States department and by large branches in New York City, each reporting to different executives. Within the United States department officers were responsible for relationships with corporate customers as well as correspondent banks and other financial institutions, two different markets. Moreover the old problem still existed of adequate coordination in customer relations between the international department, with its officers abroad, and departments handling wholesale business at the head office. This problem was further complicated in 1969, when the international department established an Edge Act subsidiary in Los Angeles.[25] While the subsidiary was limited to doing business of an international character, it dealt on the spot with many customers of the United States department.

All these matters were considered at length in the review, but the interested parties did not always reach a full consensus. In the end it was decided to replace the United States and metropolitan departments with three new line units: corporate banking, institutional banking, and personal banking, soon renamed community banking (see Figure 5).[26] Corporate banking was to handle all relationships with medium-sized and large businesses throughout the United States. Institutional banking would take over accounts of correspondent banks, saving institutions, insurance and finance companies, major church groups, and state and municipal government agencies. And personal banking would concentrate on retail service to individuals and smaller business, including administration of the domestic branch system. Both the corporate and institutional banking units would station officers in a few key branches around New York City to handle accounts that fell within their jurisdictions. The establishment of institutional banking as a separate department was expected to place greater focus on this business, and particularly correspondent banking, in which the bank had once been preeminent but had recently lost some market share.

With the separation of institutional banking, one further issue arose concerning corporate banking: whether to continue to organize the department along geographic lines with a few special industry units, or to shift completely to an industry basis. With the growing complexity of American industry, much could be said in favor of organizing along industry lines. Such a change on top of others, however, would cause serious disruption, and it was not adopted at that time. Yet as a practical matter considerable industry expertise existed among loan officers, with the auto industry being handled in the division responsible for Michigan, apparel and shipping in the New York City division, and machinery in the Midwest division. Meanwhile the special industry divisions—petroleum, public utility, and aerospace—remained unchanged, and a staff of technical directors, now covering most industries of complexity, was on hand to counsel and assist loan officers.

Organization of the international department

More complicated from a management point of view was the international department. With branches and affiliates operating diverse businesses in all parts of the world, control proved difficult. In 1970 a new organization introduced a management task approach as well as division into geographic units. Relations with correspondent banks and government institutions were placed in a separate division and directed from the head office in New York. Three heads of broad geographical areas managed branches, affiliate banks, and commercial and industrial relationships around the world, assisted by functional executives in fields such as operations and personnel, performing on a worldwide basis. Such functions as funding, foreign exchange, planning, and expansion were coordinated from the head office.[27]

Relations between corporate banking and the international department on multinational corporate accounts had been clarified but in practice were sometimes hard to carry out. The corporate banking officer served as relationship manager of an account, responsible for coordinating it throughout the world. The statutory limit on credit to a single borrower provided a compelling reason for a single point of control. But relationship managers at the head office could not always assure a customer that credit would be available in far-off places like Japan and Australia, or even Germany and the Netherlands. Country managers frequently had to weigh diverse uses for their limited resources and found it inopportune at times to meet demands from the head office.

In addition to changes in line departments, the corporate personnel function was also overhauled. Rockefeller had not been satisfied by the manner in which this function was being handled. A new human resources department was formed to include personnel administration, organizational planning, management development, recruiting, and other relevant activities.[28] The new department provided policy guidance, consultation, and coordination for all areas of the bank.

Except for specialists, most management and banking positions continued to be filled from within the bank. Midcareer hiring from outside for such positions was not yet an accepted practice at Chase, whose paternalistic approach to personnel had not been seriously altered. But officers who left the bank did return on occasion. One of these was Paul A. Volcker, who returned to Chase in 1965 as vice president in charge of forward planning after serving as deputy undersecretary of the U.S. Treasury. Volcker left again in 1969 to be undersecretary for monetary affairs, going on to become

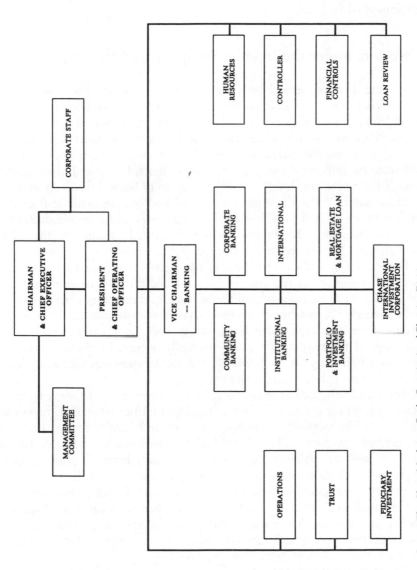

Source: The Chase Manhattan Bank, Organizational Planning Division

Figure 5. The Chase Manhattan Bank, N.A., organization, 1971.

president of the Federal Reserve Bank of New York and then chairman of the Federal Reserve Board in the difficult period of the early 1980s.

The organizational changes at Chase required shifting many officers. Much of the planning was carried out in 1970, and the new organization was implemented in 1971.

Directors under the holding company and the bank

The same directors served both the corporation and the bank, with occasional exceptions.[29] Upon becoming chairman, Rockefeller instituted a confidential survey of directors to obtain suggestions concerning the conduct of meetings and the role of directors. He found considerable dissatisfaction among some on the board, a feeling that directors were not well enough informed on important matters, were not sufficiently exposed to senior personnel below the top level, and frequently were bogged down in inconsequential detail.[30] For some years the board had met annually at Pocantico Hills with senior staff to review accomplishments and future plans. But this was not adequate. The directors wanted increased exposure to the bank's activities and the officers who managed them.

Rockefeller took these criticisms to heart and restructured the meetings. Separate sessions were required for the bank and the holding company. The great bulk of the business related to the bank, and meetings continued to be held biweekly. A number of directors favored monthly meetings, however, even if more lengthy, and the board finally made the change in early 1972. Meetings of the corporation board normally occurred only quarterly, immediately following the bank session, but special meetings following that of the bank were called when necessary.

The board delegated to members of the executive office authority for many actions on officer personnel that the board had formerly handled, requesting only that it be notified. Reporting on loans and commitments, however, constituted a problem. The volume had increased enormously over the past years. A new cut-off level was adopted, with only lines of credit, specially approved loans, or commitments involving a total of $5 million or more to be reported, compared with $1 million previously.[31] Credit officers no longer commented on many loans but selected a few that were unusual or required particular attention. More responsibility was thrust on the examining committee of the board, which surveyed the quality of credits, aided by independent auditors and examiners from regulatory agencies.

The committee structure of the board remained unchanged, with executive, examining (and audit), trust, and compensation committees acting for both the bank and the corporation. The trust advisory board established after the Manhattan merger in 1955 was discontinued in 1967. As in the past, the executive committee carried all the powers of directors when the board was not in session, and it now met regularly early each month, between board sessions.

The structure and activities of both the bank and the holding company, reaching into all corners of the world, had become increasingly diversified and complex. Even then Chase was planning a further ambitious expansion, both in the United States and abroad. And critical changes in the banking environment loomed ahead, making banking more risky. The responsibility of the directors had taken on new dimensions compared to their activities of a decade or two earlier.

Growth in an unsettled environment

The bank's new organization was designed to prepare it for a decade of widely anticipated unparalleled growth. And growth did indeed occur, as assets more than tripled by 1980. But this advance was accompanied by many unsettling developments that radically affected the environment for banking: a huge rise in energy prices, worldwide inflation and recession, disruption in the balance of payments between nations, and a breakdown of the international monetary system. Interest rates and exchange rates became increasingly volatile, adding new risks to banking. For the first time in the postwar era, sizable banking institutions failed. Chase did not escape unscathed, as an undetected overvaluation in its bond dealer account damaged its reputation.

The recession of 1970–71

The decade opened with the nation's first recession since the early 1960s, the result of a marked slowdown in defense and capital spending. The credit crunch of 1969 gave way to an easier monetary policy by the Federal Reserve and a slackening loan demand. For the first time since 1957 loans to domestic business failed to increase. Only credit extended by overseas branches and affiliates recorded a strong advance, as foreign economies continued to expand amid persistent inflation.

The recession marked a turning point for Chase and other banks in one respect: net loan charge-offs rose fourfold to $56 million, never again to return to the low levels that had prevailed over the previous three decades. The failure of the Penn Central Railroad in mid-1970 was only one of a number of defaults.[1] But it deeply disturbed the financial community and caused a flight of borrowers from the commercial paper market into major banks, particularly Chase. The bank met all calls upon it as the Federal Reserve announced that the discount window would be open for any additional needed reserves.

To assist in funding, the Federal Reserve also suspended the ceiling rate that banks could pay on large CDs of thirty to eighty-nine days' maturity, a far-reaching change that provided Chase with added flexibility.[2] Indeed over subsequent months the bank was able to ease its reliance on the Eurodollar market, substituting lower-cost CDs. With interest rates declining and money more available, the bank restored its liquidity position, depleted by the credit crunch of the previous year.

The bank under the new economic program of 1971

In spite of easier money, the economic environment in 1971 remained troublesome. Unlike earlier recessions, this time inflation intensified rather than abated. And the growing instability of the international monetary system finally created a crisis of major proportions.

As conceived at Bretton Woods in 1944, the system was built around gold and the dollar, interchangeable at a fixed price of $35 for an ounce of gold. But for many years the United States had been running a deficit in its international balance of payments and consistently losing gold. Confidence in the viability of the system steadily eroded, and the belief became widespread that the United States would be forced to devalue the dollar by increasing the price of gold.

This belief turned to conviction in the first half of 1971 as the United States began to incur a deficit in its merchandise trade balance with no relief from inflation in sight. Unease in the exchange markets finally developed into a full-fledged flight from the dollar, forcing President Nixon finally to react on August 15 with the introduction of a "New Economic Program."[3]

This new program combined action against both inflation and the crisis of the dollar. Wages and prices were frozen, soon to be followed by a system of controls, the first in U.S. peacetime history. Convertibility of the dollar into gold and other reserve assets was suspended, ending the system of essentially fixed exchange rates and leaving most currencies floating, although with some intervention.

The bank had anticipated action on the dollar. William S. Ogden, head of the international department, and the bank's economists met regularly with the executive office to assess the situation. They predicted that the dollar would be devalued but that the Eurodollar market, after a brief period of turmoil, would continue to operate effectively, and funding arrangements would not be seriously disrupted. This proved to be true. They also projected wider swings in exchange rates in a continuing unstable environment.

The authority provided to the president included control over interest rates and dividends, a power exercised by a committee on interest and dividends, headed by Arthur Burns, chairman of the Federal Reserve Board.[4] The new committee encountered no problem with interest rates for more than a year. After a brief upturn rates declined, with the prime descending to 4¾ percent in early 1972, the lowest since late 1965.

Administering the prime rate

Administering the prime rate had been a problem for Chase. The prime had become a symbol for interest rates in general, and in the eyes of many in the government and the public, major banks effectively controlled the level of interest rates through the prime rate. Pressure had been placed on Chase to hold down the prime during the credit crunch of 1969, and Representative Patman had written a widely publicized letter to Rockefeller in 1970 urging the bank to cut its rate.[5] Rockefeller's response, which was run by the bank as a full-page advertisement in the *New York Times*, pointed out that the prime rate, like the price of other products in a free market, was the result of factors influencing the supply of and the demand for bank credit. He stated further that "the bond market, the commercial paper market and other financial intermediaries all provide credit in competition with domestic banks . . . It is the interplay of rates in all these markets, domestic and foreign, which establishes the range within which banks charge their customers on a competitive basis."[6]

The letter did not make entirely clear, however, that one factor had grown in importance in determining the prime rate: the cost of borrowed money on which the bank increasingly relied. Rates for this money were volatile. The bank shortly announced that as a matter of policy it would make small and frequent adjustments in the prime rate, stating that such adjustments "have the advantage of making the rate a flexible instrument and keeping it in close alignment with other key interest rates."[7]

Other banks adopted a similar policy, and several devised formulas tying changes in the prime on a lagged basis to changes in commercial paper or other money market rates. Chase studied the formula approach but rejected it as being too mechanistic, preferring to continue to exercise an element of judgment. Over the years to come Chase often led the market in changing the prime, but sometimes it lagged. A split rate between banks for brief periods was not uncommon. The number of prime rate changes increased greatly, rising to ten in 1971 and doubling to twenty in 1973, only to explode to twenty-five in volatile 1974.

Slow domestic loan growth, rapid overseas

The president's new economic program brought a temporary respite to inflation, and the U.S economy surged ahead vigorously in the second half of 1971 and 1972. But domestic loan demand at Chase and other money center banks continued to lag. Falling interest rates again induced major corporations to resort to the capital markets, while internal cash flows were swollen by higher profits. Chase's business loans fell 9 percent from 1969 through

1972. As competition between banks became intense, innovative pricing techniques were introduced, some not altogether propitious.

Floating rates on loans, tied to changes in the prime rate, had been adopted widely as banks resorted increasingly to borrowed money for funding. Fixed-rate loans became the exception rather than the rule. But in this period of slack demand and low rates, customers naturally sought a fixed rate, especially on term loans. A hybrid was soon introduced, called a CAP rate, under which the borrower was guaranteed an average maximum rate over the life of the contract. If the floating prime rose above this maximum on the average, the lending bank absorbed the added cost. Chase did not favor such pricing but yielded to competition in adopting it in some instances to retain good customers. Later, as interest rates rose more than anticipated, the bank established reserves to finance the excess margin over the CAPs. And late in 1972, again under competitive pressure, the bank entered into a number of fixed-rate loans. These produced needed income at the time, but over much of their life could be funded only at a loss.

Although corporate demand was slow to revive, other markets remained highly active.[8] Concentration of retail business in the community banking department provided the impetus for a strong increase in loans to individuals and small business. And credit to real estate marched swiftly on, powered by a boom in construction of homes, offices, and other commercial facilities. Not only did the bank, Dovenmuehle, and the Housing Investment Corporation share in this boom, but all contributed loan opportunities to the Chase Manhattan Mortgage and Realty Trust, which underwent a quick and sizable expansion. The bank also aided the trust with direct loans and provided substantial credit to other recently established real estate trusts as well.

But no markets surpassed in strength those overseas. While corporate demand at home languished, in Chase's foreign branches and affiliates it continued brisk and vigorous. Foreign economies slowed in growth but did not descend into recession. With few exceptions, inflation remained endemic. Moreover, turmoil in currency markets led many foreign companies to turn to the Eurodollar market for credit. In consequence, credit extended abroad almost tripled to $4.5 billion from 1969 to 1972, thereby enabling the bank to report a small increase in total loans even through the period of recession.

The boom year, 1973

This pattern of loan demand to business, lethargic at home but strong overseas, altered abruptly in 1973. Early in the year corporations were already beginning to enlarge capital outlays and inventories, pushing the economy strongly upward. The Nixon program of wage and price restraints began to give way under the strains. Overseas, too, growth and inflation accelerated. The result for Chase was a worldwide upsurge in loans during the year of more than one-fourth, to a total of almost $22 billion.

All markets participated in this advance. Loans to business rose for the first time since 1969, passing their previous peak. Credit to real estate continued to grow substantially, and individuals stepped up their borrowing. But once again Chase's foreign branches and affiliates led all others, with an increase in branch loans outstanding of 86 percent to more than $8 billion. These overseas outposts now accounted for almost two-fifths of all loans extended by the bank and provided a somewhat larger share of its deposits.

Rising loan demand at home soon put pressure on interest rates and precipitated the first confrontation between banks and the committee on interest and dividends, with Chase intimately involved. The prime rate gradually recovered during 1972 from its low of 4¾ percent, finally reaching 6 percent in late December 1972, the level that had prevailed when the president inaugurated wage and price controls in August 1971. But rates on commercial paper and other sources of credit were already rising above the prime, forcing loan demand from these markets into the banks and promising to create pressures similar to those in 1969.

When the prime rate moved to 6 percent Treasury Secretary George Shultz stated publicly that the government hoped the rate would not rise above that level.[9] Arthur Burns, chairman of the Committee on Interest and Dividends, and other officials, however, had met with representatives of major banks, informing them that the committee did not intend to impose a fixed ceiling on interest rates.[10] But Burns also suggested that if the banks raised rates rapidly, Congress would likely include a tough interest control provision when it extended wage and price control legislation in the following April. Moreover, it was evident that the principal concern of the committee and of Congress lay in the cost of credit to small business rather than to large corporations.

Chase leads the way with a dual prime rate

Chase's representative at the meeting with Burns was Willard C. Butcher, who had succeeded Patterson as president of the bank. Butcher returned from the meeting convinced that further increases in the prime rate would be more acceptable if a separate, more stable rate could be established for smaller business. The bank went to work on the concept and concluded that an appropriate dividing line would be loans in excess of $500,000.

The matter came to a head on Friday, March 24, 1973, when Chase, Chemical Bank, and First National Bank of Chicago announced an increase in the prime from 6¼ percent, a level set in February, to 6¾ percent.

Simultaneously Chase stated that it would establish a graduated prime rate, with interest on loan balances up to a total of $500,000 for any single borrower remaining unchanged and linked to the existing 6¼ percent rate. Burns reacted immediately with a statement that the increase of ½ percent on loans above $500,000 was too great and called for the three banks to meet with him.[11] He also asked Chase to provide complete information on its cost of funds and be prepared to discuss its proposal for a graduated rate structure.

The following day Butcher and Rockefeller met with Burns in Washington. The bank agreed to change its proposed increase in the prime rate to 6½ percent rather than 6¾, although money market rates had reached levels normally justifying a prime of 7½ percent.[12] Burns also expressed considerable interest in Chase's concept of a graduated rate, regarding it as a highly innovative approach that distinguished between loans to large corporations with access to national money and capital markets, and those to smaller businesses which relied principally on local sources. But feeling that the Committee on Interest and Dividends needed additional time to study the implications of the plan, he asked Chase to postpone implementing it.

There the matter rested for several weeks. Then on April 16 the committee issued guidelines for bank interest rates. It noted the special role that interest rates play as a kind of balance wheel in the economy which can be used to speed up growth or slow down inflation. And it stated that bank lending charges to large corporations "may respond flexibly to changes in open-market interest rates," but that "any increase should be made in moderate steps in order to avoid disruptive market effects."[13] The guidelines also drew a distinction between the prime rate and a small-business loan rate. The latter was to apply to commercial, industrial, or agricultural borrowers whose total credit outstanding over the previous twelve months (exclusive of mortgage debt) did not exceed $350,000 and whose assets were $1 million or less, a dividing line somewhat different from Chase's.

The small business rate was to remain unchanged from the date of the guidelines and could be raised only if justified by an increase in overall costs.[14] Chase responded immediately by raising its prime rate to 6¾ percent, the level rejected by Burns several weeks earlier.[15] The rate for small business was left unchanged at 6½ percent, and so too were rates on consumer loans and home mortgages.

Yet the prime rate remained out of line, pulling loans from other markets into the banks. The problem confronting banks was again complicated by a policy of active restraint pursued by the Federal Reserve which ratcheted money market rates upward. In one important respect, however, the Federal Reserve eased the position of Chase and other banks. In May it suspended all ceiling rates on large CDs, permitting banks to bid for deposits as needed.[16] Credit crunches similar to those in 1966 and 1969 were now a thing of the past.

Once again banks were asked to institute a program of voluntary credit restraint, limiting new loans to those for productive purposes. Chase complied with this request, but administered the program only at the departmental level. The ready availability of funds (at a price) rendered unnecessary a central committee to allocate scarce funds.

As 1973 progressed, the prime marched steadily upward, reaching a peak of 10 percent in mid-September. Meanwhile the rate for small business held relatively steady, increasing only from 6½ to 7 percent. By mid-autumn signs appeared that the economy was weakening, and rates moved off their peak. But then one of those unpredictable events that affect history intervened, and the prime moved back up to close an eventful year at 10 percent.

OPEC increases the oil price fourfold

The event, or more accurately the series of events, began with the third armed conflict between Egypt and Israel in October 1973. The timing was a surprise. Rockefeller had visited Egyptian President Sadat shortly before the outbreak and received no inkling of the forthcoming attack. More unexpected, however, was the support provided to Egypt by the Arab oil producers, who placed an embargo on all oil shipments to the United States, the Netherlands, Portugal, and South Africa. The resulting shortage created an opportunity for the oil producers' cartel, the Organization of Petroleum Exporting Countries (OPEC), to raise the price of oil. By the spring of 1974 the oil embargo had ended, but Saudi Arabia's benchmark price for light oil had been lifted to $9.60 a barrel, a fourfold increase from $2.25 a year earlier.

The oil embargo and price increase produced severe strains through much of the industrialized world. The United States moved into its worst postwar recession to that time, but with inflation still exceeding 12 percent, the highest rate at that point in peacetime history. Japan also experienced recession, and major European countries realized only minuscule growth, accompanied in many instances by inflation surpassing that in the United States. Payments balances between nations were torn asunder, with OPEC nations gaining a huge surplus and oil-consuming nations running a corresponding deficit. Interest rates and exchange rates underwent wide swings, distorting normal financial relationships.

Chase, in the middle of these conflicting forces, experienced another large increase in loans. But this time the advance was centered more in the United States than abroad, as changes in interest rates again acted to divert to Chase credit demands that normally would have been met in other markets. The prime rate lagged consistently below money market rates, although it climbed to a record 12 percent in July. Meanwhile, surveillance of interest rates by the Committee on Interest Rates and Dividends came to an end in April, as Congress and the administration abandoned controls on wages and prices. The small business loan rate then rose in steps from 7½ to 9½ percent, still considerably below the prime rate.[17]

Corporations, caught in a crossfire between inflation, growing recessionary trends, inventory problems, and energy costs, not only needed more money but found traditional sources of long-term financing impaired. Chase and other major New York City banks, with substantial funds available through the money market, virtually became lenders of last resort. The bank intensified its program of loan restraint, and for the first time applied it to loans overseas. Even so, in 1974 domestic corporate loans climbed almost a third and loans in overseas branches more than a fourth, and this on top of the large increase in 1973. Worldwide loans at this point reached $27.7 billion, more than double the $13 billion at the peak of the previous boom at the end of 1969.

Real estate credit outdid all others at this time, rising by 55 percent in 1974 alone, as the industry began to experience adversity. Soaring building costs, high interest rates, and reduced sources of financing all took their toll, and housing construction fell sharply during the year. Although part of Chase's enlarged credit represented increased holdings of residential mortgages, a greater portion was extended to builders, developers, and real estate investment trusts, including the Chase Manhattan Trust.

Confidence in the creditworthiness of real estate investment trusts began to ebb, and they encountered difficulty in raising funds through commercial paper and other sources. They then turned to the banks, drawing extensively on credit lines. By the end of 1974 Chase's loans to these trusts had climbed to almost $800 million, more than a fifth of its domestic credit to real estate. And on part of the loans, as well as on other credit in the troubled industry, interest was no longer being accrued.[18]

Loan demands eased greatly in the fourth quarter of 1974 as the recession deepened. The Federal Reserve relaxed its monetary policy, and interest rates began to back down. In September, with the prime rate still at 12 percent, Rockefeller commented that the rate might decline to 10 percent by the end of the year, a prediction that fell short in time by less than two weeks.[19]

Chase Investors Management Corporation

An area of the bank little discussed thus far, pension trust, suffered in this period of inflation and recession. No other trust service had grown so rapidly through the postwar years. By 1968 Chase was responsible for $18 billion of trust investments, with two-thirds representing pension and other employee benefit funds.[20] Champion and Rockefeller, concerned that these huge investments be managed most effectively, created a separate fiduciary investment department in 1964, with John B. Bridgewood at its head. Fiduciary investment took over from the trust department all investment activities and concentrated on the fiduciary side of the business.

By 1968 the increase in trust investments had so accelerated that the department became concerned about its ability to handle effectively the volume it saw looming ahead. Private pension funds alone amounted to $7.4 billion and were projected to double in four years. The flow of new funds, along with the shifting of existing investments, amounted to more than $2 billion a year.[21] In such circumstances it became increasingly difficult to achieve results better than those registered by the broad market averages.

Troubled by problems of size, and under growing pressure from companies for superior performance, Chase in 1968 placed limits on growth.[22] The bank would subsequently discourage accounts over which it would not exercise full control. Moreover, it cut back substantially on one segment of the business, pension funds of state and local governments and public bodies. Most of these accounts were advisory in character, and the bank did not actively manage them. In offering to resign such relationships, it reduced its responsibility for funds by more than $2 billion.[23]

As the economic environment became increasingly unstable, Chase's pension trust activities encountered difficulties. For a time in the 1970s the quality of service deteriorated, and trust activities as a whole failed to earn their way. To concentrate more effectively on investments for pension trust and other benefits, Rockefeller and Patterson established a new subsidiary, Chase Investors Management Corporation (CIMC).[24] Launched in April 1972, CIMC handled all investments except some $3 billion for personal trust and other individual accounts. These remained under the trust department, with CIMC acting as an adviser.

A major advantage to the formation of CIMC was the added flexibility it afforded in compensation. Talent for investment management and research was in short supply and competition with Wall Street intense. The bank's normal scale of compensation placed it at a disadvantage in attracting and retaining outstanding personnel. But even with improved compensation, high turnover among staff continued to be a problem.

Unfortunately, formation of CIMC failed to improve Chase's investment performance, which began to fall behind that of its principal competitors. Many investment managers in the early 1970s placed a high proportion of pension funds in equities. Moreover, they concentrated on a relatively select group of large companies with a record of strong growth, called the "nifty fifty." Prices of these securities outstripped most others and reached extraordinary heights in relation to earnings. The denouement came later, with the recession of 1974–75, when these same securities experienced a relatively greater decline.

Chase's pension managers did not invest as heavily in the "nifty fifty" as others, and their performance lagged. CIMC lost accounts, especially in 1972 and 1973. Shell Oil, in shifting some $130 million, said that "investment results achieved by Chase had not been up to their standards."[25] Although the bank performed somewhat better than its competitors in the subsequent downturn, it still could not avoid a severe decline as the market as a whole dropped precipitously. By 1975 assets under management by CIMC were reduced to $5.3 billion from approximately $9 billion three years earlier (in part because of lower equity prices).[26] Loss of accounts, however, had tapered off, and CIMC began the slow process of rebuilding its reputation and clientele, described in Chapter XVIII.

Banks recycle the OPEC surplus

Chase Investors Management played a minor part in a major problem: the handling of the huge surplus on OPEC current accounts that developed from the oil price increase. This jumped elevenfold to $65 billion in 1974, and viability of the international monetary system came into question. The surplus clearly would need to be recycled to oil-consuming countries if widespread breakdown was to be avoided. It was recognized that much of this task would fall on banks, and the banks proved equal to the task.

Chase as a whole assumed a leading role in this recycling process. For many years the bank had been a major depository for the Saudi Arabian Monetary Agency, the Bank Markazi of Iran (the central bank), and the central bank of Venezuela. It also carried smaller accounts for central banks of almost all other oil producers. Now amounts channeled through these accounts increased enormously, at times exceeding $5 billion.

By and large, the great bulk of the deposits did not remain long with the bank. The oil producers shifted funds into loans and investments, chiefly at short maturities in the Eurocurrency markets and money markets of the industrial nations.[27] Smaller amounts, particularly from private sources, were invested over the long term, some through Chase Investors Management. Eurocurrency markets provided the largest single outlet for the OPEC surplus, with banks carrying out the intermediation. Chase financed part of its large growth in loans with increased Eurodollars, while it also expanded its volume of Eurodollar placings.

These placings, by which Chase borrowed Eurodollars and then lent them to other financial institutions at higher rates (and frequently at longer maturity), grew appreciably. By 1973 they averaged $3.3 billion, and in 1974 this swelled to $4.4 billion, with considerably larger amounts at peak periods. Chase at this time enjoyed an advantage in the Eurodollar market because of "tiering" in rates. As one of a select number of banks judged to be of least risk, Chase paid less for Eurodollars than many other banks, and its margin on placements widened. Tiering was increased in 1974 owing to the uncertainties created by the oil crisis and the failure of Bankhaus Herstatt, discussed below.

The bank also played a significant role in financing balance-of-payments deficits that arose as a result of the fourfold increase in the price of oil. All dollar credits, for whatever purpose, helped to finance a foreign country's payments deficit. But at this time, and through the rest of the decade, governments began to borrow directly on an increasing scale to augment supplies of foreign exchange and cover general shortfalls in international payments. Great Britain borrowed $2.5 billion for this purpose in April 1974, with Chase as one of the participating banks.[28] Credit also was extended to other countries, including Italy, although that nation preferred to channel its borrowing through state-owned companies rather than the central government.

Rockefeller and Butcher viewed these direct balance-of-payments loans with caution, not so much for reasons of credit risk but rather as a matter of principle. If governments could borrow easily to finance balance-of-payments deficits, they would not be forced to take the difficult measures necessary to eliminate the problem. For this reason Chase chose where possible to finance foreign credits that were productive in nature, especially credits for projects that would enhance exports or conserve on imports. The bank decided not to participate in some balance-of-payments credits that appeared to carry acceptable interest spreads, including one to the Swedish government, much to the distress of officers in the international department.

Closing of Bankhaus I.D. Herstatt

Uncertainties generated by balance-of-payments problems, varying rates of inflation, and differences in interest rates between countries all served to produce wide swings in foreign exchange rates during 1974. Indeed, foreign exchange markets had been volatile ever since the United States abandoned the gold standard in August 1971. An attempt was made to return to a system of fixed rates later that year in the so-called Smithsonian Agreement with the official U.S. price of gold raised to $38 an ounce. But markets remained turbulent, and the system broke down. In 1973 the United States again devalued the dollar, increasing the official gold price to $42.22 an ounce. The currencies of many countries, however, continued to float against the dollar, and a common float was attempted by the major countries of continental Europe.

These conditions of widely fluctuating rates (the dollar-deutschemark rate in 1974 moved 18 percent against the Smithsonian central rate) provided powerful temptation to speculate in foreign exchange.[29] Chase as a matter of policy avoided taking sizable speculative positions. Foreign exchange dealing around the world was coordinated and controlled by a senior officer in the international department. The volume of activity increased greatly, and spreads between buying and selling widened. Normal dealing in exchange became increasingly profitable, although more risky, and in 1974 the business generated almost $50 million in income for Chase.

But not all banks were prudent, and not all maintained effective control over their traders. A number incurred foreign exchange losses in 1974, two of particular importance to Chase: the disclosure by Franklin National Bank on May 12 of a previously undetected loss that might amount to $39 million, which contributed materially to events finally forcing Franklin to be declared insolvent; and the loss of more than $100 million by Bankhaus I.D. Herstatt in Cologne, West Germany, which led that institution, carrying $760 million in deposits, to close its doors on June 26.[30]

The demise of Herstatt affected Chase most directly, for the bank served as Herstatt's New York correspondent and clearing agent. On the day of the closing, the Herstatt account contained about $156 million in deposits, with numerous claims against the account flowing in. The German authorities had announced the closing of Herstatt at 4 P.M. local time, or 11 A.M. in New York. The officer in charge at Chase quickly learned of the development, and the bank froze the account after consulting both the Federal Reserve and the Bundesbank in Frankfort. Within days, Herstatt debtors throughout the world were seeking a piece of the $156 million held by Chase, among them a number of aggrieved American banks that had engaged in spot foreign exchange transactions with Herstatt and had delivered deutschemarks to it but had not yet been paid in dollars.

By mid-July attachments against the account totaled $174 million, and additional claims of $65 million had been made against Chase, with further potential claims of $94 million. So on July 15 the bank passed the matter over to the United States Court of the Southern District of New York, telling the court: "Chase is without means to determine the validity of the conflicting claims. Chase is in a dangerous and doubtful position and cannot safely determine to whom it is required to pay."[31]

The court took over the claims, but a settlement was not reached until February of the following year, the result then of an overall plan worked out by the Herstatt liquidator in Germany.[32] Chase itself had only a relatively small claim arising from a time deposit made by its Luxembourg subsidiary. But Herstatt's closing without honoring its spot foreign exchange obligations shocked the market. Foreign exchange transactions for a period were drastically curtailed, with trading limited to names of the highest quality. Activity subsequently recovered, but many small and medium-sized banks experienced continued difficulties.

Failure of Franklin National Bank

For Franklin National the foreign exchange loss was only a contributing factor. Franklin had bitterly opposed Chase's move into Nassau County in the early 1960s, but then had itself branched into New York City. It grew considerably, at the end of 1973 ranking as the nation's twentieth largest bank. Credit policies were liberal and loan losses greater than at other banks. In late 1973 and early 1974 adverse rumors concerning the condition of the bank began to circulate. It was known to be dealing heavily in the foreign exchange market and was thought to be dependent on foreign exchange profits to sustain earnings. Franklin delayed issuing its first-quarter report, then announced on May 10 that it would omit its dividend.[33] This was followed by disclosures of irregularities in the foreign exchange account with a possible loss of $39 million.[34]

Franklin's most serious problem, however, was a growing inability to finance itself. As with Chase and other banks, it relied heavily on borrowed money, much of it at short-term maturity. Investors became reluctant to purchase Franklin's CDs, and other banks were hesitant to lend it federal funds. After May 10 funding sources dried up, and Franklin was forced to rely increasingly on emergency assistance from the New York Federal Reserve Bank, assistance the Federal Reserve was prepared to provide inasmuch as the comptroller of the currency judged Franklin to be viable if its funding problem could be solved.[35]

By October the Federal Reserve was providing more than $1.7 billion to Franklin. Meanwhile, Chase and other New York City banks had been enlisted to aid as best they could in a prudent manner. In early June, Chase and other clearing house banks agreed to lend Franklin $250 million, but on a secured basis, chiefly through the provision of federal funds.[36]

All banks were forced to monitor their positions with Franklin closely. In the end, the inability to maintain liquidity, to fund itself, forced Franklin to the wall. On October 8, 1974, it was declared insolvent. The Federal Deposit Insurance Corporation sold the assets (including the branch system) to European-American Banking Corporation, which also assumed certain of Franklin's remaining liabilities.[37]

Chase officers spent many hours with officials of the Federal Reserve and Franklin on operating and funding problems. The closing of Franklin provided a sobering experience for American banks, including Chase, demonstrating the vulnerability of a bank dependent on borrowed money once it lost the confidence of its peers and the investing public.

Overvaluation of Chase's bond account

In early October 1974 Chase itself fell victim to an incident which, although minor in financial terms, did damage to its image. It was discovered that the bonds in the bank's bond dealer account had been overvalued by approximately $34 million at the time of discovery, and hence its earnings in previous quarters had been overstated.[38]

For purposes of financial reporting, the bank valued bonds in the dealer account at either the market price or at book value, whichever was lower. If the market price fell below book value, the difference was entered as a loss into income. Profits on bonds in the dealer account, however, were included in income only as they were realized.

Early in 1974 those responsible for the bank's investment portfolio and its bond dealer activities judged that interest rates, which had been high in late 1973, would decline well into the year, a view shared at the time by the bank's asset-liability management committee. Bond prices would then rise, creating an opportunity for profit. Large purchases of U.S. government, state, and municipal securities were added to the dealer inventory to capitalize on such a development. The inventory increased to more than $1 billion in terms of book value at one point and stood at about $800 million in early October 1974. Interest rates did decline over the first several months but then moved higher, climbing to record levels until early autumn. Rather than increasing in value, the dealer inventory declined and suffered a loss, although unrealized.

It was the practice of the bank to value the dealer inventory at the end of each month, with the senior vice president in charge of the bond dealer account responsible for the calculation. The prices of U.S. government and agency securities were readily available, but markets for state and municipal securities frequently were thin, and in some cases trading seldom occurred. Pricing such securities involved a large element of judgment, including at times extrapolation based on changes in the level of rates.[39] Over some months the head of the bond dealer account reported values for these securities at higher prices than were warranted by available market information, expecting interest rates to decline and thereby justify the price. His superior, the executive for portfolio and investment banking, had requested an audit of the account, but had been absent on a special assignment overseas. On his return, finding that the audit had been put off, he immediately reinstated it, only to be informed by the bond dealer head of the overvaluation.

This information was conveyed on Monday, September 30, to George A. Roeder, Jr., the member of the executive committee who exercised broad oversight over portfolio and investment banking.[40] Roeder told Butcher and immediately set in train steps to determine the true value of the inventory. The department itself undertook a new valuation, and Interactive Data Corporation, now owned by the bank and a source of computerized data on bond prices and yields, was called in to make an independent calculation. The bank's outside auditors, Peat Marwick and Mitchell, also played a role. All worked through Monday night and well into Tuesday, while Roy C. Haberkern, Jr., the bank's outside legal counsel, gathered information from those concerned with the dealer activity.

Rockefeller, who was in Washington attending the annual meeting of the International Monetary Fund and World Bank, was told by phone of the problem. He and Butcher were hosts that Monday evening at a large dinner, traditionally given by Chase for foreign banks and other guests, so the two men were unable to review the overvaluation until after dinner. They talked into the night.[41]

Facts continued to be gathered through Tuesday. After hosting a second dinner Rockefeller and Butcher returned to New York. Already waiting at Rockefeller's home on East Sixty-fifth Street were Roeder, Haberkern, and the executives for portfolio and investment banking and corporate communications. Perhaps it was typical of Rockefeller's low-key style that he greeted the group and insisted that those who had missed dinner have a bite to eat, prepared by Mrs. Rockefeller, before entering serious discussion. This then continued until 2:30 A.M.[42]

The group now knew the dimensions of the problem and realized that it would be necessary to make an immediate public disclosure. Aside from ethical considerations, the securities laws required such action. The group thereupon considered the outline of a statement setting forth the facts, which in more finished form was released to the public the following morning. The statement pointed out that revaluation of the trading account could cause an after-tax charge of approximately $15 million against earnings for the nine months ended September 30, 1974. Rockefeller stated: "There is no question but that extremely serious errors of judgment have been made. The resignation of the Senior Vice President in charge of Chase's bond dealer account activities has been accepted as of October 1." He indicated also that immediate steps had been taken to establish additional controls over bond trading account valuation procedures.[43]

The incident was reported on the front page of the *New York Times* and widely throughout the nation on the morning of October 3. The article in the *Times* said that the announcement had stirred the financial community, not because of the recalculation of the bank's earnings, but rather because the problem had occurred at the Chase, the nation's third largest bank. Signs of weakness in the banking system during the year had prompted depositors to gravitate toward the larger banks, including Chase.

The directors were informed at a special meeting the day of the announcement. Henceforth the bond trading inventory was to be valued separately by the bond trading group and Interactive Data Corporation, with the bank's controller adjudicating any differences between them.[44] Butcher set down as a policy that neither the bank's security portfolio nor the trading account was to take large positions of a speculative character. The security portfolio, which had also been lengthened in maturity in expectation of falling interest rates, was to be regarded as a source of liquidity and not of profit, a resolution to which, in a world of widely fluctuating interest rates, it was at times difficult to adhere.

Evolution of management

At the time of the overvaluation of the bond account, Willard Butcher had been president for almost two years. His replacement of Herbert P. Patterson in October 1972 constituted the most significant of a number of changes in top management introduced by Rockefeller as the banking environment deteriorated in the early seventies.

Butcher's appointment was prompted by dissatisfaction on the part of Rockefeller and the directors with Chase's performance in the first years of the decade. Profits had risen during the recession of 1970 and the recovery that followed, but the advance was slow, and Chase lagged behind its principal competitors. Net operating earnings reached $148 million in 1972, an annual increase of 5.6 percent from four years earlier. The gain in 1972 was small, a particular disappointment since both loans and assets had increased substantially. The return on assets fell below fifty basis points for the first time in many years.

In several respects the bank had grown less rapidly than Bank of America or First National City, then in the process of a name change to Citibank. Inevitably Chase's performance through the years was compared with First National City's by the press, security analysts, and other commentators. The margin between the two had widened, in considerable part in overseas assets and deposits because of First National City's larger network of foreign branches. But First National City had also been more aggressive in domestic lending, in 1972 reporting a slightly greater total of loans outstanding to business than Chase.[45] The head of First National City had announced a target for earnings growth of 15 percent a year, a figure given wide publicity, but an extension of results realized over the previous three years.

By mid-1972 Rockefeller concluded that a change in senior management was necessary. In May 1971 John B. M. Place had resigned as vice chairman, a vacancy not filled until January of the following year. The directors then designated Leonor F. Loree II, head of corporate staff, as vice chairman and director of the bank, in charge of worldwide banking, and Willard C. Butcher, serving as head of the International department, as vice chairman and director of the corporation, responsible for planning, expansion, and diversification.[46] Meanwhile, George A. Roeder, Jr., continued as vice chairman, finance.

The role of the president in this arrangement was of critical importance. Rockefeller was not a "hands on" chief executive, concerning himself with all aspects of the bank's operations. He could not do so, with his many outside responsibilities. And he did not view this as his proper role. Patterson, as chief operating officer, bore overall responsibility for the bank's operations, including coordination of the activities of the three vice chairmen. It was the president who frequently had to determine which matters required a decision by Rockefeller.

Yet Patterson did not assume a position of strong leadership. Perhaps owing to his temperament and inclination, his approach was somewhat passive, and in this he did not complement Rockefeller well. A director was to comment later: "David needs a tiger under him." Patterson, a well-meaning and intelligent executive, was not a tiger. As a result the executive office lacked a degree of cohesiveness.[47]

Rockefeller and the directors acted in October 1972, appointing Butcher to succeed Patterson as president.[48] Patterson did not appear reluctant to relinquish his demanding duties, and he went on to an active private life and career.

In Butcher, Rockefeller had acquired more of a tiger as president. A decisive and energetic man with qualities of leadership, Butcher was well prepared for his new responsibilities. He had spent his entire working life with the bank, after graduating from Brown University in 1947 magna cum laude and a member of Phi Beta Kappa. For a number of years Butcher served in the branch system, and in 1960, as senior vice president, he was placed in charge of fifteen of the bank's major branches in midtown Manhattan, handling both retail and corporate banking business. Later, when given an opportunity for immediate promotion to head the branch system, Butcher agreed instead to a suggestion by Champion that he transfer to the international department and gain broader experience.[49] Subsequently in 1969 he was appointed executive vice president in charge of the international department. Butcher energized the department, rapidly expanding the network of branches, subsidiaries, and affiliates.

The management committee

Upon assuming the presidency, Butcher took over direct supervision of the major lending departments as well as exercising overall responsibility as chief operating officer. After a period of orientation, he aimed to reduce the number of officers reporting directly to him. Meanwhile, younger men needed to be tested in positions of senior management. For some months in 1974 Butcher and Rockefeller studied the top management structure of the bank. The changes they wished to make would be facilitated by the approaching retirement of Loree as vice chairman.

The new organization was announced in December 1974.[50] The executive office was to be replaced by a management committee comprising Rockefeller, Butcher, Roeder as vice chairman, and four executive vice presidents: John C. Haley, John A. Hooper, William S. Ogden, and Barry F. Sullivan. Each would exercise broad supervision over a number of departments; but as members of the management committee, they also assumed an overriding responsibility to participate in formulating and carrying out the overall business policies and programs of the bank.

In practice the management committee did not differ greatly from its predecessor, the executive office. Again it was in no sense a decision-making group, as Rockefeller remained ultimately responsible for final decisions on matters of policy. But he worked in closer harmony with Butcher than he had with Patterson, and Butcher took full responsibility for the range of decisions that fell to a chief operating officer.

A riskier environment

Rockefeller and Butcher would need to maintain a trusting relationship in the period ahead, for in the early 1970s seeds were sown that sprouted both opportunities and difficulties for Chase. The OPEC increase in energy prices in particular introduced a further element of instability into the banking environment. Inflation intensified, adding to loan demands but also weakening the quality of credit. Chase doubled its loans over the first five years of the decade, but the portfolio became overweighted with troubled credit to real estate. And a large new demand abroad from persistent balance-of-payments deficits fueled controversy as to its soundness. Chase and other major banks took on the challenging task of recycling the OPEC surplus amid mounting instability in interest rates and exchange rates. Overevaluation of the Chase bond account followed, along with the failures of Franklin and Herstatt, bringing home to management the need for more effective control over new risks in banking.

Diversifying facilities at home and abroad

Expansion of facilities remained high on Chase's priority list, notwithstanding growing uncertainties and risks. During the opening of the 1970s the program was guided by Chase's first integrated long-range plan. Earlier efforts at comprehensive planning were confined chiefly to projecting the shape and size of the bank under the anticipated economic environment, with top management playing only a limited role. Rockefeller had never been satisfied with the process, so late in 1970 he, Patterson, Butcher, and the department heads became intimately involved in formulating the new plan. Their aim was to determine more precisely the mission of Chase in the period ahead, and to search out the mixture of products, facilities, and programs that would be necessary to fulfill it.

The effort proved time consuming, so much so that some managers protested that they were being forced to neglect regular business. The plan was developed in conjunction with the annual budget, which also was given added detail and precision. The results were first presented to the directors at an all-day meeting at Pocantico Hills in the autumn of 1971, with more conclusive details filled in during 1972.[1]

Program for expansion

Now that the holding company had been established, the mission of Chase could be broadened. So-called near-bank activities might be undertaken on a wider geographic scale, with offices set up around the country for personal loans, commercial finance, factoring, and real estate. Chase already provided most of these services, but not on a nationwide basis, let alone internationally. The plan adopted a new statement of mission: "To make Chase an innovative and broadly-based financial services corporation," in contrast to the more restricted concept of a commercial bank.[2]

Not that the bank and its traditional activities were to be neglected. They would continue to constitute the bulk of Chase's business. And facilities to deliver bank services would be enhanced through an ambitious expansion of branches in the city and the state as well as overseas. Corporate customers also could be handled through loan production offices and Edge Act corporations in key cities. Moreover, these could be supplemented by the acquisition of special product, finance-related companies, creating a nationwide chain of offices capable of distributing the bank's existing products as well as new products.[3]

The plan was given precision by goals established for numbers of branches, near-bank companies, affiliates abroad, and other facilities, and estimates were made of the possible growth in different products and functional areas of the corporation. The plan correctly perceived that the most rapid growth would occur overseas, and that domestic real estate activity would increase more rapidly than wholesale corporate lending. As matters later developed, expansion both overseas and in real estate proved substantially greater than anticipated, although the projection for business lending came close to the mark.

The critical importance of the economic environment also was recognized. Two "wild cards" were singled out as heavily influencing estimates: the rate of inflation and the level of interest rates. Both were substantially underestimated in the light of subsequent experience in 1973 and 1974. Nor was the energy crisis foreseen, with its severe impact on the balance of payments between nations. And the problems that eventually surfaced in real estate were not even dimly perceived at the time.

The plan was a useful, even essential, exercise, laying out the strategic direction in which the corporation and the bank would develop. It was followed by yearly updates and revisions as dictated by events. Only later in the decade, after the problems of the mid-1970s had been surmounted, was a comparable and even more ambitious effort undertaken, this time to chart the course for the 1980s.

Chase moves across New York State

On the retail side, facilities were to be expanded not only in the metropolitan area but also across New York State, a development made possible by important changes in the banking law. The first of these, in 1970, erased the legal distinction between one-bank and multibank holding companies. Then in 1971 the state legislature finally resolved the issue of statewide branching. Banks were to be permitted to branch across the state at the start of 1976, providing an adjustment period of almost five years.[4] The nine banking districts into which the state was divided would then be abolished. Meanwhile, new banks could be chartered or acquired in each district by bank holding companies.

Hardly less significant was a revision in the home office protection provision of the banking law, long a thorn in the side of Chase. After passage of the 1971 act, cities and towns containing the head office of a bank were protected from outside branching or holding companies only if their population was under 75,000 (later reduced to 50,000), rather than the former 1 million. This opened up important areas previously closed.

Within an hour after the new act was signed by the governor, Chase applied for a charter for an affiliate in Melville, Long Island.[5] This became the headquarters for The Chase Manhattan Bank of Long Island, covering both Nassau and Suffolk Counties, opened in December 1971, and the first of a series over the next three years.

Chase planned to acquire or charter a new bank in each of the seven upstate banking districts in which it was not represented. The most desirable course was to acquire an existing bank, but both the Federal Reserve and the state superintendent made it clear that they would approve only very small acquisitions. And the availability of even small banks in suitable locations at an acceptable price was distinctly limited. Over the next three years Chase chartered three new banks in Syracuse, Albany, and Binghamton, and acquired small banks in Buffalo, Rochester, Saugerties, and Canton. Each was named The Chase Manhattan Bank of its particular region.[6]

This upstate expansion did not occur without growing pains. Although the business was retail in character, each of the small city markets had its unique characteristics. And heavy competition from long-established banks and thrift institutions was augmented by other new entrants. Moreover, the need to operate separate entities added to costs and complexity of management.[7]

When it became possible at the start of 1976 to convert the system to branches, Chase lost no time in doing so. On January 1, 1976, each of the seven upstate banks, as well as The Chase Manhattan Bank of Long Island, some forty-two offices in all, were merged into The Chase Manhattan Bank, N.A. This enabled the bank to reduce costs and to reach out into larger markets. The loan limits of the small banks had been about $200,000. New business could now be cultivated and serviced directly in the middle market. Large corporate customers continued to be managed from New York, although major upstate branches acted as service centers.

Meanwhile, branch expansion in the metropolitan area accelerated. Some ninety-nine new offices were established in the first half of the decade, bringing the total to 261 in 1975 and placing the bank on a par with its competitors.[8] The bank spread throughout the suburbs, stretching from northern Westchester well into Suffolk County at the end of Long Island. All told, forty-five offices now operated in these suburban areas, where growth was concentrated and incomes were high.

The effort to acquire Dial Financial Corporation

Chase's most ambitious effort to expand domestically in the 1970s involved the attempted acquisition of Dial Financial Corporation, a medium-sized company engaged in consumer finance, with loans of approximately $300 million.[9] Headquartered in Des Moines, Iowa, it operated 461 offices in thirty-three states, primarily in the Midwest and West, with a credit life and other credit insurance subsidiary. No offices were located in New York or New Jersey, and very few in New England.

Consumer finance was one of Chase's top-rated fields for growth. Dial possessed excellent management, operated conservatively, and showed a proven record of profit. Its branch system could be the instrument for the nationwide expansion envisaged by Chase. No less important, Dial appeared to be of a size and a nature that would make the deal acceptable to the Federal Reserve Board. Dial's management was willing to negotiate, and on June 20, 1973, Chase and Dial jointly announced the signing of contracts for the acquisition.[10] The terms called for an exchange of stock, ranging from $135 million to $150 million in market value.

Again the application to the Federal Reserve was prepared with great care. The board was required to determine that any affiliation to a bank holding company "can reasonably be expected to produce benefits to the public, . . . that outweigh possible adverse effects, such as undue concentration of resources." Chase's application placed emphasis on benefits to be derived from the affiliation, including additional offices, new products, and lower rates on selected credits.[11] But care was taken also to show that no undue concentration would result, that Dial ranked only thirty-ninth among finance companies, an industry dominated by giants, with the four largest accounting for 38 percent of the business against Dial's 2 percent. Indeed, competition would be enhanced rather than reduced by the affiliation through the backing of Chase's resources.

It was with shock and dismay, then, that Chase learned on January 30, 1974, that the Federal Reserve had denied the application. The principal basis for the denial lay in a judgment by a majority of the board that the affiliation would remove the possibility of substantial future competition between Chase and Dial, and that this adverse factor was not offset by the claimed public benefits. The majority also determined that the affiliation raised the danger of creating an undue concentration of credit-granting resources, concluding that "at a minimum, this factor weighs against approval of the application."[12]

Butcher reacted to the denial immediately and with a hint of exasperation. "We are appalled," he stated publicly, "at what I consider to be a shocking decision."[13] The decision was unfair and inconsistent, he maintained, in that the board had rendered other decisions that permitted competitors (both Bank of America and First National City) to acquire important companies in the field.

The board itself may have judged the decision to be close. Certainly a minority on the board had rejected the arguments of the majority in a convincing manner on all counts. Rockefeller intervened with chairman Arthur Burns, promising to expand the benefits, and the board agreed that the application could be resubmitted with additional information.[14]

Chase increased the range of credits on which it would reduce rates. And it rebutted the board's contention that the affiliation would be anticompetitive or result in an undue concentration of resources. Officers of the bank entered into a dialogue with the Federal Reserve staff over the proposed acquisition, and the staff implied that it would support the purchase. If so, the board overruled it, for on October 31, 1974, the decision was handed down: the application again was denied.[15]

Beneath the surface much had changed. Chase had filed its initial application more than a year earlier. By late 1974 the economic environment had deteriorated. Franklin National Bank had finally succumbed, making the board cautious. Chairman Burns in a major speech urged banks to pay more attention to their internal affairs and less to expansion and diversification. Now the board had received the most recent examination of Chase by the comptroller of currency, and it pointed to significant problems in Chase's real estate portfolio and operating systems. Moreover, only four weeks before the adverse decision, the problem of overvaluation of the dealer bond account had arisen. The board let Rockefeller and Butcher know informally that these developments had played a role in their decision.[16]

The failure to acquire Dial was a bitter blow to Chase. The propitious moment to enter the small consumer loan business and to build up a nationwide network of offices had passed. Later in the decade the bank again considered this possibility but rejected it, choosing instead to start offices *de novo* on a more selective basis in terms of both location and customers.[17]

Expanding domestic facilities for commercial banking and real estate

While major attention and effort was devoted to Dial and upstate expansion, facilities for the bank's traditional wholesale banking were also enlarged. Market surveys revealed that this basic business of the bank was less strong in the Midwest and Far West than in the eastern states. So loan production offices were established, first in Los Angeles and then in Chicago and Houston. Contact officers could be closer to customers at these offices, although any credit extended had to be booked in New York. Officers could also cultivate smaller emerging growth companies in the so-called middle market, companies with annual sales of $15 million to $50 million. Chase did not attempt, however, to compete aggressively for a broad spectrum of this market, preferring to cooperate with its corrrespondent banks on credits and services to middle-sized companies.

Loan production offices also complemented Edge Act corporations set up to cultivate and handle business associated with international trade. These subsidiaries carried out transactions locally, usually dealing with contacts in a company other than the commercial loan officer. But the two found means of coordinating and supporting each other, especially in businesses that involved Chase facilities overseas. Chase Bank International in Los Angeles, the first of these Edge Act subsidiaries, was followed in 1973–74 by similar facilities in Chicago and Houston. Earlier a subsidiary had been set up in Miami, engaged principally in gathering deposits from customers in Latin America—chiefly funds seeking safe haven in the United States.

In the real estate field an additional subsidiary, Housing Investment Corporation of Florida, was organized in 1972 and in little more than a year was carrying construction and development loans in excess of $60 million. But certain other services that the holding company was expected to stimulate, especially factoring and commercial finance, failed to realize the profits and growth anticipated. In still another service, leasing, the bank also lagged, but of its own volition. Chase found that the tax benefits derived from leasing equipment were not as great as those obtained from certain other tax-exempt transactions and chose not to emphasize the activity.[18]

Information services

In addition to expanding its traditional business, Chase in the early 1970s pioneered in a field new to banks: information services. The bank was a storehouse of information, constantly replenished by reports from abroad and analytical studies by specialists in many fields. It seemed reasonable to assume that part of this information could be packaged and sold to customers. A market survey in 1970 suggested that economic analysis and forecasting was a good place to begin. Chase Econometric Associates was thus launched early in the following year, utilizing computer-based models of the economy developed by Michael K. Evans as an aid to forecasting.[19] Located in Philadelphia, the new subsidiary was modest in size but came to be a leader in the business.

Two years later an even more ambitious project was introduced in the international field—Chase World Information Corporation, specializing particularly in Eastern Europe, the Soviet Union, the Middle East, and China, all areas then opening up on a broader scale for American business.[20] The corporation soon initiated two newsletters, *East-West Markets* and *Mid-East Markets*, as well as a foreign trade service. It also provided a consulting service and prepared special studies for clients. Over the next few years many U.S. corporations were introduced into business with the Soviet Union and the People's Republic of China by expert staff from Chase World Information.

A third but quite different facility was added in 1974—Interactive Data Corporation, a computer time-sharing service that specialized in furnishing financial information to customers through remote terminals.[21] Interactive Data was immediately useful not only because of its own data base and proprietary services, but also as a vehicle for delivering financial information developed by Chase for corporate and financial planning. Over time other services were added to the Interactive Data network, whose coverage became international as well as national in scope.

The various strands of information services came to be woven together into an integrated business unit. Other companies were acquired—firms supporting freight payments and servicing mortgages among them. But the activities of Chase World Information, which at the outset appeared promising, suffered as relations with the Soviet Union deteriorated. Its two newsletters were sold, and active consulting on Eastern Europe wound down.

Chase moves to diversify overseas

Significant as were the added instruments for domestic expansion, they were overshadowed by a proliferation of new affiliates, branches, and subsidiaries created overseas. The basic structure of Chase's international network had been laid out in the 1960s (see Chapters XI and XII). Now the strategy called for the gaps to be filled and for the bank to diversify its representation in many areas so as to broaden its local services.

Over the first half of the 1970s, forty-eight new branches were started, more than three-fourths the number in place at the end of the 1960s. Many were small, covering for example the vacation isles of the Caribbean. But others were in important centers like Lyon, Copenhagen, and Taipei. And in a number of places not only were satellite branches added, but Chase representation was supplemented by special financial institutions, including merchant banks, finance companies, leasing firms, and real estate financing ventures. In many of these Chase joined other local institutions, frequently with a minority position. Such was the case with joint ventures in leasing and consulting with Mitsubishi in Japan, with discount houses in Paris and Singapore, and with leasing companies in Spain and Mexico.

In some countries where branches were not permitted, Chase employed near-bank institutions to gain representation. The Chase NBA Group in Australia had pioneered successfully in this respect. The same partners turned to New Zealand in 1972 to form a similar merchant bank, The Chase NBA New Zealand Group, again with success.[22] In the same year Chase also branched out with another major investment in Australia, Alliance Holdings, active in real estate and consumer finance, fields that fit Chase's strategic plan for expansion.[23] Chase acquired a one-third interest in the company for $12.4 million. But this venture did not achieve the same degree of success as Chase's other activities in Australia, a country that, like the United States, was suffering from a depressed real estate market in the mid-1970s. In 1984 Chase sold out its interest.

In the Far East the Philippines remained one of the few countries still lacking a significant Chase presence. Foreign branches were not permitted, but foreign participation in merchant banks was finally authorized in 1972. Chase joined the Philippine American Life Insurance Company and several local businessmen to form the Philippine American Investment Corporation, with a 24 percent interest (later reduced to 20 percent).[24] The new merchant bank initially engaged chiefly in money market operations, but soon spread into medium-term financing and other activities. Chase quickly supplemented this by expanding into consumer finance. The bank merged an interest in a finance company, held by Chase International Investment Corporation, with a much larger firm to form Filinvest Credit Corporation. By 1975 Chase had acquired a 37.5 percent interest in Filinvest, which operated as one of the largest finance companies in the country.[25]

The major objective in the Philippines, however, continued to be representation through a commercial bank. This finally became possible in 1973, when a change in the law permitted foreign banks to purchase up to 30 percent in a local bank. Chase then acquired a 30 percent interest in the Commercial Bank and Trust Company, a well-regarded institution in Manila with branches in principal centers of the country. Thus at mid-decade the bank had a three-pronged presence in the Philippines.[26]

Unlike most others, however, this representation was not destined to endure. Before the decade ended, the Philippines headed into a period of economic and political instability. Chase became dissatisfied with its minority positions in management, judging its influence to be inadequate. In 1979 the bank sold its interest in Commercial Bank and Trust Company, and followed in 1983 by disposing of interests in Philippine American and Filinvest Credit Corporations. Chase did, however, take advantage of legislation that permitted the establishment of an overseas banking unit, which served as a branch able to extend offshore credits to Philippine firms. Meanwhile the bank also kept open a representative office in Manila.

Direct presence in Canada

In the industrial world, strangely enough, Chase still lacked direct representation in the United States's immediate neighbor to the north. Branching by foreign banks continued to be prohibited in Canada, and Chase had made no effort to enter the country by other means after the breakdown of negotiations with the Toronto Dominion Bank in 1964. This gap was finally closed in

1973 by the creation of CMB Holdings, a finance company with headquarters in Toronto.[27]

The plan called for CMB Holdings to specialize in medium-term lending to major Canadian companies, a field in which Chase was believed to hold an advantage. But experience soon demonstrated that major companies were well cared for by the large Canadian banks, with branches across the continent. So CMB Holdings made slow progress, chiefly with short-term credits, funded by the issuance of short-term promissory notes in the Canadian commercial paper market, guaranteed by Chase in New York.[28]

By 1977, however, a change in the banking law appeared likely that would permit the establishment of foreign chartered banks, enabling them to accept deposits, among other advantages. In anticipation of such action, the name CMB Holdings was changed to Chase Manhattan Canada. Branches were shortly introduced into Montreal, Calgary, and Vancouver (initially little more than shells) in the expectation that they too could be included in any conversion. And a drive was mounted to build up assets, again to ensure a favorable position in chartering.

Chase Manhattan Canada did, in fact, receive its charter as a Canadian bank, although not until January 1982.[29] Meanwhile, the banking scene in Canada had changed. Canadian banks were finding it difficult to meet the full credit needs of the growing country. Chase Manhattan Canada competed more effectively for a share in the business of multinational corporations as well as medium-sized Canadian companies. Assets expanded, as did earnings, aided as elsewhere in the world by Chase's network of overseas facilities.

Chase opens up the Soviet Union and the People's Republic of China

While it was entering such countries as Canada and the Philippines, Chase also opened two giant areas previously closed to American banks: the Soviet Union and the People's Republic of China. Here David Rockefeller played a pivotal role. Rockefeller had been one of the first business leaders to engage in a dialogue with representatives of the Soviet Union. Since 1962 he had participated in a series of conferences known as the Dartmouth Group, named after the location of the initial meeting, which had been encouraged by President Eisenhower. These meetings, occurring alternately in the United States and the Soviet Union, aimed at promoting better understanding between the two countries. Rockfeller met many Soviet leaders and had lengthy sessions alone with Khrushchev and later Kosygin.[30] He also was able to call on Soviet banking officials in Moscow, in part because since the prewar years Chase had served as the U.S. bank for the Soviet purchasing mission.

American business became increasingly interested in establishing trade and economic relations with Eastern Europe and the Soviet Union in the early 1970s. The time seemed propitious for approaching the Soviet authorities about opening a representative office in Moscow. An opportunity arose when Rockefeller, attending a session of the Dartmouth Group at Kiev in July 1971, was invited with a few others to fly to Moscow to meet with Premier Kosygin. Kosygin expressed an interest in U.S. help with Soviet investment, and when Rockefeller suggested a Chase representative, Kosygin asked to have the proposal in writing.[31] Ambassador Dobrynin was supportive from the United States, and permission to open an office followed in November 1972, the first of any U.S. bank.

Alfred R. Wentworth, a senior vice president with twenty-six years' experience in the international department, was designated as the bank's representative. Wentworth, a large, outgoing man, was familiar with many areas of the world and worked well with the Soviets. Before opening the office Chase entered into the first term-loan agreement between the Soviet Union and an American bank, an $86 million credit to help finance U.S. equipment for the foundry of the Soviet's new Kama River truck plant.[32]

The bank's Moscow office, located initially at One Karl Marx Square, close to the Kremlin, opened in May 1973. Through it over the next few years passed many Americans, introduced by Wentworth to Soviet officials concerned with trade, possible cooperative arrangements, or the purchase of equipment. Not until later in the decade, as relations between the United States and the Soviet Union cooled, did activity fall off markedly.

Rockefeller visits China

Shortly after opening the Moscow office Rockefeller paid his initial visit to the People's Republic of China, the first American bank executive to enter the country since the revolution. The way had been paved as early as 1970, when, at a press conference in Hong Kong, he was asked whether the United States should establish relations with China. He responded that it was unrealistic for the United States to act "as if a country of 800 million people did not exist," and he believed it desirable that the United States open contacts with the People's Republic.[33]

After the Nixon-Kissinger initiative of 1971–72 established limited relations with the PRC, Rockefeller concluded that the time had come to explore the possibility of some activity with that country. Through Leo Pierre, Chase's representative with the United Nations, he and Mrs. Rockefeller entertained Ambassador Huang Hua (later foreign minister) and his wife at tea, the first time the ambassador had been in a private home in New York.[34] A visit to the Museum of Modern Art and a lunch soon followed. On the latter occasion the ambassador asked Rockefeller if he would like to visit the

PRC. The response was in the affirmative, and arrangements were completed for a visit in late June 1973.

Rockefeller was accompanied by Mrs. Rockefeller, Francis X. Stankard, head of the international department, Joseph V. Reed, Jr., Rockefeller's executive assistant, Mrs. Reed, and James Pusey, son of the former president of Harvard, who spoke fluent Chinese. The group spent ten days there, much of it in Peking, where Rockefeller and Stankard met with top officials of the National Bank of China, the institution responsible for foreign financial relations and transactions. They found the bank in need of modern techniques and a better understanding of international banking. Work handled by computer at Chase was frequently done by abacus in China. Other Chase officers later returned to Peking and spent many hours at the bank, conveying information on contemporary banking practices.

On Rockefeller's final evening in Peking, he and the group met for two hours with Premier Chou En-Lai. Chou, who had been well briefed on Rockefeller's visits with other officials, wanted to discuss world economics. His talks with Kissinger and Nixon, he stated, had been concerned with international political matters, but "they did not know much about economics." So among other matters, Rockefeller explained the working of the international monetary system since the breakdown of the Bretton Woods agreements in 1971. Rockefeller found Chou "an enormously well informed and cultivated person . . . one of the most fascinating and interesting people I have ever met."[35]

In his earlier session with the National Bank of China, the chairman had extended to Rockefeller an invitation for Chase to become the bank's first U.S. correspondent. Rockefeller accepted, and a formal relationship soon was established. For some time it was limited to handling such relatively simple transactions as remittances and travelers' letters of credit.[36] More extensive activities could be developed only after political relations between the two countries returned to a more normal basis. This included settlement of Chinese government balances in the U.S. blocked by the U.S. Treasury, not accomplished until 1978–79. Meanwhile, Chase World Information carried on an extensive consulting business on China, establishing an office in the Peking Hotel and introducing many U.S. corporations to officials and opportunities in this land closed to the United States for more than two decades.

The bank moves in the Middle East

Of much greater immediate significance to the bank than the Soviet Union or China was the Middle East. There Chase had little direct representation at the start of the 1970s—a branch in Beirut and a joint venture in Dubai, the Commercial Bank of Dubai, with the Commercial Bank of Kuwait and Commerz Bank of Germany as fellow shareholders.[37] A representative office in Cairo had been closed by the Egyptian government many years earlier. Chase did maintain strong correspondent relationships with banks and governments, most important with the Saudi Arabian Monetary Agency, for which the bank served as a major depository, with funds at the head office and in London. A representative office in Beirut provided regular liaison with this and other accounts throughout the area.

In 1971 the bank established a branch in Manama, Bahrain, a commercial and trade center near Saudi Arabia. And in 1973 it contracted to provide management personnel and various services for the Commercial Bank of Kuwait, its associate in Dhabi, which had urgent need of assistance—this in lieu of establishing a branch in Kuwait, which was forbidden. There matters rested until the explosion in oil prices and revenues in the winter of 1973–74 galvanized the bank into action. Over the next several years associated banks were opened in Cairo and Teheran and a branch in Amman, Jordan, supplemented by representative offices in Cairo, Teheran, and Abu Dhabi.

Of critical importance was a change in the political climate of Egypt. President Sadat had turned away from the Soviet Union and opened the economy in a limited way to private enterprise and cooperation with the West. Rockefeller visited Egypt in late January 1974 and discussed with the president Chase's plans to open branches in duty-free zones of the Suez Canal and Alexandria, as well as details of an $80 million loan that Chase was arranging to help Egypt finance the Sumed oil pipeline.[38]

As matters developed, these plans soon changed. Chase chose instead to enter into a joint venture with the National Bank of Egypt, the country's largest state bank, forming the Chase National Bank (Egypt) S.A.E. Although Chase possessed a minority share (49 percent), it provided many of the key management personnel as well as advanced operating systems and technology. The joint venture offered wider scope for commercial banking with a partner possessing excellent connections in the Egyptian business community. The new bank opened in mid-1975. It expanded well over the remainder of the decade, with branches in Cairo, Port Said, and Alexandria although the economy turned less favorable in the 1980s.[39]

Less fortunate in the end was Chase's joint-venture bank in Iran, the International Bank of Iran, established in 1975 with the state-owned Industrial Credit Bank as a partner.[40] Each partner held 35 percent, with the remainder in the hands of the public. The new bank expected to assist in the development of Iran and promote Teheran as a major financial center. Its capital funds totaled approximately $36 million (with Chase's share at $12.6 million) before it fell victim to the Iranian revolution in June 1979.

Birth of the Saudi Arabian Investment Bank

There remained Saudi Arabia, in many respects the most important country financially in the area. Chase tried for many years to gain direct representation in the kingdom. Lengthy discussions with the Riyadh Bank, a leading institution in need of assistance, were finally terminated, as was an effort to set up a Saudi Arabian finance company, opposed by local interests.

Then in 1973, as oil revenues mounted, the Saudi Arabian Monetary Agency (SAMA) suggested a quite different approach. Chase was asked to organize, staff, and manage a Saudi industrial development fund to supply interest-free or subsidized loans to small and medium-sized Saudi businesses, including local electrical utilities.[41] This would be done by Chase for a fee, while Saudi personnel were trained to take over the institution. Concurrently Chase would be permitted to establish a joint-venture investment bank, designed to provide medium- and long-term financing required by Saudi-controlled companies in the kingdom and not furnished by commercial banks. Chase's share in this latter venture would be limited to 20 percent, with other foreign participants contributing a further 15 percent and Saudi institutions and public a majority of 65 percent.

The Saudi Industrial Development Fund began operations in 1975 and over the next few years grew vigorously, helping to spread electrification through the country and extending credit to smaller business in many industries. Meanwhile, Chase gradually withdrew as Saudi-trained personnel were able to take over. By 1980 Chase personnel were no longer associated with the management of the fund, having successfully completed their mission.[42]

In contrast, considerable time elapsed before agreement was reached on the range of activities to be undertaken by the new investment bank, and it did not open its doors until April 1977. SAMA made clear that the new institution, named the Saudi Investment Banking Corporation (SIBC), was not to be a commercial bank accepting short-term deposits and extending short-term credit, other than providing temporary facilities in support of its longer-term activities. Rather it was to be exclusively a development bank contributing to the economic, industrial, and agricultural development of the kingdom's economy, an arrangement that fell short of what Chase had hoped for.[43]

Once begun, the new investment bank found a ready market for its services. By the end of 1980 its assets exceeded $4.1 billion, and it showed a respectable return on equity.[44] Branches were established in Jidda and Al Khobar, supplementing the head office in Riyadh. And supporting fee-producing services were undertaken, including project advisory services and investment and portfolio management. But still SIBC had limitations. It could not lend to existing companies that sought commercial-bank–type financing, nor could it attract the growing demand deposits of the country that provided cheap funding.

SBIC's development loans, which frequently grew out of new ventures, carried more than normal risk as economic growth in the kingdom finally slowed down. The shareholders of SBIC sought a broader charter, permitting the bank to undertake a full range of commercial bank activities. This was granted in late 1984, along with a change to a simpler name, the Saudi Investment Bank. Chase continued to own 20 percent and to provide key personnel under a technical services agreement, but the Saudi Investment Bank remained uniquely Saudi in character, with a Saudi majority on the board and a chairman selected by the Saudi Arabian Monetary Agency.

Growth of merchant banking

No activity grew more explosively in the 1970s than merchant banking, especially institutions involved in international currency markets. Chase made an early start through its initiative in 1970 in forming Orion, the consortium bank in which it held a 20 percent interest (see Chapter XII). Over the next few years the bank greatly expanded its activity, first through Libra, a consortium bank specializing in Latin American credits, and then through Chase Manhattan, Ltd., and Chase Manhattan Asia, two fully owned subsidiaries.

Libra, launched in 1972, was patterned after Orion, but with a regional focus, financing only activities that involved Latin America and the Caribbean.[45] The founding partners were those of Orion, although Chase's 26.24 percent share (later reduced to 23.58 percent) was the largest. Banco Espirito Santo e Comercial de Lisboa and the Swiss Bank Corporation, both with interests in South America, also joined the group. Still later, Banco Itau, with 450 branches in Brazil, and Banco de Comercio, then the largest private bank in Mexico, were added.

Chase provided management for Libra, with Thomas F. Gaffney, a vice president with experience in Latin America, as managing director. Headquarters were maintained in London, the center of the international market, but offices were also established in principal countries of Latin America as well as in New York City. Libra was administered conservatively in an environment that frequently proved unstable. In 1983 its assets had expanded to more than $2.5 billion.[46] Although it suffered from Latin American debt problems in the 1980s, Libra remained profitable.

Chase moves out on its own

By 1973 the extraordinary growth of the syndicated loan and Eurobond markets persuaded Chase that it should supplement its participation in Orion and Libra with a merchant bank it fully owned. To accomplish this the bank decided to utilize an institution already in existence, The Chase Manhattan Bank Trust Corporation in London. The name was changed in April 1973 to Chase Manhattan, Ltd. (known as CML), and the function was redesigned to encompass merchant bank activities.[47]

Chase Manhattan, Ltd., soon became the centerpiece for the bank's syndicated loan activities, managing and participating in large medium-term loan syndications for public agencies and private industry, including arrangements for financing special projects throughout the world. Within a few years CML added Eurobond underwriting and trading to its activities, and it engaged in financial counseling and merger and acquisition activity. In all this it competed to some degree with Orion and to a lesser extent with Libra. Paul J. Lakers served as the initial head, succeeded in late 1975 by Otto Schoeppler, a former partner in Trinkhaus and Burckhardt in West Germany. Under Schoeppler's guidance CML grew to be one of the major participants in the Eurocurrency market, which exploded in size as it recycled OPEC surpluses.

Meanwhile a sister institution, known today as Chase Manhattan Asia, was evolving in the Far East, based in Hong Kong. Its beginning was unusually modest, involving the purchase in 1972 for $6 of a charter for a merchant bank, Kam Yuan Choy Mo, that had not yet commenced operations.[48] A merchant bank in Hong Kong could carry loans with a tax advantage not enjoyed by the Chase branch, as well as undertake traditional activities. Soon the Eurocurrency markets spread to Asia, and Kam Yuan Choy Mo engaged in syndication of large loans and other merchant bank activities for customers throughout the region. In 1975 its name was changed to Chase Asia, Ltd., and later, in 1977, to Chase Manhattan Asia, Ltd. (CMAL).

By that date CMAL had become a leader in Far Eastern merchant banking. The need to provide more effective coordination between activities in Europe and the Far East was apparent, so a merchant bank group, including both CML and CMAL, was formed with Schoeppler at the head. In 1978 this group managed or co-managed loan syndications of approximately $10 billion, and by 1979 was the largest syndicate manager of any bank,[49] through the efforts of a highly professional staff able to fashion unique financing arrangements for governments, corporations, and other borrowers.

CML and CMAL did not, as a rule, take loans they syndicated directly on their own books, but they did have an advantage in placing power. Not only did Chase branches and other entities frequently participate, but even more, Chase's worldwide network of correspondent banks, including banks in the United States, provided outlets.

Orion also moved into the Far East, with its subsidiary, Orion Pacific, headquartered in Hong Kong. So here too Chase worked with two entities, frequently in competition with each other. And Chase participated in other local merchant banks in the region, in Singapore and Malaysia, as well as Australia, New Zealand, and the Philippines, as we have seen. Several of these became less useful as Chase Manhattan Asia developed, and Chase's interest was eventually sold. Finally in 1981 Chase also relinquished its interest in Orion, preferring to concentrate all efforts in a fully owned institution.

CIIC gives way to a changing environment

As Chase's merchant banks flourished, Chase International Investment Corporation (CIIC), its original development bank, decreased in importance, reflecting longer-term changes in the environment. Since its founding in the late 1950s, CIIC had for the most part maintained its initial objective of providing equity and other capital to new companies in developing nations. Over the years it had carried investments in thirty countries and agreed in principle to enter still others. By and large, investments continued to be small and were made with a "know-how" partner in the industry or service. By 1970 project loans and investments totaled $20 million, compared with $8 million a decade earlier.[50]

CIIC had not been very profitable; its return on investment through the 1960s averaged about 2.5 percent. But profit had not been the sole objective. First Aldrich and then McCloy, Rockefeller, and Victor E. Rockhill, its early president, viewed the activities of CIIC as containing an element of pro bono publico, a contribution by Chase to the process of economic development. And there had been other ancillary benefits. CIIC had introduced the first investments for the bank in a number of new countries and new markets—in Australia through the Esperance Land Corporation, in the Philippines through the predecessor of Filinvest, and in Iran and the Ivory Coast through development banks. Certain other investments, such as the development bank in Panama, were useful in support of Chase branch operations. Moreover, the CIIC personnel at the head office possessed a knowledge in depth of many countries that was drawn upon by officers and customers of other departments.

In 1970 the bank decided to shift all investments in development banks and finance companies from CIIC to Chase Manhattan Overseas Banking Corporation, the holding company for foreign subsidiaries and affiliates. Over the next few years CIIC tightened its operations and undertook additional investments, some in Europe but chiefly in Africa. Nevertheless, in terms of profitability CIIC made only limited progress in the early 1970s and then suffered a series of setbacks with the oil price increase and world recession of 1974–75. Sizable provisions for loan losses resulted in deficits. Rockefeller and Butcher, after surveying the bank's overall profit position and risk exposure, decided that CIIC should make no new commitments.[51] The subsidiary entered a period of liquidation over the rest of the decade, having pioneered in a useful activity not undertaken by any other bank, and having made a unique contribution quite out of proportion to its relatively small size.

An abortive attempt: Familienbank in Germany

Successful experience with merchant banks demonstrated anew that Chase's major strength lay in wholesale banking. The bank added yet another link in its supportive network for this activity by opening a subsidiary bank in Luxembourg, which proved especially helpful to the branches in West Germany.[52] But the strategic plan of 1971 called also for expanding overseas in retail banking. Outside the United States the bank had vigorously pursued this objective only in the Caribbean. Now it would attempt to move in Europe.

Two countries were to be the cutting edge of this initiative—West Germany and Great Britain—with the major effort centered in the former. There a new retail bank, named the Familienbank (Family Bank), was established to provide a full range of personal services, such as salary and wage accounts, installment loans, and checking and savings accounts.[53]

By the end of 1974, its first full year of activity, Familienbank was operating a network of twelve branches, with a head office in Dusseldorf. A year later the number of branches had doubled. But problems appeared. Start-up and operating costs were greater than anticipated, as were loan delinquencies. The West German economy suffered from the unexpected oil price rise, and banks became more fiercely competitive. New projections cast doubt on the long-run profitability of the enterprise.[54]

The management committee, in reviewing the position, concluded that Chase should ultimately disengage from retail banking in West Germany, and instructed the international department to determine how to do so at minimum cost. The plan finally adopted involved transferring most of the business in Chase's German branches to Familienbank, renaming that institution the Chase Bank A.G., and managing a withdrawal from the retail business over several years.[55] This enabled the bank to take full advantage of all losses for tax purposes, which would not have been possible if Familienbank had been liquidated outright. Moreover, as a foreign-owned German bank, Chase A.G. had certain other advantages over a branch. All of Chase's commercial banking business was to be carried out by Chase A.G., but a single Chase branch would continue to be maintained in Frankfort, housed and integrated operationally with Chase A.G., to handle money market and foreign exchange activities.

This reorganization took effect in September 1977, and today Chase A.G. handles the great bulk of Chase's business in West Germany. Familienbank branches were closed, and the retail business was finally liquidated in 1978. Cumulative losses after taxes amounted to more than $20 million.[56] The problems of Familienbank received wide publicity in both West Germany and the United States and reacted unfavorably on the bank's image.

Plans for retail services in Great Britain never reached full fruition. The directors in early 1973 approved establishing either a retail bank or a consumer finance company.[57] Some thirty offices were to open within four years. But a closer look at start-up costs and potential profitability soon caused the bank to reassess its position. Chase then turned to a possible participation with a company already in the business, the First National Finance Corporation, carrying consumer assets of some $280 million. A new jointly owned corporation, named the Chase Bank National (Finance), was to take over these assets. First National Finance already operated twenty-two branches in London department stores, and thirty-nine additional branches were planned for railroad stations throughout Britain.

The bank publicly announced in May 1974 that negotiations were under way with First National Finance, but it then delayed moving forward with the venture. Prospects for consumer lending in Britain appeared to be deteriorating, with the oil price shock leading to higher interest rates and rising unemployment. Finally, rejection of the Dial acquisition in the autumn of 1974 demonstrated that the Federal Reserve would not look with favor on a sizable new venture by Chase. The proposal was allowed to lapse, perhaps propitiously, for First National Finance itself subsequently encountered difficulties in a troubled British economy.

Thus Chase's first effort at retail banking in Europe ended. A decade would elapse before the bank again attempted to move into the field, but then more selectively and conservatively.

An assessment: how the bank fared against its 1971 plan

Notwithstanding the failure to expand into retail banking in Europe, and earlier to acquire Dial Financial Corporation, Chase made substantial progress toward the ambitious goals set in the 1971 plan. A network of branches was put in place across New York State, and the number of new branches added in the metropolitan area exceeded all projections. Retail banking was also strengthened in 1972 by the conversion of Uni-Card to Chase Bank-Americard (see Chapter X), continuing as a leading credit card in the city. On the wholesale side, loan production offices and Edge Act affiliates were strategically placed in the most rapidly growing regions. Moreover, the bank had taken an innovative plunge into a new field, information services, which held promise for the future.

The major domestic shortfall, and a critical one, lay in the bank's inability to develop a nationwide network of offices which could serve as distribution points for a variety of financial products. Here Chase had put all its eggs in one basket—Dial Financial—only to be thwarted again by the regulatory authority in a questionable decision. Other near-bank facilities—leasing, factoring, and commercial finance—also failed to spread as initially anticipated, in part because profitability did not appear impressive.

But the plan had called for the greatest expansion to occur overseas, and this expectation was realized. Gaps in the worldwide network were filled with near-bank affiliates, chiefly in the Philippines, New Zealand, and Canada. And the Middle East was penetrated with joint-venture banks in Egypt and Iran, branches in Jordan and Bahrain, and plans for a development bank in Saudi Arabia, the latter less than hoped for in that vital kingdom. Chase had taken the initiative in opening up the Soviet Union and the People's Republic of China to American banking. Moreover, beyond all this, throughout much of the developed and developing world, existing facilities were bolstered by diversification into merchant banks, finance companies, money market facilities, and other near-bank institutions. In particular, the founding of Chase Manhattan, Ltd., and Chase Asia, Ltd., would prove to be of the utmost importance in years ahead.

Troubled years: 1975–1976

The years 1975 and 1976 were the most difficult Chase experienced in the postwar period. The bank was not alone in this. Years of inflation, now intensified by the huge rise in the price of oil, had taken their toll. By late 1974 the U.S. economy had slipped into its worst recession since the 1930s, and the rest of the industrial world followed. Many companies, heavily encumbered with debt, failed. Real estate paid a severe penalty for speculative excess, encouraged by years of ever-rising prices. Even cities and public agencies, once considered prime investments, moved to the brink of bankruptcy.

These developments affected Chase severely. Loan losses and the volume of nonperforming loans soared for banks generally, but somewhat more so at Chase because of its greater exposure in real estate. The bank's namesake, the Chase Manhattan Mortgage and Realty Trust, moved toward ultimate bankruptcy. Earnings declined substantially, although never to a point that threatened the existing dividend. And early in 1976, along with Citibank, Chase was singled out and criticized, often unfairly, in the press. As a result, the bank's image and reputation were damaged.

Yet Chase emerged from these troubles a much stronger and healthier institution. Rockefeller and Butcher never failed to confront difficulties directly, always with the support of the directors. And in the area of public responsibility, the bank played a leading role in the struggle to salvage the finances of New York City, even at considerable cost. The bank's underlying strength, demonstrated by continued strong earnings from corporate and international business, was never threatened. By the second half of 1976 it was evident that Chase was heading into a new period of growth, resting on a more solid foundation.

Loan growth abroad, losses at home

In spite of substantial weakness in the global economy, Chase's loans continued to expand worldwide in 1975 and 1976. All of the increase occurred outside the United States, much of it related either directly or indirectly to the need of oil-consuming nations to finance balance-of-payments deficits. Chase held to its policy of favoring credit extension to private industry rather

239

than to governments. Nevertheless, its merchant banks, particularly Chase Manhattan, Ltd., and Chase Asia, were increasingly active in managing large loan syndications in which the bank participated, including many to governments and official institutions. Consequently, loans in this category had grown to $1.4 billion by the end of 1976, still little more than one-tenth of overall international loans, then totaling $13.5 billion.[1]

Many credits were provided to less developed countries, as widely dispersed as Egypt and Iran in the Middle East, Brazil and Peru in South America, and South Korea and the Philippines in Asia. Public concern began to be expressed about the exposure of American banks, including Chase, in these countries. The bank, however, monitored closely the distribution of its country risk. Almost 60 percent of total overseas credit lay in industrial countries, with Japan, Great Britain, and West Germany the primary recipients.[2] And the lion's share of the remaining credit was extended either to OPEC nations or to the more prosperous less developed countries, especially Brazil and Mexico. Loan losses incurred overseas remained relatively small and easily manageable.

At home the position of the bank was much less satisfactory. The problem did not lie in weak loan demand. Although domestic loans declined slightly in 1975, they regained their previous peak the following year, but the quality of the loan portfolio deteriorated sharply. More and more loans were placed in a nonperforming status; that is, either interest was no longer being accrued on a monthly basis, although partial cash payments were sometimes made, or the credits were renegotiated, usually for payments at a lower interest rate. Meanwhile, actual loan losses mounted to levels never before encountered.

By the end of 1975 nonperforming loans had climbed to $1.87 billion, or 6.5 percent of the worldwide loan portfolio, with the great bulk in nonaccrual status.[3] They continued to increase through the first half of 1976, reaching a peak in July of approximately $2.2 billion, after which the number began to decline, a signal to both management and investors that the worst was probably over. By the end of the year the total was reduced to $1.7 billion, or 5.6 percent of a somewhat larger loan portfolio. Meanwhile, income lost over the two years from these nonperforming assets, which the bank continued to finance, amounted to close to $100 million after taxes.

Serious as this drain on earnings was, it did not produce the same heavy impact as the escalating volume of actual loan losses. These skyrocketed to $251 million in 1975 and $269 million in 1976 (before taxes and net of modest recoveries). But again, as the end of 1976 approached, signs appeared that this hemorrhaging too would abate.

Other banks also suffered in this adverse environment. Citibank experienced an even greater volume of nonperforming loans and loss of income, although it also had a larger loan portfolio than Chase. And its loan losses in this period exceeded those of Chase, but with considerably more income to absorb them.

For Chase the major problem lay in real estate—not only in the bank's portfolio but even more in that of several of its subsidiaries: Housing Investment Corporation of Florida, Housing Investment Corporation of Puerto Rico, and, to a lesser degree, Dovenmuehle. Real estate accounted for about 80 percent of all nonperforming loans in 1975 and 1976 as well as three-fifths of the net charge-offs.

Not that corporate credits escaped unscathed. A recession as severe as that in 1974–75 was bound to have an impact, the more so since many corporations had borrowed heavily in an inflationary environment that made financing through equity difficult. One sizable corporate loss, accompanied by much publicity, occurred with the bankruptcy in 1975 of W. T. Grant, the nation's third largest chain of variety stores.[4] A group of twenty-seven banks were owed $627 million, with Chase, Citibank, and Morgan each having $97 million outstanding. Chase quickly wrote off $35 million, followed by further write-offs in subsequent months, although inventory and receivables were pledged against the loan. By the early 1980s the bank had recovered part of its write-off, losing about $33 million in principal but with a few payments yet to come.[5]

Conservative policy and declining profits

Throughout this entire period Rockefeller and Butcher insisted that the bank face reality squarely. Loans were placed on a nonaccrual basis when interest ceased being received currently, or when management believed that there was a reasonable possibility that interest would not be received on a timely basis. And a portion of a loan was charged off immediately if it became apparent that the full amount was unlikely to be collected. In this Chase differed from some competitors who, Micawber-like, procrastinated on charge-offs, only to face the moment of truth in the future.

The ultimate test was the handling of the reserve for loan losses. Provision for this reserve counted as current expense and directly affected the reported level of profits. Again Rockefeller and Butcher adopted a highly prudent course, not only providing for $520 million of net charge-offs in 1975 and 1976, but increasing the reserve for loan losses by $103 million. This raised the reserve to $324 million, or slightly more than 1 percent of all loans at the end of 1976, a relatively greater proportion than the bank's principal competitors.

In these circumstances net operating earnings declined sharply, falling to $157 million in 1975 and a low of $105 million in 1976, a drop of more than 40 percent over two years. The surprise was that the bank managed to hold the decline within these bounds. It was helped in this respect by a record earnings performance overseas, by very careful planning and control by the asset-liability management committee, and by a program of strict cost control, including the elimination of a number of unprofitable branches, products, and services.

The network of overseas branches, affiliates, and subsidiaries built under stimulus from Rockefeller in the 1960s and early 1970s proved its worth at this time by providing the lion's share of earnings in both 1975 and 1976. Indeed, excluding losing real estate operations in Puerto Rico (chiefly the responsibility of the real estate department), the net income of the international department in 1976 exceeded the $105 million for the bank as a whole.[6] Earnings flowed from all regions but were greatest in Europe and Asia, reflecting expanding loans and favorable margins in Eurocurrency financing.

Role of asset-liability management

Asset-liability management assumed a role of critical importance at this time and continued to evolve throughout the decade. Perhaps no other development demonstrated so well the changing nature of banking. A quarter-century earlier Chase had relied almost exclusively on demand deposits to finance loans and investments. Funding costs were relatively stable, as were interest rates on loans, most of which were extended on a fixed-rate basis. But by 1975 Chase was dependent on borrowed money for 80 percent of its funds, and interest rates had become increasingly volatile. Interest paid for funds represented almost two-thirds of all costs. How money was borrowed—when, in what markets, and at what maturities—had become a matter of vital concern. On the asset side, how loans were priced—floating rates, fixed rates, tied to the prime rate or Eurocurrency rates—as well as the mixture of loans and investments, was of no less significance.

Helping formulate longer-term strategy on these matters, as well as establishing week-to-week tactics, was the province of the asset-liability management committee (ALMAC). Chaired at this time by William S. Ogden, chief financial officer, the committee operated under policies laid down by Rockefeller and Butcher, and included other members of the management committee, heads of the lending and portfolio investment departments, and the chief economist.

Weekly meetings of ALMAC invariably opened with an assessment of the economic environment, with particular attention paid to the outlook for interest rates. For the question of whether interest rates appeared most likely to remain stable, to rise, or to fall, heavily influenced the guidelines developed by the committee. Specific forecasts prepared by staff for different time periods were placed before the committee for consideration. On this matter, however, the committee was not infallible. Interest rates proved notoriously difficult to predict. But the committee followed the adage, "If you have to forecast, forecast often," and it remained alert to the first faint shifts in the economic weather.

With domestic loan demand relatively weak in 1975 and 1976, and the need to minimize costs and gain income urgent, ALMAC placed emphasis on determining the least costly mix of purchased funds, along with expanding the bank's investment in securities.[7] Yet the committee also implemented a strategic policy urged by Butcher to build up the amount of medium-term borrowed money in this period of lower interest rates, even though the cost of such funds exceeded that of short-term deposits. This effort climaxed late in 1976 with the sale to Salomon Brothers of $200 million in negotiable CDs with a maturity of four years and an interest rate of 6.5 percent.[8] These longer-term deposits helped ALMAC later, for marketing reasons, to agree to a limited volume of fixed-rate loans at suitable margins.

ALMAC carried out other important functions, among them control of "placing" activity by foreign branches in the Eurocurrency markets, guidance of tax-dependent transactions, and establishment of guidelines for maturities of assets and liabilities both domestically and in foreign branches. Guidelines, formulated initially with the cooperation of managers, provided ranges within which each might operate, thereby encouraging initiative and flexibility. Moreover, managers could always seek a change in a guideline. But with branches and subsidiaries operating throughout the world, all with potential mismatches between assets and liabilities and exposed to funding risks, the bank could not afford to let each operate on its own. The guidelines system devised by ALMAC was praised by examiners as one of the most effective of any major bank.

A change in strategy

Asset-liability decisions were also guided at this time by a conscious change of strategy by Rockefeller and Butcher. For years emphasis had been placed on growth. Assets had doubled over the first half of the 1970s, but capital had not kept pace. No less serious, the return on average assets (ROA) dropped steadily from 0.61 percent in 1970 to 0.45 percent in 1974. These trends could not be permitted to continue. Part of the growth had been generated by worldwide inflation. But now Butcher announced that Chase would deemphasize growth in assets and instead stress the return on assets. Officers were to price all services so that they could be profitable, "whether . . . making a loan, managing a trust fund, giving financial advice on a massive energy project, or providing cash management to a multinational corporation."[9]

The bank then took a soul-searching look at the relative profitability of its various functions. Three in particular were found wanting: retail banking, domestic correspondent relationships, and trust and fiduciary investment. Much time and effort were devoted over the next several years to converting these into profitable operations. Meanwhile, loan officers negotiated lending margins with even greater care, although competitive pressures under conditions of slack demand limited progress on this front.

Domestic branches were scrutinized carefully with an eye to weeding out units that showed little prospect for profit. Thirteen branches were closed in 1976, and nine applications for new branches were withdrawn. These were scattered throughout the city and suburbs and included four upstate. The press reported Chase's withdrawal from Forty-fourth Street and Broadway, as well as the abandonment of its automated branch in Grand Central Station, opened in 1972 as both a laboratory for automation and as an advertisement.[10] The branch had fulfilled its original functions but in spite of heavy traffic was losing money. So with ROA in mind, it was terminated.

Other activities operating at a loss or at excessive risk were phased out. Among them, as we saw in Chapter XV, was Chase International Investment Corporation. This was joined by Chase Manhattan Capital Corporation, the subsidiary providing equity and medium-term financing to small business, which had not been managed solely on a business basis.[11] Many of its clients represented relatively new ventures, sometimes operating in minority areas with inexperienced management. Inflation and the recession bore down hard on such firms, and the corporation suffered losses even as loans and investments reached a peak of nearly $30 million in 1975. With the outlook unpromising, the decision was taken in 1976 to liquidate the portfolio.

Chase also undertook a radical departure in the corporate trust field, again to conserve costs. Back office operations in support of stock transfer, registrar, and other corporate agency functions were farmed out to an outside company, Bradford National Corporation.[12] Although Chase and other banks had performed the major part of stock transfer in the 1950s, they later began to lose market share. Large companies found it economical to handle transfers on their own computers, and computer service companies such as Bradford, with lower costs, entered the business. Moreover, the New York Stock Exchange had formed the Central Certificate Service for its members, reducing the number of certificates and increasing competition.

With these adverse trends, stock transfer, once profitable, was losing as much as $10 million a year by the mid-1970s.[13] The business was highly labor intensive, and Bradford, in a less expensive location and with lower overhead, could operate in a more cost-effective manner. Bradford provided clerical and computer functions for stock transfer and other corporate agency activities, while Chase continued to maintain the relationship with customers, marketing the services and handling all administrative responsibilities.

Savings on stock transfer, branch closings, and many other activities helped to restore ROA to acceptable levels in the years ahead. But for the moment the avalanche of losses, particularly from real estate, overwhelmed all else, and ROA in 1976 sank to 0.24 percent, its lowest in the postwar period.

Shoring up the capital position

Return on assets as an objective, rather than growth, was also dictated by Chase's worsening capital position. The corporation had gone to market in 1971 with a $200 million issue of convertible debentures. Over the next three years its assets increased almost three-fourths, but capital grew only 13 percent, and this through retained earnings. Capital ratios had deteriorated, and bank examiners were critical of this trend.

Very high interest rates in 1973 and 1974 discouraged the marketing of any new bond issue. But in June 1974 Chase seized an opportunity to gain assistance through an unusual offering. Along with Citicorp it pioneered in marketing $200 million of floating rate notes. These carried a rate tied to the interest yield on three-month Treasury bills. Although not due for twenty-five years, they also included an option for holders to reclaim payment at stated times each year after mid-1976. For this reason the notes could not be classified as capital, although they served as a close substitute. At two redemptions in 1976 more than half were cashed in. [14]

The decline in net income at middecade reduced the flow of retained earnings. This, along with the prospect of sizable redemptions of the floating rate issue, contributed to the pressure to add to capital from external sources even though the timing was poor. A two-pronged program was devised to bring a measure of relief. A $200 million issue of subordinated capital notes of the bank was successfully marketed in May 1976, followed a few weeks later by a $200 million five-year revolving Eurodollar credit for the corporation from a group of ten European banks. [15] The Eurodollar credit did not strictly constitute capital, but it provided essential backing for the corporation.

These actions relieved the immediate problem. Chase's capital position was stabilized for the time being, albeit at a lower level than desired. Over the next few years the scramble for capital would continue, especially in raising equity-type funds through ingenious financing.

A closer look at real estate problems

Problems with real estate so dominated Chase's overall performance in the mid-1970s that they merit more detailed attention. Many major banks suffered similar losses in this period, but none on the same scale. In part this reflected Chase's paramount position in the business, with real estate credits at the end of 1974 of almost $5 billion extended to homeowners, builders, and developers.[16]

Growth in this activity had been explosive, spurred on by a boom in construction that followed the economic recession of 1970. Housing became a top priority of government, and liberal financing was encouraged. Real estate investment trusts (REITs) were only one of several new sources of finance stimulated by favorable tax treatment. And the past history of real estate lulled lenders into complacency, as an inflationary environment frequently bailed out uneconomical projects.

In these circumstances excesses soon developed. Inexperienced builders and workers were drawn into the industry, and cost overruns became common.[17] Yet financing continued to be available, encouraged by wider profit margins than could be earned in other lending. Then in 1974 the environment for housing and other construction suddenly turned unfavorable. The energy crisis and record interest rates raised costs and discouraged buyers. Starts of new housing and commercial units plummeted, and selling the completed units became difficult.

At Chase for many years real estate activity had been the charge of Raymond T. O'Keefe, an officer with wide experience and an excellent reputation. O'Keefe, foreseeing the expansion that lay ahead in the 1970s, had taken the lead in founding the real estate subsidiaries in Puerto Rico, Florida, and Chicago, as well as Chase Manhattan Mortgage and Realty Trust (CMART), for which the bank served as adviser. O'Keefe retired in 1973 but remained chairman of CMART. He was succeeded at Chase by William B. Bateman, an officer with a fine record in corporate banking but with limited experience in real estate. Meanwhile, credit extended to real estate by the bank and its subsidiaries expanded from less than $2 billion at the end of 1971 to almost $5 billion three years later. In addition the bank generated the principal share of CMART's rapidly expanding loans and investments, by then in excess of $1 billion, including commitments.

Rockefeller and Butcher were fully aware of this real estate expansion and approved it. They were not conscious, however, of the extent to which personnel and administrative procedures had been stretched and strained by the rapid growth in activity. To achieve this growth, inexperienced personnel had been pressed into service; documentation and files were poorly maintained; communication between lending and administrative support areas was faulty; and follow-up on construction projects was frequently sporadic or nonexistent. In addition, lending practices in many instances were overly liberal, perhaps to the greatest degree in the Housing Investment Corporations (HIC) of Florida and Puerto Rico, both under the direction of John D. Yates, a founder of the latter, who operated relatively independently.[18]

Signs that all was not well appeared in an audit of CMART in 1974 as well as in an examination of the bank by the comptroller of currency, both of which were sharply critical. Butcher then ordered a close look at the portfolio of the bank and the real estate subsidiaries. By mid-1975 it became apparent that Chase was facing a problem of major proportions. Even then, however, the full magnitude was not evident. It would become so only as the recession unfolded, placing an increasing number of builders and developers in financial jeopardy. More and more loans were classified in a nonaccrual or loss status. By the end of 1975 net charge-offs amounted to the unheard-of figure of $109 million, while $1.3 billion was on nonaccrual and rates had been reduced on $0.2 billion.

Decline of the real estate investment trusts

Real estate investment trusts proved to be one of the most vulnerable segments of the industry. These institutions were favorite vehicles for investors since they were required by law to pay out 90 percent of earnings in dividends. But for the same reason they found it difficult to build up reserves. REITs expanded rapidly in number and assets in the early 1970s, lending chiefly for large projects like condominiums, office buildings, and shopping centers. Their funds flowed initially from the capital markets, bank loans, and commercial paper, with the latter also supported by back-up lines from banks. As developers experienced financial difficulty they transmitted it to the REITs, and by early 1974 many REITs no longer had access to commercial paper. They therefore turned increasingly to the banks, which attempted to structure credits that would permit the completion of projects in an orderly workout.

Bank loans to REITs totaled about $11 billion in 1975, with the nation's ten largest banks responsible for a considerable share.[19] Chase's REIT loans amounted to nearly $800 million (including $141 million to CMART), still less in relation to capital and total loans than at several competitors.

As the year progressed, the bank wrestled with these credits—not only those to CMART, as we shall see, but credits to almost all other REIT customers as well. By the end of 1975 more than three-fourths of REIT loans were listed as nonperforming. Losses at this point were not substantial, but many loans were no longer accruing interest, and others had been renegotiated at substantially lower rates. Losses mounted, however, in 1976 and continued to plague the bank over the next several years. All told, Chase charged off $114 million of REIT loans by 1978, a number to Florida institutions that had gone bankrupt.[20]

As the position of REITs deteriorated further in 1976, Chase cooperated with other banks to ease the burden on those that remained viable. Many loans on nonaccrual were renegotiated at sharply reduced rates. And a new procedure became widely adopted, a swap of assets between the bank and a REIT under which the bank accepted selected loans held by the REIT as partial payment of its debt. Such swaps, inaugurated by Chase with CMART and other REITs in 1976, totaled almost $140 million by the end of 1977.[21] At that point it became evident that a number of REITs could survive through supportive and at times innovative financing by Chase and other banks. But the workout was painful on both sides, and the industry never regained its full vitality or acceptance as a financing vehicle.

Real estate subsidiaries

Problems in the real estate subsidiaries, especially the Housing Investment Corporations of Florida and Puerto Rico, proved even more intractable than those in the REITs. Little control had been exercised over Yates, who was viewed as outstanding in the business, and the real estate department in New York had sparse information on loans made by the subsidiaries.

To obtain a better assessment of the situation, a team headed by Richard J. Boyle, an officer of proven experience, was sent to Puerto Rico to review the assets. Boyle arrived at Thanksgiving and found the office in chaotic condition, with credit files carrying a minimum of information and badly out of date. He remained for a fortnight, returning to report the likelihood of substantial losses.[22] A similar report came from a team in Miami, prompting William Bateman to relieve Yates of all responsibilities.

Boyle went back to Puerto Rico in January 1976, charged with putting HIC in better operating shape. Large resorts then uncompleted were involved, as well as sizable tracts of undeveloped land. Chase as a national bank could not extend credit against such land. But real estate subsidiaries of the corporation were permitted to do so. Unfortunately, the land had not always been prudently appraised; in one instance along the Puerto Rican coastline its condition was labeled as at best "damp" and uninhabitable.[23]

Boyle reorganized the Puerto Rican office and brought in a new president. But conditions in Puerto Rico continued to deteriorate and with them the fortunes of HIC, as well as real estate activities of the Chase branch. Over the next two years almost $150 million in loans on the island were charged off, and a substantial proportion of others was placed on nonaccrual status, a more damaging situation than that of the REITs.

In early March 1976 Boyle shifted his attention to Florida. There too he reorganized the subsidiary, which, with other Chase units and CMART, carried loans on land and projects principally in centers of the state that were most overbuilt.

Meanwhile Rockefeller and Butcher moved to strengthen the real estate department with transfers of some highly competent personnel while others were brought in from outside. In June 1976 Boyle returned to New York to head up the department, and John A. Hooper, chief credit officer, took over general supervision of all real estate activity as a member of the management committee. Hooper, a cautious and conservative banker, did much to steer the business into safer waters over the next few years.[24]

Chase becomes a large operator of real estate

Chase at times had properties thrust upon it by borrowers who had put up little or no equity and simply departed. But it chose also to acquire property in satisfaction of certain loans and began to foreclose on others. The bank selected these carefully, foreclosing only where it determined that it could do a better job than the developer of managing or disposing of the property.

By the end of 1975 the bank and its subsidiaries had taken over $127 million of property. These acquisitions increased throughout the next several years so that by the end of 1977 some $357 million of condominiums, apartments, office buildings, and land was under bank ownership and management, and this after almost $200 million in real estate had been sold or disposed of.[25] Much was in Florida and Puerto Rico, but the properties stretched from Manhattan to Denver and San Francisco as well.

Finding it necessary to build up a competence in property ownership and management and to do so rapidly, the bank hired outside experts and employed others on a consulting basis. By and large, Chase did not manage property itself but retained local real estate managers familiar with the special characteristics of the area. The objective was always to dispose of the property, preferably at a profit or at minimal loss.

For a while the bank worked under a certain pressure, for the National Banking Act stipulated that real estate acquired be sold within five years. This threatened to force the sale at depressed prices of properties that might increase in value over a longer period. Chase joined with other banks to urge Congress to change the law, and in 1980 the period was extended to ten years. At that time, five years after the first sizable acquisitions, Chase still owned and managed $136 million of property, after disposing of other properties for some $620 million.[26]

The Chase Manhattan Realty Trust: beginning of a downhill slide

Costly and troublesome as were the real estate activities of Chase's subsidiaries, none was more demanding of attention than the decline of the

Chase Manhattan Realty and Mortgage Trust (CMART). Chase had no ownership in the trust. But the bank had taken the initiative in founding it, given the trust the asset of its good name, and acted as adviser, generating the bulk of trust investments.

At first CMART, like other real estate trusts, appeared highly promising. As we saw in Chapter XIII, its assets grew to $750 million within three years and its share price more than doubled. The ratio of debt to equity in the trust at the end of 1972 stood at a manageable 3.4 to 1.

The first signs of potential difficulty began to appear in 1973, with interest rates climbing to unprecedented levels and shortages developing. Adam Heck, the president, recalled, "We began to see a slow-down in interest payments; builders couldn't get materials; and prices began going up, cutting into profit margins."[27] For the fiscal year ending in May 1974 profits were halved because of the need to augment the loan loss reserve. But already, on a quarterly basis, losses had developed.

Loans now were approaching $1 billion, a good proportion for work still in progress, but henceforth no new commitments would be made. Financing had become more expensive, not only as a result of rising interest rates but also because the commercial paper market was closing down for CMART and other REITs, forcing them to turn more to banks. By the spring of 1975 CMART's bank credit exceeded $750 million,[28] including some $141 million from Chase.

Meanwhile CMART's problems mounted. By May 1975 some 46 percent of its assets were no longer producing income, and it was operating at a cash loss, paying an interest rate of 3 percent above prime. Moreover, the trust required at least $200 million to finish uncompleted projects.[29] Its reserve for bad debts had been increased substantially, and its net worth had plummeted.

Chase comes to the rescue

CMART at this point clearly was headed for bankruptcy, although this was not generally recognized by the public. On the contrary, opinion was widespread that Chase would not permit the trust to fail. Bankruptcy did provide one option, but no one wanted it. And Chase decided that it would be too costly and impractical to take over CMART, even more so now that the bank and its subsidiaries had uncovered serious problems in their own portfolios. The immediate strain could be relieved, however, by action on two fronts: Chase could purchase assets from CMART, thereby providing it with necessary cash, and the creditor banks could lower their rate of interest.[30]

The proposal finally approved by the directors after intensive discussion called for Chase to purchase loans from CMART on sixteen properties amounting to $161 million and to put up another $34 million cash, all of which was needed to finish construction on uncompleted projects.[31] CMART's creditor banks, forty-one in all, including Chase, in turn would agree to lower their interest rate from 3 percent over prime (which produced a rate exceeding 10 percent) to a flat 2 percent. These measures could provide CMART with the cash it required and restore its operating margin. Even so, the outcome would be touch and go, and Boyle candidly told the board that if the real estate scene continued to deteriorate, CMART could remain in difficulty.

Final struggles of CMART

As matters developed, this help by Chase and other creditor banks could not stem the tide. Shortly after the announcement of the asset purchase and debt restructuring, CMART released the long-delayed results of its fiscal year ended May 31, 1975. It reported a staggering $166 million deficit, again chiefly because of a huge increase in the reserve for loan losses. The trust's net worth had sunk to a negative $50 million. By now, the autumn of 1975, more than two-thirds of its portfolio was earning no income.[32]

CMART at this time foreclosed on numerous properties, entering into contractual relationships with real estate firms to manage them, and it sold others to raise cash, some of them the more desirable holdings.[33] By late 1976 the loan portfolio had been further reduced to about $600 million, compared to its peak of close to $1 billion.

Throughout 1977 and early 1978 CMART continued to struggle to stay afloat. Still another swap of assets with its creditor banks was carried out; although not completely successful, it did almost halve bank debt, to less than $300 million.[34] Most troublesome, however, was $50 million in 7⅞ percent senior notes held by institutions and the public, due to mature in May 1978. The trust sought in vain to redeem these at a discount before their due date. Finally, when that day arrived CMART lacked the necessary cash to pay off noteholders and was forced to default. This in turn triggered default on its other debts, including debt to banks.[35]

CMART had worked hard to avoid this moment. Until April 1978 it appeared that it might be able to sell or swap enough assets to raise the necessary cash. But then the negotiations fell apart. Even more serious, however, was a critical decision by Chase, reached at an urgent review of CMART in February, that it should not acquire more assets to bail out the senior noteholders, for to do so might be construed as imprudent in a court of law.[36]

Chase had remained as adviser to CMART, but after 1975 the trust had expanded its own staff and relied less on the bank. Even so, Chase now worked with the trust to devise a plan for survival. This was placed before the banks and other creditors shortly after default on the senior notes and subsequently went through only minor revisions.

The plan as finally approved allocated most remaining assets among creditors, but left CMART an ongoing institution with approximately $65 million of real estate investments.[37] Chase itself received assets covering about 70 percent of its total credit (by then amounting to $49 million)—a smaller proportion of repayment than other banks—along with warrants for preferred and common stock. But the plan also called for the trust to change its name, eliminating any reference to Chase, and for Chase to terminate its role as adviser.

In May 1980 the plan was finally implemented, but only after CMART, in February 1979, had filed for bankruptcy under Chapter 11, using the court as a forum for settling conflicting claims.[38] CMART was then renamed the Triton Group, with holdings of four properties collectively valued at $64.5 million. It also possessed another asset of monetary value: a tax loss of $160 million that could be carried forward. On May 24, 1980, Chase formally ceased to be an adviser. With the change in name the trust's association with The Chase Manhattan Bank ended, a turbulent decade after it had begun.

Real estate assessed

CMART's final demise, coming two years after the end was first announced, was anticlimactic for Chase, which by then was in a phase of full recovery. The heavy cloud that hung over the bank had begun to dispel by 1977. Not until late in the decade, however, did the sun shine once again on real estate as a business. By 1980 nonperforming real estate assets were down to $350 million, a modest volume compared with the $1.5 billion that had been outstanding five years earlier.

The experience had been costly and at one point almost traumatic, with troubles piling up in the subsidiaries, the REITs, and CMART. All told, Chase charged off more than $600 million in real estate loans and other assets from 1975 through 1979, more than 60 percent of its total charge-offs in the period. Including the loss of income from nonperforming assets, the total cost approached $1 billion.[39]

Yet Rockefeller and Butcher were determined not to abandon the business, the more so now that the bank possessed a staff tested and proven by adversity. As early as 1976 they declared: "Despite recent problems, the real estate industry remains an important sector of the world economy. In the future, we will remain a major factor in this market through continuing emphasis on controlled exposure to quality borrowers around the world," a pledge reiterated in subsequent years.[40] In 1977 the bank again started making new commitments, and by the mid-1980s real estate credit exceeded $9 billion, topping the total of a decade earlier, although a smaller proportion of the portfolio.[41]

Chase becomes a target of the *Washington Post*

Problems of Chase and other banks in the troubled mid-1970s received wide publicity. As a premier institution headed by a public figure, David Rockefeller, Chase drew more than its share, with real estate takeovers, CMART, and reduced earnings all duly reported. Added to this was a steady drumbeat on the bank's involvement in the fiscal crisis of New York City (see Chapter XVII). Nothing compared in intensity, however, with a sensationalized newspaper campaign unleashed in early 1976 by the *Washington Post*, and aimed at Chase as a principal target.

The *Post*, buoyed by its exposé of the Watergate scandal in government, had come to feature investigative reporting. Even so, on a Sunday morning in early January 1976 readers were greeted by a banner headline of the type usually reserved for catastrophic events: "Citibank, Chase Manhattan on U.S. 'Problem' List."[42]

The timing and the prominence given the article were a surprise to Chase, although it had reason to expect that something negative would appear. Some days earlier a reporter from the *Post*, Ronald Kessler, had sought and been granted an interview with Rockefeller to discuss world banking trends. After a brief general discussion Kessler asked if Rockefeller was familiar with project "Victor." Rockefeller, puzzled, responded that he was not. Kessler then drew a bulky document from his briefcase, explaining that it represented a highly secret report of the comptroller of the currency listing a number of "problem banks" along with comments of the national bank examiners, and that Chase was on the list. Kessler, who had revealed by earlier questions that he was not an experienced financial reporter, asked Rockefeller if he would discuss the examiner's findings. Rockefeller refused, saying that the examiner's reports were "privileged." "If you have the information, you're not entitled to it," Rockefeller said, and dismissed him.[43]

This did not deter Kessler or the *Post*, which concluded that it could produce a story of major proportions. For the next ten days the *Post* bombarded its readers with a series of articles and editorials, many on the front page, all highly critical of banks and particularly of Chase. The *New York Times*, not to be outdone, soon followed with its own exposé.

The opening article of the *Post*, however, set the stage and was widely quoted throughout the nation and around the world. It asserted that the U.S. comptroller of the currency had compiled a "super-secret" list of problem banks, including both Chase and Citibank, holding $1 out of every $10 of deposits in the nation. The two banks had been added to the list when examinations disclosed that they possessed "inadequate" capital, and that assets of questionable value had increased sharply since previous examinations.[44]

Inflammatory as it was, the article admitted, "There is no indication that either of the giant banks . . . faces any immediate financial difficulties." And barring a worldwide catastrophe, the examiners were said to rate Chase's future prospects as "fair" and Citibank's as "excellent." Chase's current condition was said to be rated by the examiners as "poor" despite good earnings, in part because of the worldwide economic downturn, but also because of "poor" management. "Indeed they termed operating conditions at that highly respected bank as 'horrendous.' " And they claimed that although Rockefeller had made Chase's name known throughout the world, his duties required him to travel so extensively that he was not involved in the day-to-day management of the bank—a charge Rockefeller categorically denied.

Buried in the small print of the article was the acknowledgment that the information on which it was based was a year old. In reality the examination cited had been carried out some eighteen months earlier. The examiners had indeed been critical of the bank, pointing to a number of problems in the operating area and the sharp increase in classified assets, especially in real estate. But Rockefeller and Butcher, following suggestions from the board's examining committee, had gone to work on the shortcomings mentioned, and many had been corrected. This progress was recognized by the examiners in their report for mid-1975.[45] Meanwhile, the bank had embarked on a policy of building up its reserves for possible loan losses, even more than necessary to absorb large loan charge-offs. This was a matter of public record. And it had in train plans to increase capital. But none of this more positive information appeared in the *Post*.

Chase and the comptroller respond

A. Wright Elliott, head of the bank's corporate communications, first heard from Owen Frisby, Chase's Washington representative, that the *Post* story might break on Sunday morning. He directed Frisby to pick up the first edition and call immediately. Rockefeller was in Maine for the weekend and Butcher at home in Connecticut.

After hearing the story, Elliott arranged a conference call at 1:30 A.M. Sunday with Rockefeller, Butcher, and Roy Haberkern of the bank's outside counsel. Frisby read them the entire story. They recognized at once that the bank faced a major problem in public relations. Rockefeller decided to fly to New York in the morning, and the four agreed to meet at the bank to work out a response.

It was understood, however, that the principal response should come from the comptroller, James E. Smith. Smith quickly told the press:

> I am at a loss to understand what impelled the *Washington Post* to construct some routine bank examiner's reports, apparently obtained through unauthorized sources, into a front page news event—implying that Citibank and The Chase Manhattan Bank are considered problem banks by my office. I emphatically and unequivocally reject any such characterization. These two banks continue to be among the soundest banking institutions in the world.[46]

Rockefeller referred to this statement in his own comment, adding, "There is absolutely no question that The Chase Manhattan Bank is sound, vital and profitable. Any inference to the contrary is totally irresponsible." And he observed pointedly, "It is unfortunate that the *Washington Post* based its story on information taken out of context that is more than 18 months old."[47]

The *Post* continues its campaign

But the *Post* was not to be deterred; its aggressive campaign had only started.[48] Kessler wrote next about the huge foreign deposits held by Chase and Citibank and their sizable loan exposure in countries such as Japan and Italy. Later he dwelled on Arab deposits and the risk they allegedly involved. He also began to concentrate more heavily on Chase. Again he obtained surreptitiously an internal memorandum, this time from the Federal Reserve Board, which repeated the criticism from the comptroller's examination eighteen months earlier. Carried on the front page and headlined "Chase Bank Rated Poor in Exam," it contained little that was new but added to the image of disarray. It did draw from Arthur Burns, chairman of the Federal Reserve, a statement of support for the bank:

> I wish to observe that in the year and half since July, 1974, The Chase Manhattan Bank has taken numerous steps to improve all aspects of the Bank's operations that were criticized. As a result of these efforts, significant improvements in the Bank's operations have been realized. It is my judgment, based on analysis of the Comptroller of the Currency and the Federal Reserve's division of banking supervision and regulation, that The Chase Manhattan Bank is a responsibly managed and financially sound institution.[49]

Burns's statement was highlighted by the *New York Times* but only tacked onto the end of still another story by Kessler in the *Post* with the headline,

"Big Banks Found to Pay Low Taxes." By now Kessler was running out of ammunition, as evidenced by his parting shot several days later, relegated to page three: "Bank Owned by Chase Is Put on Problem List," a reference to Chase's small affiliate at Saugerties, New York, which was no longer a separate bank but had been converted into a branch on January 1.

The bank was to endure one final jab, however, and this from the *New York Times*. The *Times*, smarting from the attention commanded by its rival in Washington, uncovered its own secret memorandum, a document emanating from the Federal Reserve Board, responsible for examining bank holding companies.

On January 22, almost a fortnight after the *Post's* original blast, the *Times* in an article on page one apprised its readers of "12 Big Bank Companies on 'Problem' List of 35 at the Federal Reserve a Year Earlier."[50] Again Chase was on the list. But this time some of the sting was removed, for the list was divided into two groups—"more serious problems" and "other problem companies"—with Chase in the latter group among a number of other leading banks around the nation.

Three days later the *Times* repeated the text of the memorandum, including the full statement on Chase Manhattan. But it also printed in full a response from Rockefeller, detailing the numerous steps Chase had taken in the past year to improve operations and pointing to the third highest earnings in the bank's history, notwithstanding a $312 million provision for the loan loss reserve.[51]

Effect of the adverse publicity

And so the episode of the problem banks died out. But its effects lingered on. The market price of Chase stock, already depressed, was little affected, although the bank's image clearly was damaged, more so at home than abroad. For a time, in raising money Chase paid a small premium over rates commanded by its principal competitors. Its banking customers remained loyal, although frequent explanations of the publicity were required, troubling contact officers. Officer morale suffered at this time, and Rockefeller and Butcher were disturbed by this development. They strengthened internal communications and met regularly with senior staff, managing to draw them closer together.

The directors quite naturally were also concerned about the adverse publicity. At their regular meeting on January 21, 1976, they discussed its implications at length in an executive session with only Rockefeller among inside directors present. The minutes later included a statement by John T. Connor, head of Allied Chemical Corporation and former chairman of the bank's examining and audit committee, which revealed the board's sentiment. Connor said in part:

> In my opinion the Bank and Corporation have a very strong top management team with David Rockefeller as Chairman and Bill Butcher as President. We should let that fact be known throughout the management group. . . . As for the media criticisms, we all know that the problems described are about two years old. Starting at that time the outside Directors expressed concern to the Chairman and later to the new President. . . . Management proved to be very responsive to the suggestions made, and as a result the Chairman and the President carried out a new program that has resulted in a greatly strengthened organizational situation and sound loan programs and operating procedures.[52]

A number of months of heavy loan write-offs lay ahead. But Rockefeller and Butcher, with the support of the board, did not shrink from them. After two troubled years, 1975 and 1976, Chase entered into a period of strength and recovery that fully justified the directors' confidence.

Chase and New York City's financial crisis

F ar less costly than real estate, but much in the public eye, was Chase's involvement in New York City's financial crisis. The city's plight burst into the limelight in the early months of 1975, and throughout the remainder of the year debate raged as to whether the municipality would "go bankrupt." New York City did come perilously close to completely defaulting on certain of its obligations, and it took the combined effort of the state, the city's banks, the unions, and the federal government—with assistance, often reluctant, from City Hall—to avoid financial disaster. Chase played a significant role in this process, not only through underwriting and investing, but also through the active participation of Rockefeller and Thomas G. Labrecque, the head of Chase's treasury department, in developing and carrying out the strategy for survival.

Prelude to the fiscal crisis

The problems that erupted in 1975 were years in the making. They climaxed a decade and a half of change that affected the city and Chase in manifold ways. For a while, in the second half of the 1960s, social unrest, stimulated by racial problems and the Vietnam war, boiled over. In New York City fires, looting, and general destruction wracked parts of Harlem, the South Bronx, and Brooklyn. A nighttime bomb explosion in Chase's head office in 1969 did extensive damage.[1] And Chase's plaza became the scene of numerous demonstrations and protests.

Ethnic and economic change weakened the social cohesion of the city. The proportion of blacks and Hispanics rose to 32 percent by the end of the 1960s, compared with 22 percent ten years earlier, and the city's overall population declined as more of the middle class migrated to the suburbs. Its economic base weakened too as manufacturing moved to outlying areas where costs were lower.

Chase's own work force altered dramatically at this time. By 1969 more than 30 percent of Chase's employees were black and Hispanic, three times the proportion only five years earlier. Many of these new employees were less well educated and less familiar with work discipline, so special training programs aimed at improving productivity were devised for both workers and supervisors. Students were provided part-time work while they completed their studies, and high school drop-outs were given remedial instruction before employment.

During this time Chase mounted a series of financial programs designed to help alleviate the city's social problems.[2] Resources were channeled through the real estate and metropolitan departments, the Chase Manhattan Capital Corporation, and the Chase Manhattan Foundation. A special division coordinated lending to disadvantaged areas, with the real estate department alone committing more than $60 million in mortgage and other credit to rebuild blighted areas.

Minority businessmen were provided a combination of credit and counseling through the bank's branches and the Chase Capital Corporation. Some eighty credit analysts carried on counseling as part of their responsibilities. And Chase Volunteers for Community Action, numbering several hundred employees, devoted time after work to counseling small businesses and assisting young people. As an adjunct, the bank sponsored a street academy in a Harlem storefront, financed in part by its foundation.

The bank's foundation reached out in many directions to help minorities.[3] One-third of its grants were awarded to organizations working to improve conditions in disadvantaged areas. Many were small neighborhood self-help groups which normally lacked access to foundations. These organizations offered rehabilitation and job training to drug addicts, placed juvenile offenders and school drop-outs in jobs, and provided recreational or remedial skill facilities. On a larger scale the foundation underwrote a bookmobile with a trained librarian that traveled the streets of poor sections of Brooklyn, lending books to young and old.

At the national level, minority colleges and other organizations engaged in urban renewal received Chase grants. Probably no bank contributed as much as Chase in money and effort to help ease social problems, especially in the troubled second half of the 1960s. In doing so the bank hewed to the long-standing Chase tradition and culture. But it also recognized its own limits, and realized that meaningful progress on these problems required massive cooperation from all sectors of society.

Deterioration of New York's finances

In New York City the major financial burden fell on local government, and it proved unequal to the task. From fiscal year 1965 to 1975 the city's operating budget more than tripled, rising from $3.3 billion to $11 billion. Social programs mushroomed, prompted by racial tensions and the Great Society policies of the federal government. Welfare rolls and public employment soared, while newly muscular unions pushed up wages and benefits faster than ever before. Taxes were raised continually. As one acute observer noted, "buffeted by change, local elected officials lost control."[4]

Over the years the city's budget was balanced by an array of questionable practices difficult to discern in the complex accounting carried out by the city—a shifting of operating expenses into capital budgets, overestimation of revenues, carry-forward of doubtful receivables, and a number of other gimmicks. Although some of these practices were disclosed, their overall impact was not clearly evident. Later Chase and other underwriting banks were criticized for not adequately assessing the true budget position, which only became apparent as the tangled finances of the city were gradually unraveled. By early 1975 outstanding debt exceeded $13 billion, with more than $5½ billion at short-term maturity, highly vulnerable since much of it required roll-over through the year.[5]

For many decades Chase (and from the early nineteenth century the Bank of Manhattan) had maintained close financial ties to the city, carrying its deposits, clearing its checks, and lending it funds. As an underwriter the bank managed and participated in numerous syndications of city securities. These increased in number over the second half of 1974, and one in particular—a record $475 million bond offering in October—sold poorly.[6] Many underwriters lost money, and the interest rate on subsequent issues rose sharply, much to the distress of the mayor and the city comptroller. Then in December and January two large issues of notes went at an interest cost of 9.5 percent, the highest in the city's history.

Thomas Labrecque served as a member of the city comptroller's Technical Debt Management Committee (TDMC), along with representatives of other major underwriters. He and others impressed on the comptroller, Harrison J. Goldin, that the market was saturated with city securities. And he warned Rockefeller and Butcher that the city faced a difficult time ahead, that with $7 billion in bonds and notes to issue or refinance in 1975, "real solutions are going to be hard. . . . Most of the obvious budget moves and financing options have been exhausted."[7]

The test was to come sooner than many expected. In February 1975 Chase and Bankers Trust, as syndicate managers, were forced to cancel an offering of $260 million of tax anticipation notes. The law regarding such notes required that "at the time of such borrowing the city must have uncollected property taxes equal to the amount of the new issue plus any outstanding tax anticipation notes issued earlier." The comptroller lacked up-to-date data to ensure that this was the case, and the banks' attorneys refused to issue an opinion that the issue fully complied with the law, a shock to the comptroller, who termed the action as being "without precedent." The syndicate bids were then withdrawn.[8]

By early March the city had become hard pressed for cash and next proposed the sale of $537 million of bond anticipation notes, to be repaid with a later issue of long-term debt. This issue also was clouded by legal uncertainty owing to a suit brought by a Brooklyn Law School professor contesting the city's authority to take on additional long-term debt. Many in the syndicate dropped out. Chase and five other New York City banks, along with two investment houses, which took only 7 percent, submitted a single bid at the extraordinary yield of 8.7 percent. But before doing so, they required the state's attorney general to rule that the lawsuit was without merit and the comptroller to issue a statement concerning the lawsuit and the city's continued need for high borrowings.[9]

One final offering followed only a week later: $375 million of revenue anticipation notes. Again the underwriters were reluctant. New York City banks calculated that they now held over $1.2 billion in city securities—20 percent of their combined equity—and they told the comptroller and the mayor that they could take little more. A single syndicate was formed, including Chase, and this time it distributed to prospective buyers the "Report of Essential Facts" provided by the city, which in effect merely said that the city would continue to borrow, and along with anticipated revenue, funds would be adequate to pay off maturing debt.[10] Neither this nor the earlier issue sold well, and Chase was left with notes it did not want, soon to be frozen with losses in its trading account.

Formation of the Financial Community Liaison Group

Meanwhile, Rockefeller and the heads of other major banks had become deeply involved in the city's problem. Early in the year Mayor Beame, at breakfast at Gracie Mansion with Rockefeller and the heads of other major banks, complained that the banks were "badmouthing" the city and hurting bond sales. Rockefeller responded that the city's problem was truly serious, and suggested that rather than trade criticisms, the city and the banks should try to work together. "It would be useful," he added, "if the mayor were to invite the financial community to form a liaison committee to cooperate with the city in identifying problems and seeking solutions."[11] He recommended that Elmore Patterson of Morgan Guaranty, then chairman of the clearing house, head such a committee.

The mayor accepted the suggestion, and the Financial Community Liaison Group (FCLG) was formed with Elmore Patterson, David Rockefeller, and Walter Wriston of Citibank as the principal representatives, supported at the working level by Thomas Labrecque and other members of the Technical Debt Management Committee. These two groups then bore the brunt of the discussions and negotiations with the mayor, the governor, and other officials throughout this difficult period.

Rockefeller and the FCLG met with the mayor a number of times during

March 1975 trying to impress on him the ever-increasing difficulty of marketing city securities and the need for the city to move toward a truly balanced budget. But the mayor and other city officials still felt that the banks were short-changing the city. As Rockefeller put it, the mayor seemed to believe "that regardless of the problems that the city might have, we, the banks, as underwriters ought not to be concerned, because there was an enormous cash flow from the city's many tax sources. And this could be applied to the debt and amortization of the obligations."[12]

If the city was to pay all its bills, new borrowing would be necessary. By early April the city's plight, implying the possibility of default, was common knowledge and had become a matter of grave concern to the governor and the state legislature, which controlled the taxing power of the city. The banks seriously doubted that they could again go to the market, and their doubts were reinforced when Standard and Poors suspended its single A rating on city securities. In this aura of uncertainty the state for the first time stepped in with a loan of $369 million, advancing a payment that was not due until June.[13] Chase among others was saved from a painful decision. Not until four years later, in 1979, would the city again return to the market directly with its own securities.

Advent of Big MAC

By the spring of 1975 the city was in a desperate situation, not only with default on outstanding obligations seeming inevitable but with questions arising as to its ability to finance services. In May the Financial Community Liaison Group set forth in a letter to the comptroller the conditions necessary for a "total assistance program" including bank involvement.[14] Advances by the state and possibly the federal government would be required, along with fundamental fiscal reforms and a balanced 1976 budget. The banks could then help with a new underwriting of securities.

In one vital respect this program was already under way. Governor Carey, responding to advice from Rockefeller and others, had appointed a committee of four to come up with a plan of action. It soon recommended creation of a new state agency, the Mutual Assistance Corporation (MAC), to assist the city in financing.[15] The banks did much to shape the legislation that gave the corporation substantial powers; it could issue its own bonds, control revenues from the city's 4 percent sales tax as backing for its securities, and redesign the city's accounting system and audit its expenses. With this arsenal it was hoped that MAC could save the city from default.

Legislative agreement came in the nick of time, early on the morning of June 10, with $792 million in city notes coming due the following day. Raising the money for the notes required participation by the state, the city, and above all Chase and other banks. Indeed the banks provided almost half the total, $280 million, through renegotiation of maturing notes they already held and a $100 million bridge loan to the newly created MAC.[16]

MAC lacked authority to force the mayor to take firm action to balance the budget; that would come later with the creation of a state-dominated Emergency Financial Control Board. But the substitution of MAC bonds for short-term city notes could help the city immensely. Comprising five members appointed by the governor and four by the mayor, MAC's board performed yeoman service over the ensuing months. Felix Rohatyn, a partner in Lazard Frères, agreed to serve "for a brief transition period," but he remained until the city was on firmer financial footing, eventually succeeding as chairman and providing innovative financial leadership.

MAC's immediate objective was to raise $3 billion through long-term bonds over several months to retire about half of the city's outstanding short-term debt. The banks were to be underwriters, with Morgan Guaranty and Salomon Brothers managing a first issue, Chase and Merrill Lynch the second, and Citibank the third.

Rather to the surprise of the underwriters, the initial offering of $1 billion on June 30 was not a sellout, despite generous yields and New York City's financial institutions taking $650 million.[17] Chase was a leader among the banks, although adding further municipal securities to its portfolio at that time was painful.

The banks refuse a new bridge loan

The mayor, bowing to the inevitable, finally proposed plans to dismiss nineteen thousand employees, including three thousand sanitation workers, five thousand policemen, and two thousand firemen.[18] The sanitation workers struck, the policemen demonstrated, and the firemen carried out a job action. It was in this atmosphere that Chase and Merrill Lynch pressed forward with plans for the second MAC sale. But when the financing proved extraordinarily complicated and difficult, the underwriters finally gave up all hope of selling $1 billion of bonds. The coup de grâce was delivered when the initial issue of MAC securities began trading, only to drop ten to eleven points on the first day.

Talk in public at this time raised the possibility of the banks' making a huge bridge loan to MAC to surmount the crisis. To press upon MAC that this was no answer to what had become a desperate problem, on July 22 Thomas Labrecque and Wallace Sellers, his counterpart at Merrill Lynch, wrote an unusual letter to Thomas Flynn, chairman of MAC. Rockefeller released excerpts to the public. In part the letter said:

It makes no sense whatever to propose that the New York City commercial banks make a further bridge loan in the hope that the problems will disappear before the City needs additional funds. MAC is, in essence, a bridge, but to this point the basic problems have not been solved. . . . In order to have a chance at a solution, the following steps must be taken:

(1) An immediate, dramatic, and creditable program putting a firm, spartan control on the total expenses of the City, which is endorsed and visibly supported by the Governor and the legislative leaders, and implemented by the Mayor and the MAC Board.

(2) A highly accelerated effort on the part of MAC to put in place the monitoring and accounting efforts as authorized by the Legislation and outlined in the Prospectus.

Rockefeller added, "The facts of the matter are now clear to everyone. What is desperately needed is concrete action now. . . . Until a comprehensive program has been implemented, I see no possibility of a bank loan."[19]

This was a powerful prod at the mayor, who was under pressure from all sides. On July 31 he finally announced a comprehensive program, which was immediately endorsed by Rockefeller.[20] Included were a freeze on wages and an agreement by city unions not to seek an increase for two years, eventual elimination of 27,000 jobs, an increase in the transit fare, takeover by the state of certain city costs, and an advance bridge loan to the city from the banks. The city would install new fiscal controls and move to balance its budget over the next three years. To add credibility to his efforts, the mayor appointed Richard R. Shinn, president of Metropolitan Life Insurance Company and a Chase director, to head a new management council to advise him.

The second MAC financing

These moves improved the atmosphere surrounding the upcoming MAC financing, which was arranged after daily, almost hourly interaction between Chase, Merrill Lynch, and MAC. When it was finally carried out in mid-August 1975, the banks once again shouldered a sizable share of the burden, acquiring $350 million of new MAC bonds at a concessionary rate of 6.7 percent, more than a third of the $960 million package.[21] City and state pension funds also stepped up for a good share, and the underwriters successfully distributed $275 million to the public.

The banks also agreed to extend their holdings of city notes, which would mature between October 1975 and mid-1976—some $550 million in all—and to exchange $36 million in notes maturing in September for MAC bonds, all at bargain interest rates. But for the banks this was enough.

Rockefeller, Patterson, and William Spencer of Citibank met with the governor and told him that the banks could not take on more MAC bonds. They issued a public statement saying that in their judgment, "a further issue of MAC bonds at this time wasn't feasible and that, in view of the substantial commitments already made by the New York City banks to aid the City, there would be virtually no chance . . . of obtaining significant further commitments from that source."[22]

Chase welcomed this statement, for financing the city presented a difficult dilemma for the bank. With earnings from domestic sources declining sharply because of loan losses, the bank had cut back on its holdings of tax-exempt municipal securities in order to substitute assets that yielded a higher gross income. Later the Securities and Exchange Commission, after a study of the New York City crisis, would imply that Chase had "dumped" city securities between September 1974 and April 1975, an allegation Rockefeller forcefully denied, pointing out that of a total reduction in tax-exempt holdings in this period of $564 million, only $93 million represented New York City issues.[23]

In mid-1975, before the advent of MAC, the bank had held $245 million of city notes and bonds, the largest volume of any New York City bank. Of this some $47 million was frozen in the trading account. The subsequent drop in value of these securities reduced net operating earnings when the bank was least able to afford it. Nevertheless, Chase supported MAC vigorously and at the end of the year was carrying $188 million of its securities in its municipal portfolio as well as city notes and bonds.

The banks go along with a new program

With or without the banks, some $2 billion had to be raised in September if the city were to avoid default, and this again in a deteriorating environment as MAC's bonds slid to new lows. The expectation of default was widespread, and a *Wall Street Journal* editorial recommended it.[24] But the governor, acting as broker between the mayor, the banks, and MAC, put forward a new plan and persuaded the legislature to adopt it.

The plan had teeth in it, calling for the creation of an Emergency Financial Control Board, which in effect assumed the city's budgetary powers, much like a trustee in a corporate bankruptcy case.[25] The board would set the priorities on all expenditures, and revenue would be channeled through it. It would do what the Mayor had said he would do but hadn't done. Its chief aim was to erase the city's deficit in three years. The mayor didn't like it—he lost the power of the purse—but he had no choice in the matter.

With this plan restoring a modicum of confidence, $2.3 billion was scraped together by the state, with major help from city and state pension funds. The banks committed themselves to buying only $100 million more of MAC bonds. But with Chase as lead manager, five of the banks and two investment houses agreed to underwrite a $755 million note issue for the state. The notes were not all sold, despite a record 8.7 percent rate.[26] When they were released from syndicate three weeks later, prices dropped precipitously and yields went to 10 percent. The market now began to worry about the fiscal health of the state.

Attention focuses on Washington

With state securities showing signs of weakness, attention concentrated more heavily on possible help from the federal government. The governor, the mayor, and many bankers, including Rockefeller, had visited Washington, pleading the case for the city. Several bills were introduced into Congress, but sentiment was not favorable. "It's the classic quart of bourbon handed to the alcoholic on his promise he won't drink any more," one congressman put it. But more serious, both President Ford and Secretary of the Treasury Simon seemed adamantly opposed to any assistance.

Nevertheless, pressure on the president built up. Rockefeller and Wriston met with him in the Oval Office and presented the case for temporary aid. And Patterson, Rockefeller, and Wriston, representing the New York City banks, appeared before the Senate Banking Committee to deliver a similar message.[27] Their efforts were to no avail, for on October 29, 1975, in a speech specifically addressing the subject, the president came out flatly against any aid.[28] To all who heard him, the handwriting appeared plainly on the wall. The *New York Daily News*, in a headline remembered by voters a year later, expressed its reaction: "Ford to City: Drop Dead."

But the city, and its guardian, the state, continued to struggle. They next came up with a proposal fathered by Rohatyn that barely stopped short of default but bought essential time. Once again Chase and other banks played a key role. The program called for a three-year moratorium on the payment of principal on city notes due to mature between November and June 30, 1976, as well as a restructuring of MAC debt.[29] Individuals holding the city notes had the option of exchanging them for fifteen-year MAC bonds yielding 6 percent. And banks and the public pension funds would exchange their notes for ten-year city bonds. But they also would stretch out MAC debt by exchanging their holdings of shorter-term MAC securities for longer-term MAC bonds, all at 6 percent, considerably below existing rates. Moreover, the banks were asked to lend another $1.5 billion to the city to meet seasonal needs, and the pension funds were to invest a further large sum in MAC bonds.

Rohatyn presented this complex plan to a meeting of the banks attended by Rockefeller and Labrecque on November 13. The banks were favorably impressed, and Rockefeller announced that "Chase, along with the other clearing house banks, has agreed to participate, assuming that all the various pieces of the package can be put together."[30]

But the banks did not agree to one important provision: that they lend another $1.5 billion to the city. This would be possible, they contended, only if the loan were backed by some form of federal guarantee. Moreover, to participate in the program involved some sacrifice on the part of the banks, for they held about one-fifth of all city notes and a third of MAC debt. Chase itself now carried approximately $300 million of such securities, a large share of which had earned more than the new 6 percent coupon. Earnings after taxes were reduced by $4 million the following year in consequence.[31]

The federal government's guarantee

Added to this debt restructuring was an action no less important: an increase in a variety of city taxes to raise further revenue. The president and Secretary Simon had been kept informed of this new program, and even they were favorably impressed. The idea took root in Washington that the city could avoid default after all, and that the unions, the banks, and the taxpayers were sharing in the sacrifices that had to be made. Still unresolved was the problem of seasonal needs for finance, arising from the bunching of tax collections in the spring while expenditures were spread more evenly throughout the year. Congress and the administration began to concentrate on this issue.

Finally, at a televised news conference on Thanksgiving eve, November 26, the president announced not a change of heart but of circumstances; he would propose legislation authorizing a "temporary line of credit" to the city, up to a maximum of $2.3 billion a year to meet its seasonal requirements.[32] But there would be strings attached: the loan must be repaid at the end of each fiscal year, and the credit line would expire on June 30, 1978; the loan would not be automatic, but could be made by the secretary of the treasury only if he determined that there was a reasonable prospect of repayment; and the interest rate was to be 1 percent above the cost incurred by the Treasury in raising the money.

Within a fortnight Congress approved this legislation. But it also prepared for contingencies by passing a new bankruptcy law for municipalities. Reaction from the banks and city and state officials was one of relief, although Congresswoman Elizabeth Holtzman of Brooklyn complained that the president had behaved "like a punitive father parceling out monthly allowances."[33]

Epilogue: phase-out of the moratorium

Federal assistance began immediately, and the program worked smoothly over its duration. The worst of the city's fiscal crisis thus passed. Other problems would arise, but none as crucial as those that had been overcome. Perhaps most serious was a court test of the three-year moratorium that had been declared on the city's notes, brought against the city by the Flushing National Bank. The moratorium was upheld by two of the state's lower courts; but in November 1976, a year after it was first imposed, New York State's highest court, the Court of Appeals, ruled the moratorium unconstitutional. In doing so, however, the court also informed noteholders that they could not seek immediate measures that would disrupt the city's "delicate financial and economic balance."[34]

Somehow this new setback did not create the same sense of alarm that had gripped the city eighteen months earlier. The state, the city, the banks, and the unions all were inured to city crises. Time was required to work out a solution, accomplished over the next nine months. Individuals holding city notes were paid off in April 1977. Then in July banks and union pension funds agreed to exchange their notes for longer-term MAC bonds, while also lengthening maturities on existing MAC securities to a ten-to-twenty year range, paying somewhat higher interest rates.[35]

This restructuring of debt left Chase holding about $375 million of city securities, the great bulk of them MAC bonds. The bank continued to incur a reduction in net income after taxes of more than $4 million annually, a figure that appeared in small print in annual reports but somehow never found its way into the public consciousness.

The Urban Development Corporation

Even while the bank was embroiled in the financial crisis of the city, it found itself heavily involved with the problems of New York State. As the state became more deeply enmeshed with the city over the summer of 1975, its own credit began to suffer. By late autumn it could no longer market its securities, and for a period in early 1976, after passage of the federal loan to the city, major attention shifted to the affairs of the state.

The immediate problem centered on the plight of a number of state agencies that issued securities in their own name. These agencies, engaged in construction of housing, college dormitories, and medical and other facilities, were financed largely through the sale of so-called moral obligation notes and bonds. Such securities were backed by revenues from the projects they financed. Although they were not legally enforceable obligations of the state, statements in the prospectus and indentures led investors to assume that the legislature would make up any shortfalls in revenue necessary to honor them. Some $6 billion in such securities was outstanding in New York, and Chase and other banks had been major underwriters.[36] Now the agencies were running out of funds and might be forced to default on maturing issues.

State agency securities had already come under a dark cloud early in 1975, when one of the agencies, the Urban Development Corporation (UDC), ran into serious difficulty. The legislature had established UDC in 1968 under pressure from Governor Rockefeller, particularly to build housing for low- and moderate-income families and to improve blighted areas. Some projects had been completed, but a large number still were under construction. UDC had been badly managed and depended heavily on housing subsidies from the federal government, on which President Nixon declared a moratorium at the start of 1973. Chase participated in underwriting bonds and notes of the agency and held UDC bonds in its investment account.

Trouble started for UDC in late summer 1974, when it failed to obtain underwriting for short-term notes, which, in contrast to bonds, were not considered moral obligations of the state. Chase was then asked by the state comptroller if it could arrange financing.[37] Butcher called together a group of bankers from around the state to meet with the governor in Albany to review UDC problems. Over the Labor Day weekend an agreement was reached to underwrite an issue of longer-term bonds (considered moral obligations) as well as to extend a short-term loan. This averted an immediate crisis and, on the basis of projections given the banks, would make any additional financing unnecessary before the following spring.

On this latter count, however, the banks were misinformed. Governor Carey, shortly after succeeding to the office in early January, called Butcher to seek further help on UDC, temporarily, the governor said, until the legislature could focus on the problem.[38] Butcher again agreed and arranged for Chase, First National City, and Morgan Guaranty to provide $30 million on a very short-term basis.

But the problems of UDC continued to pile up. When an issue of $104.5 million in bond anticipation notes came due in mid-February 1975, not only did the agency lack resources to fund them, but it could not pay off the short-term bank loan and needed money to continue ongoing construction.[39]

UDC moves into (and out of) default

Mid-February came and went, leaving UDC in default. The governor installed new and more competent management and proposed a plan designed to provide financing at least to complete unfinished projects. Still another agency, the Project Finance Agency, was created, to be backed by the revenues of specific projects, as well as "moral obligation" support of the state, now of questionable value. The banks would be asked to market the securities of this agency as well as to lend direct financial assistance.[40]

Richard Ravitch, the new chairman, met with the bankers on a Sunday in late February to try to enlist their support. William S. Ogden had now taken over negotiations for Chase, aided by Palmer Turnheim, senior vice president responsible for relations with the state. The meeting broke up at 4 A.M., but only Chase returned an affirmative answer.[41]

Nevertheless the governor persisted, and the legislature on February 26, 1975, created the new Project Financing Agency in another of its midnight cliffhanger sessions. The banks were made the whipping boys for their refusal to extend additional financing. The legislature followed a few days later with an appropriation of $90 million to keep the agency in business, "but not one dollar was to go to the banks and noteholders."[42]

UDC needed $370 million in additional funds to complete projects and avoid bankruptcy. Chase remained willing to help, but some banks were adamantly opposed to further assistance so long as the $30 million loan stood in default. So the governor turned to a new source, the savings banks, which pledged a good share of the required financing. Finally on March 26, the day before UDC might be declared bankrupt, the banks agreed to lend the Project Finance Agency $140 million, with Chase taking more than its share.[43]

Nonetheless, the financing was not quite what the governor had asked for—a commitment to purchase long-term bonds of the agency. Instead it was a revolving credit at 8.5 percent interest. Moreover, the banks extracted other commitments, including repayment of the $30 million loan. But resources were now in place for the completion of UDC projects. Rather late in the day the state had fulfilled its "moral obligation."

Crisis for other state agencies

Resolution of UDC's dilemma did not end the travail of New York's agencies. Four other organizations had issued similar securities to finance construction. In early 1976, nine months after the UDC problem, these agencies also required funds to complete construction as well as to refund maturing notes and bonds. But the market had closed up on them as it had with the state itself. Rockefeller, spending Thanksgiving 1975 in Maine, told the press that a crisis was nearing, and he feared that it could be surmounted only with federal assistance similar to that promised a few days earlier to the city.[44]

As with the city and UDC, New York City banks could not walk away from the problem. They held more than $1 billion of state securities, with

Chase's $253 million the largest share. Rockefeller, Patterson, and other chief executives flew to Albany on December 10, 1975, to meet with the governor and leaders of the legislature, then in special session. The bankers urged the politicians to compromise their differences and take immediate action to provide funds for the agencies and close a gap in the state's budget. Patterson, emerging from the meeting, provided headlines for the following day, asserting, "If the necessary actions are not taken now to bolster the state's credit and to provide immediate financing for the agencies, the whole house of cards collapses."[45]

The legislature provided temporary assistance, although grudgingly. And the governor soon unwrapped a program aimed at restoring credibility to both the agencies and the state. The state's budget was to be balanced with only a token increase in expenses, and a multifaceted plan was put forth to furnish funds for the agencies to complete ongoing construction.[46] But the state also would require $4.1 billion in short-term seasonal financing, with some uncertainty now that it could be obtained.

The banks, determining to cooperate with the governor, in early March agreed to buy $1 billion of the short-term state notes for their own portfolios, as well as to roll over maturing agency issues, but only on condition that the legislature adopt both the governor's balanced budget and the full amount needed to rescue the construction agencies. The banks would then work with a special committee appointed by the governor to develop a prospectus and help market the notes to other banks and financial institutions around the nation.[47]

This unusual collaboration was carried out over the next several months, after the state legislature fulfilled its part of the bargain. At the annual meeting of Reserve City Bankers in early April, Rockefeller, Butcher, and others mounted a selling campaign for the state notes. Other New York City bankers toured the country, asking for help. The Bank of America agreed to subscribe for $100 million. Quotas from other banks were fulfilled, and both the state note issue and the financing for the construction agencies were successful. This proved to be the tonic needed by the state. In early May 1976 it returned once again to the public market, with $59 million of long-term bonds, and with Chase the lead underwriter.[48] The issue was a sell-out, and the state soon returned to normal in its financing.

Lessons of the crisis

The crisis in city and state finances had one salutary effect: it provided lessons for all involved that would be long remembered. The city learned that it could not escape the discipline of the marketplace. To gain funds in the future, it had to have its finances in reasonable order. The crisis produced reforms that placed the city on the proper path: budget and accounting systems designed to reveal its true financial status; proper disclosure to underwriters and investors; necessary cutbacks in personnel and other costs; effective controls on costs in the future; and finally, although less successfully, taxation that would sustain economic growth, not erode it. The city's economy began to improve somewhat late in the decade, and strengthened in the first half of the 1980s.

As for Chase and the other banks, they learned once again that even though they now operated multinationally, they could not escape local responsibilities. The financial health of the city and the banks remained intertwined.

Both the banks and the city discovered anew the dangers of excessive short-term financing by municipalities, not unlike that of private corporations. Also deeply impressed on the banks was the necessity for full disclosure in financing by public bodies, a practice not common prior to the crisis. Later the Securities and Exchange Commission reinforced disclosure through creation of a Municipal Securities Rulemaking Board, establishing criteria for record keeping, disclosure, and trading by underwriters and dealers.

As Chase's financial relations with the city and the state moved back to normal, the bank could look back with satisfaction at having provided essential aid to each in a critical period.

PART FOUR

Entering the eighties:
looking to the future

I n the period 1977–1981 Chase achieved a powerful recovery from its troubles of the mid-1970s. Earnings increased fourfold, only to be interrupted by unexpected losses in 1982. The upturn soon resumed, however, reaching a new peak in 1985.

Total assets and loans doubled in these years, aided in part by acquisitions (see Table 10). The bank again ranked as a leader in loans to business, as pricing of such credits underwent significant change. Services for corporations grew in complexity. Asset swaps, currency swaps, and a variety of options and futures were offered to reduce risks and costs. Investment banking gained added emphasis, much as in the 1920s, while Chase's merchant banks outpaced others in the management of large loan syndications in Eurocurrency markets.

By the late 1970s lending abroad exceeded the domestic, with less developed countries (LDCs) receiving a rising share. The LDCs encountered severe problems after 1981 in making timely payments, forcing Chase and other banks into cooperative arrangements for debt restructuring. Nonperforming assets rose in consequence, and banking, already risky, became even more so.

Chase developed a strategic plan for the 1980s and embarked on implementing it. Two markets were accorded top priority: the corporate and consumer, with concentration on the higher tiers of each. Even so, real estate, trust, correspondent banks, and financial firms continued to be courted as valued customers. Substantial resources also were devoted to

273

Table 10.   Statistical profile, 1976–1985.[a]

	Assets	Loans and Mortgages	Deposits	Equity Capital
1976	45.6	30.7	37.6	1.667
1977	53.2	35.3	43.5	1.848
1978	61.2	38.7	48.5	2.101
1979	64.7	40.4	48.5	2.306
1980	76.2	47.3	56.8	2.688
1981	77.8	51.3	55.3	2.998
1982	80.9	55.5	56.9	3.286
1983	81.9	55.9	56.3	3.576
1984	86.9	62.0	59.7	4.023
1985	87.7	61.9	61.4	4.459

	Domestic Loans and Mortgages	Domestic Commercial and Industrial Loans[b]	Overseas Loans	Income Before Security Gains (Losses) Millions
1976	17.2	6.6	13.5	105.1
1977	17.5	6.7	17.8	123.2
1978	17.7	8.0	21.0	197.2
1979	18.3	9.7	22.1	311.2
1980	20.7	10.9	26.6	364.7
1981	20.4	10.6	30.9	443.9
1982[c]	25.3	14.6	30.2	307.4[d]
1983	25.0	14.6	30.9	429.6
1984	30.0	15.8	32.0	405.8
1985	32.5	13.8	29.4	564.8

a. Year-end figures, expressed in billions of dollars.

b. Excludes short-term money market instruments in the form of Bankers Acceptances.

c. After 1981 includes domestic obligors booked in overseas offices and international obligors carried at headoffices.

d. Income after Security Gains (losses), required by Regulatory Authorities to be reported as the total after 1981.

Source: *Annual Reports* of The Chase Manhattan Corporation.

automation and nonloan products, fields in which Chase developed great skills.

Meanwhile, competition intensified as boundaries between banks and other financial institutions virtually disappeared. Chase established subsidiary banks and offices in twenty-two states, chiefly to serve consumers and medium-sized business. And the bank planned for nationwide banking within the near future.

A critical change in leadership occurred in 1980–81, when Willard C. Butcher succeeded David Rockefeller. Rockefeller's thirty-five years with Chase encompasses much of this history, representing a truly revolutionary period for banking. (A comparison of Chase in the mid-1980s with Chase in the mid-1940s is presented in the final chapter.) Radical changes occurred in products, pricing, financing, management process, and organization as the bank spread worldwide—all within a vastly different economic, competitive, and regulatory framework. Stemming from this too was a changed corporate culture that evolved over the years and helped shape the bank. These developments continued to unfold in the mid-1980s, posing for management a never-ending challenge.

Years of recovery, 1977–1981

C hase achieved an extraordinary recovery from its middecade problems in the years 1977 through 1981. Once again the bank began to move forward aggressively, and by the end of the 1970s had regained much of its lost position. Worldwide loans advanced strongly, credit losses were greatly reduced, and net income climbed sharply. None of this was accomplished without difficulty, however. It called for a more disciplined approach to management and some change in the Chase culture. Internal controls were tightened, expenses carefully monitored, and credit quality upgraded. And ineffective managers were replaced, many by new recruits from outside.

The bank was helped too by an economic environment that until late in the decade encouraged expansion. The U.S. economy advanced vigorously through 1978, slowing thereafter into a minor recession in 1980. Western Europe and Japan also grew at a good pace through much of the period. This improvement, however, came to be marred by a resurgence of inflation, with prices in 1979 and 1980 climbing at double-digit rates. A second oil shock, induced by revolution in Iran, drove prices upward, while creating large new imbalances in payments between nations, especially for less developed countries. Corporate cash positions eroded, enhancing the demand for bank credit, and governments again borrowed heavily. Interest rates soared, and exchange rates were tossed about like ships on a stormy sea. The Federal Reserve found it necessary to pursue a highly restrictive monetary policy, finally adopting new techniques of monetary control that profoundly influenced economic developments in the early 1980s.

Chase's game plan for recovery

Rockefeller and Butcher first set forth their plan for recovery at a day-long meeting with the directors at Pocantico Hills in November 1976. Chase was then ending the year with earnings at the low point of $105 million, down 42 percent from two years earlier. Loan losses and nonperforming assets had mounted to record levels. But the second half of 1976 was better than the first, and light was dimly perceived at the end of the tunnel.

The meeting at Pocantico Hills was anything but gloomy. On the contrary, the presentations were optimistic and programs appeared reasonable.

The goal that was set is perhaps best summarized in a remarkably prescient projection of earnings given by Butcher. He saw earnings rising to $310 million by 1979, up almost threefold from 1976 and representing a compounded growth rate of almost 12 percent from the 1974 peak. As matters developed, earnings in 1979 reached $311 million. But the directors can be forgiven if some were still a bit skeptical in late 1976.

Butcher presented a chart (see Figure 6) that suggested how this huge improvement would be attained.[1] It would involve combining recovery from existing problems with programs designed to bring renewed expansion. More aggressive marketing efforts were to be mounted in corporate lending, and two core businesses, retail and trust, were to be converted from loss to profit. Meanwhile, expenses were to be tightly controlled and systems and operations improved. Reaching these goals would require an infusion of capital on a regular and sustained basis, much of it from external sources.

The program was ambitious and required orchestrated action on many fronts. A most immediate and rewarding task was to reduce loan losses and the volume of nonperforming assets. This in itself would achieve almost half the targeted increase in income.[2] Progress on this score over the three years to 1979 was steady and impressive. The volume of nonperforming loans was halved from $1.7 billion to $869 million, with the major reduction in nonaccruals—that is, assets yielding little or no income. Net charge-offs of assets plummeted from a peak of $269 million to $93 million, comparable to the volume in 1974 but against an asset total half again as large. The actual provision for loan losses declined to a lesser degree, again reflecting a substantial increase in loans and the conservative policy of Rockefeller and Butcher in maintaining a prudent reserve against the aggregate.

The great bulk of this reduction in net charge-offs and nonperforming assets occurred in real estate, as that department gradually overcame its many problems. Paradoxically, no other area of the bank contributed more to the recovery of earnings than real estate, merely by bringing down its negative drag on income. Net charge-offs of business loans, both domestic and international, had already declined from the recession peak in 1975. Losses on these remained moderate over the rest of the decade, helped by the bank's policy of upgrading the quality of its loan portfolio.

Chase recovers position in the corporate market

Chase could not move ahead, however, without renewed vigor in its most important market: the extension of credit to corporate business. Here Chase's position had suffered, partly as a result of its tarnished image but also because of management's preoccupation with problems in other areas. Now that this "fix-up" period was drawing to a close, Rockefeller and Butcher set as a

Figure 6. Butcher's projection of earnings, 1976–1979.

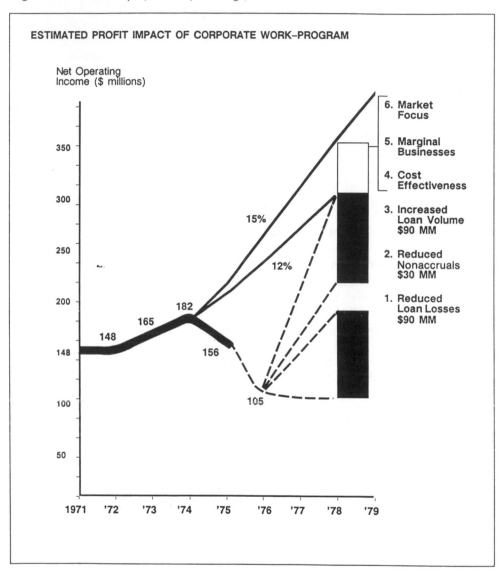

ESTIMATED PROFIT IMPACT OF CORPORATE WORK-PROGRAM

Source: Butcher presentation to directors on Chase plan for 1976–1979, Pocantico Hills, New York, November 16, 1976. Chase Archives.

principal objective the reestablishment of Chase as a premier lender to commerce and industry. Moreover, this rehabilitation was to encompass both quantity and quality. Butcher was particularly determined to weed out poor credit risks and upgrade the portfolio.

Meanwhile the corporate banking department had been strengthened in both organization and personnel. In 1976 the bank abandoned its mixture of geographic and industry divisions and organized completely along industry lines. Industry units had been the most successful in the past, especially petroleum, public utilities, and aerospace. Now teams of officers were dedicated to serving customers in specific industries across the map. These relationship managers were to be shifted less frequently, providing a new continuity in customer contacts. And experienced officers, a number recruited from outside the bank, replaced those judged to be less competent.

A new executive, James H. Carey, took over leadership of the department. Carey had been a star recruit in the mid-1950s but left the bank for management positions in other companies. He returned in 1976 and soon was designated head of the corporate bank, itself a break with tradition. Then in 1977 Carey was told to become an aggressive competitor for new business— "Get the wind back in our sails," as Butcher put it.[3]

The environment at the outset was not the most favorable. The economy was expanding, but corporations were liquid and were lengthening debt through the capital markets. And for short-term credit, the commercial paper market was undercutting banks and proving a more potent competitor than ever. Even so, Carey and his team persisted, and by 1978 they had begun to show real progress, adding important new accounts and making old ones more active. Over the year domestic commercial and industrial loans grew almost 20 percent, and this was followed by increases of almost equal proportion over the next several years. The bank regained much of its relative position as domestic loans to business rose from $6.6 billion (excluding bankers acceptances) in 1976 to almost $11 billion by the end of 1980.[4]

No less important, Butcher was able to tell the directors that the quality of the loan portfolio had returned to the level of the early 1970s and was equal to that of any other bank. And the directors were further reassured when the comptroller of the currency, in his examination letter for 1978, reported, "Loan portfolio supervision is good within all lending areas and at all levels of management," including not only corporate accounts but real estate and international as well.[5]

Revolution in loan pricing

Part of Chase's aggressiveness was manifested in loan pricing. As Carey put it, the bank had to be "on the leading edge of competition," and it was willing to match or better the rates of other banks to land credits with quality companies. Here Carey and other department heads faced a dilemma, for increased return on assets ranked as high on the list of objectives as increased market share. So when the bank stretched for a particular piece of business, it did so anticipating a favorable impact on the whole customer relationship—deposit balances, cash management, foreign exchange, and other business. Tools for measuring the profitability of various services were sharpened, and Carey insisted that an account in its entirety meet the bank's profit goal. Return on assets in the corporate bank, always among the highest, improved in this period.

This was accomplished notwithstanding radical changes in loan pricing.[6] Ever since the 1930s banks had tied interest charges on domestic business loans to the prime rate, with an additional cost in the form of compensating balances lodged with the bank. The prime rate itself had come to be related to the cost of borrowed money and was increasingly volatile, so term loans for the most part were priced on a floating rate basis.

"Cap loans," placing a ceiling on the average rate over the life of the loan, had been introduced as an innovation earlier in the decade (see Chapter XIV), but these injected an element of uncertainty into pricing that was not popular. Now more fundamental changes were forthcoming.

First to erode in the normal arrangement was the insistence on deposit balances, both for actual loan usage and for commitments or lines of credit that ensured future availability of funds. Increasingly customers were permitted a choice between providing balances or paying a fee. Chase reasoned that balances required costly reserve requirements and that payment of a fee could be more economical for both it and the borrower. Fees then became the preferred payment for many customers not already carrying adequate balances.

Even more far-reaching, the heretofore inviolate prime rate began to give way under competitive pressure, with Chase active in the change. Both commercial paper and foreign banks had made severe inroads on the demand for loans from Chase and other banks by many quality customers. Foreign banks held an advantage because until 1980 they were free of reserve requirements set by the Federal Reserve; after 1980 they could still avoid such requirements by booking loans at head offices abroad. Chase determined to meet this competition head on, although to a limited extent.

To do so the bank in late 1977 began to experiment with what it called money market loans. These included overnight loans or credits up to twenty-nine days, which were match funded and often priced against federal funds (lowest cost money), plus a spread that averaged around fifty basis points. Chase did not publicize this new type of loan product but used it in limited circumstances with key corporate relationships. News of such a change could not long be kept from the market, however. Soon both Morgan Guaranty and Wells Fargo were offering similar credits. What had been reserved for a few now was requested by many.

Money market pricing spreads to other maturities

Having once embarked on money market pricing, the bank soon extended the practice to other short-term loans, including maturities as long as one year. Again the price was related to the cost to the bank of additional funds with similar maturity. And rates for different maturities might be fixed for an agreed-upon period or might even float on a daily basis.

Programs of this type clearly had to be controlled if the bank's return on assets was not to suffer. The bank's asset-liability management committee (ALMAC) took on this task, determining the overall total of such credits and allocating it between departments, chiefly corporate and international. ALMAC also set lower limits on pricing and determined what the departments would be charged for funds under various programs. The aggregate approved by ALMAC changed in accordance with the tightness of money and the strength of demand for prime priced credit. But allocations were eagerly sought by loan officers, justified (sometimes ephemerally) by the profitability of the overall relationship. Short-term money market loans increased over time, although they constituted a relatively small proportion of the corporate bank's loan portfolio.[7]

But erosion in the role of the prime rate did not stop with short-term lending. By 1979 it had spread to medium-term domestic lending as well. Pricing of term loans in the Eurodollar market had long consisted of a spread over the cost of Eurodollars for a stated maturity. The market had come to accept as a benchmark for this purpose the three-month London Interbank Offering Rate (LIBOR), and loan rates floated in relation to it. At times the rate on term loans in the Eurodollar market fell under that of the prime in the United States. But Chase and other banks had seldom provided financing to domestic customers through the Eurodollar market, in part to protect pricing with the prime.

Exceptions to this practice soon developed. The bank began offering to term loan borrowers the alternative of loans extended by offshore branches at rates tied to LIBOR (Europricing) or domestic loans tied to the prime rate. Later still another rate option was added—a spread over the cost of negotiable certificates of deposit, a principal source of domestic funds for the bank. There were, or course, new and different risks to the borrower in connection with loans booked at foreign offices, including regulatory and political risks. Nonetheless this product was popular, and some highly valued customers were offered the best of all—the ability to select periodically from among these alternatives, enabling the customer to judge which would be lower over a specified period of time.

The prime rate diminished greatly in importance under this onslaught. Still, it remained a valued pricing tool as it continued to be a widely publicized base rate. Yet it was understood that, contrary to past history, the prime was not necessarily the lowest rate at any given time, and that different loan products were priced differently.

Return to fixed-rate lending—managing the funding gap

Aggressiveness in pricing was not the only tool employed by the corporate bank to rebuild its position. It also returned to granting medium-term loans on a fixed-rate basis, a practice discouraged for some time because of changes in the cost of borrowed money. But many customers sought such loans, and slack demand in 1976 and 1977 revived the practice. Such lending also enabled the bank to moderate the cyclical volatility of its earnings, adding loans and income at the low point of the business cycle even in the face of a possible loss later when rates for borrowed money rose.

But here too the volume and degree of interest rate risk had to be controlled by ALMAC. Allocations were established for the different departments, with corporate and international again in the forefront. And minimum spreads were required above the cost of funds for maturities matching those of the loans. By the end of 1979 the corporate department was carrying a considerable number of medium-term loans on a fixed-rate basis, while the international department, operating more in a floating-rate environment, carried fewer.

ALMAC, faced with a growth of fixed-rate lending and volatile rates for raising funds, developed what came to be known as "gap management." The "gap" represented the difference between fixed-rate assets and fixed-rate liabilities (funds to finance the assets). If this gap was positive, a part of the fixed-rate assets was financed by funds with rates subject to change. A rise in the cost of money would reduce income, while a decline in money costs would increase income. And of course if no gap existed—that is, if fixed-rate assets were equal to fixed-rate liabilities—a change in money rates would in general have little effect on costs and income. This would presumably occur if all assets were on a floating-rate basis and yields changed in step with changes in money costs. In actual practice, however, adjustments in floating rates normally lagged behind changes in money costs, decreasing earnings when interest rates rose and increasing them when rates fell.

For management purposes a distinction was drawn between the gap on long-term assets and liabilities (beyond one year) and the short-term gap.

Execution on the funding side (as well as in handling the bank's security portfolio) was carried out by the treasury department. The process grew more complicated as fixed-rate lending programs increased in number.

The bank began gap management after the mid-1970s with a considerable excess of fixed-rate liabilities (beyond one year) over fixed-rate assets.[8] This facilitated the addition of fixed-rate credits over subsequent years. By the early 1980s the volume of medium-term fixed-rate loans and investments amounted to about one-sixth of the bank's total, and had become slightly greater than the volume of medium-term fixed-rate liabilities. But managing this transition with greatest profit (as well as managing the bank's security portfolio and dealer activities) depended heavily on an accurate assessment of interest rates.

More than ever before ALMAC wrestled with this problem, examining the impact on bank earnings of a range of rate scenarios before selecting the one it regarded as most likely. Members felt reasonably confident that they could foresee the general direction of interest rate changes, although short-term movements often ran counter to predictions. Programs that leaned toward unbalanced positions were maintained throughout much of the 1977–1979 period and added to income. But in the second half of 1979, contrary to expectations, interest rates moved sharply higher and earnings were penalized. As interest rates became increasingly volatile in 1980 and 1981, ALMAC concluded that for the time being it could no longer forecast changes with confidence and moved toward more of a balance between fixed-rate assets and liabilities beyond one year.

Later, toward the mid-1980s, the development of interest rate swaps, futures, and options enabled the bank to change a gap between fixed-rate assets and liabilities relatively quickly. Interest rates became less volatile, and so ALMAC once again began to run moderate unbalanced positions.

Growth of nonlending services

Chase's improved position in the corporate market was monitored by customer surveys taken each year. These revealed impressive gains by Chase after 1976. The bank again rose to a top position as a principal bank to the large wholesale market. And it became more important to its major customers.

Much of the credit was due to the improved performance by Chase's account officers. As perceived by customers, their performance moved from the lowest among a group of leading banks in 1976 to the highest in 1979. The change to organization along industry lines was paying dividends. And so too was the infusion of new talent and leadership, along with added training.

Chase's aggressive posture on lending helped cement corporate relationships. But its officers were also able to provide a range of high quality nonlending services. Chase continued to process more money transfers than any other bank, and its foreign exchange activity grew dramatically. But no service held greater appeal than that providing money mobilization and cash management, named InfoCash.

The bank invested much time and money in developing and improving Infocash. Introduced in 1975, the service gained in favor over the years and by 1979 had more than eight hundred large corporations as clients.[9] Users managed their own accounts, as they do today, through remote computer terminals providing on-line, service furnished by Chase's subsidiary, Interactive Data Corporation. Managers could at any time determine their cash balances, foreign exchange, and investments, not only at Chase but at banks throughout the United States and major centers in Europe, and later in principal countries around the world. They could transfer balances between accounts, including foreign accounts, or invest surpluses in various money market instruments, either on their own initiative or automatically, according to predetermined programs. Either the whole or selected parts of this complex system could be utilized by a particular customer, seeking to conserve cash in an era of high interest rates.[10] Such a service, of course, became possible only with technical advances in computers and high-speed telecommunications, fields in which Chase cultivated expertise. Always a leader in the movement of money, Chase enhanced its position in the second half of the 1970s.

International loans move ahead of domestic

Although much emphasis was placed on recovery in Chase's domestic loans, the major gains continued to occur in credit generated overseas. In the five years from 1976 through 1981 loans abroad more than doubled from $13.5 billion to $31 billion, accounting for a large share of the bank's increase. As early as 1977 Chase extended more credit outside the United States than within, and the gap widened further in subsequent years. Even in the economically slack years of 1980 and 1981 foreign loans (swelled by inflation and balance-of-payments deficits) rose by nearly $9 billion, or 39 percent, almost half the total of domestic loans.

In order to manage this increasingly complex business more effectively, the bank in 1979 carried out a major decentralization. The senior executive in charge of activities in Europe and the Middle East moved to London, and another for the Far East shifted to Hong Kong. These officers possessed substantial authority and could react quickly to opportunities in their markets as they arose.

Loans to business (including state-owned firms) remained the major portion of foreign portfolios, accounting for almost two-thirds of the aggregate. The volume continued to be largest in Western Europe, Japan, and such countries as Brazil, Mexico, and Venezuela. Credit to the Soviet Union and Eastern Europe, relatively small in total, declined after 1979. And an initial loan planned for the People's Republic of China to help finance a trade center in Peking failed to materialize as that country reordered its priorities in the late 1970s.[11]

Chase's merchant banks—Chase Manhattan, Ltd., and Chase Manhattan Asia—emerged as leaders in Eurocurrency syndicated loan markets. As we saw in Chapter XV, in 1979 they were serving as lead or co-manager for the largest number of loan syndications of any international bank, generating loan opportunities for the bank itself.[12] Many of these syndications supported expansion of industry, but a number also financed balance-of-payment deficits. The bank held to its policy of according these latter credits a relatively low priority. Direct loans to foreign governments and official institutions crept upward, but their proportion in the overseas portfolio remained stable at 10 to 12 percent. Excluded from these totals, however, were credits to state-owned firms, now growing in volume.

Concern continued to be evidenced that Chase and other banks might be headed for trouble with too liberal credit to less developed countries. A House subcommittee on banking, finance, and urban affairs held hearings on the matter in April 1977, with John Haley from Chase among those testifying. Haley denied that LDC loans posed a problem and presented information on Chase's distribution of overseas credit.[13] Almost 60 percent of loans subject to country risk were then in industrialized countries, with about a third in the developing world and the remainder in OPEC and East European nations. Moreover, the great bulk of LDC credits continued to be extended to the more prosperous nations.

Yet loans to developing nations were growing at a higher rate than loans to other countries. The proportion of overseas credit to industrial countries was declining. The second huge rise in oil prices in 1979, with its accompanying inflation, soon produced a record spurt of borrowing by the non-OPEC developing world. By 1981 Chase's total exposure to these countries had climbed to more than $12 billion, or close to 45 percent of all foreign credits. Moreover, some $9.6 billion represented loans in currencies foreign to the borrowing nation, chiefly dollars, requiring the availability of foreign exchange for repayment.[14]

Rise of country risk analysis

As Chase's foreign exposure expanded, the bank began early to emphasize country risk analysis. Country risk stood apart from normal credit risk, reflecting social, political, or economic developments in a particular country that might affect the borrower's ability to repay.

A country risk committee, chaired by the bank's chief credit officer and with representatives from the international, economics, and other relevant departments, was first formed in 1975. Past and future trends in the economic and financial position of individual countries were analyzed and projected, with emphasis on the amount of foreign borrowing and factors influencing the ability to repay. Geopolitical experts for different regions also contributed judgments on political developments. Moreover, Chase's own portfolio in each country was subdivided into categories bearing different degrees of risk, among them the maturity of credits and whether they were funded with local currency or foreign currency. Foreign country managers contributed greatly to this assessment, presenting their own perceptions of the marketplace and recommending a limit for Chase exposure.[15]

It fell to the country risk committee to establish credit limits for each country, with an eye to the overall foreign risk prudent for Chase. Loans funded with foreign currency carried more risk than local currency credits because of the need for foreign exchange for repayment. With the volume of such risks increasing, the bank in 1979 established a separate unit to be concerned solely with country risk policy, and designated Francis L. Mason, most recently in charge of Western Hemisphere activities, as its head. Country risk analysis was further refined under Mason and integrated more effectively into the budgeting and planning process, becoming a key factor in the allocation of Chase resources.

Meanwhile economic conditions by 1981 had become less favorable, as growth and world trade slowed appreciably. A few countries found it difficult to repay foreign debt, notably Turkey, Poland, and Sudan. Bank leaders then banded together to reschedule and restructure bank debt, stretching out maturities and providing additional dollar credits necessary to maintain interest payments. In such cases the banks sought to involve the International Monetary Fund (IMF) not only to help with financing, but also to press upon a borrowing country a program designed to restore the nation's economic viability. This collaboration of the banks with the IMF increased greatly after 1981, as other developing countries, especially in Latin America, encountered serious shortfalls in foreign exchange (see Chapter XXII). Haley's 1977 judgment that LDC loans would not pose major problems thus proved faulty.

Turnaround in retail and trust

Chase's recovery plan also called for a turnaround in profitability of retail banking and trust services. Both had lost money, trust some $22 million and retail $36 million in 1976. Over the following three years each was success-fully converted to profit.

Trust emerged very moderately, with earnings of $5 million through cost cutting and improved programs. But retail was able to achieve a respectable profit of $24 million as the entire business underwent a substantial reconfiguration.[16] Unprofitable branches were closed, automation was ex-panded in the back office and introduced for the customer, and the bank concentrated on the most profitable segments of the market. By 1979 too Chase had formulated plans for a measured expansion of selected consumer services into other areas of the country.

The closing of unprofitable branches, begun in 1976, was pursued with vigor over the next several years; by the end of 1980 some forty-six branches in all had been shut down and applications for a number of others with-drawn.[17] Closures occurred throughout the entire metropolitan area, as well as upstate. For the first time since the early 1950s no new branches were opened.

Retail costs were also cut and service enhanced by installation of COM-ETS, the community electronic teller system, which provided tellers with access to account information across the entire branch system. Customers could now bank with equal ease at all branches.

Chase concluded that it should concentrate on upper- and middle-income segments of the retail market—professionals, executives, individuals of high net worth, and selected small businesses.[18] Three branches in upper Manhattan (later reduced to two) were devoted exclusively to highly adver-tised One Chase Banking, providing a range of banking and money manage-ment services to customers with sizable incomes. Convenience Credit was targeted to the upscale market, and Chase became the first bank in the city to offer customers a bill-paying service by phone.

Greater emphasis was placed also on card products. In 1977 Chase Bank-Americard changed its name to Chase Visa. This card in less than a decade had become Chase's most profitable retail product. Cardholders increased in number, and new holders were solicited for the first time in other areas of the country. Receivables more than doubled, exceeding $1.1 billion by 1979,[19] accounting for a good share of the steady increase in loans to individuals.

For a time in 1979 and 1980, however, Chase Visa ran into problems with profitability not of the bank's own making. Soaring interest rates raised the cost of money, but usury laws in New York State placed a cap of 18 percent on installment lending rates. Chase then mounted a two-pronged attack on the problem. Along with other banks it sought to have the state usury ceiling lifted; but it also encouraged liberalization of the banking law in another state, Delaware, aiming to establish a separate subsidiary bank free of the encumbrances of New York State.

The effort succeeded on both counts. The state usury law was suspended in late 1980, initially until 1983, when it was extended for another four years. And in 1981 Delaware acted to permit the establishment of bank subsidiaries by out-of-state holding companies.[20] No interest rate ceilings applied, and tax rates on income were substantially lower than in New York City and State. Chase immediately chartered a new national bank, Chase Bank (USA), which opened in early 1982. The new bank then became the focal point for marketing the Chase Visa card, consumer loans, and other services by mail in areas outside New York State, and it also offered a Chase money market fund, when permitted to do so by federal legislation effective late in the year.[21]

Chase Visa again became profitable, in part owing to the bank's charging a fee for the card for the first time in 1981. About 1.5 million cardholders used the service at this time. And the bank finally matched the card with its own traveler's check, the Chase Visa Cheque. Chase had first explored this business in the mid-1960s (see Chapter X), but at the time considered it only marginally profitable. Now the bank not only marketed the check through its own correspondents, but it also purchased the traveler's check business of First National Bank of Chicago. With about ten thousand sales outlets in forty countries, the check quickly gained worldwide acceptance and helped round out Chase's package of consumer products.[22]

Chase's selective approach to retail banking differed from that of some competitors, especially Citibank, which moved aggressively in all segments of the market. This difference was evident in the approach of the two banks toward the use of automated teller machines (ATMs). Chase early experimented with these, but did not find them profitable until costs changed late in the decade. At that point the bank installed 120 ATMs at sixty branches.[23] Citibank, seeking broad market share, had already made heavy use of ATMs, but at a considerable investment and in many areas not favored by Chase.

Trust improves earnings and performance

Trust's better earnings flowed particularly from its corporate agency functions. With back office operations now in the hands of Bradford National Corporation (see Chapter XVI), stock transfer eliminated a $10 million deficit. But paying stock dividends, along with acting as trustee and paying agent for bond issues, were the most profitable services.[24] These not only covered costs with fees, but also generated funds left on deposit prior to disbursement. As interest rates rose in the 1970s, such funds generated substantial income. Chase held a preeminent position as trustee for bond issues and surpassed all others as paying agent for municipal issues. With Ernest L. Loser at its head, corporate trust became the trust area yielding the greatest earnings.

Other services were reoriented and restored to profitability. In no business was the change more dramatic than in pension trust investments under Chase Investors Management Corporation (CIMC). Performance of this activity had deteriorated in the first half of the 1970s (see Chapter XIV). Banks as a whole lost market share after the stock market downturn of 1973–74. Corporations chose to divide pension funds into smaller parcels, allocating them among a number of managers, many of these nonbank firms specializing in particular types of investment. The corporation itself then became the ultimate manager, combining a number of managers to form their total.[25]

CIMC put in place a new strategy in response to this development, forming a series of smaller specialized investment funds. Each was managed by a relatively small professional staff engaged in direct contact with clients as well as selection of specific investments. Called "shops within a shop," several were holdovers from the past, one concentrating on equities of large capitalization companies and another on companies with small capitalization. A third, the intrinsic value equities shop, carried securities of small to medium-sized companies that combined high yields with favorable ratios of price to earnings and book value. Still others specialized in fixed-income securities, real estate, security options (a new investment), oil and gas properties, and international investments.[26]

A decided improvement in CIMC performance resulted from this new strategy under the leadership of a new president, Stephen E. Canter, chosen from within the ranks. The turning point occurred in 1977, with the improvement becoming even more evident in 1978, when Chase's total equity investments outperformed the widely followed stock indexes. Over the five years ending in 1982 total Chase equities rose in value an average of 87 percent, compared with 74 percent in the Standard and Poor's "500" stock index.[27] And in 1984 CIMC was singled out as a premier trust investment manager among banks.[28]

Chase's performance also was strengthened by the start of a separate investment management group in London, reporting to Canter. This dealt particularly with clients in the Middle East and Europe, including large pension funds in Great Britain interested in CIMC's special shops. A global fund, with foreign securities, was made available to clients in the United States and abroad. Growth in the foreign area proved rapid, but it represented only a small part of CIMC's overall investment responsibility. By 1985 this totaled about $17 billion, more than three times the volume of a decade earlier, with a radically changed environment and a different mix of business.

Chase becomes the leader in master trust

Some $4.5 billion of the CIMC portfolio represented short-term investments handled for another side of the trust department, the pension trust, and financial services division. The activities of this division grew phenomenally after 1978, led by aggressive marketing of a superior product, master trust. Again a favorable environment created opportunity for expansion. Pension funds continued to pile up rapidly, from $300 billion in 1977 to $800 billion in 1982.[29] Corporations spread large sums among a number of managers, including CIMC. AT&T, with some $50 billion, employed one hundred managers, while IBM, with $8 billion, used twenty-two managers and handled about $1 billion in-house.[30] Information on these investment pools had to be consolidated and performance analyzed and compared. Moreover the government required detailed reports each year, mandated by the Employee Retirement Income Security Act of 1974 (ERISA).

Master trust provided this unifying service, retaining all assets of a corporate pension fund in Chase custody, maintaining overall accounting records, furnishing analytical reports, and preparing information required by ERISA. In addition, Chase master trust made available a central investment outlet for surplus cash generated by different money managers of a large corporate pension fund.

The critical element of master trust lay in a superior data processing capability, through which Chase was able not only to keep accurate records but to generate reports to aid a corporation in the central management of its funds. A new head of trust, A. Edward Allinson, pushed the marketing and development of the service, with Edward E. Madden in charge. Madden worked closely with operations to fashion information and analytical products that could be generated from basic data provided for master trust. All told, thirty-three new products were created over four years. Some measured the performance of different managers and the pension as a whole. Others aided in investment, frequently with assistance from Chase Investors Management. Information and the ability to execute decisions were immediately available to corporations through their own computer terminals.

Chase marketed master trust vigorously, assisted at times by Rockefeller and Butcher. The result was a remarkable expansion of the business, with assets increasing from $9 billion in 1978 to more than $40 billion in 1982, including an international facility centered in London. Pension trust then contributed significantly to profits with a high return on assets.

Dramatic recovery in earnings

The improvement in retail and trust was only one of many factors that contributed to the recovery in Chase's earnings after 1976 from $105 million to $311 million in the short space of three years, and then to $444 million in 1981.[31] The gain in 1979 alone was great enough to enable Rockefeller to tell the directors, "We skipped over the $200 million bracket entirely."[32] When

Rockefeller arrived late at one board meeting, at which Butcher had announced quarterly gains, the directors rose and gave him a standing ovation in appreciation of a job well done. Stock analysts and the press began to sing a different tune about both Chase and its chairman.

Increased income flowed from many sources: larger loan volume, investments, fees, and service charges. Foreign exchange traders, operating around the globe in highly volatile markets, lifted their returns from $47 million to $123 million in 1981. This and other nonloan income was particularly welcome because it required no assets and little supporting capital. Return on average assets rose from a low of 0.24 percent to 0.59 percent between 1976 and 1981, and return on stockholders' equity more than doubled to 17 percent, both within the range of the long-term goals that had been set by Rockefeller and Butcher.

On the cost side, strict budgetary controls helped bring down the rate of advance in salary and other operating expenses. Domestic employees declined in number for several years after 1976 (partly as a result of the closing of branches), and the increase overseas leveled off. By 1981 Chase employees worldwide totaled 34,200, with some thirteen thousand at work abroad.

Moreover, as Butcher had predicted in late 1976, a sharp decline in provision for loan losses and in nonperforming assets had greatly benefited the bottom line. Provision for loan losses in 1979 of $149 million (substantially more than net charge-offs) was less than half that of three years earlier. Over the next two years the provision again increased moderately, but was readily absorbed by higher earning.

Crises in interest rates and the exchange markets

More than ever astute adjustments to changing interest rates played a significant role in determining short-run bank profitability. And as always, Federal Reserve policies largely dictated the timing and magnitude of rate changes. In these years the Federal Reserve was forced to adopt extreme measures on three occasions, and in doing so the central bank propelled U.S. interest rates to levels never before recorded.

A crisis in foreign exchange markets induced the measures in the first instance, in November 1978. Accelerating inflation in the United States along with a huge current account deficit encouraged waves of speculation against the dollar. The Federal Reserve reacted by raising the discount rate a full percent to 9½ percent and mobilizing huge foreign currency resources to intervene in exchange markets.[33] Chase's prime rate, which had advanced in measured steps to 8½ percent by May 1978, now moved upward a dozen times to 11¾ percent by the end of the year as the bank attempted to keep up with rising money costs.

The ceiling on rates, however, was not yet in sight. Soaring oil prices, record peacetime inflation, and excessive monetary expansion all came together in 1979 and 1980. A new chairman took over at the Federal Reserve—Paul A. Volcker, a Chase alumnus. Finally, on October 6, 1979, President Carter and Volcker announced a crash program, centered largely around the banks and designed to arrest inflation.[34]

Again the discount rate was raised a full point, this time to 12 percent. Marginal reserve requirements were placed for the first time on increases in the total of "managed liabilities"—large denomination time deposits with maturities of less than one year, Eurodollar borrowings, repurchase agreements, and federal funds from nonbank sources. And banks were asked to use voluntary credit restraint.

Beyond this, the Federal Reserve served notice that it would adopt a new technique for controlling monetary growth through open market operations. Emphasis would now be placed on controlling the volume of bank reserves, rather than holding short-run changes in the federal funds rate within narrow, preset limits. The money supply, and not interest rates, became the Fed's main target.

Yet even these measures failed to retard inflation, which climbed to a rate of 15 to 17 percent in the early months of 1980. President Carter then inaugurated still a third program in March 1980.[35] Included was an intensive effort, administered by the Federal Reserve, to curb the overall growth of credit, including not only business loans but consumer loans as well. And a surcharge of 3 percent was added to the discount rate of large banks, raising the level to 15 percent.

The markets immediately reacted to the Federal Reserve programs by raising interest rates still further and making them highly volatile. Chase's prime rate climbed to 15¾ percent by November 1979, and then shot up to the unprecedented level of 20 percent by early April 1980. All told the bank altered its prime forty-three times in 1980, with rates plummeting to 10¾ percent in July, only to move up to 21½ percent in December. Changes became less rapid in 1981, as the rate finally subsided somewhat to 15¾ percent in the second half.

Earlier, Volcker, in an understatement, had told bankers, "You're living in somewhat of a new world,"[36] and indeed they were, with old familiar landmarks fallen. Management of interest rates and funding costs by ALMAC and Chase's treasury department now under Wolfgang Schoellkopf, henceforth became even more difficult.

Chase in these years once again became an industry leader in setting the prime rate. In September 1977 the bank initiated a rate change for the first time since early 1975, and the press reported the banking community as being surprised.[37] Two years later Chase led all banks in rate changes. Chase used no set formula, but continued to examine the entire constellation of rates, including its own marginal and average rates on purchased funds, as well as strength in loan demand. It then exercised judgment with regard to the margin needed over the cost of funds, along with its competitive position, in setting the rate. Other banks apparently trusted this judgment, because usually, although not always, they followed Chase's lead.

Recovery in the capital position

Higher earnings were accompanied by a much-needed improvement in the capital position. Butcher, in reporting earlier to the board, had pointed out a vicious circle: "In order to have profits, we must grow; in order to grow we must have capital; in order to have capital we must have profits."[38] Now profits were increasing and along with them capital, both internally and from external sources. In five years the capital of the corporation (including the reserve for loan losses) rose by $1.8 billion to almost $4.5 billion. And the ratio of capital to total assets climbed to 5.8 percent, still less than desired but distinctly better than the ratio criticized by the comptroller at middecade.

Chase in 1981 published a pamphlet on bank capital prepared by Robert Lichten, responsible for capital planning.[39] Capital was perceived as including the reserve for possible loan losses, as well as equity and long-term debt. Within total capital a range of 25 to 35 percent for long-term debt was established as a standard.

Bolstering the equity position became especially important for Chase. It was accomplished at this time both through increased retained earnings and through issues of preferred stock, the first of these an innovative offering privately placed in 1977 to corporations holding tax-sheltered funds in Puerto Rico. This was followed in 1978 by an exchange of preferred stock for $150 million of Chase's outstanding long-term debt, opening the way for substantial new debt issues. Then in 1980 Chase pioneered with an issue of nonredeemable preferred stock, the first offered by any bank. Equity increased to 79 percent of the capital mix. Meanwhile, for the first time three debt issues were marketed abroad, one for Eurodollars and the others for deutsche marks and Swiss francs.

Capital planning now became an integral part of the management process. Even with sizable retained earnings it was necessary to go to the capital markets on a regular basis. No longer could the corporation permit assets to grow at a more rapid pace than capital, a marked change from the increasing leverage that prevailed over most of the earlier period.

Modification of the Chase culture

No less important than capital was the quality and depth of management. Here too Rockefeller and Butcher set out at middecade to achieve improvement, aided by Alan Lafley, the new head of corporate human resources. Over the following years, especially 1977–1979, policies and practices relating to officer personnel were upgraded and modernized, and a deliberate effort was made to enhance efficiency and teamwork through stronger internal communication at all levels.

Recruitment, training, and compensation practices all were overhauled.[40] College recruitment had lagged for a few years but was now stepped up. By decade's end, Chase was attracting more than two hundred well-qualified candidates each year, many with advanced degrees. They entered a credit training program which traditionally had been a pacesetter for the industry. And Chase departed from long-standing practice by hiring talented officers from outside the bank for senior management positions. Indifferent performance in positions of responsibility was not tolerated; officers who failed to measure up were terminated. The bank could no longer afford the paternalism so prevalent in the past.

A new advanced management seminar was designed for senior and middle managers, and more than 350 key decision makers, many from overseas, went through this two-week program. Still other middle managers undertook a less concentrated one-week session. Meanwhile, the appraisal and evaluation of officers' performance was sharpened, helped by better information on the profitability of different functions and units. Compensation programs were revised to reward superior performers with bonus payments of varying size, tied in part to the overall profit performance of the bank. Separate and different programs were instituted for senior and middle management.

But upgrading quality and compensation was not the sole thrust at this time. Rockefeller and Butcher sought also to draw together the management staff in a more cohesive and dedicated unit. Morale had suffered in 1975 and 1976. Now it was restored. Communication within the management group had been weak, downward from top management, laterally between different departments, and upward from subordinates to supervisors.[41] The problem of top management communication was tackled vigorously. Rockefeller and Butcher met with all levels of staff. Regularly scheduled sessions, including a meeting each Friday morning with vice presidents (taped for presentation overseas), were given greater importance. *Chase News* and the daily *Officers' Bulletin* were revamped to be more informative about the activities of different departments. And new publications, looking at Chase in greater depth, were inaugurated.

Improvement in lateral and upward communication was more difficult to achieve. Chase culture had always been somewhat parochial. But the growing integration of the corporate and international departments in handling multinational customers continued to break down lateral barriers.

Most troublesome was upward communication, especially the reluctance of subordinates to bring bad news to their superiors.[42] Outsiders had criticized this in senior management, holding Rockefeller to be too isolated and not informed of problems, and there was some merit in this allegation. Rockefeller sought to encourage a better flow of information, although not with complete success. Communication between Rockefeller and Butcher, however, was excellent; the two met regularly to review and settle issues, and held lengthy sessions outside the bank for more substantive discussions. Nevertheless at lower levels upward communication remained a problem, especially among older officers, ingrained with cautious habits of long standing.

1981: a high point for Chase

Nineteen eighty-one marked a high point in the postwar history of Chase, capping five years of solid progress. Loans, earnings, and capital all grew strongly throughout the period. The bank restored its preeminent position with major corporate business, aided in part by radical changes in the pricing of credits. Nonlending services, many based on computers, also enhanced customer relationships. And other lines of business, particularly retail and trust, were transformed from losers into profit makers.

Yet this period also saw the basis laid for new difficulties in the future. The environment for banking deteriorated as inflation became rampant. Interest rates and exchange rates grew ever more volatile, further complicating asset-liability management. Loans overseas outpaced the domestic, pushed upward in part by increased balance-of-payments deficits in less developed countries. These and further changes would affect Chase and other banks adversely in the year immediately ahead.

Chase and the revolution in Iran

In the autumn of 1979 a crisis erupted in Iran which embroiled Chase in international politics and held the potential for a huge loss on loans and other assets. Revolution late in 1978 had forced the shah from his throne and created a chaotic internal situation, one that the bank had not foreseen. Islamic clergy, liberals, and radicals all vied for power under the new head of state, Ayatollah Khomeini. The United States was proclaimed "the Great Satan" and became the bête noire of the people.

Anti-American sentiment culminated on November 4, 1979, with the seizure of the U.S. embassy in Teheran, in which fifty-two Americans were taken hostage. The Americans were held for fourteen months, a period marked by fitful spurts of frustrating negotiation. Meanwhile the claims and deposits of American banks relating to Iran were frozen. They became a major factor in bargaining for the hostages' release.

Chase had long held a primary position among American banks in Iran. Its leadership in petroleum financing had produced important relationships with the state-owned National Iranian Oil Company (NIOC) as well as with private companies operating in the country.[1] Rockefeller regularly visited the shah on his trips to the Middle East and met with him in the United States. More than any other American bank, Chase was linked in the public eye with Iran.

With the huge increase in the price of oil in late 1973, the dollar income of Iran skyrocketed. The shah embarked on a grandiose plan for industrialization, much of it to be carried out by state-owned entities. These developments greatly increased Chase's involvement with Iran in the 1970s. NIOC directed that foreign payments for its products be made through Chase. And the bank served as a major depository for Bank Markazi, the central bank, as well as a principal correspondent for Bank Melli, Iran's largest commercial bank. As much as $50 to $60 million passed through the bank each day from these sources, and aggregate deposits at times exceeded $1 billion.[2]

On the lending side, Chase Manhattan Ltd. emerged as the principal lead manager for large syndicated loans to the Iranian government and public entities. Although foreign branches were not permitted, the bank maintained a busy representative office in Teheran. And it held a 35 percent interest in the International Bank of Iran, established in 1975 (see Chapter XV).

Impact of the revolution on Chase

Chase in the eyes of most Iranians was closely associated with the shah, as well as with the business establishment that supported him. This relationship became magnified by events following the shah's departure from Iran in late 1978. The new revolutionary government lost little time in examining his records and those of public corporations with which he was identified. It alleged that payments on behalf of the monarch had been channeled through the NIOC account at Chase to a wide network of banks around the world— payments made either directly to the shah's account or to the Pahlavi Foundation, a private foundation he had established.[3] The rumor grew that Chase had handled the shah's private banking affairs and was the repository for much of his external wealth. This was false; Chase carried no personal accounts for the shah or the Pahlavi Foundation. Yet the myth persisted.[4]

Chase was further identified with the shah by public support and assistance given him by Rockefeller, Henry Kissinger (then Chairman of Chase's international advisory committee), and John J. McCloy. The recent occupant of the Peacock Throne was now a man without a country, treated as a pariah by many former friends and allies. And although the fact was not realized at the time, he was ill with incurable cancer. The State Department, not wishing to be directly involved, asked Rockefeller to let the shah know that he would not be welcome in the United States. Rockefeller recalled, "I said I thought it was a mistake, that [the shah] was a great friend of the United States and was seeking asylum and that it was in the American tradition to admit anybody under those circumstances, most particularly a friend. So I refused."[5]

During the following months Rockefeller and his administrative assistant Joseph V. Reed, Jr., helped the shah find a suitable home, first in the Bahamas and then in Mexico. Meanwhile, Rockefeller, Kissinger, and McCloy all impressed upon the State Department and the administration the basic injustice of forbidding the shah, a former ally, admittance into the United States.

This did not pass unnoticed in Teheran. The deposits left by Bank Markazi and NIOC began to decline, and the oil company shifted much of its banking activity to Bank of America's London office.[6] Then the International Bank of Iran, along with other private banks, was nationalized at the beginning of June.[7] Chase's representative office became less active, finally closing permanently, by order of the Iranian regime, after the last American staff member left the country following the seizure of the U.S. embassy.

Seizure of hostages and freeze of Iranian assets and deposits

The question of the shah's admittance into the United States was brought to a head by his illness in the summer of 1979. Joseph Reed arranged for his own personal physician to see the shah in Mexico, and the doctor recommended that he be brought to New York for medical treatment. Rockefeller, Kissinger, and McCloy again supported his entry, but the actual decision was taken by President Carter and his foreign policy advisers at a breakfast meeting in the White House on October 19.[8] The decision was unanimous after the risks were assessed. Three days later the shah was admitted to New York Hospital. This sparked intensified anti-American demonstrations in Teheran, leading to the seizure of the embassy and the hostages on November 4.

The U.S. government was fully cognizant of the position of U.S. banks in Iran, having conducted surveys among the banks earlier in 1979. The banks carried claims on Iranian borrowers amounting to $3.7 billion, but they also held much larger deposits from Iranian public sector entities, principally at their London branches.[9] Preparations had already been made for a freeze on the deposits and various other Iranian assets (about $9.0 billion in all) if advisable. Such a freeze was implemented on the morning of November 14, speeded by a remark of the Iranian prime minister, reported by local radio and picked up by U.S. government monitoring, that Iran would withdraw its deposits from American banks.

Chase was advised of the freeze early in the morning and asked to make arrangements to block all Iranian public sector accounts on its books, both at domestic and foreign offices. This was quickly accomplished, and the management committee convened to take stock of Chase's position. Information then available showed that Chase had claims on the government of Iran and other public entities of about $366 million.[10] This included $343 million in loans and other credit facilities, as well as Chase's investment in the International Bank of Iran and the small interest in the Industrial and Mining Development Bank of Iran. But the bank still held approximately $509 million in deposits from the Iranian public sector. Later, as more complete information became available, the totals would be revised somewhat, but not radically.

Complicating the picture, however, was the fact that the bulk of these loans and deposits was held overseas, especially in the branch in London. The deposits were chiefly in Eurodollars, with smaller amounts of other Eurocurrencies. Moreover almost $300 million in loans resulted from eight large syndications to public entities in which many foreign as well as American banks participated, and for which the bank served as agent.[11] The U.S. Treasury order freezing deposits extended to accounts at overseas branches and subsidiaries, a most important provision. This action, through which the U.S. government applied its regulations extraterritorially, raised a host of legal problems and disturbed foreign banks and officials.

Chase applies the right of offset

Chase waited for a day before taking action. Then on November 15 it combined all asset and deposit accounts and announced that it had offset the assets with deposits, in effect paying off all its claims against Iran.[12] At that point the regulations were not explicit in all details, and the offset was contingent on obtaining necessary approvals from the Treasury.

The deposits of some entities were not as large as their borrowings, while in others deposits were in surplus. The bank, however, considered all depositors and borrowers of the Iranian public sector to be a part of the Islamic revolutionary government, and lumped them together, an action supported by provisions of the revolutionary constitution and the decrees that expropriated or abolished the separate entities.[13] This view soon came to be called "the Big Mullah" theory.

Chase, as agent for the syndicated loans, determined that certain potential events of default had occurred, and requested instructions from the participating banks as to whether their maturities should be accelerated. These loans, with about $1.7 billion then outstanding, had some 250 banks as participants, many of them non-American and many without adequate deposits for their own offset. The necessary majority voted for acceleration in only three instances, including the largest single loan, a $500 million jumbo credit to the government of Iran.[14]

A number of participants were not happy with Chase's actions, and some questioned their propriety in the circumstances. In the case of the jumbo government loan, interest was not paid when due on November 15, since the blocking order the previous day had frozen the Bank Markazi account, which Iran had intended to use to make the payment. This default on the jumbo loan then triggered cross-default provisions in certain other agreements.

While the majority of lenders who had voted to accelerate payments under the government loan were American banks, certain European participants objected that they had not been fully informed of the circumstances. So members of this syndicate met again in London on December 7 and reaffirmed the default.[15] But meetings of other syndicates in which U.S. banks were a minority failed to make similar decisions.

The extraterritorial nature of the U.S. government's blocking orders involved major legal issues that were quickly raised in the courts. A fortnight after their issuance, Bank Markazi sued Chase in London, demanding repayment of $321 million on the grounds that the extraterritorial application of the freeze was illegal.[16] Chase instituted a suit in New York for a declaratory judgment approving its action. And the bank also counterclaimed in the London lawsuit to protect its interests. None of these suits ever came to trial as all concerned played for time, hoping that somehow the hostage crisis and the international financial mess that it had spawned would be settled.

Secret negotiations

The situation of Chase and other banks was inextricably linked to the plight of the hostages. And that crisis proved extraordinarily difficult to resolve, in part because of internal political turmoil in Iran. The U.S. government tried a number of approaches for mediation, but without success. Then in early May, John E. Hoffman, an outside counsel for Citicorp at that time engaged in a suit against Iran in West Germany, was approached indirectly by Iran's German counsel, Herbert Wagendorf, about the possibility of discussing a general financial settlement between American banks and Iran.[17] Hoffman, a partner in Shearman and Sterling, immediately reported this approach to Walter Wriston and Hans Angermueller, chairman and vice chairman of Citicorp. After consideration by the U.S. government, he was authorized to pursue the discussion, to be carried out in complete secrecy.

Hoffman soon determined that he needed an ally. He selected Francis D. Logan, Chase's principal outside counsel with Milbank, Tweed, Hadley and McCloy. Logan in turn sought and obtained approval from Rockefeller. Within Milbank, only one other lawyer, a young associate, Peggy Grieve, knew of the negotiations and assisted Logan.

Months of secret exchanges of views and negotiations then ensued, with Hoffman, aided by Logan, meeting Wagendorf and others in London, Bermuda, Germany, and elsewhere. Gradually a plan, labeled Plan C, took shape, based initially on earlier work by Hoffman and Angermueller.[18] At the outset of negotiations it had been made clear that no financial settlement would be possible without the liberation and return of the American hostages. Plan C was to cover all claims against Iran, including those of nonbank creditors. But an initial partial payment under the plan was to involve only funds held by U.S. banks at their offshore offices, as well as the syndicated loans in which both U.S. and foreign banks participated. These deposits were not tied up by attachments, as were those domiciled in the United States, and they were large enough to leave a considerable surplus for Iran after repayment of the syndicated credits and other Iranian debts. Meanwhile, deposits in Iranian accounts within the United States, on which a settlement would be carried out later, had increased substantially, as dollar receipts for oil shipped prior to the freeze continued to flow in. At Chase alone the increase amounted to about $400 million.[19]

Hoffman and Logan never knew the identity of their ultimate contact in Iran. Only later, after resolution of the crisis, was it learned that the negotiations were initiated by Ayatollah Mohammed Behesti, head of the Islamic Republican party and a dominant force in the Revolutionary Council. He was later killed in a 1981 bombing of the party's headquarters.[20]

By early autumn chances that the Iranians would agree to Plan C appeared promising. But on November 14 Hoffman, at a meeting in Dusseldorf, was told by Wagendorf that Plan C would be unacceptable, that the Iranians wanted to reconstitute financial relations with the banks. This was bitter news for Hoffman and Logan, who after months of effort were "discouraged beyond words."[21] But they began to work immediately on a new plan, this one labeled Plan D.

Plan D called for full payment of only those loans that had matured. Others would be brought up to date with payment of back principal and interest due. Future payments would be guaranteed by Bank Markazi, and certain interest-bearing deposits would be left with the banks as partial collateral.[22] Plan D was much less satisfactory to the Americans than Plan C. But by now Hoffman, Logan, and others sensed the growing political pressure in Washington for a settlement as President Carter, defeated for reelection, labored to bring the hostages home before his term expired.

Hoffman realized too that if all loans were not to be repaid, it would be necessary to involve other banks in the negotiations. So he and Logan formed a group that included the twelve U.S. banks with offshore deposits.[23] This group was brought up to date on past negotiations as well as on Plan D. They put together a figures committee and retained Peat, Marwick, Mitchell, public accountants, to assist in gathering and collating the Iranian position for each bank. All were concerned about the lack of adequate security on remaining loans outstanding under Plan D. Deputy Secretary of the Treasury Robert Carswell came to New York to press upon Wriston, Butcher, and the others the necessity to compromise.[24] He asked each bank to designate a high officer to come to Washington if necessary, with authority to make binding decisions.

Iran agrees to a settlement

The crisis came to a dramatic conclusion over the first three weeks of January 1981, a period during which the bankers were transported from hope to despair to hope, and then finally to a reality that exceeded expectations. After days of frustrating negotiations, on January 11 the Iranians suddenly announced that Plan D was unacceptable. The disheartened bankers then set about revising it. Nothing more was heard from the Iranians until January 15, when Hoffman was called to Washington. There, to his amazement, he was informed that the Iranians now wished to pay off all syndicated bank debt, reverting to the essential principles of the original Plan C. Nonsyndicated debt owed to U.S. banks would be settled by negotiation or arbitration, with payment secured by a $1.4 billion escrow fund set aside from Iranian offshore deposits and lodged in the Bank of England. Hoffman was asked to inform the banks that an 11:00 A.M. meeting would be held at the State Department the following day to resolve remaining differences.[25]

Meanwhile the bankers, anticipating some form of imminent resolution, had split up into teams. Logan and others were sent to London, where the actual transfer of funds was expected to take place. And Chase designated Thomas Labrecque, the chief operating officer, and Robert R. Douglass, the general counsel, to represent it in Washington.

Arrangements for the transfer of funds were themselves complicated, involving the banks, the Bank of England, the Federal Reserve Bank of New York, and the government of Algeria, which was now playing a crucial role as intermediary between the United States and Iran. Logan, working on arrangements in London, received a phone call at 3:00 A.M. on January 15, asking him to be on the steps of the U.S. embassy at 7:00 A.M. ready to fly to Algeria.[26] One other bank representative, Thorne Corse of Bank of America, joined him on the flight in a windowless Air Force Boeing 707, which also carried the deputy governor and chief cashier of the Bank of England, as well as U.S. Treasury and State Department representatives. Logan, unaware of the change in Iran's demands, worked during the flight on what he thought might become Plan E.

In Algiers, Warren Christopher, deputy secretary of state and chief negotiator, quickly informed the group that the Iranians were now willing to revert to Plan C as part of the overall Algiers Accords that were to provide for the release of the hostages and the settlement of claims. The actual details remained to be worked out. Logan and others, cloistered in the chancery of the U.S. embassy, worked steadily for the next five days with little sleep and almost nothing to eat. "It was certainly the most frustrating and yet important matter I've ever participated in, from moments of hope to the depth of despair," Logan later recalled.[27] Not until January 20, at the last moment, did Christopher and the Americans, consulting with Washington, manage to fashion an adequate working agreement for gaining the release of the hostages.

Disagreement over interest

A major point at issue concerned the amount of interest American banks would pay on the blocked offshore Iranian deposits. This was felt by the banks to be a matter for individual negotiation by each. Earlier, on January 9, a representative of Bank Markazi had met with each bank in New York and arranged for the payment of $670 million in interest. But the Iranians were not satisfied with the rates and demanded $800 million, a demand they continued to make even after accepting Plan C in principle. The matter was of considerable consequence to some banks, although less so to Chase. Bank of America, which had fallen heir to Chase's NIOC account, held deposits of $2.8 billion at its London branch, and therefore had the most at stake.[28]

Labrecque and other bank leaders, meeting at the State Department on January 16, wrestled with this problem, spurred on by Secretary of the Treasury Miller and Secretary of State Muskie. Labrecque called for a calculator and by an informal consensus served as defacto chairman.

The matter was ultimately resolved by determining to pay Iran the full $800 million claimed, but establishing a procedure by which the $130 million excess over the $670 million of agreed interest would constitute "disputed interest," subject to settlements negotiated bank by bank, and secured by the escrow fund at the Bank of England.[29] A more contentious issue was allocation of the $130 million of disputed interest among the banks. Bank of America had accrued a relatively low rate on its large offshore deposits and would therefore have to assume a sizable share of the deficiency. Leland Prussia, its representative, at first resisted this formula, but after conferring several times by telephone with A. W. Clausen, the chief executive, in San Francisco, he finally agreed to put up $91.5 million. Chase's share of disputed interest amounted to $11 million, a more manageable sum.[30]

Labrecque then returned to New York, but Douglass and other lawyers remained at the Treasury Department, working on arrangements for the transfer, conferring back and forth through Treasury representatives with the negotiators in Algiers, including Logan.[31] Details of the settlement accepted by the Iranians were reviewed again in Washington and Algiers. They called for reconstituting the overseas deposit accounts by reversing the offsets and including the interest, for a total of $5.5 billion. To this would be added another $2.4 billion in Iranian gold, securities, and deposits at the Federal Reserve Bank of New York, making available $7.9 billion in all.

From this some $3.7 billion of syndicated loan principal and interest was to be paid off, and another $1.4 billion was to be placed in a special escrow account in the name of the Central Bank of Algeria, held in the Bank of England, to be used to settle all nonsyndicated loans and other bank claims, including the disputed interest. The remaining $2.8 billion would return to Iran upon the departure of the hostages from that country.

Another $2 billion on deposit in accounts in the United States was by now heavily encumbered by attachments from nonbank creditors. Upon the president's order lifting the freeze, $1 billion of these funds would be returned to Iran and $1 billion transferred to another escrow account in the Netherlands, from which payment of nonbank claims would be made once verified by international arbitration.

A last-minute crisis resolved

With arrangements for the release and transport of the hostages settled, all seemed to be in place. On Monday, January 19, Christopher signed the

Algiers Accords. President Carter, anxious for the hostages' return before his term expired on Tuesday, rejoiced with all the nation. But suddenly a new problem developed in the implementation of the financial agreement.[32]

Instructions for carrying out the financial transfer were not published with the accord, but instead were contained in a separate payment order to be sent by Bank Markazi. Officials at that bank had not been fully informed of all details, and when they read the payment order for transferring the funds, they refused to approve it. The order specified the amounts to be paid to each bank, but it also included a full release of the American banks from any future obligations in connection with the deposits, not an unusual stipulation. Bank Markazi, deeply suspicious and with its records in disarray, would not assent to this. It first sent instructions inconsistent with the Algiers Accords and therefore unacceptable. The banks then agreed to eliminate the disputed section. But the new instructions for transfer, not received in London until 8 A.M. Tuesday, London time, were badly garbled.

By now the banks were under the heaviest of pressures. Secretary Miller told representatives still in Washington that they must pay. After debating briefly their potential legal vulnerability because of the garbled instructions, they decided to make the transfer. Chase, first in line, shortly after 4 A.M., New York time, instructed the Federal Reserve to transfer $460 million from its account to a special Federal Reserve account which in turn would be transferred to the Bank of England.[33] Other banks followed, providing the full $5.5 billion. Still another hitch developed in the transfer of the funds from the Federal Reserve account in the Bank of England to the Central Bank of Algeria, but this too was overcome. The exchange of funds, gold, and securities was then validated in Algeria, triggering the release of the hostages in Iran.

Logan, waiting in the chancery in Algiers, was invited to the airport to join in the welcome. He stood in the rain on the tarmac as the planes landed and viewed with high emotion the hostages descending onto neutral ground. A few hours later he himself was enroute to London in the windowless Boeing 707 with Christopher and other American negotiators, their mission at long last accomplished.[34]

Chase receives partial payment

Chase London, as the agent for eight syndicated loans, received almost half the funds returned to the banks for payment, some $1.8 billion in all. This was to be applied to payment in full of principal, and payment of interest through December 31, 1980, on all eight syndicated loans for which it served as agent. The bank retained $303 million as its own share, making the rest available for distribution to almost 250 banks around the world.[35]

The London branch received word from the head office about 10 P.M., London time, on Tuesday that the necessary funds had been received from the Federal Reserve in New York. A crew had stood by since Sunday, eating and sleeping on the premises. Telexes were sent out immediately to all participants in the credits, notifying them of receipt of the funds, again a moment of high emotion for all involved. Responses over the next several days revealed that outstandings, including interest, now stood at $1.6 billion, as Iran had continued to make normal repayments to many non-U.S. banks[36] This sum was immediately disbursed.

Chase's receipt of $303 million for its own account, while very welcome, did not cover all of its claims against Iran. There remained outstanding additional claims of some $93 million, comprising nonsyndicated credits, the bank's investment in the International Bank of Iran and the Industrial and Mining Development Bank, its claim for the $11 million of disputed interest, and a claim for interest on the syndicated loans for the eighteen days in January 1981 prior to their payment.[37] Settlement of these claims was to be negotiated with Iran, with payment made from the $1.4 billion escrow fund established for the purpose. Settlement proved difficult but was finally resolved by receipt of $92 million in June 1983.[38]

In many respects Chase and other American and foreign banks had been fortunate to receive the agreed-upon amounts at the time of the release of the hostages. Iran's last-minute decision to pay off the syndicated loans rather than restore them to current status was a surprise. No one knows who or what in the tangled internal affairs of Iran brought about this reversal. But for Chase the experience demonstrated the potential risks inherent in doing business in countries susceptible to revolutionary change. And it placed an even higher premium on adequate country risk analysis.

The computer transforms banking

Throughout the years of banking change surveyed in this history, a quiet revolution was under way at Chase in still another area: its back office operations. The advent of the computer and advances in telecommunications altered the organization and the very nature of these activities. From clerical work performed with standardized equipment, operations evolved into a highly complex business, requiring its own breed of specialized personnel. Over time, with quantum leaps in technology, the back office became increasingly integrated with the marketing departments, jointly fashioning new services and improving the quality of the old.

Central to all progress was the evolution of the computer, with its capability for electronic data processing. Banks were a natural focus for this technology, since they had to handle masses of checks, securities, and other documents, along with the attendant bookkeeping. A machine for check sorting was developed specifically for banks in the 1930s, with the Bank of Manhattan playing a role in the process.[1] This, with bookkeeping equipment, formed the mechanical basis for check handling in the early fifties. But as electronic data processing moved beyond its initial stages, Chase was determined to harness this technique for its own activities.

Early use of the computer

The bank first retained the Laboratory for Electronics in Boston, commissioning it to build a computer specially designed for bank needs. It was called Diana, after the goddess of the chase.[2] But the building of a custom-made computer proved costly, and the technology of electronic data processing was undergoing rapid change. So the bank decided instead in 1957 to rely on commercial companies specializing in computers. A new division of systems and standards was established in 1958 to develop and coordinate means for improving operating methods, including the testing and use of new equipment, manned chiefly by experts brought in from outside.

The bank's first computer, an IBM 650, was introduced early in 1959. Initially it processed the bank's clerical payroll and maintained complex records for employee benefits.[3] This served as a learning experience while work started on other applications, especially installment credit and the

Chase Manhattan Charge Plan. But the major objective was to computerize check processing and demand deposit accounting. More than 1.5 million checks passed through the bank each day, and the volume seemed to grow incessantly.

A committee of the bank's specialists studied the problem for eighteen months, and finally decided to adopt a centralized automated check handling system, using medium-scale computers and employing the Magnetic Ink Character Recognition method (MICR) recommended by the American Bankers Association.[4] This decision proved to be of great importance, for MICR checks came to be universally accepted. Even after a quarter-century of spreading bank automation, the magnetic ink check is still regarded as a most innovative accomplishment.

Two RCA computer systems with peripheral equipment (eleven computers in all) were selected for the task, along with check processing equipment from Burroughs Corporation. In March 1961 George Champion formally introduced the system, the first of its kind in New York City.[5] It would handle Chase's check flow each day and would do so more efficiently and accurately than old methods. A staff of eighteen hundred engaged in all aspects of check handling eventually would be reduced by half, although with Champion's assurance that normal attrition and transfers to other tasks would take care of those displaced.

Two years were required to complete the task. Checks processed came from the bank's 125 offices in greater New York, from the New York clearing house, and directly from other banks all over the world. Through a series of automated sorting, computing, and printing operations, checks and deposits arriving at random were reduced to an orderly pattern, by branch and by account, with bookkeeping done in printed form. This electronic check processing worked around the clock, supplying Chase's branches and head office with new balance sheets and customer records at the start of each business day. No later change was more dramatic than this early one.

Automation spreads to other areas

The computer was quickly adapted to other areas of the bank. One of the first was the stock transfer service performed by the trust department.[6] Chase performed stock transfer services for some 650 corporations throughout the country, not only keeping up-to-date records of names, addresses, and number of shares held, but also dispatching dividend checks, proxies, and necessary reports. By 1962 records on more than a million stockholders were placed on magnetic tape. Three years later the number had doubled.

Other major paper handling functions were soon automated—savings, Christmas Club, and installment credit accounts among them. By the mid-sixties twenty-seven different computer systems were at work.[7] Moreover, the computer began to spawn a set of new services, a result in part of the need to keep expensive equipment operating through as much of the day as possible. Demand deposit accounting was provided for smaller banks in the metropolitan area unable to afford a computer. And check reconciliation was undertaken for corporate customers wanting checks sorted and placed on magnetic tape for use on their own computers. For smaller companies the bank offered a complete payroll service, taking over many functions of customers' payroll departments.

To market such activities· an electronic customer service division was started. Other services were added, including rental billing and collection for large real estate operators, a clearing house for payment of airline tickets by travel agencies, and later a freight payment remittance system. The bank also gained contracts for processing state sales tax returns in Manhattan as well as the returns for New York City personal income and earnings taxes, a tribute to the comparative efficiency of its computer operations.[8]

Chase and other large banks enjoyed an initial advantage in providing these services because of their early investment and expertise in computers. But before the decade was over, this advantage began to fade. Technical improvements brought computers within reach of smaller banks, and specialized computer service bureaus sprang up. Chase found it difficult to compete with these on a cost basis. The bank eventually wound down its direct involvement in a number of early computer services, but later in the 1970s, as part of the information group, it developed others that were more advanced.

Money mobilization for large corporations, a key service, made extensive use of computers, reporting and analyzing cash positions in locations throughout the nation on a daily basis. And for individuals a computerized service in the branches, called Ticketron, provided instant reservations for entertainment events in the New York area.[9]

The computer centralizes operations

The computer had one other far-reaching impact on the bank in the 1960s: it changed the organization, bringing most accounting and transaction operations into one central unit. Previously the branches had performed their own bookkeeping and check handling, and the international department had managed its own operations units. A new bank operations department was formed in 1963 under Charles A. Agemian, with activities transferred over several years. Large savings on staff were realized, the number of employees fell from sixteen thousand to fifteen thousand over the first half of the 1960s, only to climb sharply again in the second half.

Although the computer eliminated some jobs, it created others. And it brought into the bank a new breed of personnel with special training and education. Champion was able to say in 1965 that the bank had 1,200 people working on some aspect of automation, many at jobs that did not even exist six years earlier, when the first processes were automated.[10] Many existing personnel were retrained through programs specially designed by the bank. But many also were recruited from outside—systems planners, programmers, operations research technicians, and other specialists.

The computer produced the bulk of savings in staff, but some savings were realized from a work measurement program started in the early 1960s. This program analyzed clerical tasks and developed standards to determine optimum staffing. The performance of individual employees was then recorded and measured by computer against the standard. As much as $5 million in salaries is estimated to have been saved in 1965.[11] The program developed a complex reporting system, however, and with heavy turnover and changes in the composition of staff, its usefulness eroded. By the end of the 1960s work measurement began to be phased out.

Related to work measurement was a project designed to ascertain the cost of various services. Banks had long lagged behind industry in cost accounting, and the use of computers, whose costs were shared by different departments and services, further complicated the problem. Chase was not alone in failing to know the true cost of its services and hence their profitability or lack of it. But a start was made in the 1960s with an effort to determine standard or normal costs for various products and services.[12] The result was often rough at best, with many overhead and shared costs allocated in a somewhat arbitrary manner.

In 1969 a new financial controls group began to update both the accounting and budgeting systems. As operating techniques improved, standard costs frequently had to be revised, and the approach eventually was abandoned. But it launched the bank on a lengthy development of cost analysis which in the end provided management with the tools it needed to measure the profitability of products and organizational units.

The operations center

Although computers and automation initially reduced some personnel requirements, they did not diminish the need for space. Indeed the mass of equipment in some instances increased space requirements. Aside from this, line departments were expanding their officer ranks and consequently their use of space. As a result, operations functions were being squeezed out of One Chase Manhattan Plaza into other buildings.

Confronted with this problem, the directors decided to establish a separate operations center rather than attempting to occupy a greater part of One Chase Manhattan Plaza. This would be more economical and would create the most efficient layout for computer and other activities. A new fifty-story building, erected seven blocks west of the head office and designated One New York Plaza, was selected for the purpose. In March 1967 Chase signed a lease for more than 1 million square feet, the largest at this point in New York history.[13] But the bank also obtained an option to purchase the building, which later considerably increased in value.

Chase moved into One New York Plaza in late 1969, and that building over the years continued to serve as the operations center. But even by 1969 expansion into new fields was carrying Chase into other locations. Uni-Card in the same year consolidated its operations at Lake Success on Long Island. And many staff remained at Eighty Pine Street. Other departments would also move out of the head office in coming years as the demand for space appeared insatiable.

Organizing for efficiency in the early 1970s

Changes in computer technology, telecommunications, and banking markets accelerated in the 1970s, determining the organization of the operations department, the equipment used, and even its functions. All altered substantially over the decade, but not without considerable difficulty. Operations deteriorated in quality for a while in the first half of the 1970s, contributing to the bank's problems at that time. But with a sharper focus on customer needs and stepped-up investment in equipment, performance recovered smartly by the end of the 1970s. New services were developed jointly with the marketing departments, delivery times were speeded up, and accuracy was greatly improved.

Although the centralization of operations initially reduced personnel and costs in the 1960s, as I have mentioned, this trend reversed. Barry F. Sullivan, who took over as head of operations in 1971, was then instructed to bring the function under more effective control, introducing even greater automation.[14] Sullivan set about reorganizing the department along functional lines, establishing five production groups: deposit services, owner security handling, issuer security services, data processing (including systems development), and such specialized services as letters of credit, money transfer, and cash management. These functional units cut across the marketing departments and tended to divorce line business officers from operations managers, even though satisfactory customer service depended on both.

Sullivan also introduced engineering techniques to set up more efficient production lines, eliminating paper handling where possible. He fulfilled the mandate laid down for him, and by 1973 personnel had been reduced from eleven thousand to eight thousand, even with a sizable increase in activity. But this improvement had been realized at the cost of some deterioration in the quality of service. As Sullivan put it, "In some cases we pushed too far." The problem began to show up in 1973 when corporate customers complained about delays in response to inquiries on the status of money transfers. It soon spread to the international department, where a similar shortcoming became apparent. Inaccuracies and failure to reconcile accounts developed in other areas, such as commodity finance, letters of credit, and accounts with foreign banks. "Chase did not have its checkbook balanced," one observer later commented.[15]

The problem with owner security handling

One of the most intransigent problems arose in owner security handling (OSH), the group responsible for securities held for safekeeping. At Chase this was a monumental task, with securities retained in the vault for correspondent banks and financial institutions in the United States and around the world. For years the records had been maintained in part manually and in part on an ancient Univac—so ancient that parts were no longer available. The bank scoured the country, eventually finding an old Univac and cannibalizing it.

In mid-1973 a five-year automation program was approved, and owner security handling was one of the first services to benefit. New IBM equipment was to replace the Univac, with the two systems running in parallel during the switchover. Then in February 1974 one of those unforeseen accidents occurred. The cannibalized parts of the old Univac were stored in a closet, scattered on the floor. A zealous employee, tidying up, opened the closet one day, spied all the "junk," and threw it away, soon rendering the Univac inoperable.[16]

Sullivan went ahead with the switch to the IBM computer in July 1974, even though the Univac could not run in parallel. A fully manual system was mounted. But an input problem developed with the new computer system, and massive differences appeared between the automated controls and the manual controls. "We had garbage in, garbage out, and a backlog of garbage," Sullivan recalled.[17]

A large staff was assembled from other areas to help straighten out these discrepancies. By the end of the year the differences had been reduced by three-fourths, and by mid-1975 they were relatively minor. Over the next several years the recovery of OSH was little short of dramatic. All told $12 million was invested in the most up-to-date systems and equipment. Personnel fell from two thousand to seven hundred, with savings of $18 million annually, and the bank was left with a service unsurpassed in the industry.[18]

But the bank paid a price for all this. For a time many customers were inconvenienced, and the bank's reputation for accuracy suffered. Moreover, the security handling problem contributed to another unsettling development. At the height of the changeover the examiners from the comptroller of the currency showed up for their annual visit. They found not only OSH but a number of other operating systems in the international, real estate, and accounting departments deficient, and the comptroller subsequently issued a highly critical report to the directors. A confidential summary for the comptroller's internal use, obtained surreptitiously by the press, labeled Chase's operations "horrendous."[19]

The comptroller's examination did have one salutary effect; it caused the directors to sit up and take special notice, and it galvanized Rockefeller and Butcher into even greater action. They recognized that although cost control was important, no less attention had to be paid to quality and consistency in the level of service. Additional personnel were added to operations, and several other new computer systems were successfully introduced for check processing and money transfer, although the latter took some time before it was operating efficiently. The examiner's report for mid-1975 noted distinct progress in operations, and the report a year later contained no reference to that department in the matters it called to the attention of the directors. The stories in the press about Chase's operating deficiency, appearing in early 1976, were badly out of date (see Chapter XVI).

New operating policy: organization by product

Presssure from another area also worked to bring about an improvement in operations. Receiving increased complaints about errors, the marketing departments, which were ultimately responsible to customers, took a more direct interest in operations. For products like letters of credit and collections the bank was losing market share. And yet with operations organized on a functional basis but marketing departments along product and geographic lines, it proved difficult for the two to interact satisfactorily, not only to improve service but also to develop new systems to meet marketing objectives.[20] Indeed some important products, such as cash management, had begun to depend almost exclusively on computer systems.

Rockefeller and Butcher knew that although operations had improved, the processes were not entirely satisfactory. Moreover, progress in computer techniques and telecommunications appeared to be opening up new potentials. Thomas Labrecque joined the management committee in mid-1976 and was asked to take a fresh look at the organization and activities of operations. He formed a task force, including representatives from both the operations and marketing departments, with help from outside consultants.

The result was a fundamental shift in strategy, leading to a reorganization that progressed by stages over the rest of the decade and into the 1980s.[21]

The new strategy first called for less emphasis on functions and costs of specific processes across the corporation, such as computer programming, and more on product performance and unit product costs, with an organization more along product lines. This permitted direct interaction between product managers in marketing departments and their counterparts in operations. Moreover, ultimate accountability for a product was to rest in the hands of the marketing department—for domestic money transfer and cash management in the corporate bank, for consumer deposits and loan products in the consumer bank, and for international money transfer, letters of credit, and collections in the international department, among others. These were the departments that received revenue; now they would be assigned corresponding costs. And they would need to ensure the competitive quality of their products.

The interaction of product managers in marketing and operations revealed ways to improve service and products and increase the ability to make rational investment decisions. Investment earlier had been retarded as products were lumped together and responsibility diffused.[22]

Meanwhile, the state of the art in computer technology and telecommunications continued to evolve rapidly, creating the basis for further changes in operations. Small chips no more than 1½ inches in diameter could now store information formerly requiring several thousand vacuum tubes occupying a sizable room. Microprocessors and minicomputers were developed, capable of handling data processing for specific products at reasonable cost. Advantages of scale, so compelling with large computers in the 1960s, no longer were overriding. Moreover, the transmission of data increased in ease and rapidity, not only domestically but internationally, through the beginning of SWIFT (Society for Worldwide International Financial Transactions), a cooperative venture of five hundred banks.[23]

Equipment and systems for some products could now be taken over and managed directly by a marketing unit. Such was the case, for example, with broker loans in the Wall Street division and with a number of retail consumer products. A separate operations facility for consumer banking was opened at Lake Success on Long Island, while operations at One New York Plaza concentrated increasingly on wholesale activities for corporations, banks, and other large customers, both domestic and international.

Money transfer and cash management

One series of products commanding major attention involved money transfer, a service basic to corporate customers as well as to correspondent banks and other financial institutions. Chase moved more money than any other bank, by the early 1980s handling as much as 35,000 transactions daily, with an aggregate amount in excess of $125 billion.[24] The process became increasingly automated as electronic means replaced paper and improved accuracy.

International transfers, spurred by the Eurodollar market, underwent extraordinary growth as billions of dollars flowed between banks, back and forth overseas. Determined to maintain leadership in this business, Chase formed a work group of marketing and operations officers to explore ways of improving the service. They reached out to two hundred foreign banks, surveying their needs and current problems. Out of this study emerged a concerted strategy to improve the quality of global funds transfer and to market the product more aggressively.[25]

Operations staff was upgraded in order to respond to customer queries directly rather than through marketing officers. New investments were made in technology, and seven regional service centers were established overseas. Transactions were routed through these centers, checked for accuracy, and sent on to New York. Located in the same time zone as the customer, with personnel speaking his language, the regional centers reduced errors and improved direct contact with the customer. A transfer for Shell Oil might be initiated at Chase's regional center in London, checked only against balances on a screen in New York, and passed on to Morgan Guaranty through the Clearing House Interbank Payments System (CHIPS). Later, with still further improvements in technology, Shell would be able to initiate the transaction directly through a Chase computer terminal located in the treasurer's office.

CHIPS itself underwent a radical change in 1981, with Chase a leader in the planning.[26] Participants in the system, both American and foreign, for some years had maintained a cutoff time of 4:30 P.M. for transactions. Banks then had until 10 A.M. the following day to settle their debts with one another. This left Chase and other banks with a huge overnight credit risk exposure to foreign banks around the world. To eliminate this exposure CHIPS in October 1981 converted to same-day settlement, requiring participating banks to settle their net obligations before 6 P.M., with a cutoff for transfers three hours earlier (later changed to 4:30 P.M.). This required up-to-the-minute information on transactions. Because of time differences, foreign banks incurred an added burden. Chase held seminars abroad for its foreign correspondents, helping them plan for the change. On the day of the switchover, Chase successfully cleared 35,940 transactions involving $151 billion from all over the world, an accomplishment that would have been impossible without the disciplined application of sophisticated technology to the process.

Closely related to money transfer was cash management, a series of products developed by the corporate bank in conjunction with production managers in operations. Most comprehensive was InfoCash, which steadily increased in range of service and information from 1975 onward. As we saw in Chapter XVIII, users of this service initiated transactions and obtained information through terminals in their own offices, linked to Chase's computer through the time-sharing network of the bank's subsidiary, Interactive Data Corporation. Money transfers, security transfers, and the investment of surplus funds in short-term instruments all could be initiated by the customer. Funds eventually could be transferred not only within the United States but in Europe and the Far East, and in a variety of currencies—sterling, deutschemarks, and French francs as well as dollars.[27]

Chase becomes an information intermediary

Essential to such activity was the availability of timely information; indeed, the provision of information became a service in itself. Money transfer services were packaged to include not only the transfer, but daily reports on all transfers and the status of bank accounts in different locations. Initially such reports were available to a customer through his terminal each morning, covering transactions of the previous day. Even foreign correspondent banks and corporations abroad could gain information on the status of their accounts at head office in New York. But more speedy information was demanded where possible, and Chase moved increasingly into real-time (simultaneous with the transaction) reporting. Users of InfoCash could then obtain up-to-the-minute information on dollar balances and other transactions at head office and additional locations through their Chase terminals.

Chase thus became not only a financial intermediary but an information intermediary as well. Long-standing services such as letters of credit and documentary collections were complemented by more detailed information on their current status. In such cases they were converted to substantially different products in the eyes of both customers and the bank. In the trust field, the growth of master trust was stimulated largely by the scope and timeliness of the information generated. Even in consumer banking, automated teller machines, used primarily for cash dispensing, were able to provide individual depositors with balance and transaction information.

Wherever customers responded favorably, Chase developed an information product out of transactions processing, using, for example, the transition to same-day settlement in international transfers to introduce a new product, called Same-Day Reporter, giving customers information on their own terminals about transactions cleared.[28] Product information, offered more and more on a real-time basis around the world, would be a growth business for Chase in the 1980s.

Reorganization by market

To move most effectively toward this goal, and to ensure highly responsive, high-quality service, the operations department reorganized once again, aiming at a market-oriented form of organization. Rather than organizing by clusters of similar products, operations was restructured into groups dedicated to specific markets.[29] First applied to consumer banking, this system was extended to corporate customers, domestic banks and other financial institutions, foreign banks, international's overseas activities, and securities for the trust and treasury departments.

By the mid-1980s an even finer distinction was drawn, with organization in some instances according to major businesses within a customer group. Managers of marketing departments thus gained direct control over the resources they needed. But they shared this control, in a form of "matrix management," with an overall head of operations who directed the technology to be used and provided coordination for management information and other purposes, a task carried out first by Arthur F. Ryan, who had earlier led the revamping of owner security handling, and then by Michael Urkowitz.

Continuing improvement in computer and telecommunications technology made this new organization possible. Relatively small and less expensive computers, with power formerly possessed only by large machines, were dedicated either to specific product or marketing units. Many departments had their own computers, including separate systems built for wholesale and retail check processing and demand deposit accounting. The powerful central machine that formerly performed these functions was turned exclusively to another purpose: generating information for the use and guidance of internal management.

The computer enhances management information

The computer was first adapted to management information in the second half of the 1960s. It was hoped that systems developed for handling loans, deposits, employee compensation, and other operations would generate data bases containing the basic facts about the bank's business. Top managers and those responsible for day-to-day activities might then have relevant data readily available. Progress toward this objective was realized over the years, but only slowly. For some time management information held a relatively low priority for systems design. While the use of computers for this purpose advanced, it did not reach the same level of maturity as that for serving customers.[30]

A start was made initially with automation of the accounting system, fully operative by 1970. Late in the 1960s work also began on an ambitious project to provide line officers with computerized information on their customer relationships, known as ARPAS—Account Relationship Profitability Accounting System. Development of this system continued throughout the 1970s and into the 1980s. Other projects, to aid in municipal bond bidding and trust investment, were successfully completed.

Meanwhile advances in the state of computer arts contributed materially to the ability to produce and utilize management information. Teleprocessing (the transmission of data between distant points and a central computer) and random access on-line systems permitted direct two-way communications between the user and the computer. Managers could then access product and financial information directly through remote terminals. Costs declined, and the second half of the 1970s brought a rapid expansion of information systems for use by both line managers and top management.

Major responsibility for bankwide management information was lodged in the controller's department. But the various product groups in operations also generated information for use by their line officers. Two broad objectives— providing information for general management and for customer relationships—became interrelated, with the same data base frequently serving both.

For management at all levels, one important report detailed the financial performance of departments and their units against budget. This evolved by stages over the decade. Initially many costs shared by different departments proved difficult to allocate, especially for operations. Managers were then judged on the basis of direct controllable results. The reorganization of operations into product groups largely removed this constraint, and by the late 1970s the bank had in place a system that measured not only the bottom-line profitability of various departments and their units, but also income and expenses associated with different products.

The international department, with its network of overseas branches and affiliates, posed a special challenge. Large branches had early automated their accounting, but many smaller units still performed functions manually. The bank in the late 1970s developed an automated system for uniform application by smaller and medium-sized branches. Called MIDAS (Modular International Dealing and Accounting System), it provided wholesale and retail bank accounting and processing, including loans, deposits, foreign exchange, and other transactions of importance.[31] Again, the advent of the minicomputer made such a system possible, speeding reports, reducing errors, and cutting costs.

Line managers at the head office and abroad gained access to a growing array of tools to manage customer relations. They could ascertain by way of terminals loans outstanding, deposit balances, foreign transactions, cash management, and other services. Increasingly such information was placed on a real-time basis. Some areas highly vulnerable to rapid change, such as commodity finance and broker loans, possessed their own special systems designed to provide comprehensive information. For officers with corporate accounts, however, ARPAS was not yet complete. Gaps still existed in the data on services supplied to individual customers at many locations abroad. The bank worked to eliminate these gaps, within the limits of a reasonable budget, for management information had gained greatly in priority over the short span of a half-decade.

Meanwhile the operating side of the bank, which early in the 1970s had suffered from poor performance, increased in recognition and respect. Chase stood out as a leading operating bank for both domestic and overseas customers, with special strength in such services as money transfer and cash management. By the early 1980s surveys revealed that Chase's overall operating performance ranked among the highest, a dramatic change from a half-decade earlier.[32]

Communicating through space

The nerve center for worldwide financial services and management information lay in telecommunications, messages sent in the form of voice or electronic signal from one individual to another, or directly to a terminal or computer. Indeed in the more advanced state, signals are sent directly from computer to computer. Technical advances in the field went hand in hand with those in computer technology, and Chase took advantage of them. A corporate systems group, established in 1977, raised the level of coordination and attention applied to telecommunications, and the bank devoted substantial investments to developing an integrated international voice-data network over the next several years.[33]

The voice network, called Chase-Net, inaugurated in 1981, enabled officers at the head office and in major branches around the world to dial each other directly. This private international communications system employed underseas cable, satellite circuits, microwave transmission, and other sophisticated components, with calls going through in ten seconds. Chase-Net also facilitated the use of electronic mail, with the transmission of loan agreements and other documents between different branches and offices. A word processor in London would be linked to one in New York for the transmission. And voice mail carried communications to offices in faraway time zones, storing a verbal message in a computer to be heard at a more convenient time.

Chase had long maintained teletype communications linking overseas branches with the head office and with each other. Chase-Net replaced these only in part. A foreign exchange dealers network, connecting traders in all areas with their counterparts, also continued in operation. But no less important was the electronic transmission of data. By the late 1970s an increasing volume of data moved electronically from center to center and from computer to computer through a host of channels—CHIPS, SWIFT, Fed Wire, leased wire, and Interactive Data's network among them. Much paper was replaced by electronic signals as customers and Chase officers initiated transactions.

To improve the efficiency and cost of delivery of its computer-based products and management information, in 1983 the bank inaugurated the Chase International Data Network to complement Chase-Net, the voice network.[34] This initially linked nine major centers with New York and with each other, largely employing leased lines and satellite connections. Over time it would grow to include forty-nine countries. Corporate treasurers could now use a single Chase terminal to access a number of Chase services. Telecommunications again enhanced customer relationships.

The future arrives in the office

With computer-based products, computer-based information, and computerized word processors, the office of the future arrived at Chase in the early 1980s.[35] To anyone strolling through the work areas at One Chase Manhattan Plaza, the most visible manifestation was the word processor, which replaced the typewriter at a high proportion of secretarial desks. This served as an electronic file as well as a more efficient way to prepare communications and documents. Many officers also had at their desks, or available nearby, computer terminals with screens, enabling them to call up information on customer relationships or obtain needed data. Officers in the treasury, investment, and commodity areas monitored the markets at will. And researchers accessed data to build computerized models and charts as an aid to projecting the future. Over coming years terminals and their use would multiply, but the organization and elements of the future office were already visible.

The computer complicates security

The spreading use of computers, with advances in telecommunications, produced one less favorable result: it added to the problem of security. Concern was expressed early about the possibility of using the computer for fraud or theft or to gain information on transactions illegally. A number of countries adopted legislation designed to protect the privacy and security of data, only to inhibit the free flow of information across borders in many instances.

The bank maintained strict control of physical access to computer centers. Aside from this, Chase adopted a number of measures designed to protect computer security.[36] Users of equipment were required to enter codes or passwords, built into software, to provide assurance that they were entitled to transmit or use information. And in money transfer, as well as with messages of a confidential nature, the bank employed encryption—the scrambling of information before it is sent electronically, to be unscrambled at the receiving end. Still, the possibility of a serious breach of security existed. An attempted breach did occur in 1985, when a group of young computer enthusiasts managed to gain access to a data base of Interactive Data Corporation, Chase's time-sharing subsidiary. They broke into the data base—one that did not include customer accounts—but were detected by the bank's security arrangements. The computer buffs were then traced and apprehended, although no records were altered or destroyed.

Theft of funds, both internal and external, posed a greater threat, the result in part of increased crime in New York and urban centers generally. Banks were plagued particularly by theft of securities. As early as 1956 Chase was embarrassed by the mysterious disappearance of a $1 million Treasury note, an event that received wide publicity.[37] Over the years other securities disappeared. In 1973 the bank discovered a loss of $15 million in Treasury bills, most of which was later recovered. Improved controls over security movements were installed, including an on-line computerized system called STAR, which identified the location of all financial instruments.

A computerized antirobbery system

Automation also was introduced to deter armed robbery, but this long-standing problem defied complete solution. Chase's protection in this respect evolved by stages. The first major advance followed an incident that occurred in April 1955, only a few days after the merger of Chase with Manhattan. In an operation planned and executed with great efficiency, the Woodside branch in Queens was robbed of $305,243.[38]

McCloy and Baker immediately recognized that Chase's security arrangements were woefully inadequate. A young FBI agent, Gerald Van Dorn, who had headed the investigation of the Woodside robbery, was invited to join the bank. He agreed, but only after the thieves were identified and apprehended.

Van Dorn soon introduced an innovation that became standard practice for most banks: a mounted camera that photographed a scene when automatically activated by an alarm.[39] The camera took two pictures a second, which could be enlarged to show minute details. Chase's cameras recorded a number of robberies over the years. While they may have deterred thieves during their early use, their most important contribution was in gaining conviction, for pictures served as positive proof in the courtroom.

Van Dorn also sought to improve burglar alarms. Thieves trained in military communications could bypass existing alarms. Several Chase branches, including safe deposit boxes, were robbed during weekends. Companies producing alarms were warned that if they did not develop a better product, Chase and other banks would do so themselves. A series of improvements finally resulted in a computerized alarm, with minicomputers in each branch responding to electronic signals sent out continuously from a central computer at the head office. These soon detected any unauthorized intervention or other disturbance in a branch.

None of this stopped bank robberies, which increased in number throughout the years, reaching a peak at Chase of 145 in 1979. Many were small, perpetrated by "note passers" demanding money of a teller. But a few were large, capped again in 1979 when two armed men in a stolen truck gained entrance to a Chase subbasement where a Brinks armored car was being loaded with cash.[40] After overpowering the driver and a restaurant worker dumping garbage, the thieves escaped with more than $2 million. They were never apprehended, but ten days later Brinks reimbursed the bank fully.

The computer and automation: instruments for change

Automation, powered by progress in computers and telecommunications, thus left an imprint on all aspects of the bank, even including security arrangements. Such services as check handling and deposit accounting came to be handled in astronomical volumes. Long-standing services such as cash management and money mobilization were altered in character, operating on a global basis with a host of information products to accompany them.

Many services too were handled automatically, no longer requiring intercession by a Chase officer. Corporate treasurers moved money, securities, and currencies worldwide using a Chase-related computer terminal. Pension trusts shifted funds between different managers, rewarding the more proficient. And many individuals, using automated teller machines, seldom visited the inside of a Chase branch.

The organization of operations through the years came full cycle. Prior to the computer, each department in varying degree controlled its own back office. Then from 1963 to 1970 operations were centralized, only to be decentralized again over the years, first on a broad functional basis, followed by product orientation, a market-related orientation, and finally according to major business or customer groups within markets of a department. In the process operations moved out of the back office to the front office, engaged directly with customers.

Management and line officers benefited from this evolution through more effective command of their activities, assisted by the development of sophisticated information on products, costs, and income. In the mid-1980s the process of change appeared never ending, as technological improvement promised to move operations in still newer directions.

A change in top management:
Rockefeller to Butcher

In 1980 and 1981 Chase carried out a critical change in top management: David Rockefeller retired and was succeeded by Willard C. Butcher.[1] It came as no surprise that the directors, with Rockefeller's concurrence, selected Butcher as the next chairman and chief executive officer. As early as 1977 Rockefeller had requested the directors to establish a nominating committee to deal with the succession, as well as with matters related to board membership.[2] The committee, after discussion with Rockefeller, decided to initiate a two-step succession, with Butcher to be appointed chief executive officer sometime before Rockefeller's actual retirement.

The plan was put into effect January 1, 1980, providing for an orderly transition. At the same time, Rockefeller agreed to extend his term as chairman until Chase's annual meeting in 1981, when Butcher would move into that position.

Rockefeller's retirement marked the end of an era for Chase. His career encompassed much of the span of this history. For a quarter-century he served in a position of leadership, half of it as sole chief executive. But as a member of one of America's foremost families, he also carried heavy responsibilities outside the bank. His role at the bank and his many activities outside came to be intertwined in the eyes of the public. More than most other leaders Rockefeller symbolized banking in the 1970s. He served as a lightning rod for the press and the public, drawing attention to the bank in the process. He was praised when things went right, but criticized excessively in times of adversity.

Upon his retirement, Rockefeller was hailed by the press as the world's premier banker-statesman, greeted as enthusiastically in Moscow and Peking as in London, Tokyo, or South America.[3] Much was made of the breadth of his interests. Chase's recovery in profits and image also was featured, with Butcher sharing the credit.

This had not always been the press's attitude. In the mid-1970s, with Chase mired in difficulties, security analysts had severely criticized Rockefeller. He was called an ineffectual manager and was accused of traipsing around seeing heads of state instead of administering the bank. Chase was likened to a royal court with underlings fearful of carrying bad news to the monarch. It was even suggested that Rockefeller "fire" himself. "When

David Rockefeller leaves," one bank analyst said, "Chase stock will go up 10 points." Rockefeller responded that the stock would go up 10 points *before* he left, which proved to be a gross understatement.[4] Scandinavians have a saying: "Tall trees catch lots of wind." Rockefeller was a tall tree.

Rockefeller's contributions to Chase

Aside from contributing his personal distinction, Rockefeller led the way for major changes at the bank over the years. Three of these bear particular mention. He introduced Chase to modern planning, budgeting, and other management techniques, which he consistently sought to update. He led the development of Chase into a global financial institution, which today is its most distinctive asset. And he ingrained in the bank a sense of social responsibility, a quality carried forward from Aldrich and McCloy.[5] These changes coincided with many of Rockefeller's personal concerns—his interests in international, public, and philanthropic affairs—so his activities within and outside the bank complemented each other.

Rockefeller was not a manager concerned with details. This would not have been his natural inclination even if he had been able to devote the necessary time, which was impossible given his other responsibilities. Rather he viewed his function as chief executive as being "to develop the policies and strategies of the Bank, to develop the people who could implement them . . . and to give impetus, prestige, and presence to the Bank on a worldwide basis."[6]

In such a regime the role of the president, as chief operating officer, was critical. In this respect the joint management of Rockefeller and Butcher was a partnership based on mutual trust. Butcher proved to be the "tiger" that the mild-mannered and soft-spoken Rockefeller needed to back him up. It was Butcher who saw to the details of management, including, toward the end of the 1970s, the strategic planning process. Butcher frequently fashioned courses of action, placing them before Rockefeller. But there the buck stopped. In the end it was Rockefeller who gave the final word on the crucial decisions required to restore the bank to sound health. As Butcher later put it, "There was never any question who was boss. He was."[7] Once persuaded that a course of action was desirable, Rockefeller pursued it with tenacity, reacting with quiet fortitude when faced with criticism and adversity.

Over the years Rockefeller maintained a deep interest in the process of management. When he entered the bank after World War II, it lacked even a rudimentary budget. It was Rockefeller who pressed at the time of the merger of Chase and Manhattan for an organizational overhaul and the establishment of a central staff to introduce planning, marketing, and up-to-date budgeting and personnel methods. For some years this staff reported directly to him.

Rockefeller maintained a persistent concern with personnel policies and practices. He personally helped recruit on college campuses and was a staunch advocate of salary and benefit programs that would attract and retain superior talent. But he also acknowledged that for too many years Chase had suffered from a lack of truly professional leadership in the human resource field. Not until Alan Lafley joined the bank in the 1970s were Rockefeller and Butcher satisfied that the function was in experienced and competent hands.

The personal relationship between Rockefeller and many subordinates was probably not all that he had hoped for. A kernel of truth lay in the contention that a number of officers stood somewhat in awe of him. Their reluctance to communicate bad news to higher administrative levels was a weak link in the Chase culture, frequently hampering the flow of information to Rockefeller. But he was perfectly capable of absorbing bad news without thinking ill of the messenger. Indeed his unflappability in the face of adversity was legendary. Although standing apart from most of the staff, Rockefeller was universally respected and admired for his integrity, dedication, and industry.

The record suggests that Rockefeller, like others, made his share of mistakes in the selection of personnel. He was said to be a sound judge of character but not always of ability. The turnover in senior management in the early 1970s, including the removal of Patterson as president, was great enough to occasion comment in the press.[8] But Rockefeller also reached into the ranks to advance Butcher, finally designating him for the top operating job. And he, along with Butcher, was responsible for introducing new blood into the senior management ranks in the mid-1970s and later.

Rockefeller and the internationalization of Chase

Rockefeller undoubtedly regarded the internationalization of Chase as his outstanding contribution. Certainly it was the one for which he was most noted and which best matched his personal interests and inclinations. When he entered the bank in 1946 he found an international department wedded to the concept of correspondent banking and functioning as a separate fiefdom. When he departed in 1981 the bank directly operated facilities in more than seventy countries, and international operations had become melded with the domestic.

Rockefeller not only took the lead in building the network, but he served as the bank's ambassador-at-large and most valuable marketing officer. This was the activity that prompted some criticism from outsiders, who appeared to regard his travels away from the bank as nonproductive.[9] But quite to the contrary, Rockefeller opened doors for the bank at the highest levels, paving the way for Chase representation in a number of countries. And his trips unearthed new business and cemented important professional relationships.

Rockefeller generally spent fifty days or more a year in meetings and travels outside the United States. He would visit Europe, the Middle East, and the Far East at least once every twelve months. Many trips combined receptions and calls for the bank with meetings of other organizations, most prominently the Trilateral Commission, the Dartmouth Group (involving the Soviet Union), and the Bilderberg Conference, first organized by Prince Bernhard of the Netherlands. These meetings themselves attracted top business and political leaders, and the matters discussed were of relevance to the bank. The Dartmouth Conference in 1971, where Rockefeller conferred with Kosygin, led directly to Chase's representation in the Soviet Union.

Wherever he went, Rockefeller met with heads of state—with President Sadat in Egypt, King Faisal and later his successor, King Khalid, in Saudi Arabia, and the shah in Iran; with the chancellor of West Germany, the prime minister and chancellor of the exchequer in Great Britain, the queen of Holland; and in the Far East with prime ministers, presidents, and kings.[10] Officers from the international department and corporate staff usually accompanied him. His trips were planned down to the last detail, and they invariably proved exhausting. His annual journey to the Middle East covered eleven areas in seventeen days. Rockefeller wore out his companions on such tours, for he was blessed with more than normal energy.

The Trilateral Commission and other organizations

Rockefeller's most absorbing interests were international. One associate of long standing observed: "He is more than a banker. He is an internationalist, a person who believes that the world is best served by nations working with each other."[11] This preoccupation was most evident in the organizations that Rockefeller promoted and belonged to, numbering thirty-five in the late 1970s, more than half of them international in character. They ranged from the Council on Foreign Relations, on which he served as chairman, to the National Council of United States-China Trade, on which he was a member of the executive committee. Most were established formally, but some, like the semiannual Bilderberg meetings, were structured more loosely. It was the Bilderberg sessions that first introduced him to many world leaders.

A number of organizations grew out of Rockefeller's own initiative. He observed a need and took the lead in helping to meet it. Such was the case with the International Executive Service Corps, which recruited retired executives to assist with problems of management in developing countries.

Rockefeller first put forth the idea in a speech for the bank which elicited a strong public response.[12] Still another was the Emergency Committee for American Trade, prompted by a need perceived by Rockefeller and others to protect and enhance gains realized in the Kennedy round of trade negotiations. Similarly the Center for Inter-American Relations, one of Rockefeller's earliest initiatives, fulfilled a clear-cut niche in private-sector representation for an area always of concern to the bank and to Rockffeller personally.[13]

Perhaps no organization, however, aroused more interest and suffered greater misunderstanding than the Trilateral Commission. Again this had its genesis in a talk given by Rockefeller to the bank's international financial forum, meeting in London, Paris, Frankfort, and Montreal in 1972.[14] Rockefeller suggested that with the world's nations becoming increasingly interdependent and relations more complex, it might be useful if qualified leaders in the private sector were to band together to examine some of the longer-term problems affecting world business. The fruits of this new organization might then be helpful to those engaged in formulating public policy.

The response to this suggestion revealed that others were thinking along parallel lines. A representative group from Europe, Japan, Canada, and the United States then convened and formed the Trilateral Commission. A central staff saw to the production of studies on international developments and trends. These educated members and served as a basis for discussion. The membership, carefully selected, represented a blue ribbon panel from the private sector. Among them was a former Georgia governor, Jimmy Carter, who was introduced for the first time to many international issues and experts. Later, as president, he appointed some nineteen American Trilateral members to his administration, including his secretaries of state, defense, and treasury, and his national security adviser.[15]

The prominent role of Trilateral members in the Carter administration led to attacks on the organization by ultraconservative elements in the United States. This came to a climax in the presidential election of 1980, in which the commission was accused of harboring an "elitist" group engaged in "unAmerican" activities. Rockefeller was vilified personally, and some of the vitriol spilled over onto Chase, but neither Rockefeller nor the bank gave heed to the criticism.[16]

Social responsibility and public affairs

The criticism of Chase was ironic, because the bank had long enjoyed a reputation as the most socially responsible bank in New York. Aldrich and McCloy first earned this distinction and Rockefeller enhanced it. Under his guidance with support from Champion and Butcher, the bank's contributions to community, welfare, and educational organizations were greatly expanded. And Rockefeller himself gave generously of his time to public affairs: for improvement of the city, on public advisory bodies, and in speeches and testimony before Congress.

Within the bank Rockefeller, Champion, and Butcher all took a direct interest in the contributions program. Rockefeller, and later Butcher, chaired the corporate social responsibility committee, which guided the program and allocated its resources. By the early 1980s annual contributions by Chase had increased to $6.6 million, the largest of any New York bank.[17] Chase aimed each year to contribute 2 percent of its net income after taxes earned the previous year. More than six hundred institutions benefited. And a separate international program provided grants to institutions in other countries in which Chase operated.

Over the years the grant program expanded, with recipients ranging from small neighborhood organizations in New York City to leading universities and cultural institutions. The largest single contribution went to the United Way of New York City, helping to finance a multitude of charitable and health organizations. But institutions in such diverse fields as housing, economic development, and support of America's economic system also received assistance. And money was set aside for a program specially designed to aid minority groups, particularly in the field of education.

More demanding of Rockefeller personally was his direct involvement in public affairs. At the national level he frequently called at the White House after trips abroad to report his observations to the president. He served on a number of presidential commissions concerned with such diverse matters as money and credit, trade, and international development. And he became a director of the Federal Reserve Bank of New York at a critical juncture in its affairs.[18]

Perhaps most tempting, President Nixon approached him twice—through intermediaries, as was Nixon's practice—to become secretary of the treasury, and President Carter later offered the position to him directly. He declined the first Nixon overture, since he had only recently become chairman of the bank and felt that he could not leave it. General Haig, then the president's chief of staff, conveyed the second invitation by telephone, reaching Rockefeller in Kuwait and requesting that he return immediately. Rockefeller, who had only a few days remaining of meetings with heads of state, responded that he would be back by the weekend and would like to discuss the matter personally with the president. But this was not the way Nixon operated, and Rockefeller did not see him. Later Rockefeller refused President Carter's invitation to succeed Secretary Blumenthal after a lengthy meeting with the president convinced him that they had substantial policy differences. A week later Rockefeller was asked to become chairman of the Federal Reserve Board, but he again declined, recommending instead Paul A. Volcker, who had once worked with him at Chase.[19]

Rockefeller was even more active at the local level. For many years he was the guiding force behind the Downtown-Lower Manhattan Association, doing much to shape the redevelopment of the area surrounding the bank's head office. Earlier, at the opposite end of Manhattan, he had spearheaded construction of the huge Morningside Heights housing project for middle-income families. David Rockefeller, like his brother, Governor Nelson Rockefeller, always seemed to enjoy construction of new buildings, not the least of which was One Chase Manhattan Plaza, for which he and McCloy were primarily responsible.

Rockefeller participated on many panels and commissions concerned with New York City. His greatest involvement came at the time of the city's fiscal crisis in the mid-1970s, when he served as a member of the mayor's top liaison group with the banking community. At that time too troublesome relations between business and the unions, especially in construction, constituted a long-standing problem. Rockefeller approached Harry Van Arsdale, president of the Central Labor Council of New York City, and the two agreed to establish an informal business-labor working group to review the problems of the city and gain a better mutual understanding.[20] Leaders were recruited from both business and the unions. The group met periodically, with a noticeable improvement in relations.

Personal interests and responsibilities

Even with his responsibilities at Chase and his involvement in public affairs, Rockefeller found time and energy to devote to matters related to the Rockefeller family and his own personal interests.[21] His father, John D. Rockefeller, Jr., had inscribed a set of guiding principles on a tablet that faces the main building at Thirty Rockefeller Plaza. One of these reads, "I believe that every right implies a responsibility; every opportunity, an obligation; every possession, a duty." The son appeared to adhere to this maxim. But it made for a complicated life. Rockefeller brought it within reason by using staff assistants wisely, deputizing them to represent him at meetings and on committees of lesser import. But his administrative aide still complained that he needed forty-eight hours every day and that "the weekend only brought on a new set of activities and problems."[22]

Three outside institutions claimed Rockefeller's continuing attention: Rockefeller University, the Rockefeller Brothers Fund, and the Museum of Modern Art. To these could be added Harvard University and to a lesser degree the University of Chicago, founded by support from his grandfather, John D. Rockefeller, Sr.

It was under Rockefeller's presidency and chairmanship that the Rockefeller Institute for Medical Research was converted to a university, specializing in postgraduate study and research in the natural sciences. Less demanding of time but close to his heart was Rockefeller's relationship to Harvard, his undergraduate university. He was elected twice to the board of overseers, serving a two-year term as its president. University president Nathan Pusey, and his successor, Derek Bok, were among his personal friends. Hardly a year passed that did not find Rockefeller a member of some special Harvard committee.

Contributions were determined personally, while larger projects were handled in cooperation with his brothers through the Rockefeller Brothers Fund, founded by the five brothers in 1940. A central staff at Thirty Rockefeller Center also administered business affairs for the Rockefeller family. Although the fund was organized efficiently, it too claimed a portion of Rockefeller's time, and he also served as a director of Rockefeller Center, Inc., one of the family's major business relationships.

Collecting art, chiefly paintings and sculpture, was a lifelong hobby which Rockefeller pursued in partnership with his wife, Peggy. In this the bank was a direct beneficiary. Rockefeller's own office included American, European, and Oriental paintings, along with primitive sculptures acquired in his travels. He provided the initial inspiration and leadership for the bank's own art collection and left a permanent remembrance in the large Dubuffet sculpture that graces Chase Manhattan Plaza.

Typically Rockefeller wanted others to share his enthusiasm. In 1967 he founded the Business Committee for the Arts, which did much to persuade corporations to beautify their premises with paintings and sculpture. And he accorded a high priority to his association with the Museum of Modern Art, providing leadership as its chairman throughout the 1960s and as vice chairman thereafter.

Rockefeller as speaker and commentator

No account of Rockefeller's activity with the bank would be complete without mention of his public appearances. He was in great demand as a speaker, not so much for his forensic ability, for he was not a born orator, but rather for what he represented and could contribute. His speeches ranged over many topics, usually related to national or international problems of the day, economic, financial, and political.[23] But his message at times took off on a more philosophical bent, as with "Free Trade in Ideas," presented to the Wharton School at the University of Pennsylvania, and "Values That Can Serve Mankind," to the National Conference of Christians and Jews in San Francisco. Rockefeller received many awards and was the guest of honor at many dinners, and some of the distinction brushed off onto the bank.

Butcher, in a tribute to Rockefeller carried in the bank's annual report at the time of his retirement, put many of his public activities in perspective, saying of him:

Beyond your contributions to the bank, you have given of yourself as well, on a broader scale, to the cause of national and international social and economic progress. Perhaps more than any other individual in the world today, you stand as a symbol of American capitalism. You have accepted this responsibility in the same spirit you accept all others—with pride, with decency, and with unstinting dedication. And you have discharged this responsibility by enhancing international understanding, facilitating communication and cooperation among nations, and contributing—in ways both large and small—to a better quality of life to people everywhere.[24]

Rockefeller's retirement from Chase in April 1981 was the occasion for much nostalgia. He addressed a meeting of officers in an overflowing auditorium, an event filmed for foreign presentation, and he and his wife joined the senior officers and directors and their wives for a gala dinner. At a final reception Butcher presented him with a custom-designed steering wheel for the Rockefeller yacht, which was to remind him of "all of us whom he captained with quality."[25] Rockefeller waved it aloft in response.

In retirement Rockefeller did not reduce his pace but merely altered his focus. Wanting to avoid any appearance of looking over Butcher's shoulder, he declined to serve as a director of the corporation or the bank. He did, however, agree to assume the chairmanship of the international advisory committee, replacing Henry Kissinger, who remained active as counselor to the bank and committee. In this capacity Rockefeller continued to pay a lengthy visit abroad each year, accompanied by Chase representatives and facilitating their contacts. He maintained an office at the bank, although his principal headquarters shifted to Thirty Rockefeller Plaza, which served as the command post for his many activities, public and private.

Butcher takes over

The transition from Rockefeller to Butcher went smoothly. The two had worked extremely well together through both troubled years and years of recovery. Their relationship, as we have seen, was one of partnership. "It is not David setting policy and demanding my doing. We've held a lot of hands together," Butcher remarked in looking back over the turbulent past.[26] And Rockefeller credited Butcher with many of the tough decisions that had to be made in the difficult years.

Butcher differed in temperament from the mild-mannered Rockefeller; he was more assertive and inclined to be outspoken. Although less so than Rockefeller, Butcher maintained a wide range of interests outside the bank, and was known as a staunch advocate of free enterprise with minimum government intervention. A gifted speaker, he frequently employed an apt figure of speech, often drawn from the world of sports.

Butcher's partnership with Rockefeller had prepared him well to take over the helm. At age fifty-three he was prepared to look ahead over the longer term and indeed had already played a key role in fashioning the bank's strategic thrusts for the 1980s. Although more of a "hands-on" manager than Rockefeller, he also believed strongly in delegating authority and responsibility.

This became evident in Butcher's first act as chief executive in early 1980—the disbanding of the management committee and delegating of supervisory responsibility for operations of the bank to four key officers: Barry Sullivan, Thomas Labrecque (who had joined the committee in 1976), William Ogden, and John Hooper. Sullivan would oversee corporate and international banking and Labrecque retail and institutional banking, as well as trust operations, while Ogden would continue as chief financial officer and Hooper as chief credit officer. All would report directly to Butcher, along with corporate staff executives and George A. Roeder, Jr., as vice chairman.

These appointments naturally fed speculation as to who would be named the next president. Sullivan, Labrecque, and Ogden all were widely mentioned in the press as possibilities. The field was suddenly narrowed in June of 1980, when Sullivan agreed to become chairman and chief executive of the First National Bank of Chicago, a challenging assignment inasmuch as that important bank confronted significant problems.[27]

The departure of Sullivan accelerated the change that would soon have occurred in any event, and on June 25 the new management structure was announced. Labrecque was named vice chairman and chief operating officer, to succeed Butcher as president upon Rockefeller's retirement. Ogden was also designated vice chairman, and would continue as chief financial officer.[28]

So the top management now was in place for the 1980s. Labrecque, at age forty-one, would be one of the youngest presidents in the bank's history. He also broke the Chase mold by rising to the top without experience on the wholesale side. After graduating from Villanova and entering the credit training program in 1964, he joined the treasury department. Within ten years he was heading that department, and was recognized even then as a potential candidate for president. Labrecque's experience and reputation were broadened through his participation as a key member of the comptroller's technical debt management committee during the city's financial crisis. Subsequently, on the bank's management committee, he successfully rehabilitated two of the most troubled units, the consumer (retail) and operations departments, "taking a strategic approach and then making it work," he commented.[29] Labrecque possessed the demeanor of a leader in banking. Although less outgoing than Butcher, he worked well with subordinates. The new management looked promising to bank analysts, who nevertheless speculated that Chase would be a different bank without a Rockefeller.

Moving toward nationwide banking: 1981–1985

The opening years of the 1980s witnessed a strong performance by Chase, with earnings and resources at new peaks. After five years of solid progress, however, the bank encountered an unexpected setback in 1982. Sizable losses on security-related transactions and energy credits in domestic institutional banking reduced earnings and damaged Chase's image. Nevertheless, earnings rebounded smartly, moving to record highs by middecade. Meanwhile the bank, following a strategic plan fashioned in the late 1970s, put into place new facilities and products. Both assets and the bank's outreach were enhanced, aided by significant acquisitions of other institutions.

These developments occurred against a backdrop of still greater risks for banking, intensified by widening competition from nonbank firms. Years of inflation, sky-high interest rates, and distorted payments between nations forced the world economy into recession for a period after mid-1981. Business failures and unemployment rates climbed to peaks not seen since the 1930s, both in the United States and other countries. Troublesome energy shortages, prevalent for a decade, disappeared, creating wide adjustments for oil, gas, and related industries. And declining world trade, accompanied by falling commodity prices, produced hardship for developing nations.

For the United States the downturn ended in late 1982, and was followed initially by the most rapid economic expansion since the Korean war. The U.S. advance included unusual aspects that affected other nations: inflation, beaten down by recession, remained moderate. Yet interest rates, propelled by record budget deficits, continued at unusually high levels until middecade, and the dollar gained in strength relative to other currencies. Europe recovered slowly, although its improvement became clearly evident by 1984. But many less developed countries, encumbered by heavy international debts, continued to experience serious difficulty.

The Drysdale affair

In the troublesome environment of 1982 Chase suffered major losses, completely unforeseen and widely publicized. The largest, amounting to $117 million after taxes, occurred in transactions with Drysdale Government Securities, a firm dealing in U.S. government securities.[1] In early 1982 this firm assumed the government securities position and activities of an older, established company, Drysdale Securities Corporation. The new firm ostensibly possessed a capital of $20.8 million, and the accounting firm of Arthur Andersen and Company provided an unqualified statement. Later investigations by the Securities and Exchange Commission and the Manhattan district attorney, however, revealed that the liabilities of Drysdale Government Securities had exceeded its assets at the time of its founding by more than $150 million, the result of previous losses in the government securities market suffered by Drysdale Securities Corporation.[2] The heads of both firms were subsequently indicted for fraud, pleaded guilty, and were sentenced to prison.[3]

The chief trader and owner of Drysdale Government Securities, David J. Heuwetter, built up a huge market position, gaining added working capital through an unusual practice possible at that time in the government securities market. He borrowed government securities carrying large amounts of accumulated interest, and resold the securities in the market at a price that included the interest.[4] In selling borrowed securities, Heuwetter incurred a substantial short position. He not only had to cover this position, but he also was required to pass on to lenders any interest paid out by the government during the period when he borrowed the securities.

The Securities Service Division of Chase, in the domestic institutional banking department, served Drysdale and other securities dealers by acting as an intermediary between lenders of securities and borrowers. It received securities from a lender and delivered them to a borrower. These services were also provided to Chase's own trust and custody customers who chose to lend their securities held in custody by Chase. The head of the division and his associates considered themselves to be performing the function of an agent, and not acting as a principal.[5] Later it was alleged that documentation on the transactions did not always make this relationship clear.

Drysdale Securities first became a client of the division in late 1980 after being introduced by an intermediary finder named Buttonwood Management. Over the following year and into 1982 Buttonwood assisted the division in rapidly expanding the volume of securities it provided Drysdale. In early May 1982, however, Drysdale was late in forwarding accrued coupon interest due to be paid out to security lenders. The division then informed Heuwetter that it would be necessary to wind up its relations with Drysdale.[6] Within a fortnight, on Monday, May 17, Drysdale failed to pay $160 million of accrued coupon interest on U.S. government securities it had borrowed through Chase's security service division, as well as on smaller amounts with several other banks.

Chase's top management was just completing a successful planning meeting in Woodstock, Vermont. At breakfast Sunday morning Butcher had been told that a Wall Street firm was in trouble; but, his informant added, "don't worry, we're fully secured."[7] Upon returning that afternoon, executives in charge of Chase's operations and treasury departments were urgently summoned by the head of securities services to a meeting at the head office, with Heuwetter present. It became apparent to these officers that Chase might be confronting a major problem.

Further meetings with Labrecque, Ogden, and Butcher followed on Monday. Later that day, at Butcher's initiative, he and others met at the Federal Reserve Bank of New York with representatives of securities firms and other banks to discuss the default and consider alternative courses of action. Disagreement arose as to who should bear the liability. A number of firms claimed that in providing securities, they were doing business with Chase and not Drysdale—that Chase had acted as a principal and not as an agent.[8] Butcher proposed that these disagreements be settled at a future date, and that meanwhile a pool be formed to cover the liability, with Chase providing $90 million. This proved unacceptable, however, to the securities firms.[9]

Chase takes over Drysdale's liability

On Tuesday morning, May 18, Chase released a statement that potential significant claims might be asserted against it as a result of the anticipated failure of a securities firm. The statement mentioned that firm's inability to pay $160 million of accrued interest on securities it had borrowed. But it also stated, "It is Chase's position it does not have any liability" to other firms involved in transactions with the troubled dealer.

Meanwhile Butcher, recognizing that his proposal for a pool to cover the liability would not succeed, directed Labrecque to gather all facts and explore alternatives. Chase officers, with help from Heuwetter, worked through the night to determine the full extent of Drysdale's liability. In addition to defaulting on accumulated interest, Heuwetter was unable to cover a large short position on securities he had borrowed through Chase. It appeared that some security firms might fail if the problem was not resolved, and Chase could become involved in numerous lawsuits for consequential damages. Moreover, the U.S. government securities market, already affected, faced a dangerous period ahead.

After weighing alternatives Butcher and Labrecque acted decisively. On Wednesday, May 19, Chase announced that it would pay the interest due on the Drysdale government securities processed through its security services division. Moreover, it would take over Drysdale's positions and other obligations on these securities. Chase would undertake this action "without prejudice to [its] rights against third parties." The bank anticipated an after-tax loss of about $135 million as a consequence.[10] Later, in explaining this action

Butcher and Labrecque cited the need to avoid exposure to claims for damages and to maintain order in the government securities market. But they also stated that in taking the action, Chase "intended to live up to our reputation as a responsible citizen."[11]

The bank assumed a $4.5 billion security position from Drysdale. It quickly created a hedge against the large short position, and then liquidated the portfolio. The after-tax loss was reduced to $117 million, based on a pre-tax cost of $285 million, close to that originally estimated. Chase subsequently brought an action for damages against Drysdale Government, Drysdale Securities and their principals, Buttonwood Management, and Arthur Andersen and Company, alleging that they had misrepresented the financial position of Drysdale Government when it began business. This action was settled against some of the defendants in September 1984. The settlement, along with a recovery on certain other transactions related to Drysdale, enabled the bank to add $49 million before taxes to net income in the third quarter of 1984,[12] providing at least a modicum of consolation.

Penn Square and Lombard Wall

Drysdale was not the only source of trouble for Chase in the summer of 1982. Two other problems arose in units of the same department, domestic institutional banking. One grew out of relations with a correspondent bank, Penn Square Bank, N.A., of Oklahoma City, and the other involved the failure of yet another small government securities firm, Lombard Wall.

Of the two, Penn Square clearly was the more important. That bank, with assets of less than $500 million, was declared insolvent and closed by the comptroller of the currency on July 5, 1982. Losses in the bank itself, however, were only the tip of the iceberg. Penn Square had sold more than $2.5 billion of participations in energy-related loans to other banks, including more than $275 million to Chase.[13] A high proportion of these Penn Square loans proved nonperforming, and over the next several years contributed materially to serious troubles at Continental Illinois National Bank and Trust in Chicago and Seattle-First National Bank in Seattle.

Many of Penn Square's loans were extended to independent oil and gas producers, drilling rig operators, and oil-field service companies. These credits exploded in volume after the oil price increase of 1979, and Penn Square fed a large number of participations to its correspondents. With the recession and decline in energy prices in 1981, many borrowers failed or became incapable of making regular payments. Credit analysis by Penn Square proved woefully inadequate, and banking regulators subsequently alleged that fraud and illegal banking practices had been committed.[14]

Chase's loans to Penn Square were handled exclusively by officers in domestic institutional banking, even though energy specialists in the corporate bank were well known for their expertise in assessing the creditworthiness of complicated oil and gas credits. Cross-communication between the two departments was weak, and a sense of rivalry existed. Chase charged off some $75 million of Penn Square loans before the end of 1982, and the total swelled to $161 million by 1985.

The Lombard Wall incident, in contrast, was closed out by Chase in little more than a month with no loss to the bank. Yet occurring shortly after the Drysdale and Penn Square episodes, it attracted undue attention and added to an image of disarray. Lombard, with only small capital, borrowed money through repurchase agreements with many institutions—banks, thrifts, public agencies, and corporate pension funds—and invested these funds in government securities at higher rates. On August 12, 1982, however, Lombard Wall filed for bankruptcy, with Chase listed as a creditor for $45 million.[15]

Chase did not lend directly to Lombard Wall. Rather it provided letters of credit to the firm on a secured basis, effectively guaranteeing to a lender—municipalities in most cases—payment of the interest due to it. Government security prices rose shortly after Lombard Wall filed for bankruptcy. Chase restructured its position in a manner that enabled it to avoid loss,[16] although this accomplishment received less public notice than the bank's original involvement.

Aftermath of Drysdale and Penn Square

The Drysdale, Penn Square, and Lombard Wall problems, occurring within three months, created distress at the bank and injured Chase's reputation. The bank was said by some outside commentators to be paying a premium for its borrowed money as a result—an inaccurate allegation, although the treasury department shifted more heavily to the Eurodollar interbank market and relied less on domestic CDs.[17]

Internally, Butcher and Labrecque moved with dispatch to prevent Drysdale- and Penn Square-type errors from recurring. After an investigation, nine officers resigned, including the executives in charge of institutional banking, and another senior executive resigned later after demotion. Chase subsequently sued six of the executives for damages related to losses on loan participations with Penn Square, alleging that they had been negligent. This and other shareholder suits related to Drysdale and Penn Square were settled in late 1985 by insurance company payments of $32.5 million, but without any admission of wrongdoing by the defendants.

Meanwhile, to guard against a Drysdale-type incident, in which credit risks had been inadequately assessed, risk councils were formed for each line of business, designed to provide managers a more rigorous means of understanding the risks involved in each product and operating process. Representatives from all relevant departments composed these councils. And a new division of product and production risk management was created to examine financial risks inherent in transaction processing systems.[18]

Improvements also were made in the credit review process, with more complete information made available on areas of risk concentration. Butcher and Labrecque sought to achieve greater cross-communication and horizontal coordination between departments. Training programs thereafter gave added emphasis to the policies, practices, and standards of the bank, which had been seriously violated by those who had dealt with Drysdale and Penn Square.

Nor did the lessons of the Drysdale case stop with Chase. The incident led to significant changes in the government securities market. The pricing of repurchase agreements was altered to include accrued interest, closing out access to free capital for some security dealers. Dealers now sought greater diversification in amounts of repurchase agreements outstanding to various obligors, avoiding a concentration like that of Drysdale. And the Federal Reserve Bank of New York designated a senior officer to head a new unit concerned solely with surveillance of the market.[19] Yet despite these precautions, troubles continued to plague the government securities market. Additional small firms dealing in securities were forced into bankruptcy, some the victims of sudden changes in interest rates and others of fraud.

Chase moves ahead on its plan for the 1980s

Chase's problems with Drysdale and Penn Square for a time slowed implementation of the bank's plan for expansion in the 1980s. Activity was never brought to a halt, however, and it gained renewed impetus through middecade. The plan for the 1980s, developed first under Butcher late in the 1970s and brought up to date in 1984, focused more heavily on the domestic than the international. Over the previous decade domestic loans did not quite double, but foreign credits climbed more than ninefold to $31 billion, and were now the greater. Renewed emphasis on domestic activity would help redress the imbalance.

This change also was in keeping with the times, for developments in the United States were pushing banks toward a national market. Boundaries between commercial banks and other financial institutions were becoming increasingly blurred or nonexistent. Legal changes in 1980 permitted thrift institutions to operate transaction accounts and to provide consumer credit to individuals much as Chase did. Large chains of retail stores and consumer finance companies competed in the same market on a national scale. Insurance companies increasingly provided corporate customers with medium-term credit.

But no development was more spectacular than the spreading incursion of investment firms into other fields of finance: provision of credit in all markets, management of investments, insurance, and even the establishment of quasi-deposit accounts. By 1981 money market funds, unregulated and with no ceiling on interest rates, had shot up to more than $180 billion.[20] Most funds made available limited check withdrawals. And so-called cash-management accounts combined margined brokerage accounts with unlimited check withdrawals, credit cards, and loan services, while paying considerably more on cash balances than Chase could.

Central to the plan that Chase developed to meet this competition was a revised statement of the bank's general mission, along with detailed strategic corporate objectives. The statement declared Chase to be "a broad-based international banking institution which provides a wide range of selective banking and bank-related services and products to quality customers in selected markets throughout the world."[21] The statement differed somewhat from that fashioned in the early 1970s, with the introduction of the word *selective*. Indeed Rockefeller and Butcher had already announced, "In the future the Chase will not be all things to all people in any of its markets."[22]

Still, size itself was of continued importance. The bank aimed to maintain its position as a large, leading institution, measured by assets and deposits, by scope and effectiveness of its global network, and by the broad base of quality customers in its major businesses. The two core businesses of the bank were determined to be the global corporate market and the higher tiers of the individual market. But other basic areas also were singled out for continued attention, including the middle market (medium-sized business), real estate, correspondent banking, and trust and fiduciary investment. The bank expected to grow at a rate greater than the growth of the U.S. economy. And this growth was to be accompanied by a financial performance as good as or better than that of its principal competitors. The statement presented a number of measures to assess this performance, among them return on assets in a range of 0.55 to 0.65 percent and return on equity, set after the inflation of 1980, at 15 to 18 percent. The bank also explicitly stated its aim to achieve more of a balance between domestic and international earnings, with not less than one-third derived domestically.[23]

Strategic directions for the 1980s

Chase concluded that changes in banking in the 1980s would be evolutionary rather than revolutionary, requiring strategies to be modified as events unfolded. The bank recognized that its long-standing businesses would grow and require nurturing, and that building core deposits and other sources of stable funds should command a high priority. To produce stability in earnings and improve return on assets, income from services not requiring assets—foreign exchange, trust, classical trade services, and investment banking, for example—had to expand at a strong pace.

Beyond this, a number of areas were identified for special emphasis—some in support of traditional business, but others reaching out in new directions.

- In consumer markets the bank would expand its position nationwide, developing financial products with an appeal to the more profitable segments. Utilization of card technology would be emphasized, but with local distribution centers also required. Eventually this expansion might be carried overseas, but only after the activity was firmly in place domestically.
- Worldwide private banking for individuals with high net worth, quite a different market, would be stressed, requiring integration of elements in the international, retail, trust, and corporate departments.
- On the corporate side, the bank aimed to "globalize" its relations with certain industries, primarily those operating across country borders throughout the world. Three were selected as prototypes: petroleum, mining and metals, and automobiles. This in the end would possibly call for realigning the organization for all of wholesale corporate business, so as to achieve more effective market focus.
- The national commercial market, embracing middle-sized firms, would be cultivated more intensively, but again with a limited range of products, principally leasing and commercial finance. Chase was already active in these fields, but they would be given new stimulus and geographic outreach. Factoring, an early activity for the bank, later was dropped because of relatively low earnings.
- The bank would return to a more aggressive posture in real estate, with quality in assets and performance a prerequisite. Lessons from the mid-1970s would not be forgotten.
- Similarly, Chase would strengthen its role in world trade, building on its worldwide network to increase fee income from letters of credit, classical trade business, and related transactions. These were activities Chase long had carried out, but a new and separate unit focusing directly on the market would be organized. Related to this too would be a drive to make more effective use of Chase's worldwide correspondent network, a valued resource of long standing. More could be done with correspondent banks, and on a reciprocal basis.
- Still another strategic conclusion concerned relations with foreign governments. Since this activity did not provide attractive profitable oppor-

tunities in its own right, it would be linked to institutional and corporate business, particularly in developing nations where governments played a major role in economic life.[24]

A number of these strategic initiatives were set in motion as early as 1979. These progressed through the first half of the 1980s, with some slow-down in 1982. By middecade Chase was operating a network of more than 170 offices across the United States in addition to its domestic branches.[25]

For middle-sized business, regional marketing offices served existing customers and worked with emerging growth companies. Chase Commercial Corporation handled equipment leasing and finance, with offices across the country. For investors, regional treasury offices were established to market government and municipal securities along with Chase CDs and other money market instruments. And for international business, Edge Act offices, strategically located, offered a wide range of international and trade services. A centralized trade unit was inaugurated as planned, while global private banking extended its tailored banking and asset-management services into many countries abroad. The most ambitious effort, however, reached out to individuals nationwide, providing consumer loans, home mortgages, discount brokerage, credit cards, traveler's checks, and even trust services.

Consumer offices move out of the city

Within metropolitan New York the bank continued to provide services through a network of 222 branches. The city and its environs provided the largest single consumer market in the country, and the branches produced a sizable volume of funds to finance loans. Certain branches were redesigned to concentrate on specific markets. Business banking centers in Manhattan served only small business, and separate cash-checking centers were established. Automated teller machines (ATMs) became more economical and proliferated throughout the system. These exercised an increasing impact on consumer banking, even enabling customers, through cooperative arrangements, to access their bank accounts from cities distant from New York.[26]

Chase made a special effort to cultivate individuals with high incomes, both through the trust department's private banking program and through the branch system. It designed a special program for women, and expanded its bank-by-phone bill-paying service. The bank also initiated a service that looked toward the future: a comprehensive home banking program utilizing personal computers linked by telephone to Chase's central computer. Users could transfer funds, pay bills, make balance inquiries, keep financial records, carry out stock transactions, and perform other functions. The program, called Spectrum, gained even more adherents than anticipated.[27]

But the major thrust in new facilities for consumers was in fast-growing areas outside New York. Frederick S. Hammer, then head of consumer banking, formed three subsidiaries to carry out this mission: Chase U.S. Consumer Services, Chase Home Mortgage Corporation, and Chase Bank (USA) in Delaware.

The Delaware bank, mentioned in Chapter XVIII, served as the center for marketing the Chase Visa card, consumer loans, and other services by mail outside New York State. Chase Consumer Services, by contrast, operated directly from separate offices, providing extensive credit, time-deposit, and fee-generating services to moderate- and high-income individuals and small businesses. By 1985 twenty-five offices were located in ten states, and substantial additions were planned for the period ahead. No other bank had concentrated so exclusively on this market, and the offices more than fulfilled projections. Supplementing them was Rose and Company, a prominent discount securities broker with offices in eight major cities, acquired by the bank in 1983.

Chase Home Mortgage gained an initial start by transfer to it of the three offices of Housing Investment Corporation of Florida, a company that had caused trouble for the bank in the mid-1970s. The offices now concentrated on mortgage banking for the residential and home improvement market by originating mortgages and loans, which were then packaged and sold, but with the company continuing to service them. Other offices were established and the corporation soon spread into nine states.[28]

Permission was granted to banks late in 1982 to install money market accounts (see Chapter XVIII). This, along with deregulation of interest rates, opened up new fields for growth. Chase was soon marketing new money funds and consumer CDs throughout the country, building them and other consumer deposits to more than $10 billion by 1985, compared with $1.6 billion four years earlier. This enabled the bank to reduce its reliance on negotiable CDs and afforded greater diversification and stability in funding.

Credit to consumers, bolstered by Chase Visa, climbed to $7.4 billion. Consumer banking, a loser in the mid-1970s, was contributing 20 percent of Chase's net earnings in 1984, and the bank aimed to raise this to one-third of a much larger sum over the next several years.[29]

Aggressive approach to private banking and personal trust

Relations with more affluent clients were the responsibility of private banking. This now was placed under joint administration with personal trust, and both were developed more aggressively. Private banking took over from the consumer bank two of the branches in upper Manhattan devoted to One Chase Banking, which provided individualized service to meet the needs of each client. And the bank chartered new trust companies, located in Boca Raton and San Francisco, to serve more effectively its many retired clients.

Personal trust, dating from 1919, had been marketed in a rather passive manner through the 1970s. Fees, regulated by the state, lagged behind inflation, making profitability difficult. Over the years the minimum size of accounts advanced from $100,000 to $500,000. Still, Chase was well known for personal trust and maintained one of the largest portfolios, directly managing or advising on $3.2 billion of assets in 1980.[30] A further sizable amount was held in custody for individuals, a service at Chase of recognized quality.

Since 1972 the personal trust department had handled its own trust investments, including five different commingled funds. Equity and bond funds were now turned over to Chase Investors Management, with a noticeable improvement in performance.[31] And personal trust stepped up its marketing efforts for both trusts and estates. By 1985 assets under administration had increased to almost $5 billion, in part owing to a rise in the market, but also due to new accounts flowing in.[32]

Chase spreads throughout upstate New York

Chase in mid-1984 also moved to become the major banking organization throughout New York State by acquiring Lincoln First Corporation, headquartered in Rochester. Lincoln First, with a reputation for high quality, carried assets of $4.5 billion, and operated 135 offices throughout much of upstate New York, including thirty-seven branches in Westchester County.[33] Its flagship bank, Lincoln First Bank, N.A., was preeminent in Rochester, and it maintained sizable branch systems in Syracuse, Binghamton, and other centers.

Chase's network now included 331 branches positioned to serve every major geographic and business market in the state. Lincoln First added especially to customers and facilities in the consumer and small- and medium-sized business markets. Its personal trust business, when combined with Chase's, placed the bank ahead of all others in that field, and Chase widened its margin as the largest New York bank in domestic deposits.[34]

The acquisition of Lincoln First also marked a radical shift in regulatory policies. Chase in the mid-sixties had failed to gain regulatory approval to form an upstate holding company only a fraction of the size of Lincoln First (see Chapter IX). And in 1974 the bank was turned back in its bid for Dial Financial Corporation (see Chapter XV), again a much smaller institution with no competitive relationship. Standards had indeed changed, as regulatory authorities recognized the heavy competition among various types of financial institutions, so that antitrust considerations became a less potent constraint on bank expansion.[35]

The move toward nationwide banking

With offices for corporate and commercial banking, home mortgages, consumer finance, and information services (Interactive Data), by 1985 Chase maintained business facilities in twenty-three states and Washington, D.C. Some of Chase's competitors operated in even a larger number of states. Butcher was convinced that competitive developments would eventually force changes in the law to permit conventional banking nationwide, and he moved to have Chase prepared for it.

A nationwide positioning group was formed to develop long-range plans and seek out opportunities. The group, headed by Robert R. Douglass, also monitored and participated in legislative developments. Above all it supported a change in the Bank Holding Company Law, which prohibited bank affiliations outside the home state except for states that had specifically authorized them. The group also encouraged modifications in the Glass-Steagall Act of 1933, which placed banks at a competitive disadvantage with securities firms.

The bank also sought to capitalize on opportunities for acquiring other financial concerns that fit its priorities. With this in mind in 1985 it acquired six thrift institutions (savings and loans and savings banks) in Cincinnati, Columbus, and Cleveland.[36] These state-chartered institutions had encountered difficulty because of inadequate insurance coverage of depositors. Chase quickly converted them into a full-service bank, The Chase Bank of Ohio, under a new law designed for that purpose. In still another state a change in the law facilitated creation of The Chase Bank of Maryland.[37] And in Arizona, Chase agreed to purchase Continental Bank, the state's sixth largest, centered in Phoenix, with thirteen branches.[38] All were formed as subsidiaries of the holding company, but were operated in coordination with Chase in New York.[39] Meanwhile, The Chase Manhattan Bank (USA) in Delaware, chartered three years earlier, held assets of $4.5 billion, partly the result of concentrating Chase Visa card loans more heavily in that subsidiary.

Yet in spite of this spreading system of offices, Chase and other New York banks labored under a handicap in their efforts to expand nationwide. Many states adopted legislation, upheld by the courts, that permitted acquisition of full-service banks across state lines only within a designated region.[40] These regional compacts (inaugurated first in New England and the Southeast) effectively excluded New York banks. A more restricted route, the establishment of banks with limited services (labeled nonbank banks), was approved by the regulatory authorities but blocked by adverse court decisions.[41] Nevertheless, Chase looked upon these limitations as temporary and believed it was only a question of time before Congress would adopt legislation sanctioning full interstate banking.

Filling the gaps abroad

Although Chase now placed emphasis on domestic expansion, it did not cease filling gaps in its network abroad, covering seventy-one nations or areas. Facilities were newly opened in Finland, Norway, Pakistan, Turkey, Monaco, Peru, and Uruguay. The bank moved to upgrade its representation in Australia through a new trading bank, in partnership with Australian Mutual Provident Society,[42] the country's largest insurance company. And in Spain, Chase extended its outreach through purchase of Banco de Finanzas, with assets of $265 million and branches in five cities.

The bank in 1984 also acquired full ownership of Nederlandse Credietbank.[43] In 1966 Chase had become the principal stockholder in this bank (see Chapter XII), for some years holding a 31.5 percent interest. Credietbank served Chase customers and provided the Netherlands link in the Chase network. It grew to be the fourth largest bank in that country, with assets of $4.7 billion and one hundred branches. Purchase of full ownership provided Chase a major presence in a country renowned for its international business, and permitted a more effective integration of Credietbank's resources into the Chase network.

Nor did Chase neglect relations with individuals of high net worth abroad. As we have seen, these were courted by Private Bank International. In line with its long-range plan, Chase mounted a major effort, concentrating on clients in Latin America, the Middle East, and Asia who sought a safe haven in the United States for part of their resources.[44] Some twenty-two offices for private banking were located around the world in the mid-1980s, doing a flourishing business aided by the Chase network.

Organizing for the mid-1980s

Chase put in place a revised management organization in 1984 and 1985 to carry out more effectively its long-range plan (see Figure 7). This grouped the bank's businesses into three major units, each under a vice chairman and reflecting its core markets in a manner not envisaged in earlier organizations:

- Global banking, responsible for serving corporations and institutions around the world through wholesale and investment banking.
- Consumer banking, serving individuals through Chase's credit card and consumer offices across the nation, as well as expanding retail activities abroad.
- National banking, embracing relations with U.S. correspondent banks, and with real estate, trust, investment management, private banking, and information businesses. Here the vice chairman also played a criti-

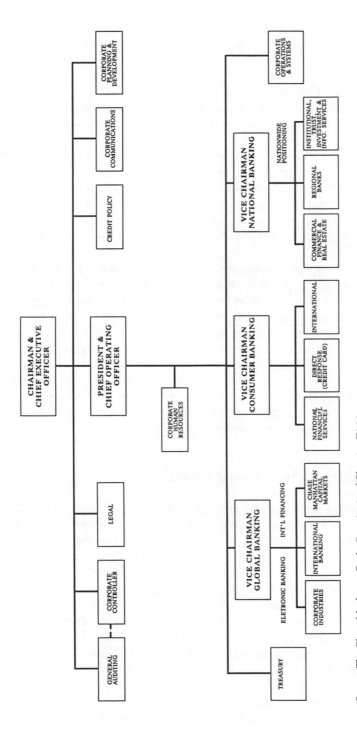

Source: The Chase Manhattan Bank, Organizational Planning Division.

Figure 7. The Chase Manhattan Corporation organization, 1985.

cal role in national expansion, establishing and overseeing full-service banks in other states as opportunities arose, with Lincoln First a role model.

The three vice chairmen, along with corporate operations and systems, human resources, and treasury activities (funding, foreign exchange, dealing and investing in securities) reported to the president as chief operating officer.

Particularly troublesome had been the melding of domestic and foreign activities with corporations, complicated further in recent years by the growth of investment banking. Relationship managers in multinational industries finally came to operate on a worldwide basis, working both through head office and foreign country managers. The vice chairman for global banking provided overall coordination and direction and planned for the future.

In one other respect management differed in a manner not reflected in organizational charts. Butcher concerned himself more directly with the internal affairs of the bank than had Rockefeller. He continued personal oversight of planning and development, as well as credit policy, corporate communications, legal and auditing staffs, and the controller. And he provided overall coordination of the different arms of top management. Although Butcher, as Chase's top representative, devoted time to looking outside, he also looked in. Rockefeller, by contrast, had concentrated largely on external relations. Butcher operated more in the style of his peers in corporate business, a manner that suited his personal inclination and was better adapted to Chase's growing complexity.

Higher earnings and growing capital

The new management arrangements were introduced as Chase completed its recovery from an earnings decline in 1982, a direct consequence of the Drysdale and Penn Square failures. Even so, its net income of $307 million, although down 31 percent from 1981, was the fourth largest in the bank's history and attested to the underlying strength of the bank's business. This became even more evident over the next several years, as net income rose to a new peak of approximately $565 million in 1985. Return on assets advanced to 0.64 percent, well within the bank's target range. Return on common equity at 13.6 percent, however, lagged behind the 1981 rate, partly because of heavy dividends to preferred stockholders.

Contribution to earnings from the international side of the bank fell markedly in this period, dragged lower by an increased volume of nonperforming loans in less developed countries. But income from domestic business recovered after 1982, more than offsetting the international shortfall.

Gains in net income were realized even as the bank strengthened its financial position through large additions to its loan loss reserve and capital. On this matter Butcher and Labrecque pursued a highly conservative policy, not hesitating to penalize earnings for greater safety. The reserve for possible loan losses climbed to $908 million, some 1.47 percent of outstandings and up about two-thirds from four years earlier. Aggregate capital rose to $7.3 billion, with common stockholders' equity at $3.8 billion. So-called primary capital (including common equity, perpetual preferred stock, mandatory convertible securities, and the reserve for loan losses) now amounted to 6.9 percent of assets, considerably above the standard recommended by the regulatory authorities.

Renewal of loan growth

Earnings were aided by increased loan growth, once recovery set in following the recession of 1981–82. Addition of the Lincoln First and Nederlandse Credietbank portfolios contributed more than $5 billion to the totals, helping to produce an overall loan increase of more than 20 percent to $62 billion. And yet the total could have been considerably larger, for Chase in 1985 sold $28 billion of loans and acceptances originated by the bank to domestic and international correspondents and other financial institutions, earning sizable fees in the process. Most were short term and would not long have remained on the bank's books. Nonetheless, the bank's assets could have been $3.6 billion greater in the absence of the program, which began in 1984 and represented a significant shift in strategy.

Chase found that lending to its top-grade borrowers was no longer profitable. Many quality companies could raise money in the market as cheaply as Chase. But a strong demand existed for quality financial assets, and Chase decided to act as a financial intermediary, serving customers at both ends of the spectrum. In deriving fee income, the bank enhanced earnings while conserving on its need for capital.

Even so, credit extended to U.S. commercial and industrial firms climbed substantially to $13.8 billion in 1985, notwithstanding the spread of commercial paper to an ever-widening group of corporations and the sale of loans to other banks. Many large domestic borrowers now chose to have loans booked at overseas offices, taking advantage of lower rates in the Eurodollar market rather than the prime rate at home. In the profitable consumer area, credit outstanding about tripled to $7.4 billion, extended both directly and through Chase Visa. And the bank continued to expand real estate financing, establishing added marketing offices for the purpose.

Financing arrangements, frequently involving a mixture of the domestic and international, required increasing skill and ingenuity on the part of officers. Interest rate swaps and currency swaps carried out with banks and customers became common, approximately $7 billion in 1985, with the volume steadily increasing.[45] And the bank became a broker of foreign exchange and interest-rate futures and options, facilitating the hedging of risks by customers. Chase's loan officers worked with the bank's capital markets group in planning and executing swaps and other complicated transactions. Investment banking, embracing syndicated loans, international bond underwriting, private placements, tax-based leasing, and mergers and acquisitions, assumed ever-growing importance and stood high on Chase's priority list for expansion. To broaden its capability in London the bank agreed to acquire two securities brokers, Laurie, Millbank & Company and Simon & Coates, as the securities industry in that center underwent restructuring and deregulation.

International lending overall did not grow at this time, as the total fell 5 percent to $29.4 billion in the four years to 1985. Credit extended in foreign industrial countries, accounting for 47 percent of the aggregate, was restrained by slow economic growth and lessened inflation. In Eastern Europe the bank's exposure declined to only a nominal amount. And the volume of loans to less developed countries (LDCs) increased very moderately, with outstandings of approximately $14 billion now exceeding the amount to industrial nations.[46]

LDC debt becomes a problem

The major portion of Chase's LDC loans, $11.6 billion in all, was extended in foreign currencies, chiefly dollars. The principal increase had occurred from 1979 to 1981, after the second oil price explosion. Many of these credits subsequently encountered difficulty, as foreign exchange became inadequate to service debt, especially in Latin America. Later banks were accused of pressing unnecessary loans on borrowing countries, exacerbating their problem. The banks did pursue a liberal policy on loans involving the more advanced developing countries, and mistaken credit judgments may have been made. But the principal difficulty stemmed from an unexpected development not foreseen by the borrowing countries or the bankers: the severity of the world recession of 1981–82, which sharply reduced world trade, commodity prices, and export earnings. In Argentina the Falklands war added to the adverse environment. Moreover, a number of less developed countries adopted fiscal and other policies that led to inflation and flight of capital, thereby further intensifying their problems.

The payments difficulty came to a head in August 1982 when Mexico surprised its creditors by informing their governments that foreign exchange reserves were exhausted.[47] Mexico had maintained an overvalued exchange rate and incurred a capital flight. At this time it owed foreign debts of more than $81 billion, with Chase a creditor for approximately $1.5 billion. A package of credits from the International Monetary Fund, the U.S Treasury, and other official sources was quickly organized to tide the country over. Shortly thereafter a committee representing the creditor banks, with Chase a member, began negotiations with the Mexicans to reschedule debt maturing through 1984, while providing $5 billion of new money to help finance interest payments. Negotiations were completed successfully in early 1983, but only after agreement by Mexico with the IMF on an economic program designed to place the nation on a path to renewed economic health.[48] Payouts of loans by the IMF and the banks were then contingent on Mexico's fulfilling certain economic and fiscal objectives.

Difficulties similar to those in Mexico soon surfaced in other countries—major Latin American nations, the Philippines, and Nigeria and many smaller countries in Africa. Brazil, with a foreign debt close to $85 billion (of which Chase was owed $2.5 billion), followed the lead of Mexico, adopting an IMF program and restructuring its bank debt, supplemented by new credits.[49] Politically troubled Argentina (owing Chase $845 million) lagged behind the others, but finally in late 1984 agreed to a rearrangement of its obligations with foreign banks.[50] These three countries, along with Venezuela, accounted for about $6 billion of Chase's cross-border debt, substantially more than its reserve for loan losses and equity. Other major banks held similar or more extreme positions, and bank share prices suffered.

The bank's nonaccrual and reduced rate (nonperforming) loans rose to $2.4 billion in early 1985, with two-thirds international. These were reduced to $2 billion by late that year, however, as Argentina cleared up its arrears. Although nonperformers represented 3.3 percent of total loans, the proportion fell considerably short of the 6.5 percent reached at the height of Chase's real estate troubles in the mid-1970s (see Chapter XVI).

By 1985 the position of many developing countries had improved somewhat. World economic recovery and austerity measures adopted under programs agreed to by the IMF proved helpful. Exports increased, imports were reduced, and efforts were undertaken to rein in internal inflation, although frequently with indifferent success. Creditor banks, represented by bank advisory groups, entered into longer-term restructuring of existing debts in some troubled countries, and aimed to do so in others.[51] Maturities due over three to five years were stretched out over ten to twelve years, with a grace period of several years on payment of principal, and interest rates were also reduced.

Mexico and Brazil required no new funds from banks to meet their interest obligation on public-sector debt in 1985. In the previous two years banks had provided these two countries almost $20 billion of new loans (Chase's share was $650 million) under joint bank-IMF programs, enabling them to avoid default and move toward greater equilibrium in external accounts. Added billions flowed to other countries.

Despite positive developments, considerable uncertainty continued to overhang the foreign debt position of many developing countries. The position of Mexico and other oil producers again weakened with a decline in oil prices. Economic and social pressures were impelling debtor governments to call for new approaches to the problem, and loans to LDCs remained a source of major concern to Chase and other banks. Meanwhile larger capital and reserves materially strengthened the bank's ability to withstand unforeseen contingencies.

The mid-1980s: a critical juncture

Thus in the mid-1980s Chase was facing both problems and opportunities. With the trauma of Drysdale and Penn Square behind it, the bank once again moved forward on an ambitious program of expansion, geared more to the domestic than the international. Indeed, nonperforming assets in developing countries placed some restraint on foreign activity, while encouraging management to continue building up reserves and capital.

Narrowing profit margins on credits of high quality also induced change, stimulating the bank to act as a broker rather than a lender in many instances. New services of an investment banking nature—asset swaps, currency swaps, foreign exchange and interest rate futures and options— enabled the bank to expand fee income. More than ever, growth in assets took a back seat to profitability.

Meanwhile the structure of banking within the United States remained in a state of flux, undergoing piecemeal deregulation, frequently forced by competition from nonbank firms. Butcher and Labrecque recognized this as a critical juncture in Chase's history and prepared the bank to move quickly as opportunities for building a national network opened up. Yet Chase maintained a narrower focus than some of its competitors, aiming at the higher tiers of its markets. Quality continued to be accorded top priority.

Forty years of change and progress

The mid-1980s brings to a close the time span of this history, a period marked by a veritable revolution in banking. The internationalization of the bank, the extension of domestic offices across the nation; radical changes in products, funding, and pricing; quantum leaps in computer and telecommunications technology—all these and a host of other developments acted to reshape Chase beyond recognition.

Banking became an increasingly risky business as the postwar years unfolded. As revealed in Table 11, borrowed money replaced demand deposits as the principal source of funds; loans climbed in place of safe government investments; international credits, many in troubled countries, matched the domestic; and the slow expansion of equity capital provided a protective shield no greater in spite of increased risks. Meanwhile, competition became more intense, not only from Chase's peers, but even more from foreign banks and other financial institutions that encroached on Chase's basic markets.

At the same time, changes in the external environment were no less radical. Over the four postwar decades a world economy of separate nations became highly integrated, with many firms and industries organized on a global basis. The industrial nations increased in affluence and number, leading to rising expectations and dissatisfaction in poorer lands. Inflation became a worldwide problem, pushing interest rates from abnormal lows to heights not previously seen. And wide swings in interest and foreign currency rates added volatility to the financial scene.

Nor could the future shape of events frequently be foreseen. Surprises erupted, like the Vietnam war and its effect on inflation, the OPEC escalation of oil prices and its damage to international payment balances, and the depth of the world recession in the early 1980s and its adverse impact on developing nations. These all exerted a powerful influence on business and finance. Chase's management had to be prepared for surprises, maintaining a flexibility in resources, operations, and outlook to cope with them.

Changing dimensions of The Chase

At the end of 1985 Chase's total assets stood at $88 billion, a far cry from the war-swollen $6 billion forty years earlier. More than two-thirds represented

Table 11.   Chase in 1945 and 1985: Major Assets, Liabilities, and Earnings (Billions of Dollars).

Major Assets				
	Year end 1945	% of Total	Year end 1985	% of Total
Total	6.1	100	87.7	100
Cash and due from banks	1.4	23	5.6	6
Placings with foreign banks	0.0	0	4.7	5
Investments	3.4	56	6.1	7
Loans and mortgages	1.3	21	61.9	71
Domestic	1.2	20	32.5	37
Commercial	0.6	10	13.8	16
Against securities	0.6	10	0.5	1
Real estate	*	*	6.3	7
Consumer	*	*	7.4	8
Foreign	*	*	29.4	34

Major Liabilities and Capital				
	Year end 1945	% of Total	Year end 1985	% of Total
Total	6.1	100	87.7	100
Deposits	5.7	93	61.4	70
Domestic demand	5.4	88	14.3	16
Domestic savings and time	0.1	2	18.4	21
Foreign	0.2	3	28.7	33
Money market instruments[a] (domestic)	0.0	0	12.3	14
Capital	0.3	5	7.3	8
Notes and debentures	0.0	0	2.8	3
Preferred stock and common equity	0.3	5	4.5	5
Net Earnings (millions $)	26.5		565	

*Minimal = Less than $75 million.

a. Federal funds purchased and securities sold under repurchase agreements, commercial paper, and other short-term money market borrowings.

Source: *Chase National Bank Annual Report, 1945*, Chase Archives. *Chase National Bank Report to the Comptroller of the Currency*, December 31, 1945, New York City Clearing House. *Chase Manhattan Corporation Annual Report*, 1985.

loans, with the major share to commerce and industry in the United States and abroad. But sizable amounts also were outstanding to real estate, individuals, and foreign governments, markets of negligible volume in 1945. Moreover, foreign credits now constituted about half of the worldwide total.

For some years Chase provided foreign credit chiefly to central banks and correspondent banks for trade-related transactions, shunning loans to industry. But the migration of U.S. customers overseas in the late 1950s and 1960s produced a change in policy. Chase's network of foreign branches, although initially expanded chiefly to serve these customers, soon came to deal broadly with local nationals as well. By 1985 the bank's overseas network was extending $29.4 billion of credit to borrowers abroad, while financing another $5 billion for U.S. customers through the Eurodollar market.

Meanwhile the government security portfolio, at $2.2 billion smaller than at the end of World War II, diminished greatly in importance as a source of liquidity became less important with the advent of borrowed money, as the banks of short-term Eurodollars acquired at lower interest rates. Maintaining liquidity became less important with the advent of purchased money, as the bank relied on the money market for added funds in the event of unexpected needs.

Indeed borrowed money—certificates of deposit, money market deposits, Eurocurrencies (mainly Eurodollars), federal funds, and commercial paper—became Chase's principal source of funding. Growth of the negotiable CD and Eurodollar markets in the 1960s proved to be seminal developments, providing invaluable means of expansion and flexibility. But the prevalence of borrowed money also changed the profit dynamics of the bank, placing a high premium on efficient money gathering and loan pricing in an environment of volatile interest rates. And it added new risks to banking, with sophisticated providers of funds able to cut off the supply if confidence in an institution wavered.

Demand deposits, the mainstay of resources through the 1950s, grew only slowly over the years, as rising interest rates encouraged minimizing such balances. Chase's net demand deposits (usable funds, net of cash and collectable items) eventually fell to less than 16 percent of its total funds.[1] And even these deposits became more costly, as legal changes in the early 1980s finally permitted banks to pay interest on the transaction balances of individuals. Still, such deposits along with savings accounts continued to be valued as less costly sources of funds.

Chase remained a vigorous competitor for savings, having surged up from a negligible amount in 1945 by a persistent willingness to pay the maximum rates permitted. Over time this policy paid off and was repeated in 1982, as banks were permitted to offer new money market accounts. Chase provided these nationwide, and funds from consumers, more stable than others, increased to more than $10 billion.

Large capital, uneven earnings

Chase's large capital of $7.3 billion in September 1985 (8.3 percent of assets) contrasted with a mere $300 million (4.9 percent of assets) in 1945. But for many years growth of this key resource did not keep pace with assets. Like other banks, Chase had increased profits by leveraging off capital. But this practice came to a end in the mid-1970s, and maintenance of adequate capital became a principal objective of management.

Sources of capital also came to be diversified. Until 1965 Chase relied solely on equity, built from retained earnings and occasional new issues. The bank then issued long-term debt, eventually including both straight and convertible instruments. But sufficient growth in equity was essential, and in this Chase faced a handicap. Through the 1970s and 1980s Chase's stock, like that of most banks, sold at less than book value. Management filled the gap with preferred stock, much of it not redeemable and classified as equity. Total equity in 1985 of $4.5 billion thus represented a fifteenfold increase from 1945, slightly more than the advance in assets.

Regulators paid increasing attention to capital adequacy, and used primary capital as a measuring rod (see Chapter XXII). Chase drew criticism from the comptroller in 1974 for inadequate capital, but over subsequent years improved its position materially. The reserve for loan losses advanced from 0.8 percent of loans to 1.5 percent in 1985 on a volume twice as large, while primary capital, measured against assets, grew from 4.1 to 6.9 percent. On both counts, Chase improved its position among its peers, although not ranking at the top. The bank placed a high priority on raising its capital ratios still further over near-term years.

Chase's net income in 1985 of $565 million produced a return on common equity of 13.6 percent, greatly exceeding the 8.8 percent in 1945 from earnings of $26.5 million. Even so, the return fell below the bank's ambitious target of 15 to 18 percent. Through the years the bank's earning performance had lacked consistency, lagging in the immediate postwar period and the early 1970s, followed by a sharp downturn in the mid-1970s and again in 1982. From 1974 to 1985 net income climbed at a rate of 10.9 percent, respectable but not outstanding. Because of sizable payments to preferred stock, the earnings per share to common stockholders increased more slowly, at a rate of 7.7 percent, less than that of many of Chase's peers.

Rockefeller and Butcher turned away from asset growth as a principal objective after the mid-1970s and placed emphasis on profitability through improved return on assets. Higher interest rates after 1950 gradually raised ROA from the depressed level of the 1940s. Chase's return of 0.64 percent in 1985 was half again as great as that in 1946–1948 and within the bank's target range. But here again management pressed for added improvement, stressing growth of fee-paying services and the sale of loans with low spreads.

Chase remained the third largest bank in the nation, as in the early postwar years, but the gap in asset size between Chase and Citicorp and Bank of America (with 1985 assets of $173 billion and $119 billion respectively) widened considerably after 1970.[2] At one time this widening gap had been a source of concern to Chase. For some years after its merger with Manhattan, the bank moved ahead of First National City in size. But with a larger international network of facilities at work in the 1960s, and Chase's inhibiting problems in the first half of the 1970s, First National City (Citibank) expanded more rapidly. Meanwhile, Bank of America sustained its expansion through large savings and other deposits from a statewide branch system in fast-growing California.

In the 1980s the three banks pursued somewhat divergent strategies. Although Chase aimed to continue to be a leading bank in size, it had become more selective in its markets, placing greater emphasis on quality and profitability. Not strictly a wholesale bank, as was the smaller Morgan Guaranty, nor a financial department store offering all services to all customers, like Citibank (and to a lesser degree Bank of America), Chase chose to occupy a place in between, with a worldwide network of facilities matched by few others.

Chase as an international bank

Chase's continuing internationalization over four decades provided its most dramatic development. In 1945 the bank operated thirteen branches in seven overseas areas, with representative offices in two others. By 1985 some seventy-one countries or territories contained Chase facilities, including branches in forty-five areas, twenty-three major subsidiaries or affiliate banks in sixteen additional areas, and fifteen representative offices.[3] And the bank maintained direct business ties through correspondents with another sixty countries. About half of its deposits were generated overseas, in keeping with a like proportion of its loans, extended especially to corporations and other business, including state-owned firms.

Chase expanded its foreign branches only slowly from 1945 to 1960, as leadership on the international side remained dedicated to correspondent banking, a tradition of long standing. But under prodding from Rockefeller the policy changed in the 1960s, with many domestic customers beginning to move overseas. By the early 1970s much of the network was in place and other nonbank financial institutions were added. Banking, and business generally, became global in character. The network then proved of great value in the troubled period of the mid-1970s, when it produced large earnings that enabled Chase to maintain its dividend.

In the 1980s Chase began to rationalize its network, filling a few gaps with new facilities, but closing or selling others with inadequate profit. Initially the bank chose to enter a number of countries through partial ownership of affiliated banks rather than branches, in order to gain resources and management quickly. Chase, however, did not find partial ownership a satisfactory relationship in many instances. Differences in objectives and management styles, along with rewards that were not commensurate with the degree of effort, led the bank to work toward full ownership. In this it succeeded in many countries, Belgium, the Netherlands, Austria, Ireland, Brazil, and Argentina among them. But it disposed of minority interests in banks in Venezuela, the Philippines, and Dubai, as well as many nonbank affiliates. Had the development of Eurocurrency and local money markets been adequately anticipated, branches rather than affiliates would have been preferred in important instances.

Ironically Chase was permitted to undertake a full range of investment banking activities outside the United States, but was barred by law from doing so within. The bank's initial partnership in Orion (1970), one of the earliest consortium banks, eventually was sold so that the bank could concentrate on two wholly owned affiliates, Chase Manhattan, Ltd., and Chase Manhattan Asia, Ltd. These greatly facilitated growth in foreign lending through participation in the development of syndicated credits involving large numbers of banks. CML and CMAL became leaders in managing or participating in the management of such credits, which usually utilized Eurocurrencies. The two investment affiliates assumed a role of growing importance in the mid-1980s, as the bank provided a broadened range of investment banking products to customers.

Escaping geographic bounds domestically

No less significant was Chase's successful effort to break its postwar geographic bounds at home. Until the mid-1950s Chase operated branches almost entirely in Manhattan, concentrating heavily on wholesale activities. The merger with Manhattan in 1955 propelled the bank throughout the city and converted it also into a sizable retail institution. Chase then worked with others to persuade the state legislature to enlarge the permissible area for branching. A hard-fought change in the law in 1960 enabled the bank to move into the city's suburbs, while a further change a decade later set the stage for branching throughout the state.

Through the years Chase was limited by antitrust policy to branch expansion *de novo*, or acquisition of only small existing banks. But here too policies changed as geographical boundaries for financial institutions generally broke down. With the acquisition of Lincoln First Corporation of Rochester in 1984, Chase became the largest branch bank in the state, operating more than 325 branches across New York.

Spreading into other states proved more difficult. Banks were blocked by long-standing legal constraints from branching across state lines.[4] But a subsidiary of a bank holding company could provide financial services through offices in other states, although not as a full service bank (both accepting demand deposits and making commercial loans), unless a state specifically authorized such activity. Chase took this route in 1969, establishing The Chase Manhattan Corporation, with the bank as its principal subsidiary.

Chase adopted a strategy for national expansion in the early 1970s, but a decade passed before a revised plan began to be seriously implemented. An early attempt to acquire Dial Financial Corporation in 1974 was thwarted by the Federal Reserve, and problems at middecade drew the full attention and energy of management (see Chapter XVI). In the 1980s, however, Chase began to spread across the nation, with facilities in twenty-three states and more than 170 offices by 1985.

Unlike most of its facilities overseas, Chase's network in the United States, apart from the head office, concentrated on upscale consumers, the middle market, and smaller business. Large corporate customers were handled from New York, with assistance from officers in regional marketing offices. Hardly less important was Chase's presence through nationwide marketing of its credit card and other products by direct mail. Expansion into selected areas of the country now claimed major attention from Chase's planners.

Yet although geographical boundaries nationwide were breaking down, the bank believed that the process would proceed by stages and not be completed in a short time. Chase aimed eventually to operate full-service banks in key regional centers, large enough to command the critical mass necessary for strong profitability.[5] It would be difficult to accomplish this de novo, given the entrenched position of existing regional institutions. Nonetheless the bank sought to take advantage of unexpected opportunities, as it did with The Chase Bank, Ohio, and Chase Bank, Maryland (see Chapter XXII). Meanwhile, acquisition of Lincoln First provided a pilot for developing controls and operating coordination with a sizable regional affiliate.

Evolution in banking products and pricing

The range of products provided to customers through Chase's expanding facilities also increased in number and variety through the decades. Extension of credit continued to be the bank's most important product, but even this underwent significant change. In the 1940s short-term credit remained highly important, much of it seasonal in nature, linked to agriculture and holiday seasons. But over the years seasonal demands greatly diminished. Term loans, including revolving credits, grew much more rapidly than short-term loans, constituting more than three-fourths of the total to domestic corporations by the mid-1980s. Projections of cash flow, along with the balance sheet, constituted a core element of credit analysis. And credits tailored to expansion needs of specific industries became common, ship loans, oil production loans, and a variety of equipment loans, among them. Specially designed credits financed huge projects, while others to foreign governments covered gaps in balance of payments.

Meanwhile competition against bank financing escalated. Commercial paper, available to only a few leading firms in the early postwar years, expanded enormously, and by the 1980s had replaced bank loans for short-term financing for a wide range of the bank's customers. Insurance companies and the capital markets, once dedicated chiefly to the longer term, shortened their maturities to the bank range. And specialized finance companies developed, meeting banks head-on in various fields.

In the face of this competitive onslaught, and with a diversity of funding sources available, the pricing of bank products also altered. For many years loans continued to be priced at a fixed rate, based on the bank's prime rate. But with the growing use of borrowed money and the increased volatility of its cost, the bank shifted to variable rates in the second half of the 1960s. Still, a portion of credits continued to be extended at a fixed rate, frequently (but not always) with funding by matched maturities.

After 1977 the prime rate, a fundamental basis for loan pricing since the 1930s, began to give way to alternatives. Money market pricing was introduced, with credits extended at a spread above the cost of funds. The prime rate came to be only one of a number of basing points. Abroad in Euromarkets, the London Interbank Offering Rate (LIBOR) was utilized. Customers frequently were offered a choice of rates based on either the prime, the cost of CDs, or LIBOR. Many domestic credits then moved offshore, financed with Eurodollars.

As competition from commercial paper forced down loan spreads in the 1980s, Chase found it more profitable to generate and sell credits, continuing to service them and enhancing income with fees. Moreover, costs or risks from volatile interest and currency rates frequently could be reduced through swaps between banks or with customers, as well as recourse to option markets. Chase engaged increasingly in these and other investment banking activities, including private placement of customers' securities, mergers and acquisitions, and abroad, bond underwriting. The line between commercial banks and investment banks grew indistinct, returning almost full cycle to the position in the 1920s (see Chapter I).

Nor was product change restricted to the corporate customer. Consumers also benefited. As a predominantly wholesale bank, Chase did not provide a full range of services to individuals in 1945, only starting installment credit the following year. But the merger with Manhattan a decade later converted the bank into a leading retail institution. Installment credit came to be supplemented by personal overdraft facilities (called cash reserve), as well as individual lines of credit. Chase's credit card (Visa), acquired in the late 1960s, grew to be its most visible instrument. For savers the bank offered a range of products—Super-Now accounts, consumer CDs, and money market accounts—once the Federal Reserve ceilings on interest rates, born of the depression in 1933, were finally abandoned in the 1980s. Consumers also benefited from technological change, as automated teller machines made cash and account information readily available.

The computer enhances the role of the back office

The bank office, no less than line departments, contributed to continuing change. The computer in particular proved to be a revolutionary instrument, naturally adapted to handling the mass of checks, securities, and other documents that flow through banks. A machine for check sorting and bookkeeping equipment formed the basis for processing checks in the 1940s and 1950s. These, along with stock transfer and other clerical operations, remained highly labor intensive. Chase first applied the computer to such activities in the early 1960s, reducing personnel in some instances by half while improving accuracy. Meanwhile a new breed of specialists was introduced into the bank, including many retrained from discontinued positions. As the volume of transactions grew ever larger, employment in the late 1960s rose to new peaks.

Automation, supported by advances in telecommunications, spread to almost all products and locations in the 1970s. Money mobilization and cash management, two key services, were greatly improved. And computers were adapted to management information purposes, generating data to assist line officers and management at all levels.

With advances in the state of the art, electronic banking became a focal point for competition between Chase and other major banks after the mid-1970s. Within a few years corporate treasurers, using terminals in their offices linked to Chase's computer, were able to monitor cash balances and initiate borrowing, investing, and foreign transactions in the United States and abroad, all without intervention by a Chase officer. For a fee the bank then packaged analytical information on these and other transactions, becoming both an information intermediary and a financial intermediary in the process.

The computer also heavily influenced trust activities, facilitating their management and execution, but also helping to create new competition. Chase and other banks held commanding positions in corporate, pension, and personal trust in the 1940s and 1950s. But their position eroded somewhat over subsequent years as new, specialized firms emerged to provide stock transfer, dividend payment, pension trust, and other services.

Pension trust grew beyond all other trust services in this period. Here the bank's investment arm, Chase Investors Management, performed less well than competitors from 1970 to 1975, but it recovered strongly by the 1980s. Chase became a leader in master trust arrangements, managing the largest volume of assets and providing a wide range of analytical information to clients.

Complex organization and management process

As the scope and nature of Chase's activities evolved, its organization and management process grew in complexity. In 1945, with the emphasis on wholesale banking, nine units reported directly to the president, who was in turn accountable to the chairman. Forty years later, nine major groups embracing a broad range of wholesale, retail, and investment banking reported to three vice chairmen serving under the president (see Chapter XXII). The chairman, aided by staff, maintained responsibility for planning, as well as providing overall coordination. And the bank operated as the major unit of a holding company, The Chase Manhattan Corporation, established in 1969.

Although the directors had not been enthusiastic about forming the holding company, it fulfilled its promise, adding flexibility in operations, financing, and expansion. The directors now exercised oversight over a highly intricate business. Size alone complicated their task. Whereas in the early postwar years, the directors reviewed all new loans of $500,000 or more, the minimum was raised periodically. It was adjusted upward again in 1981 to $25 million, permitting the board to concentrate on the more significant credits.[6]

Controlling a worldwide institution like Chase, ensuring the safety of its assets while seeking to enhance profits and plan for the future, called for a high degree of skill on the part of many managers. It could not be accomplished without what Butcher called a "disciplined management process." Here again the contrast between the present and the early postwar years was dramatic. In 1945 the bank lacked a meaningful budget, as well as management techniques associated with planning. Highly effective control was maintained over the quality of credit, however, carried out through able supervision and a committee structure designed for the purpose.

By the 1980s the management process embraced a series of interlocking committee and processes involving managers at all levels throughout the world. Short-range plans were embedded in annual budgets, developed by all marketing and staff units, with rigorous control and final approval by top management. Performance against budget was monitored quarterly. Contained in the budget also were the results of other processes. Strategic plans, the product of a policy and planning committee, resulted in programs that might run for a period at a loss and hence had to be phased in over time. Large outlays were made for improved systems and communications, with priorities established by a committee designated for that purpose.

A separate budget was drawn up for the capital side of the corporation, with funds earmarked for investment in new buildings, equipment, and acquisitions. The bank's own capital position was appraised, and plans were made to go to the market for added capital when necessary.

On the credit side, coordination and determination of policies was the responsibility of the credit risk committee, chaired by the chief credit officer, with heads of all credit-granting departments as members. A separate committee (started in 1975) asessed country risks and set limits for commitments and outstandings in all countries.

But no group carried on a more significant task at this time than the asset-liability management committee (ALMAC), with the president at its helm and vice chairmen and department heads as members. This committee, which in 1973 succeeded a long-standing portfolio investment committee, managed the broad deployment of the bank's assets and the manner of their funding. In doing so it sought to ensure a profitability through return on assets consistent with the bank's objective, while achieving the balance between operating results and strategic investments called for in the bank's budget.

The committee guarded against risks associated with changes in interest rates by setting guidelines that limited mismatches between maturities of assets and maturities of liabilities at the head office and in branches and affiliates around the world, a problem unimportant to banking from 1945 into the 1960s. ALMAC's task grew increasingly complicated, as interest rates, exchange rates, and the economy generally became more and more volatile.

Changing elements of the Chase culture

Along with organization and management process, elements of the Chase culture were altered in many ways. In 1945 the greatest value and emphasis were placed on wholesale banking, with senior leadership drawn from its ranks. International activity was also accorded a high priority, and correspondent relationships were favored over branching. Major departments operated with a high degree of autonomy, while relations with personnel were marked by a paternalistic attitude born of the Great Depression. Complementing this too was a sense of social responsibility for which Chase was noted.

In the 1980s wholesale banking, although still most prominent, no longer dominated Chase. Consumer banking, encouraged by growing affluence and the 1955 merger with Manhattan, was thrust into greater prominence. The bank grew in diversity, with such activities as real estate finance, investment banking, foreign exchange, and computer-driven products contributing significantly to income. Foreign branches and affiliates replaced correspondent banks as a favored mode of operation. And wholesale relationships, once confined largely to the domestic corporate side, with little interaction between it and the international, became a joint responsibility in a global setting.

Perhaps the greatest modification in Chase's culture occurred in relations between the bank and its officers, and in relations between the officers themselves.[7] The officer cadre changed in the 1970s, becoming more diverse in character and background. The bank moreover abandoned its paternalistic attitude toward employees, not hesitating to release officers and other staff for inadequate performance. Contrary to past practice, managerial talent was introduced from outside in senior positions wherever the bank would clearly benefit.

In the mid-1980s the bank recruited from a wide range of colleges and graduate schools and hired many individuals in midcareer, already possessing specialized experience and training. Young recruits were sought who possessed not only sharp analytical minds, but qualities of leadership and the capacity to work in a team effort, eventually to combine marketing skills with the more strictly financial. Chase, known for an internal environment that while competitive, provided opportunity for advancement and was not combative in nature, had no difficulty in attracting its share of talent.

Internal communications continued to pose problems for the bank in the 1980s as earlier. Communications had been improved by Rockefeller and Butcher, especially from the top down. Departments communicated to a greater extent with each other, impelled in part by their growing interdependence. Yet such communication continued to be inadequate, as was evident in the losses of 1982. Upward communication too, from subordinate to superiors, required strengthening.[8] The bank in 1985 launched a major effort to correct these shortcomings.

One element of Chase's culture, however, held steadfast throughout the postwar years. Successive managements placed social responsibility high on the priority list, and the bank continued to be widely recognized for this attribute. Rockefeller, Champion, and McCloy were outstanding in this respect, and Butcher pledged to maintain the same posture.

Looking ahead

Civilization, historian Arnold Toynbee has written, is the story of challenge and response. So it was with Chase. Improved products, organization, management processes, and culture—all those left the bank stronger and better positioned in 1985 than at any other time in more than a decade. But as always, further challenges lay ahead. Banking, never a risk-free business, had become ever riskier, with the large international dimension an added factor. And the industry itself faced a radical restructuring, along with the entire complex of financial services.

Butcher was asked at a meeting in 1984 what he would like to place on a lapel button to symbolize Chase. He responded with a single word, "Quality."[9] Many elements entered into that concept: a quality customer base, a highly competent staff, superior technology, and a global network for delivery. Chase was convinced that it possessed all these and worked to fuse them together in a partnership effort—partnership with customers to understand their needs, and internal partnership with staff at all levels collaborating to meet those needs.

As Chase entered the second half of the 1980s it faced the future with confidence. Management remained alert to uncertainties posed by developing country debts, a highly volatile environment, and competitive pressures greater than any yet encountered. Still the bank pressed forward, implementing its plans for the future and determined to be a quality institution worthy of its eminent name.

Directors of The Chase National Bank (1945–1955); The Chase Manhattan Bank, N.A. (1955–1985); and The Chase Manhattan Corporation (1969–1985)

Name and Affiliation	Term of Directorship
Newcomb Carlton *Chairman, Western Union Telegraph Co.*	1917–1948
Frederick H. Ecker *Chairman, Metropolitan Life Insurance Co.*	1917–1948
Arthur G. Hoffman *Vice president, the Great Atlantic and Pacific Tea Co.*	1922–1947
Malcolm G. Chase *President, Chase and Harriman, Inc.*	1925–1946
Thomas N. McCarter *Chairman, Fidelity Union Trust Company, Newark, NJ*	1925–1946
Henry O. Havemeyer *President, Brooklyn Eastern Terminal*	1926–1955
Earl D. Babst *Chairman, the American Sugar Refining Co.*	1928–1953
Francis H. Brownell *Chairman, American Smelting and Refining Co.*	1928–1951
Thomas I. Parkinson *Chairman, the Equitable Life Assurance Society of the United States*	1929–1955
Andrew W. Robertson *Chairman, Westinghouse Electric Corp.*	1929–1957[1]
Winthrop W. Aldrich *Chairman, The Chase National Bank*	1930–1953
Howard Bayne *Retired banker*	1930–1955
Bertram Cutler *Associate of John D. Rockefeller, Jr.*	1930–1947
Robert C. Stanley *Chairman, the International Nickel Company of Canada*	1930–1951
H. Donald Campbell *President, Vice chairman, The Chase National Bank*	1934–1955
Arthur W. Page *Vice president, American Telephone and Telegraph Co.*	1934–1955
Barton P. Turnbull *President, Rockefeller Center, Inc.*	1934–1948
J. Frank Drake *Chairman, Gulf Oil Corp.*	1942–1958[1]
Carl J. Schmidlapp *Vice chairman, The Chase National Bank*	1942–1955
Austin S. Iglehart *Chairman, General Foods Corp.*	1943–1955

[1] Directors of The Chase National Bank who became directors of The Chase Manhattan Bank.

James T. Lee *President, Central Savings Bank, New York*	1943–1955
Lynde Selden *Vice chairman, American Express Co.*	1943–1963[1]
Alexander N. Kemp *Chairman, Pacific Mutual Life Insurance Co.*	1944–1953
Jeremiah Milbank *Management of Investment Interests*	1944–1955[1]
Robert E. Wilson *Chairman, Standard Oil Co. (Indiana)*	1945–1958[1]
Francis W. Cole *Chairman, the Travelers Insurance Company*	1946–1955[1]
Arthur W. McCain *President, Vice chairman, The Chase National Bank*	1946–1952
Kenneth C. Bell *Secretary, The Chase National Bank*	1948
Laurance S. Rockefeller *Rockefeller Brothers, Inc.*	1947–1956[1]
Leroy A. Lincoln *Chairman, Metropolitan Life Insurance Co.*	1948–1955
Leroy A. Wilson *President, American Telephone and Telegraph Co.*	1948–1951
Joseph L. Egan *President, Western Union Telegraph Co.*	1948
Percy J. Ebbott *President, Vice chairman, The Chase National Bank*	1949–1956[1]
Cleo F. Craig *President, American Telephone and Telegraph Co.*	1951–1956[1]
Kenneth C. Brownell *Chairman, American Smelting and Refining Co.*	1951–1958[1]
Joseph A. Martino *Chairman, National Lead Company*	1952–1970[1]
John J. McCloy *Chairman, The Chase National Bank and The Chase Manhattan Bank (1953–1960)*	1953–1966[1]
Harry A. deButts *President, the Southern Railway System*	1953–1962[1]
C. R. Smith *Chairman, American Airlines, Inc.*	1953–1966[1]
Frederic W. Ecker *Chairman, Metropolitan Life Insurance Co.*	1955–1963[1]
Morris Hadley *Milbank, Tweed, Hope and Hadley*	1955
J. Stewart Baker *Chairman, Executive committee, and President, The Chase Manhattan Bank; Chairman, Bank of The Manhattan Company*	1922–1965[2]
Elliott V. Bell *Chairman, Executive committee, McGraw-Hill*	1950–1967[2]
Graham B. Blaine *Vice chairman, Bank of The Manhattan Co.*	1948–1955[2]
James F. Brownlee *J. H. Whitney and Co.*	1947–1960[2]
George W. Burpee *Coverdale and Colpitts*	1944–1958[2]
Robert M. Catharine *Chairman, Dollar Savings Bank, New York*	1944–1960[2]
J. Doyle DeWitt *Chairman, the Travelers Insurance Company*	1955–1971
William V. Griffin *Chairman, Brady Security and Realty Corporation*	1930–1958[2]

[2] Directors of the Bank of The Manhattan Company who became directors of The Chase Manhattan Bank. Beginning in 1969 directors of The Chase Manhattan Bank for the most part were also directors of The Chase Manhattan Corporation. Exceptions are noted.

Henry D. Mercer   *Chairman, States Marine Corp. Lines, Inc.*   1947–1965[2]

Ray D. Murphy   *Chairman, the Equitable Life Assurance Society of the United   1955–1957
States*

William J. Murray, Jr.   *Chairman, Executive Committee, McKesson and Robbins,   1943–1960[2]
Inc.*

Frank F. Russell   *Chairman, Cerro Corp.*   1940–1967[2]

George Champion   *Chairman, President, The Chase Manhattan Bank*   1956–1971[3]

David Rockefeller   *Chairman, President, Vice chairman, The Chase Manhattan   1956–1981
Bank*; Chairman, The Chase Manhattan Corporation

Frederick R. Kappel   *Chairman, American Telephone and Telegraph Co.*   1956–1972

James F. Oates, Jr.   *Chairman, Equitable Life Assurance Society of the United   1957–1970[3]
States*

Lucius D. Clay   *Chairman, Continental Can Co.*   1958–1963

Paul L. Davies   *Chairman, Food Machinery and Chemical Corp.*   1958–1966

J. Richardson Dilworth   *President, Rockefeller Brothers, Inc.*   1958–1981

Eugene Holman   *Chairman, Standard Oil Co. (New Jersey)*   1958–1962

Charles H. Percy   *Chairman, Bell and Howell Co.*   1958–1964

Frank O. Prior   *Chairman, Standard Oil Co. (Indiana)*   1958–1960

Whitney Stone   *Chairman, Stone and Webster, Inc.*   1958–1975

Lawrence C. Marshall   *Vice chairman, The Chase Manhattan Bank*   1960–1969

Jeremiah Milbank, Jr.   *Chairman, Commercial Solvents Corp.*   1960–1976

John E. Swearingen   *Chairman, Standard Oil Co. (Indiana)*   1960–1984

Eugene R. Black   *Former president, International Bank for Reconstruction and   1963–1970[3]
Development*

C. W. Cook   *Chairman, General Foods Corp.*   1963–1975

Gilbert W. Fitzhugh   *Chairman, Metropolitan Life Insurance Co.*   1963–1969[3]

C. Jay Parkinson   *Chairman, Anaconda, Co.*   1963–1971[3]

Stuart T. Saunders   *Chairman, Pennsylvania Railroad*   1963–1970[3]

Roger M. Blough   *Chairman, United States Steel Corp.*   1964–1969

Walter E. Dennis   *Executive vice president, The Chase Manhattan Bank*   1965–1967

C. Douglas Dillon   *Former secretary of the treasury, United States*   1966–1971[3]

J. K. Jamieson   *Chairman, Standard Oil Co. (New Jersey)*   1965–1976

Charles F. Myers, Jr.   *Chairman, Burlington Industries, Inc.*   1965–1977

[3] Director only of The Chase Manhattan Bank.

Ralph Lazarus   *Chairman, Federated Department Stores*   1966–1984

John T. Connor   *Chairman, Allied Chemical Corp.*   .   1967–1979

James A. Perkins   *President, Cornell University*   1967–1975

Herbert P. Patterson   *President, The Chase Manhattan Corporation*   1969–1972
    and The Chase Manhattan Bank, N.A.

John B. M. Place   *Vice chairman, The Chase Manhattan Corporation*   1969–1971
    and The Chase Manhattan Bank, N.A.

George A. Roeder, Jr.   *Vice chairman, The Chase Manhattan Corporation*   1969–1982
    and The Chase Manhattan Bank, N.A.

Robert O. Anderson   *Chairman, Atlantic Richfield Co.*   1969–1974

William R. Hewlett   *President, Hewlett-Packard Co.*   1969–1980

Robert D. Lilley   *President, American Telephone and Telegraph Co.*   1970–1977

Richard R. Shinn   *Chairman, Metropolitan Life Insurance Co.*   1970–1977[3]
                                                                                1977–1986

J. Henry Smith   *Chairman, Equitable Life Assurance Society of the United States*   1970–1975

Thomas A. Wood   *Chairman, TAW Leasing, Inc.*   1970–1974

Patricia Roberts Harris   *Partner, Fried, Frank, Harris, Shriver and Kampelman*   1971–1977

John H. Loudon   *Chairman of Supervisory Board, Royal Dutch Petroleum Co.*   1971–1976[4]

Willard C. Butcher   *Chairman, President, Vice chairman, The Chase Manhattan*   1972–
    Corporation and The Chase Manhattan Bank, N.A.

Leonor F. Loree, II   *Vice chairman, The Chase Manhattan Corporation and The*   1972–1976
    Chase Manhattan Bank, N.A.

Charles F. Barber   *Chairman, American Smelting and Refining Co.*   1972–1982

James H. Binger   *Chairman, Honeywell, Inc.*   1972–1980

Rev. Theodore M. Hesburgh   *President, University of Notre Dame*   1972–1981

Michael E. Carlson   *Vice President and Secretary, The Chase Manhattan Bank*   1974–1976[3]

Robert R. Douglass   *Partner, Milbank, Tweed, Hadley and McCloy*   1974[3]

Richard M. Furlaud   *Chairman, Squibb Corp.*   1974–1981

Roy C. Haberkern, Jr.   *Partner, Milbank, Tweed, Hadley and McCloy*   1974[3]

Edmund T. Pratt, Jr.   *Chairman, Pfizer, Inc.*   1974–

Coy G. Eklund   *President, the Equitable Life Assurance Society of the United*   1975–1978
    States

James L. Ferguson   *Chairman, General Foods Corp.*   1975–

John D. Macomber   *Chairman, Celanese Corp.*   1975–

[4] Director only of The Chase Manhattan Corporation.

J. Stanford Smith   *Chairman, International Paper Co.*   1975–1980

Howard C. Kauffmann   *President, Exxon Corp.*   1976–

Norma T. Pace   *Senior vice president, American Paper Institute*   1976–1982

S. Bruce Smart, Jr.   *Chairman, the Continental Group, Inc*   1976–1985

Dr. Elvis J. Stahr, Jr.   *President, National Audubon Society*   1976–1979

C. William Verity, Jr. *Chairman, Armco, Inc.*   1976–1985

William T. Coleman, Jr.   *Senior partner, O'Melveny and Myers*   1977–

James E. Olson   *President, American Telephone and Telegraph Co.*   1977–

John H. McArthur   *Dean, Harvard University Graduate School of Business*   1980[4]–
   Administration

David T. McLaughlin   *Chairman, The Toro Co.; President, Dartmouth College*   1980–

Thomas G. Labrecque   *President, Vice chairman, The Chase Manhattan*   1980–
   Corporation and The Chase Manhattan Bank, N.A.

William S. Ogden   *Vice chairman, The Chase Manhattan Corporation*   1980–1983
   and The Chase Manhattan Bank, N.A.

Alexander M. Haig, Jr.   *President, United Technologies Corp.*   1980–1981

Edward S. Finkelstein   *Chairman, R. H. Macy and Co.*   1981–

Richard W. Lyman   *President, The Rockefeller Foundation*   1981–

Robert E. Flowerree   *Chairman, Georgia Pacific Corp.*   1981–

Donald H. Trautlein   *Chairman, Bethlehem Steel Corp.*   1981–

John A. Hooper   *Vice chairman, The Chase Manhattan Corporation*   1983–1985
   and The Chase Manhattan Bank, N.A.

Phillip Caldwell   *Chairman, Ford Motor Co.*   1982–1985

David T. Kearns   *Chairman, Xerox Corp.*   1982–

Henry B. Schacht   *Chairman, Cummins Engine Co.*   1982–

Ralph E. Ward   *Chairman, Chesebrough-Pond's, Inc.*   1982–

Joan Ganz Cooney   *President, Children's Television Workshop*   1983–

Alexander D. Hargrave   *Chairman, Chase Lincoln First Bank, N.A.*   1984[4]–

Kay R. Whitmore   *President, Eastman Kodak Co.*   1984–

H. Laurance Fuller   *President, Amoco Corp.*   1985–

Robert R. Douglass   *Vice chairman, The Chase Manhattan Corporation*   1985–
   and The Chase Manhattan Bank, N.A.

Arthur F. Ryan   *Vice chairman, The Chase Manhattan Corporation*   1985–
   and The Chase Manhattan Bank, N.A.

Anthony P. Terracciano   *Vice chairman, The Chase Manhattan Corporation*   1985–
   and The Chase Manhattan Bank, N.A.

Principal Officers of The Chase National Bank, (1945–1955); The Chase Manhattan Bank, N.A. (1955–1985); and The Chase Manhattan Bank Corporation, (1969–1985)[1]

Chairmen and Chief Executive Officer

Winthrop W. Aldrich   *Chairman 1934–1953; President and Chairman of the Governing Board 1933–1934; President 1930–1933*

John J. McCloy   *Chairman 1953–1960*

J. Stewart Baker   *Chairman of Executive Committee and Co-Chief Executive 1955–1957 (also President 1955–1956); Chairman, the Bank of The Manhattan Company 1932–1955*

George Champion   *Chairman and Co-Chief Executive 1961–1969; President and Chief Operating Officer 1956–1960; Executive Vice President, Senior Vice President, head of United States Department 1952–1956; Senior Vice President, head of Commercial Banking Department 1949–1952*

David Rockefeller   *Chairman 1969–1981; President and Co-Chief Executive 1961–1969; Vice Chairman 1956–1960; Executive Vice President, Senior Vice President, head of Metropolitan Department 1952–1955; Executive Vice President, Planning and Development, 1955–1956; Senior Vice President, head of New York City branches and Customer Relations 1952*

Willard C. Butcher   *Chairman 1981– ; President and Chief Executive Officer 1980–81; President and Chief Operating Officer 1972–1979; Vice Chairman (Corporation) 1972; Executive Vice President International Department 1969–1971*

President and Chief Operating Officer

H. Donald Campbell   *1934–1945; Vice Chairman 1945–1946*

Arthur W. McCain   *1946–1949; Vice Chairman 1949–1952*

Percy J. Ebbott   *1949–1955; Vice Chairman 1955–1956; Senior Vice President Commercial Banking 1947–1949*

Herbert P. Patterson   *1969–1972; Executive Vice President, International Department 1967–1969; United States Department 1965–1967*

---

[1]Senior officers of The Chase Manhattan Bank also were appointed to the same positions as officers of The Chase Manhattan Corporation. Two exceptions are noted.

Thomas G. Labrecque   1981– ; *Vice Chairman (chief operating officer) 1980–1981; Executive Vice President, Management Committee 1976–1980 (Commercial, Institutional, Retail, Trust and Fiduciary Investment, Operations and Systems, Asset-Based Services 1978–1980; Operations and Systems, Retail and Commercial 1977; Operations and Retail Banking 1976); Portfolio and Investment Banking 1974–1976*

Vice Chairmen

Carl J. Schmidlapp   *1949–1954 (Vice Chairman, Executive Committee); Senior Vice President, Commercial Banking 1947–1949*

Lawrence C. Marshall   *1961–1969; Executive Vice President, Metropolitan Department 1955–1960; President, the Bank of The Manhattan Company 1948–1955*

John B. M. Place   *1969–1971; Executive Vice President, United States Department 1967–1969; Metropolitan Department 1965–1967*

George A. Roeder, Jr.   *1969–1982; Executive Vice President, Credit and Loan Standards 1965–1969; Metropolitan Department 1961–1965*

Leonor F. Loree II   *1972–1976 (Bank); 1972–1975 (Corporation); Executive Vice President, Corporate Staff Department 1969–1972*

William S. Ogden   *1980–1983; Executive Vice President, Management Committee 1975–1980 (Chief Fininical Officer 1976–1980; International Banking, Treasury, and Funding 1975–1976); International Banking Department 1971–1975*

John A. Hooper   *1983–1985; Executive Vice President Credit Policy 1980–1982 (Senior Executive Vice President 1981–1982); Management Committee 1975–1980 (Real Estate, Credit Policy, Lending Services, and Planning 1975–1980); Planning, Economics, and Credit Policy 1973–1975*

Robert R. Douglass   *1985– (National Banking); Executive Vice President, National Banking 1984–1985; Strategic Planning and Legal 1982–1984; General Counsel 1976–1982*

Arthur F. Ryan   *1985– (Consumer Banking); Executive Vice President, Community Banking 1984–1985; Operations and Systems 1982–1984*

Anthony P. Terracciano   *1985– (Global Banking); Executive Vice President, Chief Financial Officer 1983–1984; Sector Executive Operations, Systems, Information, and Investment Services 1980–1983; Treasury 1976–1980*

Senior Vice President (The Chase National Bank), 1945–1955, and Executive Vice President (The Chase Manhattan Bank), 1955–1985)

Edward L. Love   *Public Utility Department 1947–1952; Special Industries Department 1952–1955, Executive Vice President 1955*

Hugo E. Scheuermann   *Commercial Banking 1947–1955; Credit Policy 1955–1956 (Senior Vice President)*

Eugene R. Black   *Bond Department 1949*

Charles Cain, Jr.   *Foreign Department 1950–1955; Executive Vice President, International Department 1955–1963*

Thomas H. McKittrick   *Foreign Department 1950–1954*

John B. Bridgewood   *Trust Department 1953–1955; Executive Vice President, Investments and Financial Planning Department 1955–1964; Fiduciary Investment Department 1964–1968*

Walter E. Dennis   *United States Department 1956–1965*

Francis G. Ross   *Trust Department 1957–1971*

Harold F. Moeller   *Operating Department 1957–1962; Corporate Plans and Staff Department 1962– 1967*

Alfred W. Barth   *International Department 1961–1967*

Victor E. Rockhill   *International Department 1964–1970; President, Chase International Investment Corporation 1959–1963 and 1971–1974*

Charles A. Agemian   *Bank Operations Department 1963–1969*

Thomas W. McMahon, Jr.   *Metropolitan Department 1967–1971; Institutional Banking Department 1971–1972*

Raymond T. O'Keefe   *Real Estate and Mortgage Loan Department 1969–1973*

Robert B. Rivel   *Portfolio and Investment Banking Department 1969–1972*

Robert K. Schell   *United States Department 1968–1973*

Robert J. Pollock   *Bank Operations Department 1969–1972*

William B. Bateman   *Human Resources 1971–1973; Real Estate and Mortgage Loan Department 1973– 1975*

James W. Bergford   *Community Banking 1971–1977; International Department 1977–1983; International Financing 1983–*

James M. Lane   *Fiduciary Investment Department 1971–1972; President, Chase Investors Management Corporation 1972–1978*

James W. North   *Trust Department 1971–1977*

Charles E. Fiero   *Portfolio and Investment Banking Department 1972–1974; Monetary Missions 1975*

Roger A. Lyon   *Institutional Banking 1972–1976*

Barry F. Sullivan   *Bank Operations 1972–1974; Management Committee 1975–1980 (Retail Banking, Operations, and Information Services 1975–1976; Institutional, Fiduciary, and Information Services 1976–1978; Corporate Banking, International Banking, and Information Services 1978–1980)*

John C. Haley   *Corporate, Institutional, and Real Estate Banking 1973–1975; Management Committee 1975–1980 (Corporate, Institutional, Real Estate 1975–1976; Corporate and International Banking 1976–1978; Corporate and Institutional Relations 1978–1980); Corporate and Institutional Relations 1980–1985*

Herbert H. Jacobi   *Corporate Banking 1975*

Francis X. Stankard   *International Banking 1974–1980; Sector Executive International 1980–1984; Chairman Chase Manhattan Capital Markets 1984–*

William R. Hinchman, Jr.   *Bank Operations 1974–1978; Domestic Institutional Banking 1978–1981; Nationwide Positioning 1981–1982*

Alan F. Lafley   *Human Resources 1975–1983*

James H. Carey   *Corporate Banking 1976–1980; Sector Executive, Corporate Industries 1980–1985*

Frederick S. Hammer   *Community Banking 1977–1980; Sector Executive, Consumer Banking 1980–1984*

Richard J. Higgerson   *Sector Executive, Institutional Banking and Financial Services 1980–1982*

Wolfgang Schoellkopf   *Treasury, 1980–*

Richard J. Boyle   *Sector Executive, Commercial Banking 1984–1985; Corporate Industries, 1985–*

A. Edward Allinson   *Sector Executive, Domestic Institutional, Trust, Investment, and Information Services 1983–*

A. Wright Elliott   *Corporate Communications 1983–*

Michael P. Esposito, Jr.   *Corporate Controller 1983–*

Donald L. Boudreau   *Sector Executive International Banking 1984–*

Robert M. Lichten   *President Chase Manhattan Capital Markets and Executive for Capital Planning 1984–*

Michael Urkowitz   *Corporate Operations and Systems 1984–*

Paul T. Walker   *Credit Policy Executive 1985–*

Joseph J. Harkins   *Commercial Sector Executive 1985–*

L. Edward Shaw, Jr.   *General Counsel and Legal 1985–*

Notes

Statistics concerning the totals and various categories of assets, liabilities, income, and expense are taken from annual reports of The Chase National Bank, Chase Manhattan Bank, and Chase Manhattan Corporation for the relevant periods, unless otherwise indicated. Annual reports for 1923 and subsequent years, as well as statements of condition (assets and liabilities) for 1877 to 1923 are available in the archives of The Chase Manhattan Bank, New York. The archives also include annual reports of the Bank of The Manhattan Company for 1930 and 1933 to 1954 (after which Chase was combined with Manhattan), as well as statements of condition for Manhattan for many earlier years dating to its founding in 1799. The notes that follow list sources of information and in some instances add details to the main text.

Chapter I

1. Facts concerning the early history of The Chase National Bank are taken from documents in the archives of The Chase Manhattan Bank, chiefly Alice Timony, "A History of The Chase National Bank," 1932, and "The Chase National Bank of the City of New York 1877–1922," author unknown, a pamphlet published by the bank in 1923. Statements of condition for early years have also been utilized. The Chase Manhattan Bank devoted its March 1982 issue of *Chase News* to a brief "History of Chase, 1877–1982." This document also sets forth the early background of the Bank of The Manhattan Company, presented here in Chapter IV.
2. Statement by A. Barton Hepburn, in "The Chase National Bank of the City of New York." Cannon was president from 1887 to 1904 and chairman from 1904 to 1911.
3. Hepburn served as president from 1904 to 1911, chairman from 1911 through 1917, and chairman of the advisory committee from 1918 to his death in early 1922. He had been designated superintendent of banking of New York State in 1880 and was appointed comptroller of the currency in 1892. Hepburn also was the author of *History of Currency and Coinage in the United States* (1903), a standard text with revised editions published in 1915 and 1924 by the Macmillan Company, New York.
4. Arthur M. Johnson, *Winthrop W. Aldrich—Lawyer, Banker, Diplomat* (Boston: Division of Research, Harvard Business School, 1968), pp. 113–114.
5. William J. Shultz and M. R. Caine, *Financial Development of the United States* (New York: Prentice-Hall, 1937), pp. 501–510.
6. Ibid. See also p. 562.
7. W. Nelson Peach, *The Security Affiliates of National Banks* (Baltimore: Johns Hopkins Press, 1941), chap. 3.
8. Timony, "A History of The Chase National Bank."
9. Vincent P. Carosso, *Investment Banking in America* (Cambridge, Mass.: Harvard University Press, 1970), p. 240.
10. Timony, "A History of The Chase National Bank." See also *Chase National Bank, Annual Report, 1927.* (Annual reports are hereafter cited as *Chase Annual Report* with year of publication.)
11. The five banks, with date of merger and total assets, were the Metropolitan Bank, 1921, $57 million; Mechanics and Metals National Bank, 1925, $388 million; the

Mutual Bank, 1927, $18 million; Garfield National Bank, 1928, $21 million; and National Park Bank of New York, 1929, $266 million.

12. Timony, "History of The Chase National Bank." See also *Chase Annual Report*, 1923.

13. Senate Committee on Banking, Housing, and Urban Affairs, *Compendium of Issues Relating to Branching by Financial Institutions*, 94th Cong. (Washington, D.C.: Government Printing Office, 1976). See also Harold Van B. Cleveland and Thomas F. Huertas, *Citibank: 1812–1970* (Cambridge, Mass.: Harvard University Press, 1985), pp. 115–117.

14. *Chase Annual Report*, 1926.

15. Johnson, *Winthrop W. Aldrich*, p. 101.

16. See *Chase Annual Report*, 1923 and 1924.

17. *Chase Annual Report*, 1925.

18. Carosso, *Investment Banking in America*, p. 243. See also Shultz and Caine, *Financial Development of the United States*, p. 573.

19. Shultz and Caine, *Financial Development of the United States*, p. 596.

20. Ibid.

21. *Chase Annual Report*, 1927.

22. *Chase Annual Report*, 1929.

23. *Chase Annual Report*, 1930. See also Peach, *Security Affiliates*, pp. 95–97, for a description of the activities and growth of Chase Securities Corporation.

24. *Chase Annual Report*, 1933. See also Peach, *Security Affiliates*, pp. 164-166, and Johnson, *Winthrop W. Aldrich*, pp. 157–159.

25. Hearings before the Committee on Banking and Currency, 73rd Cong. *Stock Exchange Practices*, pt. 5, October 17–December 7, 1933.

26. Johnson, *Winthrop W. Aldrich*, p. 122. For distribution of American Express to Chase stockholders, see *Chase Annual Report*, 1934. See also, Johnson, pp. 159–160.

27. *Chase Annual Report*, 1930. The Chase-Equitable merger was accompanied by a merger into Chase of Interstate Trust Company, a much smaller institution with resources of approximately $60 million.

28. Johnson, *Winthrop W. Aldrich*, pp. 91–93.

29. Milton Friedman and Anna Jacobson Schwartz, *A Monetary History of the United States: 1867–1960* (Princeton, N.J.: Princeton University Press, 1963), pp. 328–330. See also Elvira and Vladimir Clain-Stefanelli, *Two Centuries of American Banking* (Washington, D.C.: Acropolis Books, 1975), p. 133.

30. George Champion, chairman (retired), interview with Linda Edgerly, July 7 and 12, 1978, Chase Archives.

31. See Thomas F. Huertas, "The Regulation of Financial Institutions," in *Financial Services: The Changing Institutions and Government Policy* (Englewood Cliffs, N.J.: Prentice-Hall, 1983). Also Cleveland and Huertas, *Citibank: 1812–1970*, pp. 193–197.

32. Johnson, *Winthrop W. Aldrich*, pp. 149–157.

33. Hearings before the Banking and Currency Committee, 73rd Cong. For a concise summary, see Johnson, *Winthrop W. Aldrich*, pp. 167–175. See also John Kenneth Galbraith, *The Great Crash: 1929* (Boston: Houghton Mifflin, 1961), pp. 152–155.

34. Johnson, *Winthrop W. Aldrich*, pp. 174, 220. See also *Chase Annual Report*, 1937.

35. *Chase Annual Report*, 1930–1934. See material on reduction in capital funds and reserves and statement concerning write-offs in *Reports*, 1933 and 1934.

36. *Chase Annual Report, 1938*. See also Percy J. Ebbott, former president, interview, February 18, 1960, in Crawford Wheeler, "The Chase Manhattan Story," February 1963, a series of oral history interviews with leading Chase officers of the period 1930–1955, pp. 195–196, Chase Archives.

37. Richard C. Aspinwall, vice president, economics, "Background of the Prime Rate," internal memorandum, May 13, 1981, Chase Archives. See also Friedman and Schwartz, *A Monetary History of the United States*, p. 496.

38. *Chase Annual Report, 1945*.

39. *Chase Annual Report, 1945* and *1946*.

40. *Chase Annual Report, 1945*.

41. *Chase Annual Report, 1941* and *1945*.

42. Call reports of the comptroller of the currency, December 1945, The Chase National Bank and National City Bank of New York.

43. Federal Reserve Bank of New York, *Annual Report, 1945*.

44. *New York Times*, September 26, 1944.

45. *Chase Annual Report, 1946*.

46. See Johnson, *Winthrop W. Aldrich*, chaps. 10 and 11, for detailed information on Aldrich's wartime public service.

47. Ibid., p. 349.

48. Chase National Bank, press release, April 24, 1946, Chase Archives.

49. Rockefeller Family Archives, Pocantico Hills, New York. Rockefeller had held 12 percent of the shares of the Equitable Trust Company. This holding was reduced to 4 percent of The Chase National Bank through the merger of Equitable Trust into Chase in 1930.

50. The organization of the board of directors of The Chase National Bank and later of The Chase Manhattan Bank has been taken from minutes of the board meetings for the relevant periods.

51. Chase National Bank, Manufacturers Trust, First National City Bank of New York, and Bank of America, *Annual Reports, 1945*.

52. Interview with Percy Ebbott, in Wheeler, "The Chase Manhattan Story," pp. 193–194.

53. Johnson, *Winthrop W. Aldrich*, p. 128.

54. Ibid., p. 218.

55. *Chase Annual Report, 1934*.

56. *Chase Annual Report, 1945* and *1946*.

57. James A. Jacobson, senior vice president, international (retired), interview with J. D. Wilson, December 28, 1981.

58. Chase National Bank, press release, February 8, 1945, Chase Archives.

59. David Rockefeller, interview with J. D. Wilson, July 15, 1981.

60. *Chase Annual Report, 1945* and *1946*.

61. *Chase Annual Report, 1947*.

62. George Champion, interview with J. D. Wilson, December 5, 1983.

63. David Rockefeller, interview with Linda Edgerly, October 1980, Chase Archives.

64. Ibid.

65. Victor E. Rockhill, president, Chase International Investment Corporation (retired), interview with J. D. Wilson, September 22, 1981.

66. David Rockefeller, interview.

67. Victor Rockhill, interview.

Chapter II

1. Statistical and other material for the economic background of these and subsequent years has been taken largely from annual reports of the President's Council of Economic Advisors and annual reports of the Federal Reserve Bank of New York. In addition, I have drawn on my own knowledge of economic developments gained as a practicing business economist throughout the years following World War II.
2. Chase National Bank, *Annual Report*, 1945 and 1948.
3. David Rockefeller, interview with J. D. Wilson, July 15, 1981.
4. Total loans to business by major New York City banks (reserve city member banks) are taken from Board of Governors of the Federal Reserve System, *Banking and Monetary Statistics, 1941–1970* (Washington, D.C., 1976), pp. 78–79.
5. *New York Times*, May 2, 1946; *Chase Annual Report*, 1946.
6. Percy Ebbott, interview, February 18, 1960, in Crawford Wheeler, "The Chase Manhattan Story," February 1963, Chase Archives.
7. Chase National Bank, press release, October 22, 1947, Chase Archives.
8. Federal Reserve Bank of New York, *Annual Report*, 1945.
9. *New York Times*, July 1, 1946.
10. *New York Times*, April 19, 1947, and June 6, 1947.
11. President's Council of Economic Advisors, *Annual Report*, 1948.
12. Federal Reserve Bank of New York, *Annual Report*, 1948.
13. *Chase Annual Report*, 1946.
14. Chase National Bank, press releases, November 12, 1947, for Tokyo, and December 12, 1947, for Frankfort on the Main, Chase Archives.
15. *Chase Annual Report*, 1952. The first of these Japanese military facilities was opened at Yokosuka Naval Base, twenty miles south of Yokohama, on July 5, 1951. Others soon followed.
16. Arthur M. Johnson, *Winthrop W. Aldrich—Lawyer, Banker, Diplomat* (Boston: Division of Research, Harvard Business School, 1968), pp. 322–326.
17. Ibid., p. 324.
18. Ibid., pp. 357–358.
19. *Chase Annual Report*, 1949.
20. Federal Reserve Bank of New York, *Annual Report*, 1949.
21. Johnson, *Winthrop W. Aldrich*, p. 358.
22. *New York Times*, January 12, 1950, and January 16, 1950. Later the credit to Spain was increased to $62.5 million; see Johnson, *Winthrop W. Aldrich*, p. 358.
23. Chase National Bank, press release, April 21, 1950, Chase Archives.
24. Chase National Bank, press release, January 5, 1951, Chase Archives.
25. This incident, known as the Anton Smit affair, is described in detail in Johnson, *Winthrop W. Aldrich*, pp. 273–278.
26. *Chase Annual Report*, 1949. The appointments of Ebbott as president, McCain as vice chairman, Schmidlapp as vice chairman of the executive committee, and Black and Champion as senior vice presidents were made on January 26, 1949.
27. Interview with Percy Ebbott, in Wheeler, "The Chase Manhattan Story," pp. 194–197.
28. Federal Reserve Bank of New York, *Annual Report*, 1949.
29. Federal Reserve Bank of New York, *Annual Report*, 1951.
30. *Chase Annual Report*, 1951.

31. Ibid.
32. Ibid. See also interview with Edward L. Love, October 15, 1959, in Wheeler, "The Chase Manhattan Story," p. 303.
33. Bank of America, *Annual Report, 1945* and *1952.*
34. *Chase Annual Report, 1950* and *1951.*
35. *New York Times,* August 18, 1950.
36. Chase National Bank, press release, December 31, 1951; *New York Times,* March 22, 1952.
37. *New York Times,* April 22, 1948.
38. *Chase Annual Report, 1950,* and press release, November 20, 1950, Chase Archives.
39. *Chase Annual Report, 1952; New York Times,* July 19, 1951, and August 1, 1951.
40. David Rockefeller, interview.
41. Rockefeller Family Archives, Pocantico Hills, New York.
42. Johnson, *Winthrop W. Aldrich,* pp. 361–362.
43. Chase National Bank, board of directors, April 13, 1949.
44. David Rockefeller, interview.
45. *Chase Annual Report, 1949.*

Chapter III

1. *Chase Annual Report, 1950.*
2. National City Bank of New York and Manufacturers Trust, *Annual Report, 1950.* For total deposits of major New York City banks, see Board of Governors of the Federal Reserve System, *Banking and Monetary Statistics, 1941–1970* (Washington, D.C., 1976).
3. Percy J. Ebbott to P. G. Dobson, November 28, 1951, in Arthur M. Johnson, *Winthrop W. Aldrich—Lawyer, Banker, Diplomat* (Boston: Division of Research, Harvard Business School, 1968), p. 365.
4. George Champion, interview with Linda Edgerly, July 7, 1978, and July 12, 1978, p. 26, Chase Archives.
5. *New York Times,* July 9, 1948.
6. Chase Manhattan Bank, board of directors, September 30, 1950.
7. Interview with Winthrop W. Aldrich, in Crawford Wheeler, "The Chase Manhattan Story," February 1963, pp. 89–91, Chase Archives.
8. Ibid.
9. Ibid., p. 92.
10. Ibid., pp. 93–98. See also *New York Times,* August 24, 1951.
11. *New York Times,* January 30, 1952.
12. Sidney Homer and Richard I. Johannesen, *The Price of Money, 1946 to 1969* (New Brunswick, N.J.: Rutgers University Press, 1969), pp. 147–154.
13. *New York Times,* December 18, 1951.
14. Federal Reserve Bank of New York, *Annual Report, 1951.*
15. *Chase Annual Report, 1951.*
16. Victor E. Rockhill, president, Chase International Investment Corporation (retired), interview with Linda Edgerly, September 13 and October 5, 1979, pp. 27, 32, Chase Archives.
17. *Chase Annual Report, 1952.* The pension and profit-sharing plans are described on pp. 21–24.

18. Chase National Bank, press release, December 31, 1952, Chase Archives.
19. *New York Times*, September 25, 1952.
20. Percy J. Ebbott, president, memorandum to staff, February 23, 1950, Chase Archives.
21. George Champion, interview, pp. 8–16.
22. Johnson, *Winthrop W. Aldrich*, pp. 368, 372–378.
23. Ibid.
24. John J. McCloy, interview, August 20, 1962, in Wheeler, "The Chase Manhattan Story," pp. 314-315.
25. Federal Reserve Bank of New York, *Annual Reports, 1953* and *1954*, present details on monetary policy and banking developments in those years.
26. *New York Times*, April 28, 1953, and March 18, 1954.
27. *Chase Annual Report, 1954*; *New York Times*, August 5, 1954.
28. Federal Reserve Bank of New York, *Annual Report, 1954*.
29. *Chase Annual Report, 1954*.
30. *New York Times*, February 19, 1954.
31. Chase National Bank, *Statement of Economic Benefits of the Merger of The Chase National Bank and the Bank of The Manhattan Company, 1955*, March 14, 1955, schedules A and D, Chase Archives.
32. Ibid.

Chapter IV

1. *New York Times*, January 14, 1955, lists postwar mergers of New York City banks prior to 1955.
2. *New York Times*, October 16, 1954.
3. John J. McCloy, chairman (retired), interview, August 20, 1962, in Crawford Wheeler, "The Chase Manhattan Story," February 1963, pp. 315–317, Chase Archives.
4. For the information in this section see *The Manhattan Company, Past and Present*, 1931. A Historical Sketch of the Bank of The Manhattan Company, 1943. *Background for Tomorrow—a Historical Sketch of the Bank of The Manhattan Company*, undated, pamphlets issued by The Bank of Manhattan and available in the Chase Archives. Also interview with J. Stewart Baker, former chairman of The Bank of Manhattan, in Wheeler, "The Chase Manhattan Story," pp. 126–151. In addition The Bank of Manhattan published *Manna-Hatin: The Story of New York, 1609–1930* (New York: Brearly Service Organization, 1929). A chronology, pp. 219–270, includes highlights on the history of The Bank of Manhattan. Chase Archives.
5. Figures for early deposits of The Bank of Manhattan are from statements of condition, Chase Archives.
6. J. Stewart Baker, president (retired), interview, October 5, 1960, in Wheeler, "The Chase Manhattan Story," pp. 138–142. Details concerning the development of Manhattan's branch system are taken from this source.
7. George Champion, interview with Linda Edgerly, July 7, 1978, p. 27, Chase Archives.
8. Ibid., p. 28.
9. Wheeler, "The Chase Manhattan Story," pp. 318–319.
10. Ibid., p. 319.

11. Proxy statement to shareholders of The Chase National Bank, February 17, 1955, in papers relating to the Chase Manhattan merger, p. 58, Chase Archives.
12. The pro-forma statement of Chase and Manhattan combined at the end of 1954 shows capital funds of $494.5 million. Upward adjustments in the value of certain assets were primarily responsible for an increase in capital funds at the time of merger to $514.6 million.
13. John J. McCloy, interview, in Wheeler, "The Chase Manhattan Story," pp. 321–322.
14. Ibid.
15. David Rockefeller, interview with Linda Edgerly, October 1980, p. 42, Chase Archives.
16. Wheeler, "The Chase Manhattan Story," p. 326.
17. New York Times, January 1, 1955.
18. New York Times, August 5, 1954, and October 31, 1954; National City Bank of New York, Annual Report, 1954.
19. New York Times, March 31, 1955.
20. M. A. Schapiro and Company, "Analysis of the Proposed Plan of Merger: The Chase National Bank and the Bank of The Manhattan Company," February 23, 1955, p. 16, Chase Archives.
21. Ibid., p. 14.
22. Bank of The Manhattan Company, press release, March 21, 1955, Chase Archives.
23. New York Times, January 4, 1955.
24. John J. McCloy, statement, Chase National Bank, annual meeting, January 25, 1955, Chase Archives. See also New York Times, January 26, 1955.
25. Chase National Bank, "A Statement of the Economic Benefits of the Merger of The Chase National Bank of the City of New York into President and Directors of the Manhattan Company (Bank of The Manhattan Company)," March 14, 1955, Chase Archives.
26. Section 10 of the New York state banking law.
27. "Legal Authorities for Bank Mergers," pamphlet, Journal of Commerce, New York City, 1955, Chase Archives.
28. "Papers Relating to The Chase Manhattan Merger, Effective March 31, 1955," pp. 63, 701, Chase Archives.
29. Ibid., p. 541.
30. New York Times, July 6, 1955.
31. "Papers Relating to the Chase Manhattan Merger," p. 637.
32. Chase National Bank, board of directors, March 23, 1955.
33. Letter from J. Stewart Baker, Chairman, Bank of The Manhattan Co., and John J. McCloy, Chairman of The Chase National Bank, to the Honorable George A. Mooney, Superintendent of Banks, New York State, March 23, 1955, Chase Archives.
34. Roy C. Haberkern, Jr., Partner, Milbank, Tweed, Hadley and McCloy, interview with J. D. Wilson, September 28, 1981.
35. "Papers Relating to The Chase Manhattan Merger," pp. 853–909.
36. New York Times, January 13, 1955.
37. Bank Holding Company Act of 1956, sec. 3(c)(5).

Chapter V

1. David Rockefeller, interview with Linda Edgerly, October 1980. John J. McCloy and Percy J. Ebbott, memorandum to staff, March 21, 1955, Chase Archives.

2. "Report on Management Structure and Organization" (Bower report), 1955, section on bank objectives, Chase Archives.

3. Ibid. The Bower report included recommendations in separate sections for each major organizational unit of the bank.

4. *Chase Annual Report, 1957.*

5. Bower report, section on international department.

6. David Rockefeller, interview.

7. Chase Manhattan Bank, "Commercial and Industrial Loans Outstanding, by Industry and Term," internal statistical memorandum, December 28, 1960.

8. James H. Harris, senior vice president, credit risk management, interview with J. D. Wilson, December 23, 1981, and January 18, 1982.

9. New York City Clearing House, "Report of Committee of New York City Clearing House on Causes of Persistent Erosion of Deposits from New York City," September 25, 1959.

10. *New York Times,* December 6, 1956.

11. *New York Times,* June 4, 1957.

12. *New York Times,* August 1, 1959.

13. *Chase Annual Report, 1959.*

14. Chase internal accounting records, 1960.

15. *Chase Annual Report, 1959.* The market for federal funds grew rapidly as interest rates rose and banks, including Chase, reduced excess balances with correspondents.

16. *Chase Annual Report, 1958.*

17. Chase Manhattan Bank, press release, November 14, 1956, Chase Archives. See also *Chase Annual Report, 1956.*

18. Percy J. Ebbott, memorandum to staff, January 22, 1954, Chase Archives.

19. *New York Times,* May 4, 1956.

20. Information on Chase contributions in various years is taken from minutes of the board of directors meetings for the relevant periods.

21. Chase Manhattan Bank, "A Program for Aid to Education," copy for brochure, November 5, 1958, Chase Archives.

22. Chase Manhattan Bank, board of directors, August 1, 1956 and December 12, 1956. Ebbott resigned as vice chairman on August 1, 1956, and as a director on December 12, 1956.

23. *Chase Annual Report, 1956.*

24. Ibid.

25. Chase Manhattan Corporation, board of directors, January 22, 1958. Baker resigned as chairman of the executive committee on December 26, 1957.

Chapter VI

1. Chase Manhattan Bank, press release, May 14, 1957, Chase Archives.

2. *New York Times,* November 15, 1958.

3. *New York Times,* July 12, 1957.

4. *New York Times,* January 30, 1957.

5. John J. McCloy, statement before Joint Legislative Committee on Banking, Albany, N.Y., March 13, 1957. See also David Rockefeller, statement before Joint Legislative Committee, February 18, 1958, Chase Archives.

6. *New York Times,* September 10, 1959.

7. *New York Times,* September 11, 1959.

8. *New York Times,* March 24, 1960.

9. *New York Times*, May 13, 1960. In 1984 The Chase Manhattan Corporation acquired Lincoln First Banks of Rochester, N.Y. This bank holding company earlier had acquired the National Bank of Westchester, which then became the NBW division of Chase.

10. *New York Times*, March 22, 1960, and March 23, 1960. Later Arthur Roth, chairman of Franklin National, filed suit against the state and against Chase and Chemical Bank to have the law declared unconstitutional because of Governor Rockefeller's "direct or indirect interest in various banking institutions" (*New York Times*, July 6, 1960). The law was declared invalid, but only because the court found that the legislature had violated statutory procedures: it acted in such haste that the bill had not been on the desk of members in proper form or adequate time. The act was immediately reenacted properly.

11. *New York Times*, May 15, 1960.

12. *Business Week*, October 25, 1958. *Chase Annual Report, 1958.*

13. *Chase Annual Report, 1958.*

14. Chase Manhattan Bank, press release, February 11, 1960, Chase Archives.

15. George A. Roeder, Jr., vice chairman, interview with J. D. Wilson, December 21, 1981.

16. *New York Times*, January 31, 1962.

17. Details concerning the repurchase of Uni-Serve are set forth in Chapter X.

18. *New York Times*, May 22, 1955. The banks were Chemical in New York, First National Bank of Boston, Mellon National Bank in Pittsburgh, and the National Bank of Detroit.

19. *New York Times*, May 27, 1957.

20. Norbert A. Bogdan, interview with J. D. Wilson, December 18, 21, 1981.

21. Ibid.

22. *New York Times*, May 27, 1957.

23. Victor E. Rockhill, president, Chase International Investment Corporation (retired), interview with Linda Edgerly, September 13 and October 5, 1979, pp. 17–19, Chase Archives.

24. Ibid., pp. 43–44.

25. *Chase Annual Report, 1957.*

26. Victor Rockhill, interview, pp. 47–49.

27. *New York Times*, January 23, 1958.

28. Victor Rockhill, interview, pp. 43–44.

29. Ibid., pp. 72–75.

30. Ibid., pp. 48–50.

31. Ibid., pp. 97–98.

32. Chase Manhattan Bank, "Report on Foreign Branches and International Representation," 1957, Chase Archives.

33. *Chase Annual Report, 1958.*

34. John J. McCloy, interview, August 20, 1962, in Crawford Wheeler, "The Chase Manhattan Story," February 1963, p. 344. James A. Jacobson, interview with J. D. Wilson, December 28, 1981, Chase Archives.

35. *New York Times*, July 17, 1959, and September 16, 1959.

36. *New York Times*, September 17, 1960, and September 18, 1960.

37. *New York Times*, November 30, 1960.

38. Michael P. Esposito, controller, to William S. Ogden, chief financial officer, memorandum, January 7, 1980, Chase Archives.

Chapter VII

1. Chase Manhattan Bank, board of directors, September 9, 1953.
2. John J. McCloy, interview, August 20, 1962, in Crawford Wheeler, "The Chase Manhattan Story," February 1963, pp. 328–329, Chase Archives.
3. Ibid., p. 327. See also David Rockefeller, interview with Linda Edgerly, October 1980, Chase Archives.
4. Wheeler, "Chase Manhattan Story," pp. 327–328.
5. David Rockefeller, interview. See also press release, February 23, 1955, Chase Archives.
6. David Rockefeller, interview. See also Wheeler, "Chase Manhattan Story," p. 331.
7. David Rockefeller, interview.
8. Chase Manhattan Bank, board of directors, June 15, 1955. Also *New York Times*, April 13, 1956.
9. Chase Manhattan Bank, board of directors, December 7, 1955. *New York Times*, December 8, 1955.
10. Chase Manhattan Bank, press release, March 29, 1956, Chase Archives. See also *New York Times*, March 29, 1956, and March 30, 1956. *Chase Annual Report, 1955*.
11. Chase Manhattan Bank, press release, March 29, 1956.
12. Chase Manhattan Bank, board of directors, September 26, 1956.
13. Paul E. Steinborn, vice president, construction and property management, Chase Manhattan Bank, interview with J. D. Wilson, January 21, 1982.
14. Chase Manhattan Bank, press release, January 31, 1957, Chase Archives.
15. Walter Severinghaus, project architect, Skidmore, Owings and Merrill, interview with J. D. Wilson, January 5, 1982. See also *New York Times*, June 9, 1957.
16. *New York Times*, September 10, 1959.
17. Wheeler, "Chase Manhattan Story," pp. 334–337.
18. *New York Times*, May 8, 1960.
19. Chase Manhattan Bank, press release, October 24, 1957, Chase Archives.
20. *Chase Annual Report, 1961*.
21. Ibid.
22. Wheeler, "Chase Manhattan Story," p. 335.
23. David Rockefeller, interview.
24. Chase Manhattan Bank, press release opening exhibition in Buffalo, N.Y., September 15, 1960, Chase Archives. Also Merrie S. Good, second vice president, manager, Chase art program, interview with J. D. Wilson.
25. *Chase Annual Report, 1984*.
26. *New York Times*, November 18, 1960. See also "Background Information on New Symbol," staff memorandum, September 1960, Chase Archives.
27. *New York Times*, May 7, 1964.
28. *New York Times*, September 22, 1972. See also David Rockefeller, interview.

Chapter VIII

1. Chase Manhattan Bank, board of directors, April 22, 1959.
2. Chase Manhattan Bank, board of directors, December 30, 1959.
3. *New York Times*, October 21, 1960.
4. David Rockefeller, interview with Linda Edgerly, October 1980; George Champion, interview with Linda Edgerly, July 7, 12, 1978, Chase Archives.

5. McCloy was appointed by President Kennedy as his adviser on disarmament activities from 1961 to 1963. He played a critical role in helping to resolve the Cuban missile crisis, negotiating directly with Soviet representatives. Then President Johnson named him a public member of the Warren Commission to investigate the assassination of President Kennedy.

6. The Chase Manhattan Bank, Board of Directors, December 28, 1966.

7. *New York Times*, February 20, 1961.

8. See Richard Fieldhouse, *Certificates of Deposit* (Boston: Bankers Publishing Co., 1962). See also "Certificates of Deposit," *The Federal Reserve Bank of New York Monthly Review* (June 1963), p. 82.

9. "Outlook for Chase Loans and Deposits," presentation to directors, June 1967, Chase Archives. Chase held an advantage over most banks in issuing negotiable CDs because of its wide base of corporate customers. Chase paper also carried a prime rating in the secondary market.

10. *Federal Reserve Bank of New York Monthly Review* (June 1963), p. 82.

11. See E. Wayne Clendenning, *The Eurodollar Market* (Oxford: Oxford University Press, 1970), for the historical beginnings. See also *The Eurodollar*, ed. Herbert V. Prochnow (Chicago: Rand McNally, 1970), especially chap. III, "Size, Scope, and Participants," by Frank E. Morris and Jane S. Little.

12. Bank for International Settlements, Basel, Switzerland, *Thirty-sixth Annual Report, April 1965 to March 1966*, p. 139, and *Forty-second Annual Report, April 1971 to March 1972*, p. 151.

13. Alfred W. Barth, executive vice president, international (retired), interview with J. D. Wilson, March 27, 1982.

14. Chase Manhattan Bank, weekly report to the Federal Reserve on commercial and industrial loans, January 2, 1963.

15. *Chase Annual Report, 1961*.

16. "Growth and Progress in the Mid-Sixties: Developments in Lending," presentation to directors, May 18, 1966, Chase Archives.

17. Chase Manhattan Bank, weekly report to the Federal Reserve on commercial and industrial loans, January 2, 1963.

18. *Chase Annual Report, 1964*. Also *New York Times*, August 29, 1965, section 3, p. 3, profile on Jonathan Tobey, agricultural technical director. The new group was inaugurated in 1964 by George E. Kruger, a specialist in mining.

19. Chase Manhattan Bank, press release, November 11, 1963, Chase Archives; also *Chase Annual Report, 1963*.

20. Samuel Pizer and Frederick Cutler, "Foreign Investments, 1964–65," Survey of current business, U.S. Department of Commerce (Washington, D.C., September 1965), p. 22.

21. Chase Manhattan Bank, internal accounting records.

22. *New York Times*, July 19, 1963. Less developed countries were excluded from the interest equalization tax. So too were Canada and Japan on the basis of special arrangements with those countries. The tax was not adopted until later, but was retroactive to the date of proposal.

23. *New York Times*, February 11, 1965. Banks were asked to accord priorities in foreign lending to less developed countries and to Canada and Japan.

24. Chase Manhattan Bank, presentation to the directors, May 18, 1966, Chase Archives.

25. *New York Times*, August 3, 1962.

26. *Chase Annual Report, 1964.*
27. Chase Manhattan Bank, internal accounting records.
28. Sidney Homer and Richard Johannesen, *The Price of Money, 1946 to 1969* (New Brunswick, N.J.: Rutgers University Press, 1969), pp. 150–153.
29. Robert K. Schell, "Developments in Commercial and Industrial Lending," presentation to directors, May 18, 1966, Chase Archives. See also *Chase Annual Report, 1966.*
30. *Chase Annual Report, 1966.*
31. Paul A. Volcker, "Outlook for Chase Loans and Deposits," presentation to directors, June 14, 1967, Chase Archives.
32. Federal Reserve Bank of New York, *Annual Report, 1966.*
33. *New York Times,* January 27, 1967, and November 22, 1967.
34. *New York Times,* January 2, 1968.
35. *New York Times,* June 10, 1969.
36. *Chase Annual Report, 1969.*
37. *Chase Annual Report, 1969.*
38. *New York Times,* June 24, 1969.
39. First National City Bank and Bank of America, *Annual Reports, 1965* and *1969.*
40. *New York Times,* June 10, 1965. See also George Champion, presentation to directors, May 19, 1965, Chase Archives.
41. *New York Times,* August 22, 1964.
42. *New York Times,* March 17, 1965.

Chapter IX

1. Lawrence C. Marshall, vice chairman, testimony before Joint Legislative Committee on Banking, Albany, N.Y., January 30, 1963, Chase Archives.
2. M. A. Schapiro and Company, *Bank Stock Quarterly,* June 1962, p. 10, Chase Archives.
3. *New York Times,* June 29, 1961.
4. *New York Times,* May 26, 1961.
5. *New York Times,* February 9, 1961.
6. See decision of the state superintendent of banks, October 4, 1961, Chase Manhattan Bank, "Papers Relating to the Merger with Hempstead Bank," Chase Archives.
7. Chase Manhattan Bank, "Papers Relating to the Merger with Hempstead Bank."
8. David Rockefeller, statement on Chase Manhattan-Hempstead Bank merger, before the Federal Reserve Board, Washington, D.C., January 19, 1962, Chase Archives. See also *New York Times,* January 20, 1962.
9. *New York Times,* January 31, 1962.
10. Chase Manhattan Bank, "Papers Relating to the Merger with Hempstead Bank."
11. Board of Governors, Federal Reserve System, "In the Matter of the Application of The Chase Manhattan Bank for Approval of Merger with Hempstead Bank," April 30, 1962, *Federal Register,* May 4, 1962. See also *New York Times,* May 1, 1962.
12. Ibid.
13. Chase Manhattan Bank, presentation to directors, May 19, 1965, Chase Archives.
14. Chase Manhattan Bank, presentation to directors, June 12, 1968, Chase Archives.
15. Ibid.
16. *New York Times,* January 26, 27, 1961, and May 4, 1962.
17. Chase Manhattan Bank, "Papers Relating to Upstate Holding Company," 1964,

Chase Archives. Also J. D. Wilson, memorandum to Lawrence C. Marshall, September 11, 1963, Chase Archives.

18. Chase Manhattan Bank, press release, July 15, 1964, Chase Archives.
19. "Papers Relating to Upstate Holding Company," see memorandum on plan of reorganization, September 9, 1964.
20. Ibid.
21. Ibid. Letter from secretary, board of governors, Federal Reserve System to Dewey, Ballantine, Bushby, Palmer and Wood, attorneys, February 25, 1965. "Papers Relating to Upstate Holding Company," Chase Archives.
22. *New York Times*, March 30, 1965.
23. Letter from George Champion to directors, March 16, 1965, "Papers Relating to Conversion to a National Charter," Chase Archive.
24. Letter from J. Stewart Baker to directors, April 12, 1965, "Papers Relating to Conversion to a National Charter."
25. Legal opinion from Dewey, Ballentine, Bushby, Palmer and Wood, June 30, 1965, "Papers Relating to Conversion to a National Charter."
26. Letter from Champion to directors, July 2, 1965, "Papers Relating to Conversion to a National Charter."
27. *New York Times*, July 15, 1965.
28. *New York Times*, July 16, 1965.
29. *New York Times*, October 6, 1965.
30. Chase Manhattan Bank, board of directors, October 20, 1965. See also *New York Times*, October 21, 1965.
31. "Papers Relating to Proposed Affiliation with Liberty National Bank, Buffalo," Chase Archives. Letter to George Champion from board of governors, Federal Reserve System, November 3, 1965, Chase Archives.
32. M. A. Schapiro and Company, *Bank Stock Quarterly*, December 1965.
33. Letter from Federal Reserve Board to Department of Justice, January, 1966. File on Papers Relating to Proposed Affiliation with Liberty National Bank, Milbank, Tweed, Hadley and McCloy, New York.
34. *New York Times*, February 17, 1966. See also *The Wall Street Journal*, February 17, 1966.
35. Ibid.
36. *New York Times*, April 8, 1966.
37. *New York Times*, May 5, 1966.
38. In 1984 Chase was permitted by the Federal Reserve Board to acquire the Lincoln First Corporation, headquartered in Rochester, with assets of $4.2 billion and operating 135 offices, including thirty-seven branches in Westchester (the former National Bank of Westchester); see Chapter XXIII.

Chapter X

1. Chase Manhattan Bank, report of committee on traveler's checks, March 17, 1960, Chase Archives.
2. One of the company's subsidiaries, American Express Warehousing, was engaged in the storage of vegetable oils and other commodities. It leased storage tanks from another company, Allied Crude Vegetable Oil Refining Company, and issued warehouse receipts for vegetable oils stored by Allied and other companies. Allied had borrowed from financial institutions with these receipts as collateral. When Allied

filed for bankruptcy, it was revealed that the oil it had supposedly stored, and which backed the warehouse receipts, did not exist. The tanks were empty. Additional warehouse receipts had been forged. All had been lost through unsuccessful speculation in commodity futures by the president of Allied. Huge sums—as much as $80 million—were involved in this salad oil scandal. *New York Times*, November 20, 22, 1963, concerning bankruptcy of Allied Crude Vegetable Oil Refining Company. See also *New York Times*, December 31, 1963, for subsequent bankruptcy of American Express Warehousing Corporation, and September 22, 1964, for American Express Company settlement offer to creditors.

3. Recommendation concerning Chase Traveler's Checks, John D. Wilson, director of corporate planning, August 12, 1965, Chase Archives.

4. Ibid. The growth of Traveler's Check sales from 1965 to 1970 was estimated to be at a rate of 5 percent. Over the next several years sales escalated to a 14 percent rate, but then slowed down somewhat.

5. Charles A. Agemian, executive vice president and controller, memorandum to George Champion, September 1965, Chase Archives.

6. Report on a proposed Chase Traveler's Check, December 1967, Chase Archives.

7. *New York Times*, September 23, 1965.

8. Memorandum, concerning acquisition of Diners Club, Inc., November 17, 1965, Chase Archives.

9. Ibid.

10. Chase Manhattan Bank, press release, November 17, 1965. *New York Times*, November 18, 1965.

11. Roy C. Haberkern, Jr., Milbank, Tweed, Hadley and McCloy, letter to Donald F. Turner, assistant attorney general in charge of the antitrust division, December 29, 1965.

12. *New York Times*, December 31, 1965.

13. *New York Times*, December 31, 1965, and January 1, 1966.

14. John J. McCloy, memorandum on telephone conversations with Donald F. Turner, Assistant Attorney General, concerning Chase's proposed acquisition of Diners Club, April 11, 1966. Files of Milbank, Tweed, Hadley and McCloy.

15. *New York Times*, April 13, 1966.

16. Report of committee exploring *de novo* general purpose credit card, Barry Sullivan, chairman, September 30, 1966, Chase Archives.

17. Memorandum, findings and recommendations concerning local card business, January 16, 1967, Chase Archives.

18. Metropolitan department, recommendation on overdraft banking, September 20, 1966, Chase Archives.

19. Memorandum, findings and recommendations concerning local card business.

20. Arthur E. Peterson, marketing officer, memorandum to Paul G. Tongue, vice president, May 1, 1969, Chase Archives.

21. Memorandum, recent developments in the local credit card field, September 27, 1968, Chase Archives.

22. Ibid.

23. T. W. McMahon, Jr., executive vice president, Metropolitan banking, memorandum to Champion, Rockefeller, and Marshall, negotiations with American Express Company to Purchase Uni-Serv Corporation, November 27, 1968, Chase Archives.

24. Chase Manhattan Bank, press release, December 18, 1968, Chase Archives. See also *New York Times* and *The Wall Street Journal*, December 19, 1968.

25. James H. Harris, senior vice president, credit risk management, interview with J. D. Wilson, February 10, 1982.
26. Paul G. Tongue, memorandum, Chase Manhattan affiliation with BankAmericard, August 19, 1971, Chase Archives.
27. *New York Times*, January 20, 1972.

Chapter XI

1. *Chase Annual Report, 1960* and *1969*.
2. George Champion, interview with Linda Edgerly, July 7 and 12, 1978, Chase Archives. George Champion, speech to Economic Club of Detroit, press release, May 23, 1960, Chase Archives.
3. David Rockefeller, interview with Linda Edgerly, October 1980, Chase Archives.
4. Ibid. Also William S. Ogden, vice chairman, interview with J. D. Wilson, May 22, 1982.
5. Alfred W. Barth, executive vice president, and Roy C. Haberkern, Jr., Milbank, Tweed, Hadley and McCloy, "Report on Banco Hipotecario Lar Brasileiro, S.A.," October 24, 1961, Chase Archives.
6. C. A. Agemian, controller general, memorandum to Champion, Rockefeller, and Marshall, January 29, 1962. Also A. W. Barth, memorandum to Champion and Rockefeller, March 16, 1962, Chase Archives. Banco Lar had included as income "internal interest" which it had charged against construction in process, including that of its own branch offices. It had also taken into income a percentage of the profit realized on property that had been sold but was still under construction. See also C. A. Agemian, memorandum to Champion and Rockefeller, March 14, 1962, Chase Archives.
7. Chase Manhattan Bank, press release, April 30, 1962, Chase Archives.
8. Chase Overseas Banking Corporation (CMOBC), International Subsidiaries and Affiliates of the Chase Manhattan Group, investment summaries, 1984, Banco Lar Brasileiro, international department. These summaries present balance-sheet and income statistics for 1983 and in some cases 1984, and record the development of Chase investment in each foreign subsidiary and affiliate from the bank's initial participation.
9. CMOBC investment summaries, 1984, Banco Lar Brasileiro.
10. A. W. Barth, C. A. Agemian, and R. C. Haberkern, "Report on Banco Mercantile y Agricola," n.d., Chase Archives. Also CMOBC investment summaries, 1980, Banco Mercantile y Agricola, and R. C. Haberkern, Jr., interview with J. D. Wilson, May 12, 1982. Although Chase in effect acquired 51 percent of Banco Mercantile, Barth arranged through Rothschild's in Paris for 2 percent of this to be held through the Swiss Bank Corporation and a Panamanian firm controlled by Rothschild's, thereby ensuring voting control.
11. T. A. Conigliaro, memorandum to Rockefeller and Butcher, January 9, 1980.
12. Chase Manhattan Bank, press release, January 18, 1965, Chase Archives. Also Roy C. Haberkern, Jr., interview.
13. William S. Ogden, affidavit, December 1970, concerning sale by Chase Manhattan Overseas Banking Corporation of 51 percent stock interest in Banco Continental, Lima, Chase Archives.
14. William S. Ogden, interview. Also Chase Manhattan Bank, press release, August 28, 1970, Chase Archives.

15. Chase Manhattan Bank, press release, August 2, 1967, Chase Archives.
16. "Proposal to Acquire a Majority Position in the Banco Argentino de Comercio, Buenos Aires, Argentina," memorandum to Chase Manhattan board of directors, June 19, 1968, Chase Archives.
17. CMOBC investment summaries, 1980, Chase Bank, S.A. Also Kenneth A. Murdoch, vice president, interview with J. D. Wilson, May 12, 26, 1982.
18. Ibid.
19. "Proposal to Acquire Banco Atlantida of Honduras," memorandum, September 15, 1966, Chase Archives. Also Chase Manhattan Bank, press release, December 27, 1966.
20. CMOBC investment summaries, 1980, Inversiones Atlantida, S.A.
21. *Chase Annual Report, 1960, 1962, 1965,* and *1968.*
22. Memorandum, Nationale Handelsbank N.V., James A. Jacobson to Charles Cain, Jr., October 31, 1962, Chase Archives.
23. Memorandum on visit of C.F. Karsten, Rotterdamsche Bank, with C. Cain, Jr., in New York, February 4, 1963.
24. Letter to Nationale Handelsbank, N.V., from C. Cain, Jr., June 5, 1963, Chase Archives. Also letter to David Kennedy, chairman of Continental Illinois National Bank, from C. Cain, Jr., April 26, 1962.
25. *New York Times,* May 10, 1975. Before Saigon fell, Chase flew out a large number of its Vietnamese staff with their families and relocated them in the United States and other countries.
26. C. A. Agemian, memorandum to Champion and Rockefeller, February 16, 1965, Chase Archives.
27. Ibid.
28. *New York Times,* May 29, 1969.
29. Victor E. Rockhill, president, Chase International Investment Corporation (retired), interview with J. D. Wilson, May 24, 1982.
30. *New York Times,* May 14, 1975.
31. Victor E. Rockhill, interview.
32. *New York Times,* March 20, 1965. See also *New York Times,* December 6, 10, 1966. *New York Times,* May 24, 25, 1969, and *New York Times,* February 16, May 8, and May 28, 1968.
33. Chase Manhattan Bank, statement on Chase's policy on South Africa, April 18, 1978, public relations department.

Chapter XII

1. This report on strategy for international representation came to be known as the Fiero-Koons report, September 23, 1963, Chase Archives.
2. David Rockefeller, interview with Linda Edgerly, October 1980, Chase Archives.
3. Ibid.
4. "Proposal for Joint Participation in Banque de Commerce, Belgium, with Banque de Bruxelles of Belgium," report to Chase Manhattan directors, November 24, 1965, Chase Archives.
5. "Agreement in Principle and General Policy Guidelines Concerning a Joint Venture between the The Chase Manhattan Bank and the Banque de Commerce," October 1965, Chase Archives.

6. Francis L. Mason, senior vice president, country risk policy, interview with J. D. Wilson, May 26, 1982.
7. Agreement between The Chase Manhattan Bank, Pierson, Heldring and Pierson, and N.V. Nederlandsche Credietbank, November 21, 1966, Chase Archives.
8. CMOBC investment summaries, 1980, Nederlandsche Credietbank.
9. Tilghman B. Koons, vice president, international, interview with J. D. Wilson, May 24, 1982.
10. *The Wall Street Journal*, December 23, 1983; see Chapter XXIII for details.
11. T. B. Koons, memorandum to Champion and Rockefeller, concerning Privat-und Kommerzbank, A.G., Vienna, Chase Archives.
12. "Proposal to Acquire 75 percent Interest in Privat-und Kommerzbank, Austria," memorandum to directors, February 16, 1966, Chase Archives.
13. CMOBC investment summaries, 1984, Chase Manhattan Bank (Austria), A.G. The bank assumed this name in 1974.
14. Victor E. Rockhill, president, Chase Manhattan Overseas Banking Corporation, Bank of Ireland, memorandum to A. W. Barth, executive vice president, international, May 17, 1965, Chase Archives.
15. "Proposed Chase-Bank of Ireland Joint Venture," memorandum to directors, February 15, 1968, Chase Archives. See also Chase Manhattan Bank, press release, August 12, 1984.
16. CMOBC investment summaries, 1984, Chase Manhattan Bank (Switzerland).
17. Karl Lasseter, vice president, international, interview with J. D. Wilson, June 8, 1982.
18. Ibid. See also investment review of Chase Manhattan Bank (Switzerland), international department, January 1980.
19. Frank E. Salerno, vice president, international, interview with J. D. Wilson, June 28, 1982.
20. CMOBC investment summaries, 1984. This institution, named the International Investment Corporation of Yugoslavia, was started in December 1969. Partners include fifteen Yugoslav banks, the International Finance Corporation, four U.S. banks, and thirty-eight West European banks. Its primary function is to promote direct foreign investment in Yugoslavia through project analysis and development, including finding suitable partners. Its assets of about $10 million are relatively small. Chase has provided leadership, with a former officer, Paul J. Lakers,, as president.
21. Victor E. Rockhill, president, Chase International Investment Corporation (retired), interview with Linda Edgerly, September 13 and October 5, 1979, pp. 55–70, Chase Archives.
22. *New York Times*, April 27, 1965.
23. Chase Manhattan Bank, press release, December 18, 1969, Chase Archives.
24. Chase-NBA, Group, Ltd., investment review, international department, July 1978.
25. David Rockefeller, interview.
26. J. W. Bergford and T. B. Koons, memorandum, "Grand Alliance Task Force, Chase Manhattan, National Westminster, Royal Bank of Canada," July 24, 1969, Chase Archives.
27. Chase Manhattan Corporation, press release, October 29, 1970, Chase Archives.
28. CMOBC investment summaries, 1980, the Orion Group.
29. Foreign branch statistics are taken from international accounting reports for June 30 and December 31, 1969.

30. Barry Sullivan, chairman, First Chicago Corporation, interview with J. D. Wilson, June 19, 1982.
31. John C. Haley, executive vice president, corporate relations, interview with J. D. Wilson, June 14, 1982.
32. Leo S. Martinuzzi, senior vice president, information services, interview with J. D. Wilson, July 20, 1981.
33. Ibid.
34. Chase Manhattan Bank, press release, August 6, 1965, Chase Archives.
35. David Rockefeller, interview.
36. James J. Phelan, vice president, international, interview with J. D. Wilson, June 28, 1982.
37. Chase Manhattan Overseas Banking Corporation, statement of condition, December 31, 1969. See also Chase Manhattan Corporation, *Annual Report, 1969*, on assets and deposits of associated and affiliated banks.
38. Chase Manhattan Overseas Banking Corporation, statement of condition and statement of income and expense, December 31, 1969.
39. Chase Manhattan Bank, internal accounting records.
40. Chase Manhattan Corporation, *Annual Report, 1971*, p. 16. Earnings included Chase's equity percentage in the net income of associated banks in which Chase held a 20 percent or more equity ownership.

Chapter XIII

1. Bank Holding Company Act of 1956, section 2(a).
2. *New York Times*, July 3, 1968.
3. "One-Bank Holding Company," memorandum to directors, December 13, 1968, Chase Archives.
4. *New York Times*, June 14, 1969.
5. *New York Times*, January 9, 1969.
6. *New York Times*, March 26, 1969.
7. Chase Manhattan Bank, press release, September 18, 1968, Chase Archives. See also *New York Times*, September 19, 1968.
8. Chase Manhattan Bank, press release, December 4, 1969, Chase Archives.
9. *New York Times*, September 23, 1969.
10. Chase Manhattan Bank, press release, October 29, 1969, Chase Archives.
11. George A. Roeder, Jr., vice chairman, statement before House Banking Committee, Washington, D.C., May 7, 1969, Chase Archives.
12. *New York Times*, November 6, 1969.
13. *New York Times*, January 30, 1970.
14. *New York Times*, April 2, 1970.
15. Prospectus for offering of securities for Chase Manhattan Mortgage and Realty Trust, June 4, 1970, Chase Archives.
16. Ibid.
17. *New York Times*, May 27, 1970.
18. *New York Times*, January 1, 1971.
19. *New York Times*, May 28, 1971. See also *Federal Reserve Bulletin*, May and July 1971.
20. *New York Times*, October 31, 1968.
21. Chase Manhattan Bank, board of directors, October 27, 1971.

22. Chase Manhattan Bank Foundation, *Annual Report, 1969.*
23. *New York Times,* October 31, 1968.
24. Chase Manhattan Corporation, *Annual Report, 1969.*
25. Ibid.
26. Chase Manhattan Corporation, *Annual Report, 1970.*
27. Chase Manhattan Bank, organizational chart for the international department, 1970, Chase Archives.
28. *Chase Annual Report, 1970.*
29. Six directors of the bank chose not to be directors of the holding company when it was established in order to avoid any possible conflict of interest in the future. They remained directors of the bank, however.
30. "Relations between The Chase Manhattan Corporation and Bank and Their Outside Directors," memorandum May 28, 1969, Chase Archives.
31. Chase Manhattan Bank, board of directors, July 19, 1969.

Chapter XIV

1. *New York Times,* June 22, 1970.
2. Chase Manhattan Corporation, *Annual Report, 1970.*
3. *New York Times,* August 15, 1971. See also Federal Reserve Bank of New York, *Annual Report, 1971.*
4. Ibid.
5. *New York Times,* September 10, 1970.
6. *New York Times,* September 16, 1970.
7. Chase Manhattan Bank, press release, April 23, 1971, Chase Archives.
8. Chase Manhattan Corporation, *Annual Report, 1972.*
9. *New York Times,* December 29, 1972.
10. Willard C. Butcher, chairman, interview with J. D. Wilson, February 18, 1983.
11. *New York Times,* March 24, 1973.
12. *New York Times,* March 26, 1973.
13. *New York Times,* April 17, 1973.
14. The committee on interest and dividends introduced a limit on bank profit margins to justify an increase in the small business loan rate and various other fees and rates. The profit margin was determined as the ratio of net operating income before taxes to gross operating income (both on a fully taxable basis). Banks could not exceed the average of the best two of the previous four years.
15. *New York Times,* April 18, 1973.
16. Federal Reserve Bank of New York, *Annual Report, 1973.*
17. *New York Times,* September 14, 1974.
18. *Chase Annual Report, 1974.*
19. *New York Times,* September 18, 1974.
20. "Policies for Fiduciary Investments," presentation to directors, June 12, 1968, Chase Archives.
21. Ibid.
22. Ibid.
23. Stephen E. Canter, president, Chase Investors Management Corporation, interview with J. D. Wilson, April 11, 1983.
24. *New York Times,* February 7, 1972. See also Chase Manhattan Corporation, *Annual Report, 1972.*

25. *New York Times*, July 29, 1972. Information on Chase's investment policy from 1968 to 1975 is from Stephen E. Canter, interview.
26. Chase Investors Management Corporation, internal accounting records.
27. Federal Reserve Bank of New York, *Annual Report, 1974*.
28. *New York Times*, April 21, 1974.
29. Federal Reserve Bank of New York, *Annual Report, 1974*.
30. *New York Times*, June 27, 1974.
31. *New York Times*, August 14, 1974.
32. *The Wall Street Journal*, February 27, 1975.
33. *New York Times*, May 11, 1974. For other information on the failure of Franklin National Bank see Federal Reserve Bank of New York, *Annual Report, 1974*; J. F. Sinkey, Jr., "Collapse of Franklin National Bank of New York," *Journal of Bank Research*, 7 (Summer 1976), 113–122; *Adequacy of the Office of the Comptroller of the Currency's Supervision of Franklin National Bank*, Report of House Committee on Government Operations (Washington, D.C.: Government Printing Office, 1976), 42, 94–1669; and Joan Edelman Spero, *The Failure of the Franklin National Bank: Challenge to the International Banking System* (New York: Columbia University Press, 1980).
34. *New York Times*, May 13, 1974.
35. Ibid.
36. *New York Times*, June 12, 1974.
37. *New York Times*, October 9, 1974.
38. *New York Times*, October 3, 1974.
39. Roy C. Haberkern, Jr., Milbank, Tweed, Hadley and McCloy, interview with J. D. Wilson, September 13, 1982.
40. Ibid.
41. *Fortune Magazine*, November 1974.
42. A. Wright Elliott, executive vice president, corporate communications, interview with J. D. Wilson, January 26, 1983.
43. Chase Manhattan Bank, press release, October 2, 1974, Chase Archives.
44. Roy C. Haberkern, Jr., interview.
45. *New York Times*, June 4, 1972.
46. *New York Times*, January 13, 1972.
47. David Rockefeller, interview with Linda Edgerly, October 1980, Chase Archives.
48. *New York Times*, October 13, 1972.
49. Willard C. Butcher, interview.
50. Chase Manhattan Corporation, press release, December 19, 1974, Chase Archives.

Chapter XV

1. Chase Manhattan Bank, "The Long Range Plan: 1971," Chase Archives.
2. Ibid.
3. Ibid.
4. *New York Times*, June 5, 1971. Holding companies acquiring a bank in another banking district could add no new branches in the first year and only two annually until 1976, restricting the pace of expansion.
5. *New York Times*, April 29, 1971. Prior to establishing its affiliate in Melville, Long Island, Chase attempted to charter a new bank in Garden City, the head office location of Long Island Trust Company. A provision in the new banking laws,

however, prohibited bank holding companies from chartering new banks in towns covered by "home office protection." Melville was an alternate choice.

6. In Syracuse the Bank of Central New York opened in December 1972. The Bank of Greater Rochester, based on the acquisition of the Bank of Caledonia, also opened in December 1972. The Bank of Mid-Hudson, in Saugerties, resulted from the acquisition of the Saugerties National Bank and Trust Company in 1973. In Buffalo the Bank of Western New York followed from the acquisition of the Lincoln National Bank in July 1973. The newly chartered Bank of Eastern New York opened in Albany in October 1973, and the Bank of Northern New York, based on the acquisition of the First National Bank of Canton, opened in that town in March 1974. The final subsidiary, the Bank of the Southern Tier, newly chartered, began in December 1974. A press release on each of these banks is available in the Chase Archives.

7. Dennis C. Longwell, former president of The Chase Manhattan Bank of Central New York, interview with J. D. Wilson, September 29, 1982.

8. The Chase Manhattan Bank directory, November 1975, Chase Archives. Branch statistics for other New York City banks are taken from Moody's *Bank of Finance Manual*, Moody's Investors Service, Inc., New York, 1976.

9. Dial Financial Corporation, *Annual Report*, 1972, Chase Archives.

10. *New York Times*, June 21, 1973. See also *New York Times*, March 13, 1973, for terms of transactions. The planning, negotiations, and dealings with regulatory authorities for Dial were headed by Leo S. Martinuzzi, Jr., senior vice president, corporate development.

11. Schedule 5 (public benefits) of application by The Chase Manhattan Corporation to the Federal Reserve Board for approval of the acquisition of Dial Financial Corporation, Chase Archives.

12. *New York Times*, January 31, 1974. See also Federal Reserve System, "The Chase Manhattan Corporation: Order Denying Acquisition of Dial Financial Corporation," January 30, 1974, Chase Archives. The majority voting against the acquisition included Chairman Burns and governors Mitchell, Brimmer, Bucher, and Holland. Governors Daane and Sheehan strongly supported the application.

13. Chase Manhattan Bank, press release, January 31, 1974.

14. Memorandum for reconsideration by the board of governors of the Federal Reserve System of its denial of the application of The Chase Manhattan Corporation to acquire Dial Financial Corporation, Chase Archives.

15. *New York Times*, November 1, 1974. See also Federal Reserve System, "The Chase Manhattan Corporation, Order Denying Acquisition of Dial Financial Corporation," October 31, 1974, Chase Archives.

16. Leo S. Martinuzzi, Jr., senior vice president, corporate development, interview with J. D. Wilson, September 21, 1982.

17. In 1982 the Federal Reserve approved the acquisition of Dial by Northwest Bancorp, although Dial had grown to be the country's eighth largest consumer finance company. *New York Times*, July 29, 1982.

18. The volume of tax-exempt assets that the bank could hold was limited by the amount of its profits. Chase found that the income from state and municipal securities, certain tax-exempt foreign assets, and other sources exceeded that from many leveraged leases. The bank specialized particularly in vendor leasing—providing equipment manufacturers with a leasing facility for customers. See *Chase Annual Report*, 1976.

19. *New York Times*, March 27, 1971. See also Chase Manhattan Bank, press release, February 8, 1971, Chase Archives.
20. *New York Times*, July 18, 1973.
21. Chase Manhattan Bank, press release, June 21, 1974, Chase Archives.
22. Chase Manhattan Bank, press release, February 1, 1972, Chase Archives.
23. *New York Times*, March 23, 1972.
24. Chase Manhattan Bank, press release, November 15, 1972, Chase Archives.
25. CMOBC investment summaries, 1980, Filinvest Credit Corporation.
26. James H. Bish, senior vice president, international, interview with J. D. Wilson, September 28, 1982.
27. CMOBC investment summaries, 1980, Chase Manhattan Canada.
28. Alfred R. Wentworth, senior vice president, international (retired), interview with J. D. Wilson, October 6, 1982.
29. Frank E. Salerno, vice president, international, interview with J. D. Wilson, October 6, 1982.
30. David Rockefeller, interview with Linda Edgerly, October 1980, Chase Archives.
31. Ibid.
32. *New York Times*, March 22, 1973. An equal credit was extended by the U.S. Export-Import Bank, which took the longer maturities.
33. David Rockefeller, interview.
34. Ibid.
35. Ibid.
36. Richard A. Fenn, vice president, international, interview with J. D. Wilson, October 6, 1982.
37. Chase sold its interest in the Commercial Bank of Dubai in the late 1970s, incurring a loss.
38. *New York Times*, February 5, 1974.
39. The Chase National Bank (Egypt) received government approval in October 1974. See *New York Times*, October 16, 1974.
40. Chase Manhattan Bank, press release, June 30, 1975, Chase Archives.
41. Chase Manhattan Bank, investment review of Saudi Investment Banking Corporation, December 4, 1981, Chase Archives.
42. Anthony B. Neidecker, second vice president, international, interview with J. D. Wilson, September 21, 1982.
43. Investment review of Saudi Investment Banking Corporation.
44. CMOBC investment summaries, 1980, Saudi Investment Banking Corporation.
45. *New York Times*, October 17, 1972. For greater detail see Chase Manhattan Bank, press release, October 16, 1972, Chase Archives.
46. CMOBC investment summaries, 1980, Libra Bank.
47. Chase Manhattan Bank, press release, June 11, 1973, Chase Archives.
48. Chase Manhattan Bank, board of directors, August 15, 1973. Also James H. Bish, interview.
49. *Chase Annual Report*, 1978. Also Otto Schoeppler, president, Chase Manhattan, Ltd., interview with J. D. Wilson, October 8, 1982.
50. Victor E. Rockhill, "Report on Chase International Investment Corporation," May 1971, Chase Archives. Statistics on profitability are also taken from this source.
51. John B. Perfumo, vice president, international, interview with J. D. Wilson, October 8, 1982.

52. CMOBC investment summaries, 1980, Chase Manhattan Bank Luxembourg S.A., initial investment on March 21, 1973.

53. Chase Manhattan Bank, press release, May 25, 1973, Chase Archives. Familienbank opened for business in November 1973.

54. Chase Manhattan Bank, postcompletion audit, Familienbank, October 1975.

55. Neal J. Farrell, senior vice president, international, memorandum to management committee on Familienbank, March 4, 1977, Chase Archives.

56. Chase Manhattan Corporation, *Annual Report, 1976* and *1978*.

57. Chase Manhattan Bank, board of directors, January 17, 1973.

Chapter XVI

1. Chase Manhattan Corporation, *Annual Report, 1976*.

2. Ibid.

3. Statistics in this chapter on nonperforming loans and loan losses, including their various categories, are taken from *Chase Annual Reports* for the relevant periods.

4. *New York Times*, October 3, 1975.

5. Anthony J. Blunda, vice president, credit risk services, interview with J. D. Wilson, August 17, 1983.

6. *Chase Annual Report, 1976*.

7. *Chase Annual Report, 1975* and *1976*. Also Kathleen T. Smith, vice president, financial planning, interview with J. D. Wilson, November 1, 1982.

8. *Chase Annual Report, 1976*.

9. Report on Chase annual meeting, 1975, *New York Times*, March 26, 1975. See also *New York Times*, March 26, 1976.

10. *New York Times*, February 21, 1976. Information on branch openings and closings is from quarterly reports to the board of directors.

11. Robert D. Hubbard, president, Chase Manhattan Capital Corporation, interview with J. D. Wilson, October 13, 1982.

12. *New York Times*, July 24, 1976.

13. A. Edward Allinson, executive vice president, institutional, trust, investment, and information services, interview with J. D. Wilson, April 11, 1983.

14. *Chase Annual Report, 1976*.

15. *New York Times*, April 17, 1976. Also see Chase Manhattan Bank, press release, May 18, 1976, Chase Archives.

16. The estimate of almost $5 billion in real estate credit includes mortgages, credit to real estate investment trusts, domestic credit to builders and developers classified under the heading "real estate," as well as under the heading "commercial and industrial," real estate credit in Puerto Rico (including Housing Investment Corporation of Puerto Rico) and in foreign countries, and credit extended by Housing Investment Corporation of Florida and Dovenmuehle.

17. Richard J. Boyle, executive vice president, commercial sector, interview with J. D. Wilson, October 26, 1982.

18. Ibid.

19. *New York Times*, October 20, 1975.

20. Figures for Chase REIT loans are presented in annual reports of the Chase Manhattan Corporation for 1975 through 1978.

21. *Chase Annual Report, 1977*.

22. Richard J. Boyle, interview with J. D. Wilson, November 8, 1982.

23. Ibid.
24. Two key positions in real estate were filled by Gregory L. Brennan, who became chief credit officer, and Joseph H. Quinn, who headed property disposal.
25. *Chase Annual Report, 1977.*
26. *Chase Annual Report, 1977* through *1980.*
27. *New York Times,* November 7, 1975.
28. The Chase Manhattan Mortgage and Realty Investment Trust (CMART), *Annual Report, 1975.*
29. Chase Manhattan Bank, report to board of directors, July 24, 1975.
30. Ibid.
31. Ibid. See also *New York Times,* October 2, 1975. Most of the loans on the sixteen properties acquired from CMART were paid by 1980. On only one was the bank forced to take over property and incur a loss.
32. *New York Times,* November 7, 1975.
33. *New York Times,* November 14, 1976.
34. *The Wall Street Journal,* February 25, 1977, and April 22, 1977. Also Richard J. Boyle, interview, November 8, 1982.
35. *New York Times* and *The Wall Street Journal,* May 3, 1978. See also *New York Times,* May 23, 1978.
36. Richard J. Boyle, interview, October 26, 1982.
37. Chase Manhattan Bank, memorandum to board of directors, June 21, 1978.
38. *The Wall Street Journal,* February 23, 1979, January 16, 1980, May 27, 1980, and June 6, 1980. Final settlement of CMART was held up by disagreement between holders of senior debt, subordinated debt, and shares of beneficial interest (similar to common stock) on distribution of assets and participation in continuing ownership.
39. Estimate of real estate losses derived from *Chase Annual Report, 1975* through *1980.*
40. *Chase Annual Report, 1976.*
41. Chase Manhattan Corporation, *Annual Report, 1985.*
42. *Washington Post,* January 11, 1976.
43. Fraser Seitel, vice president, public affairs, interview with J. D. Wilson, December 2, 1982.
44. These and subsequent quotations are drawn from the article appearing in the *Washington Post,* January 11, 1976.
45. Arthur Burns, chairman of Federal Reserve Board, in *New York Times,* January 16, 1976.
46. *New York Times,* January 12, 1976. Smith had been informed of Ronald Kessler's visit by both Chase and Citibank, and so was forewarned of the *Washington Post* article.
47. Ibid.
48. See *Washington Post,* January 12, 14, 15, 16, 18, and 20, 1976.
49. *New York Times,* January 16, 1976.
50. *New York Times,* January 22, 1976.
51. *New York Times,* January 25, 1976.
52. Chase Manhattan Corporation, board of directors, January 21, 1976.

Chapter XVII

1. *New York Times,* November 11, 12, 1969.
2. See *Chase Annual Report, 1969, 1970,* and *1971* for description of Chase's programs

to improve New York City environment, including E. J. Kahn, Jr., "A Quiet Kind of Revolution," *Annual Report, 1971.*

3. See The Chase Manhattan Foundation, *Annual Reports, 1967–1970,* Chase Archives.

4. Charles R. Morris, *The Cost of Good Intentions: New York City and the Liberal Experiment* (New York: W. W. Norton, 1980). See also Securities and Exchange Commission, staff report on transactions in securities of the City of New York, Committee on Banking, Finance, and Urban Affairs, House of Representatives, August 1977. "Going Broke the New York Way," *Fortune Magazine,* August 1975. Fred Ferretti, *The Year the Big Apple Went Bust* (New York: Putnam, 1976). Also *The City in Transition: Prospects and Policies for New York,* Final Report of the Temporary Commission of City Finances, Ayer Co., 1978, and David Mermelstein and Roger Alcaly, *The Fiscal Crisis of American Cities* (New York: Random House, 1977). The *New York Times* examined the crisis retrospectively in five articles on June 30 and July 2, 4, 6, and 8, 1985.

5. *New York Times,* May 16, 1975. A study by the congressional budget office, "New York City's Fiscal Problem: Its Origins, Potential Repercussions and Some Alternative Policy Responses," November 10, 1975, places New York City's debt on June 1, 1975, at $14.7 billion, including $5.3 billion short term and $9.4 billion long term. Hearings before Senate Committee on Banking, Housing, and Urban Affairs, October 9, 10, 18, and 23, 1975.

6. "Going Broke the New York Way."

7. Briefing memorandum for David Rockefeller, January 8, 1975, cited in Securities and Exchange Commission, staff report.

8. *The Wall Street Journal,* March 3, 1975. Also "Going Broke the New York Way."

9. *New York Times,* March 7, 8, 1975. See also "Going Broke the New York Way."

10. *New York Times,* March 14, 1975. See also *New York Times,* May 17, 1975, for total holdings of city securities by major banks.

11. David Rockefeller, interview with J. D. Wilson, November 30, 1982.

12. David Rockefeller, testimony before the Securities and Exchange Commission, July 29, 1976.

13. *New York Times,* April 4, 1975. See also *The Wall Street Journal,* April 4, 1975.

14. *New York Times,* May 29, 1975.

15. *New York Times,* May 30, 1975.

16. *New York Times,* June 10, 11, 1975.

17. *The Wall Street Journal,* July 1, 1975.

18. *The Wall Street Journal,* July 2, 1975.

19. Chase Manhattan Bank, press release, July 24, 1975, Chase Archives.

20. *New York Times,* August 1, 1975.

21. *New York Times,* August 8, 1975.

22. *New York Times,* August 28, 1975.

23. David Rockefeller, testimony before SEC. Also Rockefeller, statement at hearing before the New York State Assembly Standing Committee on the Banks, October 17, 1977.

24. *The Wall Street Journal,* September 4, 1975.

25. *New York Times,* September 10, 1975.

26. *New York Times,* September 11, 1975.

27. Elmore Patterson, David Rockefeller, and Walter Wriston, joint statement before the

Senate Banking, Housing, and Urban Affairs Committee, October 18, 1975, Chase Archives. Also David Rockefeller, interview.
28. *New York Times*, October 30, 1975.
29. *New York Times*, November 13, 14 and 15, 1975.
30. *New York Times*, November 15, 1975.
31. *Chase Annual Report, 1976.*
32. *New York Times*, November 27, 1975. See also *The Wall Street Journal*, November 28, 1975.
33. *New York Times*, November 28, 1975.
34. *New York Times*, November 20, 1976. See also *The Wall Street Journal*, November 22, 1976.
35. *New York Times*, July 26, 1977.
36. *New York Times*, February 25, 1975.
37. Palmer Turnheim, senior vice president, Chase Manhattan Capital Markets, interview with J. D. Wilson, November 24, 1982.
38. Ibid.
39. *New York Times*, February 25, 1975.
40. *New York Times*, February 26, 1975.
41. Palmer Turnheim, interview. See also *New York Times*, February 27, 1975.
42. *New York Times*, March 6, 1975.
43. Palmer Turnheim, interview. See also *New York Times*, March 27, 1975.
44. *New York Times*, November 28, 1975.
45. *New York Times*, December 11, 1975.
46. *New York Times*, February 8, 1976.
47. *New York Times*, March 5, 1976. Also David Rockefeller, interview.
48. *New York Times*, May 11, 1976.

Chapter XVIII

1. Presentation by Willard Butcher on Chase's Plan for Recovery, 1976–1979, to Chase board of directors at planning meeting, Pocantico Hills, New York, November 16–17, 1976.
2. Comparative statistics on nonperforming loans, net charge-offs of assets, and provision for loan losses are taken from Chase Manhattan Corporation, *Annual Report, 1979.*
3. Willard C. Butcher, remarks at Chase Manhattan Corporation, board of directors meeting, November 16, 1977.
4. Chase Manhattan Corporation, *Annual Reports, 1976* and *1980*, show domestic commercial and industrial loans to be $9.2 billion and $11.0 billion in the two respective years. These figures, however, include bankers acceptances, which can be purchased in the open market. Excluding these results is an increase in commercial and industrial loans from $6.6 billion to about $10.9 billion.
5. Willard C. Butcher, remarks at Chase Manhattan Corporation, board of directors meeting, January 17, 1979, Chase Archives.
6. Henry E. Prunner III and Avram Stein, vice presidents, interview with J. D. Wilson, January 5, 1983. Mr. Prunner served as head of the division of loan pricing and product development for corporate industries, with Mr. Stein as his deputy. They provided details of changes in loan pricing.

7. Avram Stein, interview with J. D. Wilson, January 3, 1984.
8. Kathleen T. Smith, vice president, financial planning, interview with J. D. Wilson, February 10, 1983.
9. *Chase Annual Report, 1979.*
10. Chase Manhattan Bank, press releases, March 2, 1978, December 8, 1978, and September 14, 1979, Chase Archives. See also Chase Manhattan Corporation, *Annual Report, 1981.*
11. *New York Times*, May 31, 1979.
12. Otto Schoeppler, president, Chase Manhattan, Ltd., interview with J. D. Wilson, October 8, 1982.
13. *New York Times*, April 7, 1977.
14. *Chase Annual Report, 1981.*
15. Chase Manhattan Corporation, *Annual Report, 1978.* See also *Annual Report, 1980*, and article by Francis L. Mason, senior vice president, country risk policy, *Chase Directions*, Spring 1982, Chase Archives.
16. Willard C. Butcher remarks to board of directors budget meeting, January 16, 1980, Chase Archives.
17. Thomas G. Labrecque, executive vice president, presentation to board of directors, Woodstock, Vermont, October 16, 1979, Chase Archives.
18. *New York Times*, November 19, 1978. See also Thomas G. Labrecque, presentation to board of directors, November 16, 1977, and October 16, 1979, Chase Archives.
19. *Chase Annual Report*, 1976 and 1979.
20. *New York Times*, February 4 and March 17, 1980.
21. Thomas A. Conigliaro, president, The Chase Manhattan Bank (USA), "The Delaware Banking Experience," *The Bankers Magazine*, January–February, 1983.
22. Frederick S. Hammer, executive vice president, consumer banking, interview with J. D. Wilson, March 15, 1983.
23. *Chase Annual Report, 1979.* See *New York Times*, November 19, 1978, for Chase and Citibank retail strategies.
24. Ernest L. Loser, senior vice president, corporate trust services, interview with J. D. Wilson, April 11, 1983.
25. Stephen E. Canter, president, Chase Investors Management Corporation, interview with J. D. Wilson, April 11, 1983.
26. Ibid.
27. Chase Investors Management Corporation, internal accounting records.
28. *Institutional Investor*, April 1984.
29. Edward E. Madden, senior vice president, pension trust and financial services, presentation to meeting of Chase officers, September 1, 1982.
30. Information on master trust from Edward E. Madden, interview with J. D. Wilson, April 18, 1983.
31. Earnings figures presented represent income before security gains or losses. These were tantamount to net operating earnings and were those used most widely by stock analysts and others in measuring the financial performance of banks. After 1981, however, regulatory agencies required banks to report net income (earnings after security gains or losses) as the single measure of earnings. Chase reported net income of $116 million in 1976, $303 million in 1979, and $412 million in 1981.
32. David Rockefeller, presentation at budget meeting of board of directors, January 16, 1980, Chase Archives.

33. *New York Times*, November 2, 1978. See also Federal Reserve Bank of New York, *Annual Report, 1978*.
34. *New York Times*, October 7, 1979. See also Federal Reserve Bank of New York, *Annual Report, 1979*.
35. *New York Times*, March 15, 1980. See also Federal Reserve Bank of New York, *Annual Report, 1980*.
36. *New York Times*, October 10, 1979.
37. *New York Times*, September 14, 1977.
38. Willard C. Butcher, presentation at board of directors meeting, November 16, 1977, Chase Archives.
39. "Capital Planning: Debt Management," Chase Manhattan Bank, 1980. See also section on capital management in *Chase Annual Report, 1980*.
40. Alan F. Lafley, executive vice president, corporate human resources, interview with J. D. Wilson, January 12, 1983.
41. Ibid. Also A. Wright Elliott, executive vice president, corporate communications, interview with J. D. Wilson, January 26, 1983.
42. Alan F. Lafley and A. Wright Elliott, interviews.

Chapter XIX

1. Francis X. Stankard, executive vice president, international banking, interview with J. D. Wilson, January 26, 1983.
2. Ibid.
3. Roy Assersohn, *The Biggest Deal* (London: Methuen, 1982), p. 72.
4. Francis X. Stankard, interview.
5. *America In Captivity*, special issue of *New York Times Magazine*, May 1981, p. 37.
6. Francis X. Stankard, interview. See also *Iran: The Financial Aspects of the Hostage Settlement Agreement*, Committee on Banking, Finance, and Urban Affairs, House of Representatives, July 1981, p. 8.
7. *New York Times*, June 9, 1979.
8. Assersohn, *The Biggest Deal*, p. 35.
9. Ibid., pp. 80, 317–320. Iranian deposits held by all U.S. banks at the end of 1980, prior to the ending of the freeze, amounted to about $7.5 billion. This included interest earned for a period of approximately fourteen months as well as deposits that flowed in as a result of oil payments subsequent to imposition of the freeze.
10. *Chase Annual Report, 1979*. A note to financial statements on p. 67 presents information on Iranian assets and deposits held by Chase on November 15, 1979, and the offset put into effect by the bank.
11. Albert L. Lalonde, vice president, international banking, interview with J. D. Wilson, January 28, 1983.
12. *New York Times*, November 16, 1979.
13. Francis D. Logan, partner, Milbank, Tweed, Hadley and McCloy, interview with J. D. Wilson, January 31, 1983.
14. Ibid.
15. *New York Times*, December 8, 1979. Also Francis D. Logan, interview concerning action on this and other loan syndications.
16. *New York Times*, December 21, 1979.
17. Assersohn, *The Biggest Deal*, pp. 134–143. See also *Iran: Financial Aspects of the Hostage Settlement Agreement*, pp. 30–32.

18. *Iran: Financial Aspects of the Hostage Settlement Agreement*, pp. 32–34. Also Assersohn, *The Biggest Deal*, pp. 139–143 and 156–160.
19. *Chase Annual Report, 1980*, p. 65.
20. Assersohn, *The Biggest Deal*, p. 168.
21. Francis D. Logan, interview.
22. *Iran: Financial Aspects of the Hostage Settlement Agreement*, p. 34.
23. Francis D. Logan, interview.
24. Assersohn, *The Biggest Deal*, pp. 202–203. See also *Iran: Financial Aspects of the Hostage Settlement Agreement*, p. 34.
25. Ibid. See also Assersohn, *The Biggest Deal*, pp. 277–280.
26. Francis D. Logan, interview.
27. Ibid.
28. Assersohn, *The Biggest Deal*, pp. 240–242, 302–306. See also *Iran: Financial Aspects of the Hostage Settlement Agreement*, p. 36.
29. Thomas G. Labrecque, interview with J. D. Wilson, February 11, 1983. See also Assersohn, *The Biggest Deal*, pp. 304–306.
30. Chase Manhattan Corporation, *Annual Report, 1980*, p. 65.
31. Francis D. Logan, interview. See also Assersohn, *The Biggest Deal*, pp. 317–320.
32. *Iran: Financial aspects of the Hostage Settlement Agreement*, p. 46–48. See also Assersohn, *The Biggest Deal*, pp. 322–328.
33. Assersohn, *The Biggest Deal*, p. 328.
34. Francis D. Logan, interview.
35. Frank R. Reilly, senior vice president, administrative services, interview with J. D. Wilson, January 31, 1983.
36. Ibid.
37. Chase Manhattan Corporation, *Annual Report, 1980*, p. 65.
38. *New York Times*, July 9, 1983. Settlement was reached in June but announced on July 8, 1983.

Chapter XX

1. J. Stewart Baker, interview, in Crawford Wheeler, "The Chase Manhattan Story," February 1963, pp. 143–144, Chase Archives.
2. Charles Block, vice president, consumer operations services, interview with J. D. Wilson, January 19, 1982.
3. *Chase Annual Report, 1958*.
4. *Chase Annual Report, 1959*.
5. Chase Manhattan Bank, press release, March 17, 1961, Chase Archives.
6. Chase Manhattan Bank, press release, May 25, 1961, Chase Archives.
7. "Increasing Efficiency in Operations," presentation to directors, May 19, 1965, Chase Archives.
8. *Chase Annual Report, 1965*.
9. *Chase Annual Report, 1970*.
10. George Champion, commencement address, Millikin University, Decatur, Ill., June 6, 1965, Chase Archives.
11. "Trends of the Future," presentation to directors, May 18, 1966, Chase Archives.
12. Charles Block, vice president, operations department, interview with J. D. Wilson, June 21, 1982.
13. *Chase Annual Report, 1967*.

14. Barry F. Sullivan, chairman, First Chicago Corporation, interview with J. D. Wilson, December 28, 1982.
15. "The Three Year Deadline at 'David's Bank,' " *Fortune Magazine*, July 1977.
16. Barry F. Sullivan, interview. See also "Three Year Deadline."
17. "Three Year Deadline."
18. Arthur F. Ryan, executive vice president, corporate operations and systems, and Charles Block, interview with J. D. Wilson, August 17, 1983.
19. *Washington Post*, January 11, 1976. See also Chapter XVI, the section entitled "Chase Becomes a Target of the *Washington Post*."
20. Michael Urkowitz, senior vice president, product/production risk management, interview with J. D. Wilson, March 24, 1983.
21. Thomas G. Labrecque, president, interview with J. D. Wilson, February 11, 1983. See also *Chase Annual Report, 1977*.
22. Arthur F. Ryan and Charles Block, interviews.
23. Ibid.
24. Michael Urkowitz, interview.
25. Michael Urkowitz, Arthur F. Ryan, and Charles Block, interviews.
26. *Chase Annual Report, 1981*, pp. 15–16.
27. Michael Urkowitz, interview. See also *Chase Annual Report, 1981*.
28. Arthur F. Ryan, "Integrating Technology with Business Strategy in the Production Base," presentation to Chase board of directors, October 19, 1981, Chase Archives.
29. Michael Urkowitz, Arthur F. Ryan, and Charles Block, interviews.
30. Arthur F. Ryan and Charles Block, interviews. I am indebted to them, as well as to Michael Urkowitz, for facts concerning the development of management information at Chase.
31. Chase Manhattan Bank, *Chase Directions*, Spring 1979, pp. 13–15, Chase Archives.
32. Arthur F. Ryan and Charles Block interviews.
33. Elaine R. Bond, "Systems, Technology, and the Information Revolution," presentation to Chase board of directors, October 19, 1981, Chase Archives.
34. Chase Manhattan Bank, *Chase News*, March 1983, Chase Archives.
35. Bond, "Systems, Technology," See also Jerry D. Lambo, "Officer Automation/Productivity Program," presentation to Friday weekly officer meeting, June 20, 1983, Chase Archives.
36. Chase Manhattan Bank, *Chase Directions*, Spring 1979, pp. 24–25.
37. *New York Times*, March 12 and 16 and September 11, 1956.
38. *New York Times*, April 7, 1955.
39. Gerald J. Van Dorn, vice president, protection (retired), interview with J. D. Wilson, April 13, 1983.
40. *New York Times*, August 22, 1979.

Chapter XXI

1. *New York Times*, December 20, 1979.
2. Chase Manhattan Corporation, board of directors, December 21, 1977.
3. *New York Times*, April 5, 1981.
4. "The Analysts vs. The Chase: Can David Ever Get His Act Together?" *Institutional Investor*, July 1976, p. 22.
5. Rockefeller himself mentioned these changes in informal remarks at the opening dinner of the planning meeting of senior officers at the Homestead, Hot Springs,

Virginia, May 15, 1980. He added a fourth change to which he believed he had made an essential contribution: namely, realization of the vital importance of highly qualified human resources and the need for professional skill in ensuring it. Rockefeller then named certain aspects of banking to which, with hindsight, he felt he had not given adequate recognition. These included formal asset-liability management, the importance of quality control on assets, and the need to push the development of systems, including use of computers.

6. David Rockefeller, interview with J. D. Wilson, May 4, 1984.
7. Willard C. Butcher, interview with J. D. Wilson, February 18, 1983.
8. See, for example, "The Chase at Ebb-Tide," *New York Times*, June 4, 1972.
9. "The Three Year Deadline at 'David's Bank,' " *Fortune Magazine*, July 1977.
10. See "David's Connections," *Institutional Investor*, May 1981, p. 117.
11. Barry F. Sullivan to Associated Press at time of Rockefeller's retirement, April 20, 1981.
12. Keynote address to International Management Congress in New York, September 16, 1963. Chase Manhattan Bank, press release, September 16, 1963, Chase Archives.
13. Chase Manhattan Bank, press release, February 5, 1965, Chase Archives.
14. "David Rockefeller Talks About Chase," *The Bankers Magazine*, Autumn 1977, pp. 31–32.
15. Ibid.
16. David Rockefeller, interview with J. D. Wilson, March 2, 1983.
17. "Community Involvement: The Chase Approach," annual report of The Chase Manhattan Bank Corporate Responsibility Activities, 1981, Chase Archives.
18. Rockefeller became a class A director of the Federal Reserve Bank of New York on December 22, 1972. He was reelected to serve until December 1976. Earlier, from December 1971 to December 1972, Rockefeller had represented the second Federal Reserve district on the board of governors' federal advisory council.
19. David Rockefeller, interview, March 2, 1983.
20. David Rockefeller, interview with J. D. Wilson, November 30, 1982.
21. Many of the details on Rockefeller's activities related to his personal interests and those of the Rockefeller family were provided in the interview of March 2, 1983.
22. Ambassador Joseph V. Reed, Jr., former vice president and assistant to the chairman, interview with J. D. Wilson, December 29, 1982.
23. A list of Rockefeller's speeches and public statements is available in the Chase Archives.
24. Chase Manhattan Corporation, *Annual Report, 1981*.
25. Comments of Rockefeller and Butcher at final reception with Chase officers, Chase Archives.
26. *New York Times*, December 9, 1979.
27. *New York Times*, June 25, 1980.
28. *New York Times*, June 26, 1980. Ogden took early retirement in 1983 and became chairman of the Continental Illinois Bank and Trust in 1984. Hooper was appointed vice chairman in 1982 and retired in 1985.
29. Thomas G. Labrecque, interview with J. D. Wilson, February 11, 1983.

Chapter XXII

1. For a description and discussion of Chase's loss on Drysdale government securities see The Chase Manhattan Corporation, *Annual Report, 1982*, pp. 3, 35; *The Wall*

Street Journal, May 19, 20, 21, and June 11, 1982; *New York Times*, May 19, 20, 21, 1982; *Barrons*, May 24, 1982; *Institutional Investor*, September 1982; and Martin Mayer, *The Money Bazaars* (New York: E. P. Dutton, 1984), pp. 222–231.

2. *The Wall Street Journal*, July 28, 1983; *New York Times*, July 28, 1983.

3. *The Wall Street Journal*, February 10, March 30, 1984; *New York Times*, February 10, 1984; *New York Times*, March 18, 1985.

4. *The Wall Street Journal*, May 20, 1982. See also *Institutional Investor*, September 1982.

5. Arthur F. Ryan, executive vice president, corporate operations and systems, interview with J. D. Wilson, July 19, 1984. The securities service division began to provide service to outside clients in 1979. Earlier the division had worked only internally in the bank as part of the custody function, receiving and delivering securities. The head of the division and his associates were experienced in operations and had no training in credit evaluation of the firms they dealt with, since none was believed necessary in their capacity of acting solely as agent.

6. *The Wall Street Journal*, July 28, 1983.

7. Willard C. Butcher, interview with J. D. Wilson, July 19, 1984.

8. Arthur F. Ryan, interview. A number of security firms claimed that in providing securities which Chase furnished Drysdale, they had entered into repurchase agreements (RPs) with Chase, and that Drysdale, in turn, had obtained the securities by entering into reverse repurchase agreements (reverse RPs) with Chase. RPs and reverse RPs are the most common method of financing trading in the huge government security market. Under an RP a dealer or holder of government securities gains cash by selling securities to a buyer, with an agreement to repurchase the securities at a specific price and at a specific date in the future. The date may be the next day or some later time. The buyer in effect has made a loan to the seller collateralized by the securities. In the case of a reverse RP, the buyer acquires securities by purchasing them for cash, with an agreement to resell the securities at a specific price and at a specific date in the future. The purchaser in effect has borrowed the securities for a fixed period, providing cash as collateral. With an RP the original holder of the securities pays an interest rate (RP rate) for the cash received, and this is included as the difference between the initial sales price of the securities and the agreed-upon price at which the securities will be repurchased (or in the case of reverse RPs, resold). The original holder of the securities in turn is entitled to the interest paid by the issuer (the U.S. Treasury) when due. It was the inability to pay this interest that brought Drysdale's problems to a head. Security firms, by claiming that they had entered into repurchase agreements with Chase, alleged that Chase, not Drysdale, was liable for the interest due them.

9. Willard C. Butcher, interview.

10. *The Wall Street Journal* and *New York Times*, May 20, 1982. See also *The Wall Street Journal* and *New York Times*, May 19, 1982, for Chase's first statement on Drysdale.

11. Chase Manhattan Corporation, *Annual Report*, 1982.

12. *New York Times*, October 16, 1984. See also *The Wall Street Journal*, October 16, 1984.

13. *The Wall Street Journal*, July 2, 6, 7, and 8, 1982. *New York Times*, July 6, 8, and 9, 1982. Penn Square began in 1960 as a local shopping center bank. By 1974 it held deposits of $30 million. The bank then changed dramatically, opening a separate oil and gas loan department and hiring scores of officers from other banks. Over the next eight years it grew eightfold.

14. *The Wall Street Journal*, January 13 and July 2, 1984. For a detailed account of Penn Square see Marc Singer, *Funny Money* (New York: Knopf, 1985); Philip L. Zweig, *Belly Up* (New York: Crown, 1985).
15. *The Wall Street Journal* and *New York Times*, August 13, 1982.
16. *New York Times*, August 27, 1982. Anthony P. Terracciano, chief financial officer, interview with J. D. Wilson, July 11, 1984.
17. Anthony P. Terracciano, interview.
18. Arthur F. Ryan and Anthony P. Terracciano, interviews. See also interview with Thomas G. Labrecque, in "Lessons from Drysdale," *American Banker*, December 30, 1982.
19. *The Wall Street Journal*, August 20, 1982. See also Federal Reserve Bank of New York, *Annual Report*, 1982.
20. *New York Times*, December 4, 1981.
21. General statement of mission, 1978, Chase Archives.
22. Chase Manhattan Corporation, *Annual Report*, 1977.
23. General statement of mission, October 1984, Chase Archives.
24. Willard C. Butcher, "Chase's Strategic Directions for the 1980s," presentation to board of directors, Woodstock, Vermont, October 16, 1979, Chase Archives.
25. See Chase Manhattan Corporation, *Annual Report*, 1984, for list of offices.
26. *New York Times*, April 8, 1982. Chase in early 1982 helped form a cooperative arrangement with nearly one thousand banks in fifty states through which customers of each bank could carry out banking transactions or obtain cash from automated teller machines through other members. This integrated network, called the Plus System, enabled Chase and other members to provide service to customers on a nationwide basis, beyond the confines of its own branch system. Later in 1985 Chase also joined a similar cooperative network, called the New York Cash Exchange, that included eight banks serving New York City, New York State, and Connecticut.
27. Chase Manhattan Corporation, *Annual Report*, 1981 and 1984.
28. Frederick S. Hammer, executive vice president, consumer banking, interview with J. D. Wilson, March 15, 1983. See also *Chase Annual Report*, 1985.
29. Willard C. Butcher, remarks to Chase officers, June 7, 1984, Chase Archives.
30. Hans P. Ziegler, senior vice president, domestic private banking, interview with J. D. Wilson, June 15, 1983.
31. Chase Investors Management Corporation, internal accounting records.
32. Hans P. Ziegler, interview with J. D. Wilson, September 1985.
33. *The Wall Street Journal*, December 22, 1983.
34. Report to weekly officers meeting, April 27, 1984, Chase Archives. See also Federal Reserve Board order approving acquisition of Lincoln First Banks by The Chase Manhattan Corporation, May 14, 1984.
35. A number of changes occurred in the regulatory approach to competition among banks in the 1970s and early 1980s. Regulators moved away from the concept of potential competition, partly as a result of adverse court decisions. Moreover, definition of the relevant geographic market was broadened by the Federal Reserve to include the Standard Metropolitan Statistical Area, embracing both New York City and the suburbs, rather than a local area (Westchester). Thrift institutions also were added in measuring concentration, and more emphasis was placed on use of the so-called Herfindahl-Hirschman index as the unit of measure for concentration. See John D. Hawke, Jr., "Public Policy toward Bank Expansion," in *Handbook for Banking Strategy*, eds. Richard C. Aspinwall and Robert A. Eisenbeis (New York: John Wiley and Sons, 1985).

36. *New York Times*, May 8, 22, 1985.
37. *The Wall Street Journal*, April 9, 1985, and *New York Times*, October 23, 1985.
38. *New York Times*, October 18, 1985.
39. Chase was less fortunate in Pennsylvania. An investment had been made in Equibank, in Pittsburgh, in 1981, with an option to purchase the bank whenever Pennsylvania law permitted it. But the condition of Equibank deteriorated, and the law barring out-of-state banks was not changed. To facilitate additional capital infusion from other sources, Chase agreed to accept repayment for part of its investment and abandon its option. *The Wall Street Journal*, October 4, 7, 1984.
40. *New York Times* and *The Wall Street Journal*, June 11, 1985.
41. See *The Wall Street Journal*, March 30, 1984, October 16, 1984, and December 26, 1984. See also editorial, *New York Times*, December 26, 1984. So-called nonbank banks arose as a result of a quirk in the laws that limited a bank's ability to accept deposits to a single state. A bank was defined as accepting demand deposits and making loans. A consumer (nonbank) bank did one or the other, but not both. Chase applied for twenty-six charters in sixteen states for such institutions, but the authority of regulatory agencies to issue such charters was denied by the courts.
42. Chase sold its interest in Chase-NBA Group and Chase-NBA Securities to its partner, the National Bank of Australia, to avoid possible conflict of interest.
43. *The Wall Street Journal*, December 23, 1983.
44. Chase Manhattan Corporation, *Annual Reports*, *1979* and *1980*. For 1985, Chase Manhattan Bank, internal records.
45. For a discussion of interest rate swaps see Julian K. Walmsley, "Understanding Interest Rate Swaps," *The Bankers Magazine*, July–August 1984. See also *New York Times*, February 7, 1985.
46. *Chase Annual Report*, *1984*. Although total loans in overseas offices in 1985 were $34 billion, some $5 billion of these had U.S. firms as the ultimate obligor. Loans with foreign obligors amounted to $29.4 billion. Of these about $14 billion was extended to less developed countries. Of the $29.4 billion approximately $29 billion was in overseas offices and $400 million at the head office.
47. *New York Times*, August 20, 21, 1982. For a full discussion of the debt problem, see *Annual Report of the President's Council of Economic Advisors*, *1984*, section on "Third World Debt Problem" (Washington, D.C.: U.S. Printing Office, 1984), p. 71. See also Darrell Delamaide, *Debtshock* (Garden City, N.Y.: Doubleday, 1984).
48. *New York Times*, February 25, March 4, 1983.
49. *New York Times*, February 26, March 1, 1983.
50. *The Wall Street Journal*, December 3, 1984, and *New York Times*, December 3, 5, 1984. See also *The Wall Street Journal* and *New York Times*, June 12, 1985, for Argentine agreement with International Monetary Fund.
51. *New York Times*, September 8, 1984; *The Wall Street Journal*, September 10, 1984. Banks agreed to restructure Mexico's foreign debt due through 1989 on more liberal terms. Similar restructuring was agreed to or under negotiation with Brazil, Venezuela, the Philippines, Chile, and Ecuador.

Chapter XXIII

1. Included at the end of 1985 were $7.926 billion in net interest-free domestic demand deposits, 0.763 billion NOW accounts, and $1.939 billion in overseas demand deposits, or $10.628 billion in all. This represented 15.6 percent of $68.067 billion total funds then employed.

2. Citicorp and BankAmerica, *Annual Reports, 1985.*
3. Chase Manhattan Bank, internal statistics.
4. The McFadden Act, passed in 1927 and amended in the Banking Act of 1933, permitted national banks to branch in cities or towns or elsewhere in a state, wherever state laws authorized state banks to do so. This in effect placed limits on branching under the authority of the individual states. The Douglas Amendment to the Bank Holding Company Act of 1956 restricted a bank holding company to owning full-service banks (banks that accept demand deposits and make commercial loans) only in the state in which its head office is located, except where a state specifically authorizes bank holding companies domiciled in other states to own banks within that state. Certain multistate bank holding companies then existing were permitted to continue owning banks in states where they operated.
5. Robert R. Douglass, executive vice president, remarks at meeting of senior officers, May 2, 1985, Chase Archives.
6. Chase Manhattan Bank, board of directors, February 18, 1981.
7. Alan F. Lafley, executive vice president, corporate human resources, interview with J. D. Wilson, January 12, 1983.
8. Ibid. Also A. Wright Elliott, executive vice president, corporate communications, interview with J. D. Wilson, January 26, 1983.
9. Willard C. Butcher, remarks to Chase officers, June 7, 1984, Chase Archives.

Index

Abu Dhabi, representative office in, 231, 256
Affluent individuals, as 1980s target group,
    339, 340, 341, 344
Africa
    Standard Bank acquisition in, 169–171
    CIIC in, 235
Agemian, Charles A., 62, 79, 406
    and charge card, 94, 95
    Virgin Islands sale arranged by, 100
    and American Express relationship, 153
    and Banco Lar in Brazil, 164
    operations department under, 308
Agnelli, Giovanni, 183
Albers, Josef, 112
Aldrich, Nelson, 14
Aldrich, Winthrop, 4, 14–15, 19–20, 43, 399,
    404
    retirement of, 8, 51–52, 53
    and investment-commercial separation, 16,
    53
    on wartime finance, 17
    and McCain, 20
    Mexico City branch closed by, 23
    and public utilities department, 23
    and John Wallace, 23
    and Eugene Black, 24
    strategic conception of, 24–25
    and David Rockefeller, 26
    Latin American trip of, 33–34
    and Hong Kong branch, 36
    and trading-with-enemy case, 36
    and bank growth, 39
    Middle East trip by, 41
    and branch system, 43–44
    and first Manhattan merger attempt, 44–45
    and Chase earnings performance, 45–46
    and interest rates, 46
    and employee benefit package, 48
    organizational changes by, 50–51
    and McCloy, 52
    as ambassador to Great Britain, 52, 53
    contributions by, 53–54
    remaining objectives laid down by, 54, 103,
    118
    and charitable contributions, 85
    as internationalist, 97

and One Chase Manhattan Plaza, 103
and American Express, 150
and CIIC, 235
and social responsibility, 323, 326
Algeria, in U.S.-Iran negotiations, 302
Alliance Holding, 226–227
Allinson, A. Edward, 290, 407
ALMAC (asset-liability management commit-
    tee), 242, 243, 281, 282, 283, 292, 361
American Express Bank and Trust Company
    and Chase National, 12, 14, 15, 150
    Uni-Card of, 94–95, 158–160
    traveler's checks of, 150, 151, 152, 153–154
    fraud against, 151, 153, 385–386n.2
    and credit cards, 154, 155
American Foreign Banking Corporation, 13
American Overseas Finance Corporation
    (AOFC), 95–96
American Overseas Investing Company, 96
Anderson, Robert O., 402
Angermueller, Hans, 300
Antitrust law
    and Chase-Manhattan merger, 67–68, 69–
    70, 71
    and credit-card acquisitions, 155–156
    and upstate holding company, 188
    as lessened constraint, 342, 356
    See also Banking law; Regulation of banking
Arab-Israeli conflict (1967), 129
Arab-Israeli conflict (1973), 208
Arcturus, 98
Argentina
    representative offices in, 33, 163
    Chase acquisitions in, 163, 164, 166, 167,
    356
    Falklands war in, 348
    foreign-debt problem of, 349
ARPAS (Account Relationship Profitability
    Accounting System), 316–317, 318
Arthur Andersen and Company, 333, 335
Art
    at One Chase Manhattan Plaza, 111–112
    Rockefeller's interest in, 111–112, 329
Asia. *See* Far East
Asset-liability management committee (AL-
    MAC), 242, 243, 281, 282, 283, 292, 361

409